Understanding Energy Security in Central and Eastern Europe

The purpose of this book is to move beyond the approach which views energy as a purely geopolitical tool of the Russian state and assumes a 'one size fits all' approach to energy security in Central and Eastern Europe (CEE). It argues that in order to fully understand Russian involvement in the regional energy complex, the CEE–Russian energy relationship should be analysed in the context of the political and economic transitions that Russia and the CEE states underwent. The chapters on individual countries in the book demonstrate that, although Russia has and will continue to play a substantial role in the CEE energy sector, the scope of its possible influence has been overstated.

Wojciech Ostrowski is a Senior Lecturer at the University of Westminster.

Eamonn Butler is a Senior Lecturer at the University of Glasgow.

Routledge Contemporary Russia and Eastern Europe Series

For more information about this series, please visit: https://www.routledge.com/Routledge-Contemporary-Russia-and-Eastern-Europe-Series/book-series/SE0766

Identity and Nation Building in Everyday Post-Socialist Life
Edited by Abel Polese, Jeremy Morris, Oleksandra Seliverstova and Emilia Pawłusz

Cultural Forms of Protest in Russia
Edited by Birgit Beumers, Alexander Etkind, Olga Gurova and Sanna Turoma

Women in Soviet Film
The Thaw and Post-Thaw Periods
Edited by Marina Rojavin and Tim Harte

Russia – Art Resistance and the Conservative-Authoritarian Zeitgeist
Edited by Lena Jonson and Andrei Erofeev

Ruptures and Continuities in Soviet/Russian Cinema
Styles, characters and genres before and after the collapse of the USSR
Edited by Birgit Beumers and Eugénie Zvonkine

Russia's Regional Identities
The Power of Provinces
Edited by Edith W. Clowes, Gisela Erbslöh and Ani Kokobobo

Understanding Energy Security in Central and Eastern Europe
Russia, Transition and National Interest
Edited by Wojciech Ostrowski and Eamonn Butler

Russia's Far North
The Contested Energy Frontier
Edited by Veli-Pekka Tynkkynen, Shinichiro Tabata, Daria Gritsenko and Masanori Goto

The City in Russian Culture
Edited by Pavel Lyssakov and Stephen M. Norris

Understanding Energy Security in Central and Eastern Europe
Russia, Transition and National Interest

Edited by
Wojciech Ostrowski and Eamonn Butler

LONDON AND NEW YORK

First published 2018
by Routledge
2 Park Square, Milton Park, Abingdon, Oxon OX14 4RN

and by Routledge
711 Third Avenue, New York, NY 10017

Routledge is an imprint of the Taylor & Francis Group, an informa business

© 2018 selection and editorial matter, Wojciech Ostrowski and Eamonn Butler; individual chapters, the contributors

The right of Wojciech Ostrowski and Eamonn Butler to be identified as the authors of the editorial material, and of the authors for their individual chapters, has been asserted in accordance with sections 77 and 78 of the Copyright, Designs and Patents Act 1988.

All rights reserved. No part of this book may be reprinted or reproduced or utilised in any form or by any electronic, mechanical, or other means, now known or hereafter invented, including photocopying and recording, or in any information storage or retrieval system, without permission in writing from the publishers.

Trademark notice: Product or corporate names may be trademarks or registered trademarks, and are used only for identification and explanation without intent to infringe.

British Library Cataloguing in Publication Data
A catalogue record for this book is available from the British Library

Library of Congress Cataloging in Publication Data
Names: Ostrowski, Wojciech, editor. | Butler, Eamonn, editor.
Title: Understanding energy security in Central and Eastern Europe: Russia, transition and national interest / edited by Wojciech Ostrowski and Eamonn Butler.
Description: Abingdon, Oxon ; New York, NY : Routledge, 2018. | Series: Routledge contemporary Russia and Eastern Europe series ; 81
Identifiers: LCCN 2017049658| ISBN 9781138120341 (hardback) | ISBN 9781315651774 (e-book) | ISBN 9781317311034 (mobipocket)
Subjects: LCSH: Energy security–Europe, Eastern. | Energy security–Europe, Central. | Energy industries–Political aspects–Europe, Eastern. | Energy industries–Political aspects–Europe, Central. | Energy policy–Europe, Eastern. | Energy policy–Europe, Central.
Classification: LCC HD9502.A2 U494 2018 | DDC 333.790947–dc23
LC record available at https://lccn.loc.gov/2017049658

ISBN: 978-1-138-12034-1 (hbk)
ISBN: 978-1-315-65177-4 (ebk)

Typeset in Times New Roman
by Taylor & Francis Books

Printed and bound by CPI Group (UK) Ltd, Croydon CR0 4YY

For Tessa and Graham

Contents

List of tables ix
List of contributors x
Acknowledgements xiii
List of Abbreviations xiv

1 Introduction 1
  WOJCIECH OSTROWSKI

PART I
Analytical framework 15

2 Energy security in Central and Eastern Europe: An IR theoretical dimension 17
  ROLAND DANNREUTHER

3 Debating transition 32
  TERRY COX

4 Russian energy companies and the Central and Eastern European energy sector 52
  SYLVAIN ROSSIAUD AND CATHERINE LOCATELLI

PART II
Case studies 71

5 Czech Republic 73
  RICK FAWN

6 Romania 93
  ANCA-ELENA MIHALACHE

7 Poland 116
  WOJCIECH OSTROWSKI

8	Bulgaria	138
	DIMITAR BECHEV	
9	Hungary	155
	EAMONN BUTLER	
10	Baltic States	178
	GIEDRIUS ČESNAKAS	
11	Serbia	202
	MILOS DAMNJANOVIC	
12	Conclusion: Central and Eastern European energy security – more than Russia	222
	EAMONN BUTLER	
	Index	232

List of Tables

4.1	Main Russian oil companies, by level of production in million barrels a day	58
4.2	Russian gas production by producer	60
4.3	Russian oil companies' main investments in CEE and Baltic countries	63
4.4	Dependence of CEE countries on Russian gas, 2014	64
4.5	Gazprom's main investments in CEE and in the Baltic states	65
5.1	Transparency International, Corruption Perceptions Index 2014: Results	80
7.1	Polish-Russian Energy Relationship 1989–2015	119
11.1	Relations with Russia and Serbia's Energy Sector	206

Contributors

Anca-Elena Mihalache has graduated from the University of Aberdeen, MSc Energy Politics and Law. She is a former Senior Analyst at Energy Policy Group, a Romanian think-tank specialising in energy policy and energy security. She currently holds the role of Oil and Gas Policy Officer at the Department for Business, Energy and Industrial Strategy (BEIS) in the United Kingdom.

Dimitar Bechev is Research Fellow at the Center for Slavic, Eurasian and East European Studies in the University of North Carolina at Chapel Hill as well as a Senior Nonresident Fellow with the Atlantic Council. He is the author of *Rival Power: Russia in Southeast Europe* (Yale University Press, 2017) and has written extensively on EU external relations, the politics of the Balkans and Turkey, Russian foreign policy. His articles have appeared in the *Journal of Common Market Studies, Problems of Post-Communism, East European Politics and Societies*, amongst other periodicals. Dr. Bechev is the founder of the European Policy Institute, a think-tank based in Sofia, Bulgaria, and he contributes policy analysis to *Oxford Analytica, The American Interest, Foreign Policy, Al Jazeera Online*. He holds a D.Phil. from the University of Oxford.

Terry Cox is Professor of Central and East European Studies, School of Social and Political Science at the University of Glasgow, and Editor of *Europe-Asia Studies*. His primary research interests are in the comparative social policy and political sociology of the Central and Eastern European region with a special focus on civil society, interest representation and social welfare. His research has been published in various journals and edited collections. His most recent book is *Civil Society and Social Capital in Post-Communist Eastern Europe* (Routledge, 2015).

Rick Fawn is Professor of International Relations at the University of St Andrews. Among his dozen books is *International Organizations and Internal Conditionality: Making Norms Matter* (Palgrave Macmillan, 2013), on how normative, resource-poor intergovernmental bodies can still encourage and influence recalcitrant member states. He is currently working on Visegrad regional cooperation.

List of contributors xi

Roland Dannreuther is Professor of International Relations at the University of Westminster. His research interests include security studies, energy politics and the regional politics of Russia, Middle East and Central Asia. His recent publications include *Energy Security* (Polity, 2017), *Global Resources: Conflict and Cooperation* (Palgrave, 2013) (co-edited with Wojciech Ostrowski); *International Security: The Contemporary Agenda* (Polity, 2013); *China, Oil and Global Politics* (Routledge, 2011) (co-authored with Philip Andrews-Speed); and *Russia and Islam: State, Society and Radicalism* (Routledge, 2010) (co-edited with Luke March).

Wojciech Ostrowski is a Senior Lecturer in International Relations at the University of Westminster and Director of the MA programme, Energy and Environmental Change. His research concentrates on the areas of energy security, political economy of resources and international relations with a regional focus on Central Asia and Eastern Europe. He is the author of *Politics and Oil in Kazakhstan* (Routledge, 2010 and 2011), and an author and co-editor of *Global Resources: Conflict and Cooperation* (Palgrave, 2013).

Eamonn Butler is a Senior Lecturer in Central and East European Studies, School of Social and Political Science at the University of Glasgow. His primary research interest is the European Union and post-2004 enlargement studies. His recent work has focused on energy security within the Central and Eastern European region and he has published on energy sector relations between corporations, the EU and its member states, and third parties, including Russia. His research has been published in *Geopolitics, Europe-Asia Studies, International Journal of Energy Security and Environmental Research, Routledge Yearbook of Central and Southeastern Europe*, and EUISS Reports. He is the political science editor for *EuropeNow Journal* and sits on the editorial board of *Europe-Asia Studies*.

Milos Damnjanovic is the Head of Research and Analysis at BIRN Consultancy, a part of Belgrade-based BIRN Ltd. Prior to coming to BIRN, he worked as a consultant for a number of local and international organisations and companies, including GIZ, NALED, Eurasia Group and Oxford Analytica. From 2011 to 2015 he was an Associate with the South East European Studies at Oxford (SEESOX) programme at the European Studies Centre of the University of Oxford. Damnjanovic is also the Serbia Country Author for Freedom House's *Nations in Transit* publication. From 2005 to 2011, Damnjanovic completed a D.Phil. in Politics at St Antony's College at the University of Oxford, working on democratisation in Serbia and Croatia during the 1990s.

Catherine Locatelli is a CNRS Research Fellow at the University of Grenoble Alpes (Grenoble Applied Economics Lab, France). Her research relates to the Russian energy sector, primarily to the reform of the oil and gas industry. In particular, she studies Russia as a major supplier of hydrocarbons, especially to the European Union. She analyses the consequence of Russian internal developments in the energy industry on the international energy sector.

Sylvain Rossiaud is Lecturer in Economics at the University of Grenoble Alpes (Grenoble Applied Economics Lab, France). His teaching relates to oil and gas economics. His academic interest includes the institutional dynamic governing the Russian oil industry. His current research focuses on institutional comparative analysis of neoliberal reforms in the oil sector.

Giedrius Česnakas has a Ph.D. in political science and works as Associate Professor and the Head of the Department of Political Science at the General Jonas Žemaitis Military Academy of Lithuania and a Lecturer at Vytautas Magnus University. His primary research interests are energy security and energy diplomacy of Russia. For his dissertation 'Energy Resources in Russia's Foreign Policy towards Belarus and Ukraine (2000–2012)' he was awarded by the Lithuanian Academy of Sciences with the award for the best research of young scientists in the areas of the humanities and social sciences. He has published in a number of scientific journals and publications of leading think-tanks in the United States.

Acknowledgements

Our thanks go first to the Faculty of Social Sciences and Humanities, University of Westminster for sponsoring an authors' workshop, which allowed us to develop key ideas discussed in this book. We also gratefully acknowledge the support of the ESRC/AHRC backed Centre for Russian, Central and East European Studies (CRCEES) for providing funding early on in the project to support a follow up authors' workshop. We would also like to thank representatives from the European Commission DG Energy, the Czech, Slovak and Polish Permanent Representations to the EU, Central European Energy Partners, PERN, 'Przyjazn' S.A. Poland, European Policy Centre Brussels, Weglokoks Poland, and the European Institute for Security Studies for attending the knowledge exchange event in Brussels that fed into the writing of this book. Finally, we are indebted to our co-authors since without their enthusiasm and dedication for the project there would be no book.

List of Abbreviations

ASE	AtomStroyExport
BBL	Oil Barrel
BCM	Billion Cubic Metres
BEH	Bulgarian Energy Holding
BN	Billion
BRELL	Belarus, Russia, Estonia, Latvia and Lithuania
BRUA	Bulgaria-Romania-Hungary-Austria
BSP	Bulgarian Socialist Party
CEE	Central and Eastern Europe
ČEZ	České Energetické Závody
CMEs	Coordinated Market Economies
COMECON	Council for Mutual Economic Assistance
DANS	National Security Agency
DIICOT	Directorate for the Investigation of Organized Crime and Terrorism
EC	European Commission
EPS	Elektroprivreda Srbije
EU	European Union
EURATOM	European Atomic Energy Community
EWRC	Energy and Water Regulatory Commission
FDIs	Foreign Direct Investments
FKgP	Független Kisgazdapárt
GDP	Gross Domestic Product
GERB	Citizens for European Development of Bulgaria
GHG	Greenhouse Gas
GIPL	Gas Interconnector Poland – Lithuania
GWh	Gigawatt Hour
HAP	Hydro Accumulation Plant
HFT	Hungarian Finance & Trade Corp.
HP	Heat Plant
IBRD	International Bank for Reconstruction and Development
IEA	International Energy Agency
IGA	Inter-government Agreement

List of Abbreviations   xv

IKL	Ingolstadt – Kralupy nad Vltavou–Litvínov
IMF	International Monetary Fund
IOCs	International Oil Companies
IPS/UPS	Integrated Power System/Unified Power System
IR	International Relations
B/D	Barrels Per Day
KDNP	Kereszténydemokrata Néppárt
KMG	KazMunayGas
KTB	Corporate Commercial Bank
LMEs	Liberal Market Economies
LNG	Liquefied Natural Gas
LNGT	Liquefied Natural Gas Terminal
MCM/Y	Million Cubic Meters Per Year
MDF	Magyar Demokrata Fórum
MEBOs	Manager and Employee Buy-Outs
MIÉP	Magyar Igazság és Élet Pártja
MNCs	Multinational Corporations
MoU	Memorandum of Understanding
MRF	Movement of Rights and Freedoms
MSZP	Hungarian Socialist Party
MT	Megatons
MVM	Magyar Villamos Művek Zártkörűen működő Részvénytársaság
MW	Megawatt
MZSP	Magyar Szocialista Párt
NATO	North Atlantic Treaty Organisation
NEC	National Electrical Company
NIS	Naftna Industrija Srbije
NOCs	National Oil Companies
NPP	Nuclear Power Plant
NPS	Nuclear Power Station
OECD	Organisation for Economic Co-operation and Development
PGNiG	Polskie Górnictwo Naftowe i Gazownictwo
PiS	Prawo i Sprawiedliwość
PKN	Polska Kompania Naftowa
PO	Platforma Obywatelska
RES	Renewables Energy Sources
RFE/RL	Radio Free Europe/ Radio Liberty
SCC	Stockholm Chamber of Commerce
SEE	South-East Europe
SLD	Sojusz Lewicy Demokratycznej
SZDSZ	Szabad Demokraták Szövestsége – a Magyar Liberális Párt
TAL	Transalpine Pipeline
TAP	Trans-Adriatic Pipeline
TCM	Trillion Cubic Metres

TEP	Third Energy Package
TOE	Tonnes of Oil Equivalent
TPPs	Thermal Power Plants
TSOs	Transmission System Operators
TWh	Terrawatt Hour
UCTE	European Continental Network
UN	United Nations
US	United States
WB	World Bank
WTO	World Trade Organization

1 Introduction

Wojciech Ostrowski

1.1 Energy security and Central and Eastern Europe

According to the classical definition, energy security has three main components: reliability of supply, affordability of supply and environmental sustainability. Energy security is a term that was coined in the mid-1970s, thereafter its prominence steadily declined through the 1980s and the 1990s and some scholars argued that it was no longer relevant (Youngs 2009). Yet, in recent years the issue of energy security has risen again to the very top of the international agenda. Highly volatile oil prices, resource nationalism, the diminishing power of International Oil Companies (IOCs), the rise of emerging powers and their 'Hybrid' National Oil Companies (NOCs), corruption scandals and riots in energy-rich countries, military interventions in the oil states as well as technological breakthroughs such as the shale revolution in the USA, all played their part (Yergin 2011; Goldthau 2016). In effect, the period from 2003 until 2014 was often compared and contrasted with that of 1973–1986 the last time that the issue of energy featured highly on the international security agenda (Dannreuther 2015). European states were also affected by the developments in the international energy arena. Yet, the politics of energy security in the 2000s and 2010s played out very differently in the Western and Eastern parts of the European continent.

In the 1990s in Western Europe very few policy makers were preoccupied with the issue of energy security, primarily due to low energy prices and Russia's 'opening' to Western capital. In 2001 the European Commission (EC) in its Green paper warned member states that the status quo would not endure forever and that they should look more closely at the issue of energy (Commission of the European Communities 2001). The rapid increase in energy prices in 2000s had a serious impact on industry and individual customers, and exposed Western energy companies to pressure from empowered producing countries seeking to renegotiate contracts concluded in the 1990s (Vivoda 2009; Wilson 2015). Yet, in Western Europe the shock of the 2000s was not as profound as in the 1970s. The western part of the continent no longer depended on a single region for its oil supplies (i.e. the Middle East) and had begun looking for ways to move towards renewable energy (Vogler

2013; Bradshaw 2014). In essence, the energy crises of the 2000s were limited to the problem of affordability, whereas reliability of supply – despite all the noises – played a rather marginal role (Noël 2008; Goldthau and Witte 2009; McGowan 2011).

High-energy prices affected Central and Eastern Europe (CEE) economically as much as Western Europe. However, in the case of CEE, reliability of supply also quickly emerged as another important issue. These concerns were motivated by the widespread belief that an assertive Russia, which emerged under the first presidency of Vladimir Putin, would use energy in order to either bend states in the region to its will or simply to intimidate them (Balzer 2005; Stegen 2011). The fact that Russia cut off energy supplies to some post-Soviet states in the 1990s and that Russian-owned companies took over installations, such as pipelines and refineries in some of the poorest post-Soviet republics as a way of paying energy debts, seemed to point towards an alarming pattern (Nygren 2008; Galbreath 2008). Furthermore, throughout the early 2000s the Russian state did very little to alleviate those anxieties. The pursuit of aggressive resource nationalism and the destruction of privately owned energy companies inside Russia persuaded many in the West that the Russian state was consolidating its power and that energy would become a cornerstone of a new geopolitical policy (Baev 2007; Goldman 2008; Gustafson 2012).

In the late 1990s and early 2000s, debates concerning CEE energy security overwhelmingly focused on Ukraine and Belarus. Both states occupied a strategic place in the Soviet and in the post-Soviet Russian energy complex and both states found themselves on a collision course with the Russian energy companies and the state during the 2000s (Balmaceda 2007; Chow and Elkind 2009; Högselius 2013). The two infamous Russian–Ukrainian gas wars (2006 and 2009), which became global news, were the most precarious moments in the whole saga (Stern 2006; Hafner and Bigano 2009). At the same time, the overwhelming focus on Ukraine and Belarus meant that other CEE states were sporadically a subject of equally intense academic and journalistic investigations (Balmaceda 2008; Lough 2011; Krastev 2015). This assumed that the energy relationship between Russia and post-Soviet republics mirrored those of the larger CEE region and that Moscow would be equally able and willing to use the energy weapon in order to advance its political goals (Lucas 2014). In short, the tactics used towards post-Soviet republics could be applied towards post-socialist states with a similar geopolitical objective in mind. The legacy of this thinking was clearly visible during the 2014 Ukrainian crises (Biersack and O'lear 2014; Gros 2015; Kozak 2016).

1.2 Purpose of the book and key findings

The purpose of this book is to move beyond a realist approach which views energy as purely a geopolitical tool of the Russian state and assumes a 'one size fits all' approach to CEE energy security. The individual contributions to this volume mainly concentrate on the post-socialist states where energy security has been understudied and is poorly understood when compared with reports available on Belarusian, Ukrainian or Central Asian energy dilemmas (Anceschi 2008; Ostrowski 2010; Luong and Weinthal 2010; Balmaceda 2013). To this end we ask the question of what role Russia plays in the CEE energy sector and how did the Russian–CEE energy relationship develop since the early 1990s? We argue that in order to fully understand Russian involvement in the regional energy complex, the Russian–CEE energy relationship should be analysed in the context of the political and economic transition that both Russia and the CEE states underwent. Thus, we assert that questions on which energy security analysis normally centre – such as a country's energy mix, its transport system, and energy vulnerabilities – have to be considered along with questions related to the post-communist transformation, interactions between emerging post-socialist elites in Russia and the CEE region, as well as general governance structures. Furthermore, we contend that the role of energy companies is particularly important for an analysis of the energy security complex, because the involvement of Russian private, state-owned or intermediary energy companies in CEE have been often considered as a way for the Kremlin to gain a foothold in a country and prevent diversification away from Russian energy supplies. Such explanations have also constituted an important part of the geopolitical narrative. Yet, the involvement of Russian energy companies has not been investigated in any great depth in the case of post-socialist states and their impact is poorly understood.

The individual contributions to this volume demonstrate that dependency on Russian energy supplies and the involvement of Russian private, state-owned or intermediate companies in the CEE region have significantly differed from country to country and have been, if anything, decreasing in recent years with a few notable exceptions. The reason for perpetuating linkages between CEE countries and parts of the Russian energy sectors are multi-layered and are best understood when scrutinised on a case-to-case basis. Yet, there are some clear patterns. In the last twenty-five years or so, the level of involvement of Russian private and state-owned companies in the CEE region has varied from relatively low in the case of Czech Republic and Romania – two states which strongly resisted engagement with the Russian companies and treated them with deep suspicion – to relatively high in the case of the Baltic Republics and Serbia. In the cases of Poland and Bulgaria one of the most controversial elements of the Russian–CEE energy relationship has been the existence of intermediary gas and oil companies which were created throughout the 1990s. The non-transparent nature of these companies often fuelled suspicions regarding their role and the potential pressure that the Russian state might seek to exercise through them on the political and economic environment of the CEE states. However, the individual chapters demonstrate that the companies, which have caused so much anxiety, were generally bodies set up by Russian and regional elites in order to enrich themselves. In short, old fashioned rent seeking rather than political domination was the main reason behind some of Russia's most controversial 'energy' ventures in the CEE region.

The book demonstrates that while a geopolitically driven analysis is not without merit – in particular in the case of Baltic Republics – the Kremlin-centred analysis overstates the strength of the leverage that Russia has had over these countries. In other words, there have been fewer pressure points in the CEE energy complex than commonly assumed. For instance, Russian gas, which has been at the centre of much of the analysis concerning the regional energy security, is much less significant in the overall regional energy mix. Indeed, in a number of the cases reviewed in this book, domestically produced coal still plays a hugely important role. Furthermore, in the majority of cases, the CEE states were also able to resist significant Russian involvement in the energy sector and managed to push for diversification away from Russian supplies. The key element in this strategy has been a new energy infrastructure which was constructed with notable financial and political involvement of the EU.

Another important part of the equation concerning the Russian involvement in the CEE countries was the state of the Russian energy sector during the transition. In the 1990s the country's oil sector underwent a chaotic privatisation and a clique made up of ex-communist apparatchiks and directors captured the gas sector. In effect, the sector descended into a state of disarray, reducing any real threat that it could be used as an efficient 'energy weapon' by the state. Throughout the 2000s, Putin's energy strategy sought to address this disarray and mainly focused on renationalising the Russian oil industry, while at the same time redefining the relationship with key post-Soviet transit states (Belarus and Ukraine). At this point in time, the CEE energy sector remained largely marginal to this project.

We acknowledge that the Russian energy sector will certainly continue to play an important part in the CEE energy complex in the years to come. However, controversies regarding Russian involvement, with the exception of Serbia and perhaps Hungary, are unlikely to dominate debates concerning regional energy security to the same extent as in the 2000s and the early 2010s. Rather, as various contributions demonstrate, the key disputes in the years to come will focus on the EU's approach to energy markets and climate change agenda. Therefore; the centre of the debate regarding the CEE energy complex has started to shift from Moscow to Brussels. How the CEE states respond to this development will be critical to understanding future regional energy sector policy and security.

1.3 Structure of the book

1.3.1 Part I: Analytical framework

The first part of the book frames the discussion surrounding the issue of CEE energy security. The first three chapters demonstrate that in order to fully understand the dynamics shaping energy security, we will have to move beyond standard explanations and bring to the fore scholarly debates that have been hitherto marginal to energy studies, but which have the capacity to shed a new light on the key drivers shaping the CEE–Russian energy relationship. Roland Dannreuther, in the opening chapter, argues that in the scholarly literature discussions concerning the CEE–Russian energy dynamics have been contextualised within the framework of the EU–Russian energy relations, which until the mid-2000s appeared to be relatively stable. This was because Russia, after the collapse of the Soviet Union, remained a reliable supplier of energy to the European states. Yet, this sense of stability unravelled between 2004 (Yukos affair) and 2009 (second Ukrainian gas crises) and resulted in strengthening more alarmist voices regarding the reliability of Russian supplies. In his chapter, Dannreuther demonstrates that classical International Relations (IR) theories usefully captured a range of narratives that were put forward in order to describe the politics of energy in Europe. In essence, the actions of the Russian state were interpreted as being realist while the EU, with its focus on cooperation and consensus building, was largely viewed as a liberal actor. Those two narratives played an important role in shaping our understanding of the underlying forces governing the energy security relationships in Europe including the CEE region. Yet, Dannreuther suggests, the classical IR schools do not accurately depict all the drivers that have influenced CEE–Russian energy dynamics and as such other critical factors have to be taken under consideration, including (a) the need to recognise the agency and independence of the CEE state themselves and not treat the region as a strategic vacuum at the mercy of Russia and the EU; and (b) the need to incorporate the role of non-state actors, most notably the CEE and Russian energy companies. The two following contributions elaborate further on the points made by Dannreuther by focusing on the way in which the CEE region has developed politically and economically after the collapse of the Soviet Union and the strategies of the Russian energy companies in the region.

Terry Cox's wide-ranging contribution, which draws on a succinct analysis of transition studies literature, demonstrates that any serious discussion concerning energy security and policy in the CEE region and the relationship with Russia should start with the recognition of the fact that while all the states in the region underwent a form of transition, the outcomes vary significantly from country to country. To allow us to unpack the reasons for those different outcomes, we need to consider various issues, such as economic liberalisation, privatisation and the character of ownership, in addition to issues of state capture and corruption. Cox, through his exploration of a variety of policy sectors, notes that questions concerning the formation and development of new elites and the renewal and circulation of old elites are closely connected to questions of economic viability, state effectiveness and most importantly privatisation. Cox also argues that the political and economic transformation that the states in the CEE region underwent cannot be divorced from the international environment and neo-liberal economic orthodoxy which dominated economic thinking in the region until the 2000s and which, as we show elsewhere in the book, still plays an important role in the energy sector. Furthermore, it is important to keep in mind that the transition did not occur in an institutional vacuum and that the paths followed by countries before the transition started matter a great deal for the final outcome. This point is particularly significant in the case of energy systems and their operations which are based on long-term projects, arrangements and links that cannot be easily broken. Cox, in his contribution, further demonstrates that the study of the politics of transition also allows us to understand why, in several cases, the state retained a greater ownership share of the energy sector and why even the most liberal CEE countries proved to be reluctant to either completely privatise or open their energy sectors to foreign investments. Finally, the discussions that have taken place in the last twenty-five years or so, within the realm of transition, shed light on the issue of corruption and state capture which, as the individual chapters in the volume demonstrate, are an important element for understanding the CEE–Russian energy dynamic.

The discussions concerning the Russian energy sector often focus on the Kremlin, petrodollars and the way in which they are spent by the regime in order to maintain the status quo. Yet, the existing studies devote relatively little time to the industries that generate the actual rent. This is an important omission since the study of the industry brings to the open dynamics which may otherwise get lost. The contribution by Sylvan Rossiaud and Catherine Locatelli underscores this point. They demonstrate that the Russian oil and gas sector is far from static and that it underwent fundamental changes during the last two decades. The authors also note that it is important to take into account the very significant difference between the oil and gas industries. In their chapter, Rossiaud and Locatelli argue that instead of concentrating solely on the Kremlin and the politics of post-Soviet Russia, we should pay much more attention to the economic drivers. Furthermore, we should recognise that Russian companies – in particular, Lukoil – to a large degree failed to penetrate the CEE energy sector. At the same time, Rosneft, the number one Russian oil company, remained absent from the CEE downstream market. The authors also demonstrate that Russia is a very attractive supplier of gas to the CEE region due to the proximity of these markets and the relatively low production and transport costs. In short, despite everything that has been said regarding diversification in the CEE region, the simple reality is that Russian gas is extremely competitive for a number of countries. As a result, Rossiaud and Locatelli note, commercial considerations should be given greater weight in an analysis of the choices made by CEE actors regarding their energy security. At the same time, we should also more closely scrutinise the actions of Gazprom, its strategy aimed at maximising gas rent and its responses to the liberalisation of the EU gas market.

1.3.2 Part II: Case studies

The case studies discussed in the second part of the book demonstrate that, although, Russia has and will continue to play a substantial role in the CEE energy sector, the scope of its possible influence has been overstated. Most importantly, Russian gas plays a much smaller role in the CEE energy mix than has often been assumed. The CEE countries began devising different projects aimed at diversification away from Russian energy supplies, in some cases as early as the 1990s. The Czech Republic was most successful at adopting this strategy while others followed its footsteps in the 2000s with the help of the EU. The Romanian political elites, supported by the local population, firmly rejected any involvement of Russian companies in the country's energy sector. In the case of Bulgaria, Poland, and more recently in the case of Hungary, the corrupted nature of the transition led to the creation of a conducive environment for the involvement of Russian energy actors who in tandem with local political elites established rent-seeking, intermediary companies. The presence of those companies was viewed as part of the Kremlin's strategy aimed at dominating the CEE energy complex, but there is a lack of evidence to show that this was generally the case. At the same time, the legacy of the scandals and struggle that those companies generated had an important impact on various strategies being pursued by the individual states vis-à-vis Russian actors. In the case of the Baltic Republics and Serbia, the Russian energy companies managed to penetrate the energy system to a much greater extent than in other states in the CEE regions, albeit, for very different reasons. The Baltic Republics due to their historic Soviet ties and relative isolation from the European energy system did not have much choice but to actively engage with Russian companies. Serbia, which until the mid-2000s followed similar trajectories to Poland or Bulgaria, began collaborating with Russian companies after the Russian state actively supported Serbian efforts aimed at blocking Kosovo's independence.

Rick Fawn argues that in order to understand the actions of the Russian companies in the Czech Republic we have to first and foremost understand the dynamics of the (non)privatisation process. The Czech energy sector, as in the case of other big countries in the CEE region, was not privatised and remained in state hands. This meant that it enjoyed relative immunity from Russian pressure. Fawn argues that Russian energy companies attempted, at various stages, to engage with powerful political actors and sought to influence the country's energy policy through them. However, this strategy has not been very successful. He also demonstrates that the Czech Republic, which heavily depends on coal within its total primary energy mix, has since the late 1990s, taken substantial measures to diversify energy supplies. Those measures included the construction of gas pipelines, facilities and the expansion of gas storage. Furthermore, as in the case of other CEE states, an important breaking point in the story of Czech energy security was EU accession. At the same time, Fawn argues, corruption has been a major problem at the heart of the Czech energy sector. The Czech national energy champion, České Energetické Závody (ČEZ), a state-within-a-state-like company, was captured by the country's energy elites and used to their own benefit. Also, these elites were able to use ČEZ to unduly influence the political life of the country throughout the transition period.

Anca-Elena Mihalache, in her contribution, demonstrates that Romania's energy mix is both diverse and balanced, with coal, natural gas and oil being extracted locally. As such, the main problems affecting the Romanian energy sector are not primarily political but rather technical, with ageing infrastructure and the lack of repairs being at the top of the list. Mihalache goes on to argue that the key to understanding the dynamics governing the Russian–Romanian energy relationship is the legacy of Ceausescu's policies, which aimed at gaining economic and political independence from Moscow during the Communist era. In the post-1991 period the old Communist policy found its manifestation in the actions of Romanian elites who blocked Russian and Western capital from entering the country, including the energy sector, with the Romanian public largely supportive of the policy. Thus, as in the case of the Czech Republic, the state remained a dominant actor in the energy sector while local elites captured the sector and engaged in rent-seeking activities. The Russian investments, as in the case of Poland or Bulgaria discussed in the following sections, were not driven by any political agenda but were rather aimed at making a quick profit predominately via asset stripping. There is also no proof that Russian businesses held privileged relations with political parties or decision makers. Finally, Mihalache demonstrates that, in recent years, various protectionist measures, which initially shielded the country from Russian penetration, have led to a clash with liberally oriented EU institutions.

Wojciech Ostrowski, in his chapter, argues that Polish energy security was never threatened directly by the Russians because the state, as in the Czech Republic and Romania, retained control over the energy sector and because coal plays a key part in the country's energy mix. He further stresses that various geopolitically centred explanations did not pay sufficient attention to domestic politics and to the broadly understood transition politics. Ostrowski argues that the study of domestic politics puts a spotlight on the corrupted environment of the 1990s and early 2000s, which allowed Polish and Russian political, commercial and private actors to engage in rent seeking activities. The collusion between the two sets of actors had a detrimental effect on the way in which the debate concerning Polish energy security has developed and on the broader political and economic relationship between Russia and Poland. Ostrowski further demonstrates that the division and infighting between the 'anti-Russian' post-Solidarity camp and the 'pro-Russian' post-communist camp, coupled with corruption scandals that brought to the open murky dealings between the Russian oil and gas sectors and Polish political actors, have continued to generate interest in the country's energy security and further fuelled concerns about Russian's real intentions. The Ukrainian–Russian 'gas wars' in the mid-2000s entrenched a negative view of the Russian oil and gas sectors and gave the energy security debate a truly geopolitical dimension, albeit not for long. Since the late 2000s the EU, similarly to other countries in the CEE region, has played an important dual role in the Polish–Russian relationship, facilitating reconciliation between two parties, whilst also aiding Polish efforts aimed at diversifying away from Russian oil and gas supplies.

Dimitar Bechev, in his chapter, argues that Bulgaria, which does not consume huge quantities of energy and which, in theory, should be able to diversify away from Russian supplies, is stuck in an imbalanced relationship with Russia due to the collaboration between the country's key domestic players and Russian energy companies. Bulgaria's dependence on Russian energy supplies and the fact that Russian companies play an important role in the country's energy complex derives from structural problems at the heart of the country's political system, including state capture, corruption and rent seeking. Thus, Bechev argues that the problem of energy security goes beyond the issue of import dependency. He shows that a central issue is a lack of transparency and of real competition. As in the case of Poland, the Russian–Bulgarian energy trade was conducted in the 1990s through various shady intermediary companies; the influence of which only declined in the early 2010s. Yet, these energy relationships were not wholly dominated by Russians. As the case of South Stream demonstrates, the state could, if it wanted to, extract concessions from the Russians. In a similar vein, despite various privatisation waves since the late 1990s, the Bulgarian state has remained a critical player in the country's energy sector. This has given Bulgaria significant leverage, but also meant that – as in the Czech and Romanian cases – a large share of the contracts were awarded to insiders without proper competition and that political appointees led state-owned enterprises. Finally, the Bulgarian accession to the EU in 2007, as in the case of others in the region, had an important impact on the development of the country's energy security calculations.

In his chapter, Eamonn Butler explains that Hungarian energy policy increasingly reflects a statist agenda, where in the post-EU accession period, Budapest has made moves to resist foreign ownership of its energy sector where possible, and 'rebuild those government positions that were given up in the previous years due to short-term fiscal considerations or even less transparent or meaningful reasons.' This, Butler suggests, is a direct attempt to respond to a transition era privatisation strategy that is deemed to have not been beneficial for the Hungarian state. Recent policy decisions, such as cutting the cost of energy for the domestic user, thus affecting profit opportunities, has discouraged ongoing commitments from foreign investors, particularly key Western firms, who have started to withdraw. This has begun a process of opening the country up to a backdoor renationalisation of the energy sector across infrastructure, imports and retail. Butler highlights that this resistance to foreign ownership also extends to Russia and the country has sought to restrict direct Russian ownership and shareholdings. The case of MOL/Surgutneftegaz provides a clear example of such active resistance. However, Hungary also recognises that Russia remains its largest energy supplier and that it needs to maintain a pragmatic approach to its partnership with Russia. This has been the standard political attitude throughout the entire post-communist era and post-2010 the government has become even more willing to work with Russia. Engagement in projects such as South Stream, the development of new gas storage facilities and the award of a contract to build an extension to Hungary's nuclear power station at Paks, all provide evidence of a strong relationship. At the same time, this has opened Hungary up to significant criticism and suggestions about a lack of transparency in its dealings with Russia. Furthermore, a willingness to challenge the EU in favour of Russia appears to have placed the country well within the Russian zone of influence in the region. Butler, however, suggests that we should not necessarily take this at face value and that a better understanding of Hungarian energy policy, vis-à-vis its commitments to the EU, national energy needs, the reality of day-to-day party politics, and the legacy of its transition, all contribute to a complex situation where a less rigid relationship with Russia exists.

Giedrius Cesnakas's chapter discusses the Baltic Republics, which are the only countries discussed in this volume to be part of the Soviet Union and subsequently become EU and NATO member states. Cesnakas demonstrates that the dependence of the Baltic Republics on Russia varies from case-to-case, with Estonia being least dependent, followed by Latvia, and then Lithuania being the most vulnerable. Lithuania was particularly hard hit by disruptions and oil supply cut-offs throughout the 1990s and Russian companies also attempted to take over parts of the Lithuanian oil infrastructure. But such attempts were resisted. A similar situation could be seen in Latvia. Yet, this does not mean that Russian companies were entirely absent from the Baltics. As part of the privatisation process, the three Baltic Republics ended up selling most of the shares in their national gas companies to Russian companies. This move was driven by an expectation that the inclusion of Russian companies in the ownership structure of the Baltic's natural gas companies would ensure lower prices and stability of supply. This promise has not been always fulfilled. Furthermore, as in other cases covered in this book, throughout the 1990s, most of the gas trade between Russia and Lithuania was conducted through intermediary companies. Unlike in other cases, however, those powerful intermediaries were able to use their financial capabilities to influence politics via links with political parties and the media, while people with connections to the ex-KGB loomed in the background. However, the power of the intermediaries in the Baltic region declined by the early 2010s. The game changer in the Russian–Baltics republics dynamic was the accession of the three countries to the EU. This created the necessary conditions for the development of energy projects that had previously been lacking. As a result, interconnectors, diversification and renewable energy projects have been completed or are on track. Over time, the region has become more resilient to external threats as dependence on Russia's resources has decreased and market-based rules expanded.

Milos Damnjanovic demonstrates that Serbia is the only country in the CEE region which since the late 2000s has increased its energy insecurity by essentially 'handing over' its oil and gas sector to Gazprom. This move was due to special political circumstances which were not replicated in other countries. Having said that, until the late 2000s, the story of the Serbian–Russian energy relationship, despite Serbia's international isolation in the 1990s, was not that different to other countries in the region. The post-socialist evolution of the Serbian energy sector was accompanied by the presence of Russian intermediary companies, involved in the sale of natural gas, and an increase in the prevalence of corruption scandals in the energy sector. As with other states in the region, the energy sector also largely remained in the hands of the state. Yet, the relationship between the Serbian and Russian energy relationship moved to a different level after 2007. Moscow's attempts within the United Nations (UN) and other international organisations to block recognition of Kosovo's independence changed the political dynamics between the countries. The provision of this vital support from the Serbian perspective coincided with an intensification of the energy relationship between Russia and Serbia which led to the 2008 deal with Gazprom. As a result of the agreement, the Russian company now controls Serbia's oil and gas extraction, as well its oil refining capacities and much of its oil retail sector. In addition, the Serbian energy sector depends on a single pipeline through which Russian gas is piped. Consequently, towards the end of the 2010s, Serbia, which traditionally enjoyed a high degree of energy security – with coal accounting for over half of its energy mix – found itself exposed to pressures from Russia which now possessed very strong leverage. In short, Serbia has trodden a diametrically opposite path from the other countries in the region under discussion here.

The individual contributions to this book demonstrate that while Russia will undoubtedly continue to play a very important role in the CEE energy complex in the years and decades to come, the most important decisions concerning regional energy policy will be increasingly made in Brussels. This situation will create both opportunities and problems for the CEE countries. On the one hand, the CEE states as full members of the EU – with the exception of Serbia – will be increasingly able to shape the EU's policies and upload their policy ideas via mechanisms such as the Energy Union. However, on the other hand, the CEE states could find they need to follow the lead of the European Commission and key Western member states on a wide range of issues including market liberalisation, energy transition and climate change. This new situation will inevitably create political tensions between the CEE states – all of which have their own national interests and political dynamics – and the Commission regarding energy policy. The opening of energy policy infringement procedures against Bulgaria and Hungary already provide some evidence of such tensions. However, unlike the discourses addressing the perceived Russian threat produced throughout the 1990s and the 2000s, it is unlikely that we will see the same type or level of anxiety about the EU and suggestions that actors such as the Commission are a threat to the CEE states' energy interests.

References

Anceschi, L. (2008). *Turkmenistan's foreign policy: Positive Neutrality and the consolidation of the Turkmen regime.* (London: Routledge).
Baev, P.K. (2007). 'Russia aspires to the status of "energy superpower"', *Strategic Analysis,* 31(3), pp. 447–465.
Balmaceda, M.M. (2007). *Energy dependency, politics and corruption in the former Soviet Union: Russia's power, oligarchs' profits and Ukraine's missing energy policy, 1995–2006.* (London: Routledge).
Balmaceda, M.M. (2008). 'Corruption, intermediary companies, and energy security: Lithuania's lessons for Central and Eastern Europe', *Problems of post-communism,* 55(4), pp. 16–28.
Balmaceda, M.M. (2013). *The politics of energy dependency: Ukraine, Belarus, and Lithuania between domestic oligarchs and Russian pressure* (Vol. 40). (Toronto: University of Toronto Press).
Balzer, H. (2005). 'The Putin thesis and Russian energy policy', *Post-Soviet Affairs,* 21(3), pp. 210–225.
Biersack, J. and O'Lear, S. (2014). 'The geopolitics of Russia's annexation of Crimea: narratives, identity, silences, and energy'. *Eurasian Geography and Economics,* 55(3), pp. 247–269.
Bradshaw, M.J. (2014). *Global energy dilemmas: energy security, globalization, and climate change.* (Cambridge: Polity).
Chow, E. and Elkind, J. (2009). 'Where east meets west: European gas and Ukrainian reality', *The Washington Quarterly,* 32(1), pp. 77–92.
Commission of the European Communities (2001). *Green Paper: Towards a European Strategy for the Security of Energy Supply.* (Brussels: European Commission).
Dannreuther, R. (2015). 'Energy security and shifting modes of governance', *International Politics,* 52(4), pp. 466–483.
Galbreath, D.J. (2008). 'Putin's Russia and the 'New Cold War': interpreting myth and reality', *Europe-Asia Studies,* 60(9), pp. 1623–1630.
Goldman, M.I. (2008). *Petrostate: Putin, power, and the new Russia.* (Oxford: Oxford University Press).
Goldthau, A. and Witte, J. (2009). 'Back to the future or forward to the past? Strengthening markets and rules for effective global energy governance', *International Affairs,* 85(2), pp. 373–390.
Goldthau, A. (ed.) (2016). *The handbook of global energy policy.* (Chichester: John Wiley & Sons).
Gros, D. (2015). 'The price of oil and Soviet/Russian aggressiveness'. *CEPS Commentary,* 16 January.
Gustafson, T. (2012). *Wheel of fortune.* (Harvard JMA: Harvard University Press).
Hafner, M. and Bigano, A. (2009). *Russia-Ukraine-Europe gas crisis of January 2009: causes, lessons learned and strategies for Europe.* (Milan: Fondazione ENI Enrico Mattei).
Högselius, P. (2013). *Red gas: Russia and the origins of European energy dependence.* (London: Palgrave).

Kozak, M. (2016). 'War in Ukraine opens Europe's eyes to energy security', 18 July 2016, available at: www.financialobserver.eu/poland/war-in-ukraine-opens-europes-eyes-to-energy-security/, accessed 2 September 2017.

Krastev, I. (2015). 'What Central Europe thinks of Russia'. *International New York Times*, 28 April 2015.

Lough, J. (2011). *Russia's Energy Diplomacy*. (London: Chatham House).

Luong, P.J. and Weinthal, E. (2010). *Oil is not a curse: Ownership structure and institutions in Soviet successor states*. (Cambridge: Cambridge University Press).

Lucas, E. (2014). *The new Cold War: Putin's threat to Russia and the West*. (London: Palgrave Macmillan).

McGowan, F. (2011). 'Putting energy insecurity into historical context: European responses to the energy crises of the 1970s and 2000s', *Geopolitics*, 16(3), pp. 486–511.

Noël, P. (2008). 'Challenging the myths of energy security'. *Financial Times*. 10 January 2008.

Nygren, B. (2008). 'Putin's use of natural gas to reintegrate the CIS region'. *Problems of Post-Communism*, 55(4), pp. 3–15.

Ostrowski, W. (2010). *Politics and oil in Kazakhstan*. (London: Routledge).

Stegen, K.S. (2011). 'Deconstructing the "energy weapon": Russia's threat to Europe as case study'. *Energy Policy*, 39(10), pp. 6505–6513.

Stern, J. (2006). 'The Russian-Ukrainian gas crisis of January 2006'. *Oxford Institute for Energy Studies*, 16, pp. 5–12.

Vivoda, V. (2009). 'Resource nationalism, bargaining and international oil companies: challenges and change in the new millennium', *New Political Economy*, 14(4), pp. 517–534.

Vogler, J. (2013). 'Changing conceptions of climate and energy security in Europe', *Environmental Politics*, 22(4), pp. 627–645.

Wilson, J.D. (2015). 'Understanding resource nationalism: economic dynamics and political institutions', *Contemporary Politics*, 21(4), pp. 399–416.

Yergin, D. (2011). *The quest: Energy, security, and the remaking of the modern world*. (London: Penguin).

Youngs, R. (2009). *Energy security: Europe's new foreign policy challenge*. (London: Routledge).

Part I
Analytical framework

2 Energy security in Central and Eastern Europe
An IR theoretical dimension

Roland Dannreuther

2.1 Introduction

The most popular and influential understanding of energy insecurity in Central and Eastern Europe (CEE) highlights the threat posed by Russia, drawing implicitly from the classical realist tradition in International Relations (IR). Russia is perceived as a revisionist state, seeking to challenge the regional and international order. The CEE states are particularly vulnerable because the region has historically been a zone of Russian influence. The most significant economic power that Russia possesses is its role as a major oil and gas producer; the CEE states are vulnerable since they are highly dependent on imports of these energy resources from Russia. The main anxiety is that Russia's strategic approach to the CEE region includes the willingness to use this energy vulnerability as an instrument for political diplomacy and coercion (Baev 2007; Baran 2007; Lough 2011). Such coercive uses of energy as a political weapon can be public and visible, as evident in Russia's conflict with Ukraine and the major gas disputes that have occurred there, most notably in 2006 and 2009. But such malign influence and manipulation of its role as an energy exporter can also be perceived to be more hidden and subtle, such as the use of corrupt economic and political networks to undermine the independence of the states in the region.

This relatively simple realist and geopolitical framing of the problem of energy security in CEE is made more complicated by the inclusion of the European Union (EU). In contrast to Russia, the EU is presented as embodying a fundamentally different understanding of international relations, rejecting the realist and geopolitical approach and promoting instead the liberal norms of cooperation, integration and the peaceful resolution of disputes. The EU is conceptualised as a 'normative power' which eschews the traditional state-centric and nationalistic approach that characterises Russian policies and behaviour (Bretherton and Vogler 2006; Manners 2006; Sjursen 2006). Instead of energy resources being viewed as attributes of national power and interests, the EU promotes them as potential sources for expanding free trade and regional integration and, more generally, for supporting democratic values and freedoms. For the EU, energy security for CEE comes from the liberalisation of the energy sectors, the overcoming of obstacles to regional energy flows and cooperation, and supporting diversification of energy imports so as to reduce the vulnerability of reliance on foreign supplies (Youngs 2009; Goldthau and Sitter 2014).

CEE energy insecurity is incorporated into the representation of a wider conflict between Russia and the EU. This involves a clear ideological and political dimension that mirrors the classical division in IR theory between the realist and liberal traditions (Averre 2009; Kuzemko 2014). Russia is viewed as wedded to the traditional realist model of a state using all its attributes of power, which include its energy resources, as a means to enhance its regional and global ambitions for great power status. In contrast the EU is viewed as a liberal power, constructed on the rejection of the use of force, the overcoming of national and sovereign interests through cooperation and integration including in the energy sector, and the promotion of a liberal model of economic prosperity and democratic values.

The issue of energy security in CEE is, therefore, wrapped up in this broader Russian–EU political context. This not only involves the CEE states but also, and with greater potential for escalation, the former Soviet neighbourhood states, most notably Ukraine, Belarus and the South Caucasus. In 2014, the underlying tensions between Russia and Ukraine exploded most dramatically with the Russian annexation of Crimea and the Russian-supported secessionist rebellion in East Ukraine (Kropatcheva 2011; Tsygankov 2015).

This predominantly geopolitical framing of the issue of energy security in CEE is undoubtedly powerful and captures important dimensions of the underlying reality. However, as with all theoretical constructs, it also involves a simplification of that reality which can hinder a better understanding of the complexities and nuances of the underlying economic and political dynamics. The danger is not only that this framing embodies only a partial truth, but also that it can exacerbate the sources of conflict that it is seeking to describe and overcome. Therefore, the objective of this chapter is to set out this more complex and nuanced reality and thereby to qualify this dominant geopolitical understanding of CEE energy security.

This chapter has two main sections that provide this more detailed and contextualised understanding. The first section provides a differentiated historical context which highlights that EU–Russian relations and European energy security concerns have changed significantly over time. There is no timeless and eternal reality of Russia as a threat to European energy security. Rather, there are differing and frequently shifting European perceptions of the extent of the Russian threat. In fact, it is argued that in the period since 2008 the anxieties and fears over Russia and energy insecurity in the CEE states have significantly declined. The second section brings out further aspects of how IR theoretical frames need to be qualified. This involves, first, incorporating the differences between the CEE states in terms of their dependence on Russia for energy imports and the differences in their overall energy mix. These national differences have a significant effect on the relative sense of vulnerability of these states towards Russia. Second, the agency and autonomy of the CEE states themselves should also not be forgotten. The CEE states are not powerless in the face of Russian and EU power and they generally have a strong resolve to assert their independence and autonomy, which is reflected in their energy policy priorities. These are often more complicated than a simple opposition to Russia and an embrace of the EU. And, third, any account must include the role of non-state actors, most notably energy companies, in developments in the energy sector in the CEE states. Recognition of their role again qualifies the dominant state-centric geopolitical framework.

2.2 The historical context

Three distinct periods of post–Soviet Russian–EU relations in the context of energy security and its impact on CEE can be identified. The first is the immediate post-Soviet period in the 1990s; the second is the period from the 2000s up to the 2008 economic crisis, the period coinciding with the first two terms of Putin's presidency; the third period is from 2008 up until the present day. Each of these periods has distinctive characteristics reflecting the changing policy ambitions and objectives of both Russia and the EU as well as broader changes in the global political economy of energy. All of these have, in turn, direct impacts on how the states of CEE have perceived their relative energy insecurity and the extent and degree of their anxieties over the behaviour of Russia.

The first period of the 1990s, in the aftermath of the dissolution of both the Warsaw Pact and the Soviet Union was necessarily a period of immense political and economic change, generating high levels of insecurity and anxiety on both sides of the former Iron Curtain. However, in the specific area of energy, there was also a significant degree of continuity and an expectation of building upon existing patterns of cooperation and integration. The energy sector was the key area where Europe and the Soviet Union had already engaged in significant economic and political cooperation from the 1970s onwards. The development of the vast Soviet gas resources in north-western Siberia had been very much a joint project, where the Soviet Union provided a reliable source of gas for European markets in exchange for Western technology and expertise to build the pipelines and compressor stations required to transport that gas. During this late Soviet period, Moscow had gone to considerable lengths to insulate these Soviet–European energy relations from broader geopolitical developments and to thereby demonstrate its reliability as an energy supplier (Högselius 2013).

There was, therefore, already a Soviet legacy to post-Soviet Russia of the perception of a country determined to be a 'reliable energy supplier' and not wanting to allow geopolitical factors to undermine a vital trading relationship. The 1990s was also a period of low oil prices dropping at one point to a historic low of under $10 a barrel in 1999. In this context of what appeared to be a new regime of low prices, the dominant economic approach promoted the liberalisation of the energy sector, openness to foreign equity, and the privatisation of state-owned oil companies. The Russian government in the 1990s followed, to a considerable extent, this liberalising move, in particular breaking up the autarchic oil sector through privatisation and inviting foreign capital and ownership. The result was, by the end of the 1990s, a much more complex array of private and state-owned companies with an ambition to develop an internationally competitive energy sector. The EU strongly supported these economic reforms and promoted, in its own turn, a multilateral framework for cross-border cooperation in energy trade, including sensitive areas such as transit and investments. In 1994, the Russian government signed the Energy Charter Treaty (ECT) which, if implemented, would have effectively meant the extension of European norms of trade and openness to Russia's domestic industry (Haukkala 2014).

Overall, the general perception among the European capitals during the 1990s towards Russia was relatively benign, in that Moscow was seen to be making the right moves in terms of its energy reforms and that, despite the evidence of resistance, there was a certain inevitability of its gradual absorption of European values and norms. The main areas of tension were, moreover, primarily in the political and military spheres and the principal Russian concern was the North Atlantic Treaty Organization (NATO) rather than the EU, with strong opposition to NATO enlargement and the NATO interventions into Bosnia and Kosovo (Dannreuther 1999–2000). The EU and the prospect of EU enlargement was generally viewed in Moscow in a more favourable light and even as a potentially positive counter-point to the US drive for NATO enlargement (Tumanov et al. 2011).

Energy-related conflicts were still apparent, but these were predominantly local in nature, primarily among the neighbouring former Soviet countries, such as the Baltic states, Ukraine, Belarus and the South Caucasus. The shift from the Soviet system of subsidised energy supplies to imposing commercial rates based on international prices created significant economic problems in these newly independent states, exacerbated by the general difficulties of the transition period. The willingness of the Russian government to reward those states which were perceived to be politically loyal, through keeping their energy prices lower; and inversely to raise prices for those countries moving away from the Russian sphere of influence, inevitably politicised these energy relations, heightening regional energy security concerns (Newnham 2011; Smith Stegen 2011). The incomplete, chaotic and highly corrupted nature of the Russian economic transition process was also manifested in shadowy intermediary companies which engaged in rent-appropriation of the energy trade so as to reward elites in both Russia and the client states. This was also inevitably viewed as a clandestine vehicle for Russia to maintain its power and influence in those countries which it had formerly controlled.

Despite these growing sources of anxiety over energy security among the former Soviet states and more generally in CEE, the view from the EU and the major European capitals was still relatively benign, viewing this as more 'teething problems' in the process of transition than as a fundamental threat to European energy security. However, this complacency shifted dramatically in the second period which started in the early 2000s with the transition from the Yeltsin to the Putin presidency. The major catalyst for this was the resolve of the new president to re-assert Russia's ambitions to be a great power and to reverse the decentralising dynamics of the Yeltsin era. This shift was most notably marked in the energy sector by the state take-over of one of the most successful private Russian oil companies, Yukos, in 2003 and the subsequent sentencing of the company's CEO, Mikhail Khodorkovsky, to a long period in prison (Thompson 2005; Sakwa 2008). This initiated a process of increased state control over the oil industry, mirroring the control which had never been relinquished in the gas industry, and the assertion of the political primacy of the state over all other actors, including powerful economic interests (Goldman 2008; Bradshaw 2009). These moves towards a more assertive state control of the industry initiated a paradigm shift in the EU from viewing the Russian government as moving, if slowly and inconsistently, towards the liberalisation agenda promoted by the EU, to seeing it as deliberately attempting to undermine and subvert it.

This shift in perceptions over the nature of the domestic reforms in Russia was paralleled by growing anxiety over Russian behaviour towards its neighbourhood, including the CEE states. With EU enlargement in 2004 and 2007 incorporating CEE states as new EU members, complementing their accession to NATO, Russia no longer viewed the EU as potentially more accommodating to Russian interests than NATO. Moreover, in a number of the former Soviet countries, most notably Ukraine, the geopolitical tension between the West and Russia increasingly became centred on the conflict between the EU and Russia, reflecting the internal tensions within Ukraine over whether its destiny lay with Europe or with closer relations with Russia. The historic role of Ukraine as the major transit country for Russian gas to reach its European markets became a major trigger point for this broader deterioration in Russian–Ukrainian and Russian–EU relations. The longstanding dispute over Ukraine payments for its gas imports from Russia spilled over in 2006 and 2009 into temporary suspensions of gas flows into Ukraine. This led to the interruption of supplies of gas to European markets which affected the CEE states most strongly. Even though this interruption did not last very long, it was highly symbolic and indicated that Russia could no longer be trusted as a reliable supplier who would always prioritise economic over political interests.

The late 2000s was, therefore, the period when the perception of Russia as a geopolitical threat to energy security was at its strongest. The Ukraine gas crisis in 2009 had been preceded by the Munich Security Conference in 2007, when Putin had articulated in the strongest form to date of Russian opposition and disillusionment with the West, which was then followed in 2008 with the intervention into Georgia. All of this appeared to confirm the realist view of Russia as a revisionist power determined to use its energy power to further its political objectives.

However, it is notable that in the period since 2008, the energy dimension of the European–Russian conflict has diminished. There are a number of factors behind this. The first is that the economic recession in 2008 heralded a significant drop in oil prices, bringing to an end the seemingly inexorable rise in oil prices from 2000 onwards which had reached its peak at $147 a barrel. With the decline of oil prices, which culminated in prices dropping to below $30 a barrel in 2014, the relative power of Russia as an oil and gas producer significantly declined. Reduced demand in key European markets, which was not only driven by economic conditions but also by the resolve to 'decarbonise' the European economy through promoting modern renewable energy sources (RES) in the energy mix, meant that European demand for Russian gas could no longer be guaranteed. The additional factors of the 'shale gas' revolution in the United States, and the growing global role played by Liquefied Natural Gas (LNG) supply, meant that Russia potentially faced a much more competitive environment (Goldthau and Boersma 2014). As a consequence, Europe's relative bargaining power, despite the decline of its own domestic gas supplies from the North Sea, increased. The result was that the Russian stake in defending its image as a 'reliable supplier' became a more critical economic and political objective.

A second factor was that the reforms in the domestic Russian energy sector began to stabilise and to be consolidated by the end of the 2000s. The Russian state had, certainly, strengthened central state control over the sector and had significantly reduced the independent power of the private oil companies and their owners (the so-called 'oligarchs') while also making Russia a less welcoming place for foreign investment. However, this was not unique to Russia and mirrored a broader global development of 'resource nationalism' among energy producers so as to capture a greater share of the more abundant rents at a time of higher prices (Bremmer 2009; Vivoda 2009). However, as Locatelli and Rossiaud (2011) argue, these Russian reforms were not primarily driven by a desire to re-assert a Soviet-style autarchic structure but to re-balance the relationship between companies and state so as to resolve some of the dysfunctional results of the reforms of the 1990s which also had been perceived to be illegitimate by much of the Russian population. The end-result of the stabilisation of the Russian energy sector, even if it gave the state a stronger role, was a greater degree of stability and coherence in Russian energy policy. One important consequence of this was the significant decline of the role of the shadowy intermediaries, and a return to more direct state-to-state or company-to-company negotiations, which reduced the perception among CEE states that the Russian government was using such intermediaries for malign political purposes.

The third factor behind the decline in the perception of energy insecurity in relation to Russia was the corresponding strengthening of the EU's own reach and power as an energy actor. In reality, the EU's authority in the European energy sector has always been circumscribed by the powers accorded to the member states to determine their national policies and priorities, as explicitly written into the 2007 Lisbon Treaty. Nevertheless, the succession of EU energy initiatives or 'packages' from 1998 onwards, with the second and third packages in 2003 and 2009 respectively, expanded the role of the EU in promoting the liberalisation of European energy markets, in breaking up state monopolies, and in supporting regional integration and greater diversification of supplies. The accession of the majority of the ECE states as full members of the EU also meant that they could benefit from the greater bargaining power that membership provided as compared to negotiating directly with Russia. As Ostrowski and Cesnakas note in the chapters in this volume on Poland and the Baltic states, the reassurance and the need to conform with the EU's regulatory framework helped these countries to gain confidence in their energy relations with Russia and thereby to reduce perceptions of energy insecurity. In certain areas, the EU was also willing to assert itself in a more typically quasi-realist manner, such as in promoting an alternative Nabucco gas pipeline and in directly taking on Gazprom's ambitions in Europe through applying EU competition law (Goldthau and Sitter 2014).

By the mid-2010s, the EU's energy relationship with Russia was on a much stronger foundation and the anxieties and concerns of the CEE states in relation to their energy security had been significantly alleviated. But this was also happening during a period when the more general military and political relationship with Russia was becoming more rather than less intense. The extent of the deterioration of the general political climate was confirmed with the Russian annexation of Crimea in 2014 and the Russian support for secessionist forces in East Ukraine. In these conditions of the most serious threat to European security since the end of the Cold War, it was notable that, as compared to the much less serious conflicts between Russia and Ukraine in 2006 and 2009, anxieties over energy security were less prominent or apparent (Casier 2016). The relative 'silence' over the threat to energy supplies reflects a return to Cold War practice. As during the 1980s, both Russia and Europe saw it as in their mutual interest to 'insulate' energy from broader military, political and economic developments. As in the Soviet period, energy had become a key joint interest to promote the potential for cooperation despite the deterioration of the broader relationship.

2.3 Energy security in CEE – qualifying the IR framework

This chapter has argued that understanding the historical evolution of Russian–European energy relations is critical for understanding how the perceptions of Russia as a geopolitical threat to European energy security is context-specific and changes over time. In terms of IR theory, this does not reject the general characterisation of Russia as operating according to broadly realist principles, or that the EU conforms more closely to the liberal model. Rather, it is true that the actual concrete manifestation of these attributes reflects a more complex and differentiated reality. The danger of assuming a simplistic or deterministic geopolitical/realist frame is that it misses this greater complexity and fails to recognise the potential for constructive cooperation that can emerge and survive even a severe deterioration in the general political and security relationship.

In addition to this greater historical sensitivity, accounts of CEE energy security which utilise an IR theoretical framework need also to incorporate other critical considerations and factors if they are to provide a more accurate and sophisticated understanding of the underlying reality. Three such factors include how IR theoretical lenses are more applicable to some energy resources rather than others; the need to recognise the agency and independence of the CEE states themselves and not treat the region as a strategic vacuum at the mercy of Russia and the EU; and the need to incorporate the role of non-state actors, most notably the energy companies.

2.3.1 The energy mix in CEE

It is first important to recognise that when the issue of energy security is discussed in relation to Europe and the CEE states, the dominant concern is over the security of gas supplies. This focus on gas is not surprising since there are genuinely greater international security concerns for Europe over the supply of this particular energy resource. The reason for this is ultimately due to its physical characteristics; gas is far less dense and energy-rich than liquid petroleum – for a given volume at standard pressure, it contains only a fraction of the heat content of oil. The consequence is that gas is more difficult and more expensive to transport than oil. The only way that gas can be transported over land is by pipelines and this 'tyranny of distance' has meant that gas has a number of regional, rather than truly global, markets. Large gas projects are also highly capital intensive and, given the size and complexity of these projects, states are inevitably involved. The development of the gas pipeline network from the Soviet Union to Western Europe in the 1980s is paradigmatic of the intense state-to-state negotiation and cooperation required. Gas trade, in contrast to oil, generally requires long-term contracts if it is to be feasible, principally because of the capital-intensive projects and the need for long-term guarantees of supply and demand to make the trade worthwhile for both buyers and sellers.

All of these factors contribute to make Russian exports of gas to European markets particularly politically sensitive. There is the need for a cooperative relationship so as to sustain the continual flow of gas which is in the interest of both producers and consumers. The fact that even a short-term interruption can have major and immediate impacts places a significant pressure to avoid any deterioration in relations having a knock-on impact on gas supplies. The way that gas pipelines cross over other countries, so-called 'transit' states, adds to the more general energy security concerns. Transit states in trans-continental gas pipeline routes are critical sources of vulnerability as they have the power to disrupt flows of gas and have an incentive to bargain for improved terms, which is exacerbated by there being no clear international agreement about what the terms and financial benefits for transit states should be (Stevens 2009). It is not surprising, in this context, that Ukraine, through which most of Russia's gas to Europe flows, has been at the epicentre for European energy security anxieties (Kropatcheva 2011; Feklyunina 2012). Russian attempts to reduce this vulnerability by developing alternative pipeline routes, such as with Nordstream and the ambitions to develop South Stream, have themselves been sources of significant political sensitivity (Baev and Overland 2010). More generally, determination of the appropriate price for gas supplies for Russia, and Russia's natural preference for long-term contracts, are themselves sources of political contestation as there is only a regional and not an international pricing benchmark.

It is not surprising, therefore, that gas supplies from Russia are the most significant focus for the issue of energy security in Europe and that this is reflected in the IR literature on European energy security. However, this focus on gas needs to be qualified by the recognition that gas only represents one element in the overall European energy mix. Although gas is a vital part of Russia's trade with the EU, representing 42 per cent of Europe's gas imports, Russia also exports 33 per cent of Europe's oil imports and 26 per cent of its hard coal imports. In reality, the revenues that Russia receives from its oil exports are significantly higher than those for its gas exports. However, these oil exports generate far less energy security concerns, primarily because oil is a much more fungible commodity and European states can relatively easily ensure supplies from other producers on the global market and can also store these supplies at much lower cost. As such, the Russian capacity to use its oil supplies as a geopolitical tool are more limited than for its gas supplies. This is even more the case for coal where there are ample global supplies and storage is even less costly.

The nature and extent of Russian energy power is also brought into a more realistic perspective when the broader European energy situation is more clearly defined. Overall Russian energy resources contribute to approximately 20 per cent of the EU's energy consumption and 10 per cent of its electricity. Certainly, a number of CEE states rely 100% on the gas supplies from Russia – Estonia, Lithuania, Latvia, Bulgaria and Slovakia. However, when these gas supplies from Russia are considered as a share of the overall national energy consumption, only four CEE states rely on more than 25 per cent of their energy consumption from Russian gas imports – Hungary, Lithuania, Latvia and Slovakia.

In practice, all CEE states rely upon a diversity of different energy resources in their energy mix, either produced domestically or imported from a variety of different producers. The decisions about what the exact nature of this energy mix should be remains a matter of national sovereign determination and energy security is only one element in this. Price and economic competitiveness, along with environmental concerns, also influence the decisions made. Despite the potential energy security risks, Russian gas is often economically competitive, when compared for example with LNG imports. Similarly, a decision to diversify away from Russian supplies by using more coal has significant environmental consequences, which potentially cancel out the energy security gains. In short, CEE states can legitimately take the decision to import Russian gas despite the increased energy security risks because of the other benefits that it provides, not least to domestic energy consumers.

2.3.2 The CEE states as autonomous actors

Overall, when the more general geopolitical context is qualified by focusing on more strictly national perspectives of energy security, the picture of Russia as an overbearing energy superpower is less evident. This suggests, more generally, that it is helpful to give more prominence to these national perspectives than is often the case when adopting the traditional IR theoretical traditions of realism and liberalism. There is a certain tendency in these IR approaches, in particular with realism, to treat smaller states as powerless against the predations of the great powers and to view states like those in CEE as pawns in a great game between the major external powers, in this case between Russia and the EU. The problem with this is that it tends to reduce the autonomous power of these sovereign states to make their own decisions. It also fails to recognise that even small states have a capacity to manipulate or play off external powers so as to protect their specific national interests.

This is particularly relevant in the case of CEE. The states of this region are generally either small or medium-size whose historical memories are of incorporation into the peripheries of larger empires. The latest of these was as satellites of the Soviet Union so it is not surprising that the perception of continued threat from Russia remains a live concern. The intensity of this sense of threat is, however, historically conditioned and varies across the CEE region. There is, for instance, a significant difference in threat perception in Poland and the Baltic states, where the Russian threat is generally viewed as existential, and Bulgaria and Serbia, where more positive images of Russia are evident. As Ostrowski notes in this volume, the Polish perception of the Russian energy threat has little connection with the actual reality of Poland's energy situation which is only marginally dependent on Russian imports. In contrast, in Serbia, as Damnojovic argues in this volume, the perception of Russia as a protector of its broader political and strategic objectives culminated with a willing submission to Gazprom to take over most of its oil and natural gas sector.

There is value, in this regard, to highlight a third strand of the classical IR theoretical tradition which includes a more radical dependency perspective, articulating the interests of states which have had a history of external domination and control. This tradition emphasises how poorer less developed states are vulnerable to exploitation and the perpetuation of conditions of dependency when incorporated into structural conditions of inequality (Prebisch 1963; Hinnebusch 2003). Operating within this perspective, the inclusion of the

CEE states into the EU, which was welcomed as a form of liberation from the previous Soviet legacy, has not meant that there is an unquestioning agreement with the broader EU integrationist ambitions.

In the area of energy policies, a number of the key EU policy objectives can be seen potentially to threaten significant national energy security interests. An example of this is how the energy security provided by the freedom to use the ample coal supplies found in many CEE states, which provides a significant degree of energy security, is threatened by the climate change-driven decarbonisation objectives of the EU. For Poland, this is perceived as arguably a greater threat to its energy security than that posed by Russia. Similarly in Estonia, the pressure from the EU for climate change mitigation has threatened electricity production which primarily uses indigenous shale oil supplies. More generally, the EU's liberalisation policies in the energy sector threaten to increase prices for consumers, which is particularly sensitive for CEE states where a larger proportion of incomes is spent on energy supply than in other more prosperous EU member states.

The dependency perspective is valuable when considering those CEE states where a desire for national autonomy and independence in energy matters is particularly strong. Romania has had a long tradition as a domestic energy producer and a country where there is a strong resistance to any significant foreign control over its energy sector. In Hungary, the populist political agenda of the Viktor Orbán government is translated into a 'Hungary-first' policy which prioritises Hungary's national interests even if that means favouring Russia over other external suppliers. Although Hungary and Romania might be extreme cases, all of the CEE states are capable of utilising or manipulating the 'Russian threat' so as to strengthen their own specific national interests. For Poland, the image of Russia as a geopolitical threat has been used to defend its own coal industry against EU pressure, despite the environmental damage it causes, because of the presumed benefits that it provides for overcoming the energy insecurity of Russian imports.

2.3.3 *The role of non-state actors*

Another important qualification to the dominant geopolitical framing is the need to include not only states but also non-state actors who play a significant role in European energy relations. The most important of these are the energy companies, both Russian and Western, who in practice are significantly more important actors in terms of the commercial business of European and CEE energy trade than are states. There is also no simple mapping of the interests of states with the interests of their national energy companies. This is the case for state-owned Russian companies as well as for private Western energy companies. Unlike states with their necessarily complex set of competing interests, companies have a necessarily narrower focus on commercial success and profitability. Such a focused commercial logic does not easily map onto the state-centric assumptions of IR theory.

In the case of the more ambitious Russian oil and gas companies, a significant strategic goal is to become global energy players and this means making acquisitions and gaining a presence in foreign markets. State control of energy prices within Russia means that higher profits can often be made more easily in foreign rather than in domestic markets. These companies can, therefore, be considered to be seeking as much to 'escape' from the state as to be obedient 'instruments' of the state, though clearly there is also a mutual interest for the Russian government to support the external objectives of their energy companies.

For these Russian oil companies, there is also nothing particularly exceptional about CEE other than it is a region where it could be expected that they might have a strategic advantage given the historical links and connections. In practice, however, the political sensitivities raised by the attempts of Russian companies to secure energy assets in the region has tended to limit the ability of these companies to realise their ambitions. As a consequence, as Rossiaud and Locatelli note in this volume, the only major oil Russian oil company that has been consistently active in the downstream CEE oil sector has been Lukoil but it has suffered a number of disappointments and, with the fall in oil prices, has been looking to disengage from the region even more. Gazprom has had a stronger rationale to move further into the European downstream market, primarily to maximise the gas rents that it obtains, and to limit the impact of EU liberalisation, rather than any state-directed political objectives. Again, as with the Russian oil companies, Gazprom's ambitions have been constrained by concerns over energy security and the EU's resolve to use its competition policy to limit the market power of the Russian gas monopoly. In its struggle with the European Commission, Gazprom has not simply resorted to a state-backed geopolitical approach but has also adopted an array of technocratic and legalistic approaches to support its interests (Romanova 2016). As with any company, Gazprom's main interest has been to secure its economic and commercial interests which ultimately requires accommodation and compromise rather than unresolved confrontation.

Like their Russian counterparts, the interests of Western European energy companies cannot simply be assumed to coincide with the interests of the EU and their respective states. German companies like E.ON Ruhrgas and BASF/Wintershall, and Italian companies like ENI, have a long history of mutually advantageous commercial relations with the Russian energy sector and their profits and future prospects are linked to maintaining these good relations and ensuring access to upstream Russian oil and gas (Lough 2011). This more benign relationship with Russia also reflects, to some degree, differing national perspectives where the larger Western European countries that have traditionally imported the greatest volume of Russian gas have significantly less fears and concerns over energy security than the smaller more vulnerable CEE states and thus less interest in disrupting European–Russian energy relations. In general, private Western oil companies do not make a hard and fast distinction between Russia and other oil-producing parts of the world where business conditions are often even more difficult and challenging than in Russia. Indeed, many of these companies, like BP or Total, see the Russian energy sector as attractive and with greater prospects than found, for example, in many of the energy-rich Middle Eastern states.

2.4 Conclusion

This chapter has highlighted how the issue of Russia and energy insecurity in CEE tends to be analysed, whether implicitly or explicitly, within the framework of a geopolitical or realist approach. This Russian geopolitical threat is then contrasted with the counter-actions and policies of the European Union which is taken to represent the anti-realist liberal model. There emerges, as a consequence, a picture of a continuing and unresolved conflict between a normative EU and a realist and aggressive Russia with energy as a major cause and the CEE as a major site for that conflict.

Although this application of high-level IR theoretical frameworks has advantages for identifying the implicit assumptions that underpin public and elite perceptions, such frameworks can also caricature and over-simplify the more complex reality of Russia's energy role in the region. Such a simplification includes, critically, how the energy relationship between Russia and Europe, and with the CEE states more specifically, changes over time and is continually being negotiated and adapted to the differing external and internal conditions. It was noted, in this regard, that Russian–European distrust and anxieties over energy security were most acute in the early to mid-2000s but then become less politically sensitive from the 2008 economic recession onwards. Even with the severe deterioration in the overarching European–Russian political relations over the 2014 annexation of Crimea, with the imposition of EU sanctions, the energy dimensions of these relations have not been affected and have been, to some extent, insulated from the broader politico-strategic relationship. Similarly, in CEE the level of anxiety over energy insecurity has not generally become larger or more prominent due to the Russian actions in Ukraine.

The other major weakness of adopting an implicit IR theoretical framework is that this naturally tends to focus on the large external actors, the so-called 'Great Powers'. Realist theory, in particular, places its attention on states and on the balance of power which is primarily about the balance between the largest and most powerful states. What is lost in this analysis is the independent power and autonomy of the smaller or medium-sized states, which generally characterise the CEE states, in the face of this overarching regional conflict between the EU and Russia. Certainly, these states have gained in significantly increased bargaining power by becoming EU member states and this has helped to give them the confidence to negotiate and act more forcefully in their relations with Russia. However, this has not meant that they have become unquestioning pawns of the European Union or the larger European states. Rather, they have preserved and increasingly want to assert their sovereign independence which includes engaging with Russia in the energy sector, if it is perceived to be in their national interest to do so. In general, where Russia has been successful in developing or extending its energy presence in the CEE states this has been at the invitation and through the sovereign decision of these CEE states rather than by means of geopolitical imposition or manipulation. In this sense, energy security in CEE is mainly about what the CEE states make of it.

References

Averre, D. (2009). 'Competing rationalities: Russia, the EU and "shared neighbourhoods"', *Europe-Asia Studies*, 61(10), pp. 1689–1713.
Baev, P.K. (2007). 'Russia aspires to the status of "energy superpower"', *Strategic Analysis*, 31(3), pp. 447–465.
Baev, P.K. and I. Overland (2010). 'The South Stream versus Nabucco pipeline race: geopolitical and economic (ir)rationales and politicla stakes in mega-projects', *International Affairs*, 86(5), pp. 1075–1090.
Baran, Z. (2007). 'EU energy security: time to end Russian leverage', *The Washington Quarterly*, 30(4), pp. 131–144.
Bradshaw, M.J. (2009). 'The geopolltics of global energy security', *Geography Compass*, 3(5), pp.1920–1937.
Bremmer, I. (2009). 'State capitalism comes of age: the end of the free market?', *Foreign Affairs*, 88(3), pp. 40–55.
Bretherton, C. and J. Vogler (2006). *The European Union as a global actor*. (London: Routledge).
Casier, T. (2016). 'Great game or great confusion: the geopolitical understanding of EU-Russian energy relations', *Geopolitics*, 21(4), pp. 763–778.
Dannreuther, R. (1999–2000). 'Escaping the enlargement trap in NATO-Russian relations', *Survival*, 41(4), pp. 145–164.
Feklyunina, V. (2012). 'Russia's international images and its energy policy. An unreliable supplier?', *Europe-Asia Studies*, 64(3), pp. 449–469.
Goldman, M. (2008). *Oilopoly: Putin, Power and the rise of the new Russia*. (Oxford: Oneworld Book).
Goldthau, A. and T. Boersma (2014). 'The 2014 Ukraine-Russia crisis: implications for energy markets and scholarship', *Energy Research and Social Science*, (3), pp. 13–15.
Goldthau, A. and N. Sitter (2014). 'A liberal actor in a realist world: The Commission and the external dimension of the single market for energy', *Journal of European Public Policy*, 21(10), pp. 1452–1472.
Haukkala, H. (2014). 'Towards a pan-European energy order? Energy as an object of contention in EU-Russian relations', *OGEL* 12(4).
Hinnebusch, R. (2003). *The International Politics of the Middle East*. (Manchester: Manchester University Press).
Hogselius, P. (2013). *Red Gas: Russia and the Origins of European Energy Dependence*. (Basingstoke: Palgrave Macmillan).
Kropatcheva, E. (2011). 'Playing both ends against the middle: Russia's geopolitical energy games with the EU and Ukraine', *Geopolitics*, 16(3), pp. 553–573.
Kuzemko, C. (2014). 'Ideas, power and change: explaining EU-Russian energy relations', *Journal of European Public Policy*, 21(1), pp. 58–75.

Locatelli, C. and S. Rossiaud (2011). 'A neoinstitutionalist interpretation of the changes in the Russian oil model', *Energy Policy*, 39(9), pp. 5588–5597.
Lough, J. (2011). 'Russia's energy diplomacy', *Chatham House Briefing Paper*. REP RSP BP 2011/01. The Means and Ends of Russian Influence Abroad Series May 2011, Available at: www.chathamhouse.org/sites/files/chathamhouse/19352_0511bp_lough.pdf, accessed 11 August 2017.
Manners, I. (2006). 'Normative power Europe reconsidered: beyond the crossroads', *Journal of European Public Policy*, 13(2), pp. 182–199.
Newnham, R. (2011). 'Oil, sticks and carrots: Russia's energy resources as a foreign policy tool', *Journal of Eurasian Studies*, 2(2), pp. 134–143.
Prebisch, R. (1963). *Towards a Dynamic Development Policy for Latin America*. (New York: United Nations).
Romanova, E. (2016). 'Is Russian energy politcis towards the EU only about geopolitics? The case of the third energy package', *Geopolitics*, 21(4), pp. 857–879.
Sakwa, R. (2008). *The Quality of Freedom: Khodorkhovsky, Putin and the Yukos affair*. (Oxford: Oxford University Press).
Sjursen, H. (2006). 'The EU as a normative power: how can this be?', *Journal of European Public Policy*, 13(2), pp. 235–251.
Smith Stegen, K. (2011). 'Deconstructing the "energy weapon": Russia's threat to Europe as a case study', *Energy Policy*, 93(10), pp. 6505–6513.
Stevens, P. (2009). *Transit Troubles: Pipelines as a Source of Conflict*. (London: Chatham House).
Thompson, W. (2005). 'Putting Yukos in perspective', *Post-Soviet Affairs*, 21(2), pp. 159–181.
Tsygankov, A. (2015). 'Vladimir Putin's last stand: the sources of Russia's Ukraine policy', *Post-Soviet Affairs*, 31(4), pp. 279–303.
Tumanov, S., A. Gasparishvili and E. Romanova (2011). 'Russia-EU relations, or how the Russians really view the EU', *Journal of Communist Studies and Transition Politics*, 27(1), pp. 120–141.
Vivoda, V. (2009). 'Resource nationalism, bargaining and international oil companies: challanges and change in the millennium', *New Political Economy*, 14(4), pp. 517–534.
Youngs, R. (2009). *Energy Security: Europe's New Foreign Policy Challenge*. (London: Routledge).

3 Debating transition

Terry Cox

3.1 Introduction

If, as the chapters of this book suggest, the energy security of the countries of Central and Eastern Europe (CEE) is determined to some extent by the character of governance and relations between key elite actors in the field, then it can be argued that these questions in turn are affected by the overall character of the society and economy of each country. Furthermore, as divisions have been emerging between CEE countries on questions of energy security and supply, it seems relevant to examine these questions in the context of differences between the CEE countries in the character of their post-socialist economies and polities, something that has not been explored in any great detail within general regional energy security literature. Among the many aspects of these differences are questions of the extent of the liberalisation of the economy, the character of ownership and of privatisation, the character of post-socialist elites, relations between state and economy including issues of state capture and corruption, and the relation of national economies to their wider international context.

Since the end of Communist rule and the dismantling of the distinctive economic and social institutions of the 'state socialist' system, the post-socialist societies of Eastern Europe have undergone processes of transformation that share some general similarities, but also display some significant contrasts. In each society the distinctive institutions of 'state socialism' gave way to institutional frameworks based on market economics. Eastern Europe's political structures underwent extensive changes following the collapse of the ruling Communist parties; these included major shifts in economic and social policy, and dismantling the old systems of centralised bureaucratic management of the economy, extensive state ownership of the means of production, and the bureaucratic allocation of goods and services. In their place, a new system emerged, comprising in varying degrees private ownership and regulation based on market forces so that prices were determined by the market. Subsidies on consumer goods (including energy) and services were largely removed, measures were introduced for the privatisation of state-owned companies, and more generally the majority of property is now held in private hands. At the same time, the domestic economies of the region have been exposed, each in slightly different ways, to international influences as they have sought advice, investment and expanding trade with other countries and international institutions. Accompanying the economic changes have been parallel political reforms so that competitive elections between political parties provide the main mechanism for the selection of governments and the articulation of the preferences of the electorate.

3.2 Transition or transformation?

Initially, in the early 1990s, the debate on these changes was dominated by a neo-liberal understanding of the process as one of 'transition' which assumed an endpoint that would be western-style capitalism 'without qualifying adjectives'. The main discussion focused on the mechanisms for achieving this given end rather than on the possibility that there might be different outcomes. Moreover, it was generally assumed that with the collapse of communist rule the new strategies could be pursued within an institutional vacuum free from any constraints from communist legacies.[1]

However, by the mid-1990s, it had become apparent to most observers that the processes of post-communist change were actually more complex and were leading towards different outcomes, an issue that was particularly noticeable within the regional energy sector. In order to understand this greater variability, a clearer focus was required on the determinants of the changes rather than only on the strategies and mechanisms of change, and alternative understandings were proposed which saw the process as one of 'transformation', entailing the idea that the endpoint could not be predetermined and a range of possible outcomes was conceivable. To begin with, description of the variation was seen in terms of the extent of progress of different countries towards the establishment of market capitalism. For example, it was suggested that by the mid-1990s three groups of countries could be identified in terms of the extent of their economic and political transformation (Csaba 1996). More dramatically, for Gati (1996: 11–12), the three emerging groups could be described as 'leaders', including the Czech Republic, Hungary and Poland and perhaps the three Baltic states of the former Soviet Union; 'laggards', including Bulgaria and Romania; and 'losers', including some of the countries that had emerged from the former Soviet Union and Yugoslavia. Quite soon however the idea emerged that different countries were not necessarily at different stages of capitalist development, but were consolidating as different types of capitalist economy.

Moreover, the neo-liberal approach was criticised for ignoring historical legacies. For example Laszlo Bruszt (1992: 57) proposed that a deeper analysis of transformation must include 'the differences in the structural and institutional legacies of these regimes, linking the modalities in transformative politics to the differences in the paths taken before and during the transition to democracy'. The influences of the paths taken before and during transformation were subsequently explored in more detail for Czechoslovakia, Hungary and Poland by Ekiert (1996) and Cox and Mason (1999). The focus of these studies and of David Stark (1990, 1992) was not on the influence of legacies in isolation, but on the relations between different social actors, elite and non-elite, in adapting and building on the legacies in the building of new institutional arrangements. As Stark (1992: 21) argued, 'actors who seek to introduce change require resources to overcome obstacles to change. This exploitation of existing institutionalized resources is a principle component of the apparent paradox that even instances of transformation are marked by path dependence.'

3.3 Explaining the variation in post-socialist regimes

Since the late 1990s, as the extent of variation in post-socialist regimes became apparent, an equally varied literature has emerged attempting to identify the main factors explaining why different countries in the region have developed in different ways. In general, many of these studies have focused on different aspects of political and cultural influences, including political institutional factors (see, Ostrow 2000; Lewis 2002; Haughton 2005; Ganev 2007; Kopecky 2008), the negative consequences of high levels of political polarisation for economic transformation and effective governance (Frye 2010), the significance of social capital and civil society development (see, Ekiert and Kubik 1999; Howard 2003; Uhlin 2005; Cox 2014), and the influence of international institutions especially the European Union (EU) (see, Jacoby 2004; Vachudova 2005).

In contrast to these approaches, which tend to see economic factors as dependent variables in relation to political and cultural factors, other approaches have given greater emphasis to economic influences and the international economic environment in which new regime formation has taken place. Consideration of economic influences has been the particular focus of three comparative studies of post-socialist forms of capitalism by Connolly (2013), Myant and Drahokoupil (2011), and Martin (2013).

Connolly has offered an analysis on the basis of the hypotheses that economic factors determine the variations in transformation outcomes. First, he suggests, 'developments in the wider international economy affect the prospects for domestic structural economic change which in turn shapes the development or otherwise of greater levels of economic competition' (Connolly 2013: 217). Among the more significant developments, Connolly suggests, were changes in the behaviour of multinational corporations, changes in international production networks, the role of international institutions, and fluctuations in world prices for raw materials and manufactured output. In his country studies he finds confirmation of this hypothesis; for example, in that fluctuations in the prices of commodities, especially hydrocarbons, was the most important variable in explaining Russian political economy, while the diffusion of manufacturing through multi-national companies (MNCs) had a significant influence on economic restructuring in Estonia and Romania, and in CEE more widely.

Second, Connolly hypothesises that 'higher levels of technological sophistication and competition throughout the economy cause political development along more open-access lines' (Connolly 2013: 218). The main features of open-access orders he suggests, are 'the dominance of impersonal, universally enforced legal frameworks in which competition between organisations is conducted in a more open manner', whereas limited-access orders are characterised by 'selective application of rules, both at the elite level and within wider society, and by the channelling of competitive tendencies through informal, personalistic ties and relationships' (Connolly 2013: 43).

In reference to his separate country studies, Connolly suggests the evidence supports this hypothesis on the whole. He took Belarus as an example of a concentrated industrial structure under state ownership and control, Romania as a country making a slow start in economic transformation but then achieving significant development of privatisation, increased foreign investment and a growth of medium- and high-level technology-based production, and Estonia as a country with rapid privatisation and foreign inward investment, and extensive market competition in all sectors of the economy. Relating economic data to political and social data he finds that Belarus had the lowest levels, Romania medium levels and Estonia the highest levels of inter-sectoral competition in the economy, citizen participation in politics, freedom of expression and association, consistent rule of law governing the activities of the government, control over corruption and capacity for collective action among independent groups. This allows him to conclude that 'the argument that economic competition causes greater political competition does appear to be supported by the evidence' (Connolly 2013: 218), and more broadly this supports his argument that "higher levels of technological sophistication and competition throughout the economy causes political development along more open-access lines' (Connolly 2013: 218).

However, other evidence produced by his study suggests such an explanation is not completely adequate and that a range of other factors are also important in explaining why stronger democracy, a more open and active civil society and generally a more open-access social order have developed during post-communist transformation in some societies rather than others. The other significant factors he suggests, include two other economic factors, the rate of investment and the nature of the privatisation process, and also the particular character of political parties, civil and business associations, business–state relations.

Other studies that explore the significance of economic factors as the main determinants of post-socialist regime variation have explored the question more specifically within the framework of the 'varieties of capitalism' debate. Within this general approach, different typologies of capitalist transformation have been proposed, each representing a distinct coherent form of capitalism, drawing on different criteria for the classification of countries. An influential study in the development of this approach in general was the pioneering work of Hall and Soskice (2001) on varieties of capitalism among the more advanced capitalist economies of the world which proposed a basic distinction between liberal market economies (LMEs), typified by the USA, and coordinated market economies (CMEs), typified by Germany, each with distinctive forms of capital market, production system and system of governance. An alternative approach was developed by Amable (2003: 171–181) based on a longer list of variables including product and labour markets, finance and employment, and also social characteristics of welfare and education. This identified five different types of capitalism: market-based, social democratic, continental European, Mediterranean and Asian. However, although there has been much debate on whether variations on their basic typology can be used for the study of the post-socialist forms of capitalism detailed studies of the region have tended to opt for different approaches.[2]

Instead of drawing directly on approaches created for the analysis of developed capitalist economies, Myant and Drahokoupil have proposed using data on the integration of the CEE economies into international economic relations more generally as the dependent variable, and relating it to independent variables such as state capacity, the rule of law, corporate governance, the stability of the financial system, the clarity of business ownership and the extent of separation between business and politics (Myant and Drahokoupil 2011: 300–301).

In attempting to operationalise their approach Myant and Drahokoupil identified six different forms of international integration that could be related to the internal features of the CEE economies in different ways in order to categorise different forms of emerging capitalism. First, 'the most secure form of international integration, offering the highest incomes, was the export of high-value products'. This was based mainly on foreign direct investment (FDI) by MNCs and depended on the existence of a skilled workforce, a 'complex web of links to other organisations' and a high level of state capacity (Myant and Drahokoupil 2011: 303). Such conditions were found primarily in the Visegrad countries and to a lesser extent in the Baltic countries, and later to some extent in South-East Europe (SEE). Second, but much less common, were examples of high-value exports by domestically owned companies without FDI, mainly represented by some Slovenian companies and a few in the Czech Republic. Third, was the subcontracting to MNCs of the manufacture of lower value goods for export where only lower skill levels were required. This was important in the Visegrad countries temporarily in the early 1990s, and more important in the Baltic and SEE countries later on (Myant and Drahokoupil 2011: 304–305). Fourth, was the export of raw materials and semi-manufactured goods. This was of some importance to the CEE countries to begin with, but less so later. Fifth, was dependence on remittances, aid and borrowing from international financial institutions which was mostly found within the region under discussion here in some countries in SEE. Sixth, were different forms of international integration based on 'financialised growth' or, in other words, 'by foreign borrowing and financial inflows to support private sector activity including consumption and imports' (Myant and Drahokoupil 2011: 307). These forms were less important for the Czech Republic, Slovakia and Poland, but more so for Hungary, the Baltic and the SEE countries (Myant and Drahokoupil 2011: 307–310).

By combining these forms of international integration with key internal characteristics of each country, such as its property rights, the role of the state and relations between the state and main elite actors, Myant and Drahokoupil are able to propose five sets of combinations which provide the basis for five suggested varieties of capitalism in post-socialist economies, three of which are of relevance to the countries discussed here. First are 'FDI-based market economies' with export sectors based on manufacturing by foreign-owned MNCs and are characterised by democratic political systems. These are represented by the Visegrad countries. Second are 'peripheral market economies' which are also democratic and have a legal and institutional basis for business activity but weakly developed domestic economies compared to the first group, often based on financialised growth and remittances. This group includes some SEE and Baltic countries, with some, such as Estonia, developing so that they move towards membership of the first group. Myant and Drahokoupil's fifth group, of 'remittance and aid-based economies', include some SEE countries (along with some former Soviet countries). This group comprises low income economies with a weak basis for further development, domestic economies with a preponderance of small-scale trading and a poorly developed institutional base and infrastructure to attract MNCs. Movement out of this group would depend on a country's ability to strengthen this base for business development, most likely into the 'peripheral market economy' group.[3]

Although the authors do not provide definitive lists of the countries in each group, it seems likely that, of the countries discussed in this book, the Visegrad countries would belong to the 'FDI-based market economies', the Baltic countries and probably Romania and Bulgaria to the 'peripheral market economies', and Serbia would be on the boundary between the peripheral and the 'remittance and aid-based economies' (Myant and Drahokoupil 2011: 310–312).

A different approach again is taken by Roderick Martin (2013) who argues that although the variety of capitalisms approach offered an important critique of the 'standardised conception of post-socialist capitalism' of the Washington Consensus, it underestimated the degree of internal diversity within individual national capitalist systems. The East European post-socialist forms of capitalism were different from western forms for a number of reasons, not least because they resulted from an 'interaction between pre-existing socialist structures and early 1990s models of liberal market capitalism', and also because they were shaped by state intervention in favour of varying forms of liberalisation and privatisation in the post-socialist period, and by 'international influences – ideological, institutional and financial' such as from the World Bank, the IMF and the EU. The result, according to Martin, were "segmented systems" (Martin 2013: 238).

He identifies four segments of East European economies: state, privatised, *de novo* and international. These segments are present in each economy, although their relative weight and pace of developments differs between countries. The state segment was of particular importance to begin with, in the early 1990s, but continues to exist in all countries of the region to varying degrees. It comprises firms 'in national or local government ownership, with financial resources acquired from the state, investment strategies determined by the state, and operating under a form of disintegrating chartered monopoly' (Martin 2013: 281). The privatised segment consists of firms that were transformed from state-owned, including complex forms of ownership by other state firms, to a variety of forms of private ownership determined by varying state policies of privatisation, and often maintaining corporate links with the state (see below for further discussion). The *de novo* segment comprised new start firms that were 'privately owned, with capital internally generated or acquired from relations and friends, and open market relations with primarily local and national product markets', and having quite distant relations with the state. The international segment 'comprised corporately and institutionally owned multinationals, financed through international transfer, and related to product markets via intra-firm linkages, leading to international markets' (Martin 2013: 282). As is shown within the various cases explored in this book, examples of each of these are to be found within the energy sector.

In contrast to the focus on the economic aspects of regime variance, the work of Bohle and Greskovits (2012) puts more emphasis on political and social factors in developing a political economy of capitalist diversity in the CEE countries. By focusing more on elite policy choices within the context of economic and structural constraints, they can be seen as building on the approaches for the study of the early transformation period by scholars such as Ekiert, Stark and Bruszt discussed above. Their approach was to begin with the '*initial choices* of transformation strategies by political and technocratic elites' and to trace how such choices were both constrained by socialist and pre-socialist legacies, and also 'shaped by the transformative capacities of states and state-society relationships', while keeping in mind that 'legacies of the past do not act on political outcomes directly. Rather, their influence is mediated by how policy makers and citizens perceive this inheritance' (Bohle and Greskovits 2012: 4).

The ways in which the interactions between actors' choices and perceptions and historical legacies actually impact on the formation of specific regimes and the particular nature of the characteristics and problems of such institutional arrangements are in turn affected by the wider international economic and political environment in which the transformation processes take place (Bohle and Greskovits 2012: 4–5). Within this context the elite choices to be made in adopting a national development strategy involve achieving some kind of balance between the requirements of support for markets to operate freely as proposed by neo-liberal approaches, to provide compensation or support to citizens from the insecurities and threats to their life chances that market forces entail as supported by European versions of welfare capitalism, and attempts to involve labour in policy choices and decision making through corporatist ideas.

On the basis of this approach Bohle and Greskovits arrive at the following categorisation of different regime types. Their first group of 'pure neo-liberal regimes' comprised Estonia, Latvia and Lithuania to begin with. Bulgaria and Romania, which started as weak states with no clear regime, later joined this group. These countries successfully established market economies but provided little support for businesses and low levels of social welfare support to compensate for the effects of the market. Instead, popular support was gained through promoting the idea of a restoration of national identity that had been suppressed in the Soviet period and exclusion of non-nationals from citizen rights.

In contrast the second group of 'embedded neo-liberal regimes' comprised the Czech Republic, Hungary, Poland and Slovakia to begin with, and was later joined by Croatia as that country gained a more effective state. These countries liberalised their economies, offered support for the privatisation of domestic companies and encouraged FDI by foreign MNCs, and at the same time sought to retain a reformed version of their social security and welfare provisions to soften the effects of market transformation for their citizens and avoid the development of any concerted opposition to the reforms.[4]

Beyond the three coherent regime forms, the authors also discuss a fourth group of countries, mainly in SEE, of weak states. These were countries where, especially in the 1990s, political elites faced too many constraints on their ability to choose a reform programme and the 'required manoeuvring capacities' were in short supply. The result was 'social disintegration and political crisis' (Bohle and Greskovits 2012: 183–4). From the late 1990s Bulgaria and Romania were able to adopt more coherent strategies and moved towards 'the neo-liberal pattern of radical stability-oriented institutions of macro-economic coordination, minimal taxation and a meagre welfare state', while Croatia following the disruption of the post-Yugoslav wars, opted for a strategy closer to embedded neoliberalism by policies 'protecting selected social groups and some of its industries from the vagaries of marketization' (Bohle and Greskovits 2012: 183). In turn the stabilisation trends in these three countries was reinforced by the prospect and then the achievement of EU membership, but overall the influence of the EU on SEE has been more complex and contradictory.

While 'improvements in the indicators of fiscal deficit, inflation, FDI flows, and the quality of governance, the macroeconomic coordination capacities of Bulgaria, Romania and Croatia' were strengthened, the 'logic of integration at different speeds' imposed by the EU on the wider SEE region 'exacerbated regional fragmentation since the material and spiritual ties between the would-be EU insiders and the remaining outsiders were partly weakened and partly transformed by the fact that the weak or quasi-states' of the Western Balkans were left behind (Bohle and Greskovits 2012: 220).[5]

3.4 Differences between the CEE countries in the character of their post-socialist economies and polities

As noted above, in the course of attempting to identify general varieties of capitalism or regime types, key issues have included the character of post-socialist elites in each country and their relation to questions of privatisation, the character of ownership and relations between state and economy, and the quality of governance, including issues of state capture and corruption. These feature not only in discussion of the differences between the regime types, and between weak states and those that had begun to consolidate into identifiable regime types, but also of differences between countries within the same grouping.

3.4.1 Elites and privatisation

The issue of the formation and development of new elites and the renewal and adaptation of old elites has been a central feature of regime development throughout the CEE region and is closely connected to questions of economic viability and state effectiveness in each country.

Intrinsic to questions of elite formation have been both the transfer of political power and the transformation of property relations, including the character of processes of privatisation. The process has involved a range of different old and new elite groups. It included the partial transformation of the communist-era political and economic elites, and the emergence of new political and economic elites, all with their different cross-cutting agendas. The interplay of these different groups in the pursuit of their interests took different forms and shaped the outcomes in different ways, not only between the different variants of capitalist development discussed above, but also between countries within each type. Moreover, the domestic-level processes were deeply affected by their relation to inward investment by foreign owners and the relation of the East European countries to the international economy.

In most countries property transformation was achieved through a combination of different approaches to property transfer and privatisation, the most commonly used being mass voucher privatisation, where the adult population received vouchers from the state to be exchanged for shares on formerly state-owned companies; manager and employee buy-outs (MEBO) which ranged from measures to enable all employees to buy a holding in their place of employment to schemes that favoured the managers mainly or entirely; and direct sales to new owners who in most cases were foreign owners since there was little capital available in the domestic population for such purchases (Myant and Drahokoupil 2011: 237–238).

In East Central Europe the old political elites already contained strong reformist elements that had been sympathetic to market reform under communist rule, and were now in favour of transforming property relations. In Hungary they were close to the centre of state power at the time of the political transition in 1989, while in Poland and Czechoslovakia they had been partially suppressed respectively by the imposition of military rule in the 1980s, and the restoration of more conservative communist rule by Soviet armed intervention in 1968. However, as events unfolded in 1989, in each case the reform communist elements were able to negotiate political reforms to reach a peaceful compromise with new oppositional elites resulting in open competitive elections, the subsequent peaceful transfer of power between parties representing these different elites, and despite differences over the approach to be taken, an acceptance by all sides of property transformation and privatisation which enabled the transformation of elements of old economic elites and the emergence of new ones.

The predominant form of privatisation depended on the character of the dominant political elites and the state of the economy at the time when the measures were introduced. In Czechoslovakia, where the new political elite drawn from former opposition circles held sway and the new rulers had inherited almost no international debts, voucher privatisation was adopted and regarded as the most democratic and socially just method. Subsequently however, in the Czech Republic, 'sales by initial owners led to the consolidation of vouchers in the hands of investment funds, in turn largely owned by Czech banks, owned by the Czech state' (Martin 2013: 109).[6]

In contrast, in Hungary, where the new political elite had inherited high levels of debt and regarded its repayment as a priority, although locally privately owned companies emerged as a result of insider privatisation involving complex forms of ownership networks between companies, the main form was direct sales to private, foreign owners. In Poland, where there was also a high level of international debt but the new political elite found it expedient to accept debt relief from its creditors, a combination of direct sales and MEBO was adopted (Bohle and Greskovits 2012: 141–146). This 'resulted in combination of domestic and foreign ownership, with higher levels of domestic ownership in the long run than in the Czech Republic or Hungary ... [and] a higher level of employee ownership in the short run, with subsequent on-sales, primarily to managers' (Martin 2013: 109).

In Estonia, Latvia and Lithuania, new political elites came to power with pro-market economy and distinctly nationalist outlooks shaped by their struggles to separate from the Soviet Union and establish independent countries. Furthermore both Estonia and Latvia had large Russian minorities who made up large shares of industrial workers and managers in the population. For these new political elites direct sales were preferred to MEBOs, with voucher privatisation use as a secondary strategy as a means of restricting the share of ownership achieved by the Russian population (Bohle and Greskovits 2012: 122–123).

In south-east Europe, in contrast to the East Central European and the Baltic countries, sections of the old political elites succeeded in holding on to power, often by adopting new more democratic names, images and ideologies, as in Romania and Bulgaria, or more nationalist aims and ideologies as in

Serbia. This enabled them to maintain many of their existing links and networks with communist era economic managers. The new political leaderships sought to defend the interests of the old state enterprise lobbies and introduced forms of insider privatisation, by a combination of manager-oriented MEBOs and voucher privatisation through which the elite maintained managerial control, thus allowing old political and economic elites to maintain their predominance, and also producing a largely fragmented ownership structure (Bohle and Greskovits 2012: 198–199). In Romania specifically, gradual mixed-method privatisation 'left considerable influence to insider managers, with the state retaining wider ownership' than in the Czech Republic, Hungary or Poland (Martin 2013: 109).

The different national patterns of property change contributed to the variations between countries in eastern Europe, and to some extent these variations have remained. However, in all countries international influences have resulted in a significant growth in foreign ownership whatever initial approach to privatisation was chosen. A combination of the influence of international economic organisations, and of the EU, and the opportunities offered by transnational companies and world markets, especially in meeting the need for investment capital, led to an increase in the significance of foreign ownership. This built on the already strong presence of foreign ownership in Hungary and the Baltic countries, but also affected the other CEE countries through inward investment in complex manufacturing and the financial sector. For example, in the Czech Republic, the state-owned banks that had bought up the shares resulting from voucher privatisation, were in turn privatised and sold mainly to foreign owners. While in the CEE countries much of the foreign investment was stable, in contrast, weaker SEE states with less dependable economic infrastructure only attracted 'impatient foreign capital' unwilling to commit to longer-term investment (Bohle and Greskovits 2012: 93, 170–172, 206–209).

3.4.2 A capitalism without capitalists?

Although it is widely accepted that transformation has resulted in the predominance of some kind of capitalism throughout CEE, there is much debate on whether the economic elites who exercise power over the economy are best characterised as a class of owners or as managers. Although a widely held view in the early years of the transformation process was that the old political elites of socialism were converting their political capital into economic capital to become a new economic elite or capitalist class (Staniszkis 1991; Hankiss 1990), subsequent work revealed the process of elite transformation to be more complex.

According to Iván Szelényi (Eyal et al. 1998) and his colleagues who analysed the social backgrounds of the new economic elite on the basis of studies in the Czech Republic, Hungary and Poland, members of the ruling political elite had been downwardly mobile, while those who benefitted were the second rank, technocratic elite (Eyal et al. 1998: 117, 120).[7] Thus, it was not the old political elite that was becoming the new economic elite, but economic managers, who had often been members of the ruling party and who had benefited from the social capital that party membership provided. This seemed to suggest that capitalism in CEE was in Szelényi's words, a 'capitalism without capitalists'. The idea gained further support from Stark and Bruszt (1998: 137–165) who suggested privatisation had created recombinant forms of property, by which he meant a process whereby former managers were active in both the state and private sectors, but centralised their assets in the private sector and their liabilities in the socialist sector.

As Nigel Swain (2011) has commented, 'that manipulations of this type took place is not in doubt. It was one of the features of Hungarian "spontaneous privatisation" and Polish "*nomenklatura* privatisation" that their early post-socialist governments tried to stamp out; it continued into the later 1990s in the Czech Republic where the term "tunnelling" was invented to describe it; in Romania and Bulgaria the term "parasitic privatisation", describing essentially the same process was in use throughout the 1990s' (Swain 2011: 1679). However, further research would suggest that capitalist owners did emerge from privatisation and new business development in the longer term. Data collected by Szelenyi and his team in 1996, for Hungary only, suggested first, that analysis of the same firms as investigated in 1993 showed a sharp decline in public ownership at the expense of foreign ownership, and second, there had been a growth in domestic private ownership of middle-sized firms between 1993 and 1996 (Eyal et al. 1998: 116).

Further research on Hungary on the background of the new economic elite by Laki and Szalai (2006) supported this view. They suggested that after 2000 while small business was predominantly privately owned, big business was controlled by multinationals or state-owned companies, and a third category between the two was mainly owned by Hungarian companies, which were owned in turn by other Hungarian companies or by groups of private individuals. Although the earlier career of the new owners was not mainly in party or state structures and state organs, party membership was not irrelevant: around a third of those interviewed admitted to party membership (Laki and Szalai 2006: 325–326). A similar picture was found in other countries in the region, including Bulgaria, the Czech Republic, Hungary and Poland (Róna-Tas and Böröcz 2000: 223; Słomczynski and Shabad 1996: 175–177). Furthermore, Johnson and Loveman (1995) in their study of new Polish entrepreneurs, found that 85 per cent had worked previously in managerial positions in the state; some left before 1980, but more did so over the course of the 1980s and 1990s. Many had been involved in Solidarity (Johnson and Loveman 1995: 107–112).

Thus, although it seems clear that despite the background of the new economic leaders as managers predominantly in the socialist state economy, a significant section of them did become capitalist entrepreneurs. However, although capitalism in CEE was therefore not a 'capitalism without capitalists', a further question concerns the relative influence of owners in relation to managers over key company decisions. According to Martin (2013: 108), 'although private owners secured rights to control their assets, to realise the usufruct from their use, and to transfer ownership, they experienced difficulty in exercising effective strategic control'. Moreover, ownership did not lead to the dominance of owners over managers, but rather to interdependence between them and a balance of power. While managers could draw on expertise and experience, 'the power of owners was limited by external political influences and internal structural arrangements' (Martin 2013: 110). And in relation to foreign owners,

> managers were able to mobilise external resources, including state and public opinion, in conflicts that arose between national blockholders and foreign shareholders ... Owners of CEE enterprises were diverse including foreign portfolio investors, foreign individuals, foreign banks, foreign and domestic corporations, domestic institutions and individuals, and the state. For foreign investors, exit rather than engagement was the major means of responding to dissatisfaction with corporate performance.
> (Martin 2013: 110, 112)

3.4.3 Corruption, state–business relations and the role of the state

Behind the question of the relative influence of owners and managers, a consistent presence has been the role of the state. Although the role of the state changed between the early 1990s and more recent years, the state remained involved in the management of the economy in various ways, including continuing direct ownership, sponsorship of strategic industries, organising the processes of privatisation, and appointing members to the boards of banks and public utilities. As noted above, managers have been able to draw on state support in their relations with owners, while at the same time, the state has been a major influence in organising the transfer of assets to owners and attracting foreign owners and investors into ECE national economies.

However, while the state has remained a major influence on the economy, its close involvement in economic relations has raised questions about how far in turn it is subject to particular economic interests, and in particular to accusations of corruption (Kotkin and Sajo 2002). As Martin has commented, 'In the absence of effective markets, the allocation of ownership rights involved the state in decisions that differentially affected the rights and economic interests of groups and individuals, inevitably leading to accusations of favouritism (at best) and corruption (at worst) from disadvantaged groups' (Martin 2013: 289).

According to Hellman et al. (2000), although companies and other economic interests have sought to exert influence over the state around the world, it has developed to a significant extent and has taken a variety of forms in the countries undergoing post-socialist transitions. Hellman et al. distinguished between three different forms: influence, corruption and state capture. Corruption mainly involves relatively small-scale bribery in relation to the implementation of existing laws, rules or regulations. Offe (2004: 78) expands on this to suggest that corruption may be defined as bribes for favourable policy decisions or the exchange of decisions for some payment, and it can be analysed in terms of four categories of bribes: in exchange for permission to sell illicit goods; in exchange for favourable administrative decisions; bribes to secure lenient treatment regarding official regulation of business; soliciting a bribe for favours by those in decision-making positions (Offe 2004: 81–83).

Sometimes however, economic interests may seek outcomes in their favour in a more organised or systematic form, in order to change policy or alter the rules of the game, and this for Hellman et al. (2000) may be distinguished as influence rather than corruption, if it is effected, for example, by political leverage, or as state capture if it is achieved by means of payments to state officials or politicians. On the basis of research by Hellman et al. (2000) using World Bank data, they concluded that 'state capture and influence are in evidence in all transition economies', but that such economies can be divided into two types according to whether 'the impact of state capture by a narrow group of firms is quite widely felt by firms throughout the economy' (a capture economy), or whether 'firms may seek to influence the state through capture, but there are constraints which prevent the state from distorting the legal and regulatory framework to the advantage of a few powerful firms' (Hellman et al. 2000: 32).

In capture economies, the strategy of state capture tends to be adopted by '*de novo*' firms trying to compete in a market dominated by influential incumbent firms with close historical and formal ties to the state and substantial advantages in terms of market share' (Hellman et al. 2000: 32). The research investigated the extent to which firms in different transition economies reported capture in each of six dimensions of parliamentary legislation, presidential decrees, the central bank, criminal courts, commercial courts, and political party finance. Of the countries discussed here it found that for the late 1990s, Bulgaria, Croatia, Latvia, Romania and Slovakia had high levels of state capture, while the Czech Republic, Estonia, Hungary, Lithuania and Poland had low levels (Hellman et al. 2000: 9).

However, as Innes (2014) has argued, the increasing economic difficulties facing governments of the region in the past ten years has given rise to new pressures within the countries with low levels of state capture as defined by Hellman et al. In addition to what Innes describes as the 'corporate state capture' identified by Hellman et al., where business interests 'buy' the services of governing politicians and state officials, some of the countries that exhibited low capture of this kind, have now experienced 'party state capture' where 'parties re-politicize the state in pursuit of political monopoly' (Innes 2014: 88). While mounting economic pressures have maintained pressure for high levels of corporate state capture in countries where this was already prevalent, in some countries with low capture, where politics had been characterised by electorally aware, professional party competitions, economic problems coinciding with the electoral decline of the social democratic left parties. This has allowed parties claiming to act in the national interest to come to power, introduce measures to alter constitutional checks and balances in favour of a strong state, and drive through their own policy agendas. This has happened particularly, Innes argues, in Hungary under Fidesz and Poland under the Law and Justice Party (Innes 2014: 91).

3.4.4 Globalisation, national economies and financial nationalism

As noted above, to a significant extent economic transformation in CEE was a process of international adjustment as well as a process of internal reforms, as international institutions, foreign governments, and companies (especially multinationals) supplied the knowledge, practical assistance, and the means to help domestic government achieve economic transformation. In this there were significant differences between the countries of the region. For example, to begin with in the early 1990s Hungary was the most international in outlook as successive governments provided favourable trading conditions and tax incentives to multinationals. By the 2000s Hungarian banks were almost entirely foreign-owned and around 80 per cent of GDP was accounted for by both imports and exports. Poland also provided favourable terms for international trade and foreign investment from the early 1990s but retained a larger domestically owned economy than Hungary. In contrast the Czech Republic liberalised foreign trade later, in the late 1990s and offered less encouragement to inward foreign investment, although it developed close ties with German manufacturing companies. Romania's reorientation to international markets and foreign investment also began in the late 1990s and remained at lower levels than the Central European countries. According to Martin, 'the major sources of capital, technology, social organisation, and economic culture were Western, both US and Western European' (Martin 2013: 293), although 'Russia's importance as a major source of natural gas and oil for the region ensured that its influence survived, and Russian investment increased in the region in the new century' (Martin 2013: 195).

At the same time, greater international links brought problems as well as benefits: 'with increasing dependence upon multinationals', countries in the region 'became subject to the competitive pressures operating upon Western-European economies, subordinated to the international strategies of major multinationals' (Martin 2013: 193). This meant that, although EU membership gave the EU member countries of the region greater political influence than countries with peripheral economies usually enjoyed, they were nevertheless 'incorporated into the global economy as peripheral parts of the European region, heavily dependent upon foreign markets and foreign investment' (Martin 2013: 196).

However, 'the international financial crisis and lower foreign investment after 2008 reduced the incentive for CEES governments and enterprises to follow through the logic of convergence on liberal market capitalism' (Martin 2013: 293), in a context where ironically, following accession, the leverage of the EU on its new member countries had declined. Following the financial crisis of 2008, the state has been a major player in shaping the direction of national economic development and asserting the interests of their national economies in the face of international influences and interests.

In this context, as noted by Johnson and Barnes (2014), there has been a significant trend towards economic nationalism, which they define as 'a strategy that employs financial levers – including monetary policy, currency interventions, and other methods of interaction with local and international financial systems – to promote the nation's unity, autonomy and identity' (Johnson and Barnes 2014: 2). This strategy has become increasingly popular with governments across the region, although Hungary remains the prime example so far. Here, it emerged first, as a consequence of the undermining of the hitherto predominant neo-liberal strategies of the Socialist governments since 2002 by the severe austerity required in exchange for support from the IMF and the EU and the subsequent surge in popularity of the nationalist-populist positions of Fidesz. Then, once in power, the Fidesz government adopted five key policy choices against the advice of international institutions: to preserve the national currency and make it the exclusive means of exchange internally; to control monetary policy to reduce the independence of the central bank; to give preferential treatment to 'insider' financial institutions and banks; and to repay loans and avoid further borrowing from international institutions and to reject the advice such institutions would give (Johnson and Barnes 2014: 4–6). Against expectations, Johnson and Barnes argue, these policies have been successful partly because of the tolerant attitude of international bond markets which have regarded the extent of Hungarian government deficits as acceptable and investment in Hungary as an acceptable risk (Johnson and Barnes 2014: 21–25).

It remains to be seen how long-lasting or generalisable the Hungarian policies will be, but as Johnson and Barnes comment, the Hungarian experience demonstrates that 'financial nationalist policies can be pursued in the heart of Europe, without automatically undermining economic development goals' (Johnson and Barnes 2014: 29). And such policies may become more attractive to governments in the region in the context of the broader range of international influences that are available to CEE policy makers, offering different models of development, including Putin's Russia, and more especially, given its relatively greater success as a model, China.

3.5 Future prospects

It should be noted that most of the research for the analyses discussed in this chapter was conducted prior to or just after the financial crisis of 2008 and its aftermath, and therefore too soon for definitive conclusions to be drawn concerning whether the directions towards regime consolidation will continue or be disrupted by the weight of economic problems and their social and political consequences. While the forms of capitalism that have emerged in

Central and Eastern Europe since 1989 were based on the model of liberal market capitalism that was dominant at the end of the 1980s, it remains an open question as to whether such a model will remain influential, or even whether capitalism in the forms developed so far will persist. As Martin (2013: 299) has commented:

> How far alternative models of capitalism will develop depends upon national political preferences and the response of the EU, international investors, and multinational corporations. Such responses are less likely to be determined by the logic of models of capitalism than by national political structures, the economic interests of multinational corporations, and the productive capacities of enterprises.

And as Bohle and Greskovits (2012: 274) suggest:

> In the light of all this it remains to be seen whether any combination of the developments presented here will ever add up to an overarching settlement. If this fails to happen, the loose framework of partial compromises [internationally] ... . will mirror the fragmentation observed in national arenas... With the global crisis still unfolding, there is great uncertainty regarding the course capitalist development is about to take.

Notes

1. Examples of the predominant 'transition' approach included Aslund (1995), Balcerowicz (1995), Gelb and Grey (1991), Fischer and Gelb (1991), and Sachs (1993).
2. For further discussion of the application of the varieties of capitalism approach for the economies of post-socialist Eastern Europe see Lane and Myant (2007).
3. The other two groups apply more to parts of the former Soviet Union. They are 'oligarchic or clientelistic capitalism', with authoritarian political systems and a closer relation between business and politics than the other groups, and 'order states' with authoritarian political systems, substantial state ownership of the economy, and limited development of the legal and institutional basis for business activity.
4. A third type of coherent new regime was represented by one country only, Slovenia, which pursued the marketization of domestic industries and the promotion of new domestic businesses with relatively little foreign involvement, while maintaining high levels of welfare provision and retaining a form of tripartism in policy making inherited from the Yugoslav system.
5. Unfortunately, in the analysis of Bohle and Greskovits (2012), as is the case with other studies discussed here, the question of distinctions between the 'EU-outsider' states of SEE is not explored further, and in particular, of how far Serbia should be categorised along with its smaller neighbours or whether it is beginning to show any signs of consolidating in the direction of any of the more coherent regime types proposed by the various authors.
6. For further discussion of the economics of Czech privatisation and its outcomes, see Myant and Drahokoupil (2011: 238–244). For a detailed analysis of the politics of privatisation in the Czech Republic in comparison with Russia, and in particular the role of ideology in influencing decisions on how to privatise, see Appel (2004).

7 Russia, Bulgaria and Slovakia were also included in the research, but not in the analysis presented in the book.

References

Amable, B. (2003). *The Diversity of Modern Capitalism*. (Oxford: Oxford University Press).
Amsden, A., Kochanowicz J. and Taylor L. (1994). *The Market Meets its Match: Restructuring the Economies of Eastern Europe*. (Cambridge MA: Harvard University Press).
Appel, H. (2004). *A New Capitalist Order: Privatization and Ideology in Russia and Eastern Europe*. (Pittsburgh; PA: University of Pittsburgh Press).
Aslund, A. (1995). *How Russia Became a Market Economy*. (Washington DC: Brookings Institute).
Aslund, A. (2002). *Building Capitalism: The Transformation of the Former Soviet Bloc*. (Washington; DC: Brookings Institution).
Balcerowicz, L. (1995). *Socialism, Capitalism, Transformation*. (Budapest: CEU Press).
Bohle, D. and Greskovits, B. (2012). *Capitalist Diversity on Europe's Periphery*. (Ithaca; NY: Cornell University Press).
Bruszt, L. (1992). 'Transformative Politics: Social Costs and Social Peace in East Central Europe', *East European Politics and Societies*, 6(2), pp. 55–72.
Connolly, R. (2013). *The Economic Sources of Social Order Development in Post-Socialist Eastern Europe*. (London: Routledge).
Cox, T. and Mason, B. (1999). *Social and Economic Transformation in East Central Europe: Institutions, Property Relations and Social Interests*. (Cheltenham: Edward Elgar).
Cox, T. (ed.) (2014). *Civil Society and Social Capital in Post-Communist Eastern Europe*. (Abingdon: Routledge).
Csaba, L. (1996). *The Capitalist Revolution in Eastern Europe*. (Cheltenham: Edward Elgar).
Ekiert, G. (1996). *The State Against Society: Political Crises and Their Aftermath in East Central Europe*. (Princeton; NJ: Princeton University Press).
Ekiert, G. and Kubik, J. (1999). *Rebellious Civil Society: Popular Protest and Democratic Consolidation in Poland*. (Ann Arbor: University of Michigan Press).
Eyal, G., Szelényi, I. and Townsley, E. (1998). *Making Capitalism without Capitalists: Class Formation and Elite Struggles in Post-Communist Central Europe*. (London: Verso).
Fischer, S. and Gelb A. (1991). 'The Process of Socialist Economic Transformation', *Journal of Economic Perspectives*, 5(4), pp. 91–105.
Frye, T. (2010). *Building States and Markets After Communism*. (Cambridge: Cambridge University Press).
Ganev, V. (2007). *Preying on the State: The Transformation of Bulgaria after 1989*. (Ithaca; NY: Cornell University Press).
Gati, C. (1996). 'The Mirage of Democracy', *Transition*, 2(6), pp. 6–12.
Gelb, A. and Grey, C. (1991). *The Transformation of Economies in Central and Eastern Europe: Issues, Programs and Prospects*. (Washington; DC: World Bank).
Hall, P. and Soskice, D. (2001). *Varieties of Capitalism*. (Oxford: Oxford University Press).
Hankiss, E. (1990). *East European Alternatives*. (Oxford: Clarendon Press).

Hardy, J. (2009). *Poland's New Capitalism*. (London: Pluto Press).
Haughton, T. (2005). *Constraints and Opportunities of Leadership in Post-Communist Eastern Europe*. (Aldershot: Ashgate).
Hellman, J. (1998). 'Winner Takes All: The Politics of Partial Reform', *World Politics*, 50(2), pp. 203–234.
Hellman, J., Jones, G. and Kauffmann, D. (2000). 'Seize the State, Seize the Day: State Capture, Corruption and Influence in Transition', *World Bank Policy Research, Working Paper No. 2444*.
Higley, J. and Lengyel, G. (eds) (2000). *Elites after State Socialism: Theories and Analysis*. (Oxford: Rowman and Littlefield).
Howard, M. (2003). *The Weakness of Civil Society in Post-Communist Eastern Europe*. (Cambridge: Cambridge University Press).
Innes, A. (2014). 'The Political Economy of State Capture in Central Europe', *Journal of Common Market Studies*, 52(1), pp. 88–104.
Jacoby, W. (2004). *The Enlargement of the EU and NATO: Ordering From the Menu in Central Europe*. (New York: Cambridge University Press).
Johnson, S. and Loveman, G. (1995). *Starting Over in Eastern Europe: Entrepreneurship and Economic Renewal*. (Boston, MA: Harvard Business School Press).
Johnson, J. and Barnes, A. (2014). 'Financial Nationalism and Its International Enablers: the Hungarian Experience', *Review of International Political Economy*, 22(3), pp. 535–569.
Kopecky, P. (ed.) (2008). *Political Parties and the State in Post-Communist Europe*. (London: Routledge).
Kornai, J. (1998). *From Socialism to Capitalism*. (London: Social Market Foundation).
Kornai, J. and Rose-Ackerman, S. (eds) (2004). *Building a Trustworthy State in Post-Socialist Transition*. (Basingstoke: MacMillan).
Kotkin, S. and Sajo, A. (eds.) (2002). *Political Corruption in Transition*. (Budapest: Central European University Press).
Laki, M. and Szalai, J. (2006). 'The Puzzle of Success: Hungarian Entrepreneurs at the Turn of the Millennium', *Europe-Asia Studies*, 58(3), pp. 317–345.
Lane, D. (2014). *The Capitalist Transformation of State Socialism*. (Abingdon: Routledge).
Lane, D. and Myant, M. (ed.) (2007). *Varieties of Capitalism in Post-Communist Countries*. (Basingstoke: Palgrave).
Lewis, P. (ed.) (2002). *Party Development and Democratic Change in Post-Communist Europe: the First Decade*. (London: Routledge).
Martin, R. (2013). *Constructing Capitalisms*. (Cambridge: Cambridge University Press).
Myant, M. and Drahokoupil, J. (2011). *Transition Economies: Political Economy in Russia, Eastern Europe and Central Asia*. (Hoboken; NJ: Wiley).
Offe, C. (1991). 'Capitalism By Democratic Design? Democratic Theory Facing the Triple Transition in East Central Europe', *Social Research*, 58(4), pp. 865–892.
Offe, C. (2004). 'Political Corruption: Conceptual and Practical Issues', in Kornai, J. and Rose-Ackerman, S. (eds), *Building a Trustworthy State in Post-Socialist Transition*. (Basingstoke: MacMillan).
Ostrow, J. (2000). *Comparing Post-Soviet Legislatures: A Theory of Institutional Design and Political Conflict*. (Columbus: Ohio State University Press).
Przeworski, A. (1995). *Sustainable Democracy*. (Cambridge: Cambridge University Press).

Róna-Tas, A. and Böröcz, J. (2000). 'Bulgaria, the Czech Republic, Hungary and Poland: Pre-socialist and Socialist Legacies among Business Elites' in Higley, J. and Lengyel, G. (eds.), *Elites after State Socialism: Theories and Analysis*. (Oxford: Rowman and Littlefield).

Sachs, J. (1993). *Poland's Jump to a Market Economy*. (Cambridge; MA: MIT Press).

Sájo, A. (1998). 'Corruption, Clientelism and the Future of the Constitutional State in Eastern Europe', *East European Constitutional Review*, 7(2), pp. 54–63.

Schoenman (2005). 'Captains or Pirates? State-Business Relations in Post-Socialist Poland', *East European Politics and Societies*, 19(1), pp. 40–75.

Słomczynski, K. and Shabad, G. (1996). 'Systemic Transformation and the Salience of Class Structure in East Central Europe', *East European Politics and Societies*, 11(1), pp. 155–189.

Staniszkis, J. (1991). *The Dynamics of Breakthrough*. (Berkeley: University of California Press).

Stark, D. (1990). 'Privatisation in Hungary: From Plan to Market or From Plan to Clan?', *East European Politics and Societies*, 4(3), pp. 351–392.

Stark, D. (1992). 'Path Dependence and Privatisation Strategies in East Central Europe', *East European Politics and Societies*, 6(1), pp. 17–54.

Stark, D. and Bruszt, L. (1998). *Postsocialist Pathways: Transforming Politics and Property in East Central Europe*. (Cambridge: Cambridge University Press).

Swain, N. (2011). 'A Post-Socialist Capitalism', *Europe-Asia Studies*, 63(9), pp. 1671–1695.

Uhlin, A. (2005). *Post-Soviet Civil Society: Democratization in Russia and the Baltic States*. (Abingdon: Routledge).

Vachudova, M. (2005). *Europe Undivided: Democracy, Leverage and Integration After Communism*. (Oxford: Oxford University Press).

4 Russian energy companies and the Central and Eastern European energy sector

Sylvain Rossiaud and Catherine Locatelli

4.1 Introduction

A common constraint governs the definition of policy on energy security in Central and Eastern European (CEE) countries: their asymmetric energy interdependence with Russia means they are potentially vulnerable and exposed to the 'Russian risk' (Binhack and Tichy 2012). For historical, economic and political reasons CEE countries are still – albeit to differing degrees – very dependent on Russian gas and oil imports. The relations established within the Comecon framework which shaped the region's oil and gas pipeline network help explain this dependence.[1] Furthermore, in view of production and transport costs, Russia remains very competitive for these countries, which may in turn complicate their efforts to diversify by adopting more expensive alternative energy sources.

Since at least the mid-2000s – and especially following the two Russia–Ukrainian gas crises of 2006 and 2009 – much of the literature on European Union (EU) energy security has focused on analysis of the Russian risk and possible ways of mitigating it. Realistic analysis tends to highlight the way in which the Russian state sustains and manipulates the vulnerability of the EU's CEE and Baltic states members. Therefore, Russian energy policy is generally interpreted in light of its use of energy as a political instrument (Newnham 2011). Such analysis seeks to highlight the extent to which the route taken by a new pipeline or the price of Russian hydrocarbons reflects the Russian state's geopolitical interests in its perceived sphere of influence. In response to EU or NATO enlargement, and informed by the Russian elite's view of a 'multipolar world' that should be structured around independent power centres, two key objectives purportedly underpin Russian energy policy (Braun 2012; Fedorov 2013):

i) Keeping CEE and Baltic countries under control by fragmenting and isolating them from EU or NATO countries; by multiplying the number of gas pipelines bypassing transit countries and/or rewarding the more compliant ones, while manipulating gas prices (Orban 2008).
ii) Boosting the power of the Russian state by instrumentalising downstream investments made by national champions Gazprom and Rosneft.

According to critics of the realist current found in international relations theory (Dannreuther 2013), focusing exclusively on the interests of the Russian state can only provide a partial picture of the factors which have enabled Russian actors to structure the regional energy complex. Importantly, it needs to be acknowledged that the Russian state is not the only actor in regional energy relations. These two issues are analysed further in this chapter.

First, at the beginning of the transition process, the rationale behind reform was to 'create' new vertically integrated actors, with international reach, capable of competing with western oil and gas companies operating abroad. The Soviet legacy explains why CEE countries were the preferred target for investment by Russian firms, notably through the purchase of shares in networks and companies (refineries, distribution companies, utilities, etc.). The prime objective of this chapter is to understand the changes which have occurred since the early 1990s in the determinants, modalities and results of Russian hydrocarbon companies' efforts to engage within and structure the CEE energy complex.

Second, it is simplistic to assert that the behaviour of Russian oil and gas companies has only been driven by state interests. Admittedly, in view of the initial goals of reform, the behaviour of the new actors, and the coordination mechanism between them and the state, yielded some 'unexpected results'. The political, economic and institutional environment in Russia at the start of the transition process explains why it was difficult for independent firms to emerge. But the internal balance of the political economy then changed, altering the behaviour of Russian firms at home and their international development strategy. In particular, changes also occurred abroad through the liberalisation and integration of gas markets in the European Union. This institutional rupture exerted considerable influence on Gazprom's strategy in CEE countries. Our second objective is consequently to grasp the way in which internal and external changes shaped Russian companies' international growth strategy. Two questions are asked: What points of rupture are we likely to see? How do the various periods in this process explain the behaviour of Russian companies with regard to their international growth strategies in CEE countries?

Although oil and gas narratives are different, we may highlight two main points of interest starting with the difficulties encountered during attempts to normalise relations between the companies and most CEE states. The downstream strategies of Russian companies were only limited in scale, despite the interests of Russian actors and the opportunities which arose when the various target countries started privatisation (Poussenkova 2010). Most CEE countries sought to contain the expansion of Russian firms. The second point concerns the rupture observed from the mid-2000s onwards. Regarding oil, tighter state control at home – thanks to the increasingly central role played by the public company Rosneft – resulted in two key changes. On the one hand the domestic market witnessed relative normalisation of the Russian companies' behaviour. On the other hand, public and private Russian companies found it increasingly difficult to penetrate the CEE downstream market. As for Gazprom, the third EU Energy Package, coupled with reforms at home and a gas bubble in the European market, forced the publicly owned company to adapt its downstream strategy in the European market.

This chapter is organised as follows: The first part presents the changes in the organisational and institutional framework of the Russian hydrocarbon industry. We present the original mode of organisation resulting from reform in the early-1990s and its adjustment to suit the Russian economic and institutional environment. The second part of the chapter focuses on the wider CEE regional strategies of Russian companies.

4.2 Emergence of Russian oil and gas companies

The hydrocarbon sector in Russia has seen major changes since 1991 and the collapse of the Soviet Union, in terms of both its organisation and institutional framework. This process has been different in oil and gas. Unlike the gas industry, the mass privatisation programme launched at the beginning of the 1990s affected oil assets. The result now is nevertheless an organisational framework centring on powerful state-owned companies, with Gazprom in natural gas and Rosneft in oil. These two enjoy indisputable market power over the Russian market, given the scale of their production and control of infrastructure (in the first case). But they are far from being monopolies, with competitive fringes occupying substantial segments of the oil and gas markets and disputing their dominant position. This market structure came about through a process which gradually sought to bring organisation models into line with the specific features of the Russian institutional and economic environment (Locatelli and Rossiaud 2011).

4.3 Oil reforms drivers

Two key features marked reform of the oil industry during the early years of the transition process. The first one related to reorganisation of oil assets. The objective was to set up vertically integrated companies engaging in all aspects of the sector from exploration to downstream operations. These would replace the oil and gas ministries characteristic of the hierarchical organisation enshrined in a centrally planned economy. Lukoil, Yukos and Surgutneftegaz were the first vertically integrated oil firms established on the basis of former Soviet associations (Lane and Seifulmulukov 1999). Re-organisation of the oil industry gave rise to 14 financial holdings, with either federal or regional reach (Khartukov and Starostina 2000). Private shareholders held a majority share in the main companies: Lukoil (started in 1993), Surgutneftegaz (1993), Yukos (1993), Slavneft (1994), Sidanko (1994) and the Tyumen Oil Company (1995).[2] The state-owned company Rosneft and three regional companies, Tatneft (1994), Bachneftekhim (1995) and KomiTek (1994), were smaller.[3]

The second feature concerned the swift transfer of ownership of the newly established companies to private investors. According to the instigators of reform, privatisation was a priority for economic and political reasons. In economic terms this meant changing the incentives for new owners in order to secure the conditions for the renewal and growth of oil and gas output through substantial productivity gains. It was important to end the old extensive growth model, which maximised output to the detriment of building up reserves, despite the latter being the only guarantee of long-term hydrocarbon production in the future (Gustafson 1989). The challenge was to use the definition of private property rights as an incentive for efficient behaviour which would guarantee long-term growth in the hydrocarbons industry. It was particularly important to refocus the attention of firms on large-scale exploration strategies, particularly in areas near Russia's 'border zones'. In political terms, rapid privatisation seemed necessary in order to form interest groups favourable to further reform. Keen to maximise the value of their assets, the new owners would be inclined to favour reforms designed to consolidate their ownership rights and establish state regulation by contract and the rule of law. The reorganisation and privatisation process was supplemented by oil laws defining new modes of coordination between the state and new private-sector actors. Various formal laws were passed on regulation through competition and contracting. These measures were supplemented by the subsoil law of 1992, which defined rights of access to hydrocarbon resources through a licence-based, two-key regime jointly managed by the federal state and regional governments (Kryukov and Moe 1998; Skyner 2006).

4.4 From the constitution of a private oligopoly to the emergence of a powerful state-owned oil company, Rosneft

The Yukos affair (2003–2004) marked a break in the political economy of the Russian oil industry, with the shift from a free-market organisation, rooted in the reforms initiated at the start of the transition process, towards tighter state control by means of Rosneft.

4.4.1 The two privatisation phases and the unexpected results of reform

Two phases need to be distinguished in the transfer of ownership of oil assets to private investors. These phases led to a separation between two types of private oil company in terms of shareholder structure. The first phase, starting at the end of 1992, corresponded to mass privatisation through the issue of vouchers. The authorities adopted a complicated approach. On the one hand, they opened the way for corporate insiders – members of the former management – to take control. But at the same time, the two-tier nature of privatisation made it difficult for parent companies to properly control subsidiaries working on exploration and production. Under these conditions the only Soviet-oil-industry insiders to succeed in consolidating control over their subsidiaries were Vagit Alekperov (Lukoil) and Vladimir Bogdanov (Surgutneftegaz). In contrast, the failure of other former Soviet managers to achieve effective integration – in particular in the case of Yukos and Sibneft – opened the way for them to be taken over by outsiders (Gustafson 2012).

The second privatisation phase (1995–1997) was marked by the loans-for-shares scheme which enabled oligarchs to consolidate ownership of the leading oil companies. The scheme was based on an arrangement decided by the authorities. Russian banks made loans to the state. In exchange, the latter transferred the shares in oil companies it still held to the banks as collateral; initially for a three-year period. When the state failed to pay back the loans, the banks gained permanent ownership of the assets. In this way, Mikhail Khodorkovsky took control of Yukos and Roman Abramovich gained Sibneft. The consolidation process which followed in the 1990s included the take-over of KomiTek by Lukoil, VNK by Yukos, Slavneft by TNK, and Sibneft then Sidanko by TNK. This led to the emergence of an oligopoly centring to a large extent on industrial and financial groups owned either by Russian banks (Yukos, Sibneft and TNK) or by insiders (Lukoil and Surgutneftegaz). By 2003 these five companies controlled 73 per cent of Russian oil production and more than 60 per cent of exports, whereas the weight of companies in which the state held a majority share was marginal (Locatelli 2006).

The loans-for-shares scheme prompted much comment and criticism due to allegedly corrupt auctions and prices well below the true value of assets. It represented a break in Russia's systemic transformation, convincing public opinion at home that the privatisation of oil assets was illegitimate. As such it paved the way for two key factors in the political economy of Russian oil until the Yukos affair: the very short-term strategies adopted by oligarchs for managing their assets; and conflict between the centres of political and economic power, the latter brought into existence by privatisation.

There is now plenty of documentary evidence that the 'transplantation' (Goldschmidt and Sweyrnert 2006) of market institutions in Russia entailed some 'unexpected results' at a systemic level (Roland 2000). These results mainly concern the economic forces driving reform. Contrary to what Russia had hoped, the 1990s reforms did not enable the oil industry to end the unbalanced resource management characteristic of the Soviet system, with the highest possible output and exports, and low investment in exploration. On the one hand, the new actors certainly rationalised their operations and invested in brownfield sites, yielding increased production from 1999. This was achieved through partnerships with oilfield service companies, enabling the modernisation of production technology. On the other hand, the conditions for renewing the reserves were not guaranteed (Dienes 2004). Despite this being its initial aim, the privatisation process did not allow progress towards a pattern of growth that would secure its long-term development. A distinction must be made between Yukos, Sibneft and TNK, on the one hand, and Lukoil and Surgutneftegaz, on the other. Oligarchs did their utmost to maximise the short-term value of assets. The main explanation for such behaviour lay in the insecurity of private property rights (Hedlund 2001; Tompson 2008). They failed to fulfil their functional role in reducing uncertainty in an institutional context marked by the absence of the rule of law and other institutions capable of complementing and securing such rights. In contrast, Alekporov and Bogdanov were less inclined to invest in modernising and streamlining their companies. They, nevertheless, continued exploring new reserves (Dienes 2004).

The observation concerning the unexpected results of reform is equally valid for the political goal behind the quick privatisation of assets. As an interest group the oligarchs were hostile to effective regulation by contract and the rule of law. With regard to both taxation or coordination by contract, they sought to keep the law as vague as possible in order to further their strategy of cash and asset stripping (Hare and Muravyev 2002; Hoff and Stiglitz 2004). Coordination by contract proved ineffective due to the lack of adequate enforcement capacity. The main provisions contained in the licences, thanks to which the federal state could have directed and guided the strategies of oil companies, proved inoperative. The state found itself unable to deploy effective progressive taxation based on company profits, which would have given firms an incentive to step up exploration in border zones.

Due to the ineffectiveness of formal coordination institutions, relations between the new private actors and the state were determined by a very particular hybridisation of the formal market institutions with informal rules and behaviour inherited from the Soviet period. First, in the context of the economic crisis and demonetisation which characterised the early years of the transition, the new actors resorted to barter and non-payment of debt within the framework of informal networks overlapping with those dating from the Soviet era. We then see coordination by bargaining between companies and the various political and administrative echelons. But compared with the Soviet era the focus of bargaining had shifted from negotiating production programmes and allocation of inputs to the assignment of privileges in terms of tax breaks and access to the Transneft export network (Kryukov 2001). Lastly, as a corollary of coordination by bargaining, the federal authorities resorted to regulation by arbitrary decisions and threats. Threats focused on the withdrawal of licenses and even moves to reclaim ownership of assets. The failure of the federal authorities to promote the rule of law mirrored the lack of demand on the part of the oligarchs, the Yukos affair being the most obvious instance of this trend.

Here again we may make a distinction between the way various private companies responded to such hybrid regulation, depending on their ownership structure. In keeping with a path-dependence rationale, business leaders with a Soviet background such as Alekporov or Bogdanov were more likely than oligarchs to make allowances for the state's economic and political interests. Lukoil and Surgutneftegaz thus succeeded in striking a balance in their operations between the demands of the federal authorities and a business rationale. Keen to build genuinely independent firms, the oligarchs were less receptive, setting in motion a vicious circle, with all actors rejecting formal rules, and companies increasingly resorting to short-term strategies.

4.4.2 The political economy of Russian oil after the Yukos affair

The changes in the organisation of the oil industry which started, at the latest, during Vladimir Putin's second term of office as president, were due to the difficulties the authorities had in dealing with the crisis in exploration and capturing oil rent in a free market. The shifts in the oil model undoubtedly reflect increasingly direct state control over the industry (Pleines 2009). Primarily, the takeover of assets belonging to certain private companies – notably by way of the Yukos affair – made Rosneft, as a large state-owned conglomerate, possible.

This process was completed following the acquisition of all the assets of TNK-BP, making Rosneft one of the largest oil companies in the world, in terms of both production (over 4m barrels a day, see Table 4.1) and reserves. It is also being extended through the discretionary re-allocation of exploration and production licences in favour of public companies (Rosneft, GazpromNeft and Gazprom) and through their joining consortiums previously dominated by private firms (for instance Gazprom's involvement in the development of Sakhalin-II, to the detriment of Shell). Lastly, this process has been accompanied by changes in the legal and competitive framework governing the various operators' access to resources. The two-key licence system has been scrapped, giving full control to the federal state. Public companies enjoy preferential treatment for access to oil fields in Russia's border zones. These

Table 4.1 Main Russian oil companies, by level of production in million barrels a day

	Oil companies	2009	2011	2014
Private companies	Lukoil	1.80	1.73	1.99
	TNK-BP	1.41	1.44	–
	Surgutneftegaz	1.18	1.22	1.2
	Slavneft (50% private, 50% public)	0.31	0.36	0.33
	RussNeft	0.24	0.26	0.15 (2012)
State-owned companies	Rosneft	2.41	2.28	4.16
	Gazprom Neft	0.59	0.6	1.05 (1)
Regional companies	Bashneft	0.25	0.3	0.4
	Tatneft	0.52	0.52	0.53
Total		**9.96**	**10.22**	**10.58**

Sources: Individual companies based on author analysis.

Notes: (1) To obtain total production, add 0.17mB/D, representing GazpromNeft's share in Slavneft, to 0.12mB/D, representing GazpromNeft's share in Tomskneft VNK.

changes have substantially increased the relative weight of state-owned companies in oil production (see Table 4.1).

Over and above the change in the structure of ownership rights, in what respect does this reform represent a rupture in the political economy of Russian oil at home? First, this reform undoubtedly reflects a change in the balance of power in Russia's elite, marked by the growing influence of the *siloviki*, in particular, Igor Sechin. It would nevertheless be a mistake to reduce the Yukos affair to just a shift in the balance of power at home. Advocates of a free market also supported consolidation of Rosneft. Furthermore, greater state control has brought on a period of increasingly effective coordination by contract. The authorities used Rosneft as a benchmark, thus enhancing information-sharing with operators. The Russian authorities have started a learning process, curtailing the conflict-ridden, discretionary re-negotiations of the 1990s. They have altered the beliefs of private companies concerning the credible commitment of the state, prompting them to change their approach to exploration accordingly. Indeed, the third change in the behaviour of Russian companies concerns their management of reserves. Actors, both public and private, and international companies are now engaged in exploration work (Henderson 2011), emblematic of the relative normalisation of their behaviour compared to their international peers.

4.5 Gazprom, the dominant company in the Russian gas market

In terms of its organisation the gas industry took an altogether different course from its petroleum-based counterpart. The production associations making up the Soviet gas ministry were brought together to form Gazprom, a vertically integrated company with the state as its initially dominant (38 per cent) and ultimately majority shareholder, from the 2000s onwards. At the beginning of the century a raft of liberal reforms based on the European model, involving de-integration and more competition, was debated then shelved. However, in recent years an original type of reform has been framed in an effort to normalise Gazprom's behaviour by subjecting it to competition at home.

4.5.1 Debate on reform of the gas industry

At the start of the transition process, re-organisation of the industry gas prompted lively debate in Russia. Up to 1993 two competing approaches were advocated. One sought to maintain a centralised, integrated gas industry. Broadly supported by Gazprom management, this approach was in stark contrast with the liberal stance backed by reformers, determined to end the state-owned monopoly over gas production. Many members of the government, led by Yegor Gaidar, supported re-organisation along these lines. Taking his cue from reform of the oil industry, the energy minister, Vladimir Lopukhin, sought to split Gazprom into several parts. The appointment of Viktor Chernomyrdin as prime minister confirmed consolidation of Gazprom.

60 *Sylvain Rossiaud and Catherine Locatelli*

Chernomyrdin, who had headed the Soviet gas industry ministry and handled the setting up of Gazprom, was firmly opposed to breaking up the monopoly (Khripunov and Matthews 1996).

In the early 2000s the new minister of economic development, German Gref, tabled a liberal reform programme involving de-integration and tougher competition (Ahrend and Tompson 2004). Restructuring projects centred on vertical de-integration of Gazprom, the aim being to separate production and transport functions (in keeping with a patrimonial-unbundling rationale) so as to isolate competitive segments from those enjoying a natural monopoly. From a competitive point of view, the aim was also to set up six production companies based on those wholly owned by Gazprom. Though reduced to its role as a transporter, operating as a natural monopoly under state ownership and subject to regulation allowing third-party access to the network, Gazprom would nevertheless have retained its position as the only gas exporter, this being the sole concession to the European model. In a final stage (2007–2013), Gazprom would have limited itself to just its export business (Locatelli 2003).

Nevertheless, the feasibility and credibility of this reform based on the EU's de-integrated, competitive model was impeded by the accumulation of substantial non-payments and low gas prices. These two mechanisms led to regulation by quantities, disregarding any concern for profit or costs. The company enjoyed preferential access to the rent from exports to the European market, enabling it to fund investment. In exchange, it was required to fulfil the long-term, take-or-pay contracts passed with European countries.

4.5.2 Independent firms dispute Gazprom's market power

The structural changes in the Russian market now cast doubt on this model. There is no question of vertically de-integrating Gazprom, but the state wants to subject the company to competition, in particular, to impose norms on its behaviour (Locatelli 2014). Independent firms – private gas companies and oil companies with reserves they wish to monetise – have thus become key players in the Russian market. However, they lack access to the international market (except Rosneft and Novatek, which export liquefied natural gas to Asia).

Significant increases in regulated prices have opened the way for greater competition in the Russian gas market.[4] Between 2006 and 2010 these prices increased by 124 per cent for industrial customers, and 121 per cent for residential consumers. This rise has gradually ended the price differentials

Table 4.2 Russian gas production by producer

Gm^3	1996	2006	2007	2008	2009	2010	2011	2012	2013	2014
Gazprom	564.7	556.0	548.6	549.7	462.2	506.6	509.8	479	480	445
Others	38.3	100.2	104.1	113.9	120.2	141.7	160.7	176	188	134
Total	603	656.2	652.7	663.6	582.4	650.3	670.5	655	668	579

Sources: Gazprom; Russian Energy Ministry.

between the regulated market, supplied by Gazprom, and the 'free' market mainly supplied by independent firms and oil companies (and in a marginal way by Gazprom itself, particularly in the case of its 'new gas'), enabling competition in the industrial and electrical sectors at least, between Gazprom and other gas operators. In some niches of the gas market the latter can now compete on equal terms with Gazprom (Henderson 2013). This change is gradually allowing a more competitive gas market to take shape, no longer managed exclusively with a view to rationing, but increasingly with a market rationale. Competition between Gazprom and the other gas operators has also come about through stricter control over access to Gazprom's transport network. It should be borne in mind that the gas-pipeline network is a natural monopoly, so rules on third-party access are a necessary pre-condition for introducing competition to this market. Third-party access organises free access to the transport network on equal terms for all producers. This system has existed in Russia since 1997, but initially it was rarely enforced or subject to the whims of Gazprom, it being the only one to hold information on the rate of use of transport capacity. It seems that this situation is now changing (Yafimava 2015).

4.6 The strategies of Russian energy companies in Central and East Europe

The largest Russian companies have persistently asserted themselves as 'real' energy companies in international hydrocarbon markets. Limited at home by institutional and economic conditions specific to the Russian transition, they have looked abroad to derive the greatest benefit from exports and maximise the associated rent. To this end they have sought to deploy international growth strategies, the better to maintain and secure their export sales. As former members of the eastern bloc, CEE countries represented the prime target for experimenting with such policies. However, the results were uneven. We shall start by reviewing the forces driving international development of Russian oil companies in Central and Eastern Europe, and the corresponding results. Then we shall look in greater detail at Gazprom's downstream strategy, subsequently thrown into doubt by EU rules on energy markets and, more broadly, by issues of energy security. The latter have proved a determining factor in relations between Gazprom and the CEE countries with regard to gas.

4.6.1 International growth strategy of Russian oil companies in Central and East Europe

In the 1990s the international development strategies of Russian oil companies diverged. Surgutneftegaz, Sibneft and TNK-BP concentrated on the home market, whereas Lukoil and, to a lesser extent, Yukos developed abroad. In particular, this led to investment in the downstream oil sector in CEE countries (taking shares in refining industries and filling stations).[5] Lukoil was successful in this respect, as can be seen from Table 4.3.

Two economic rationales presided over such investments. First, direct access to foreign markets was a priority, given the low price of petroleum products at home and the problem of non-payment. Second, the acquisition of refineries enabled Lukoil and Yukos to delay CEE countries' attempts to diversify sources of supply and thus set prices that reflected their market power. It is essential in this respect to bear in mind the legacy of economic and technological interdependence left over from the days of Comecon (Balmaceda 2013). At the start of the transition process, in addition to the concentration of oil imports from Russia, this interdependence resulted in two types of vulnerability in the oil supply chains of CEE countries. Relations between the USSR and satellite countries organised crude-oil supply systems. The Druzhba pipeline, for instance, still carries an essential part of the oil supply to this region. Furthermore, local refineries were only viable if they processed large volumes of Russian crude oil. The interdependence left over from the Soviet era therefore explains why it made economic sense for Russian companies to take control of these facilities. At the same time, such moves represented a significant threat to target countries. Petr Binhack and Lukas Tichy (2012) point out that Lukoil's investments in the downstream oil sector in the Czech Republic could only be a source of concern for its authorities. This move could have led to a Russian firm gaining control of the only refinery equipped to process crude oil from sources other than Russia.

Many countries consequently saw Lukoil's investments in downstream oil as a threat to their energy security. Two additional factors drove this process. The first related to the fact that Lukoil was seen as an instrument of Russian foreign policy. As already stressed, Alekporov was always sympathetic to state interests, at home and abroad. The second factor was the vulnerability of CEE countries, which could be instrumentalised to promote investments by Russian companies. The most symptomatic example was Transneft's repeated stoppage of supplies during privatisation of Mazeikiu Nafta in Lithuania, apparently to favour its takeover by Yukos (Duncan 2007).

In the 2000s efforts to secure supply severely limited Russian investments. In 2002 Lukoil failed in its attempt to buy the Gdansk oil refinery in Poland. It also failed to buy a stake in the Lithuanian Mazeikiu Nafta refinery in 2005. These two examples are illustrative of the difficult normalisation of relations between Russian companies and some CEE states (Pleines 2006). Furthermore, with the fall in oil prices, Lukoil has announced plans to re-organise its downstream business, which may lead to it disengaging from large parts of its activities in the Baltic states, Czech Republic, Slovakia, Hungary and Ukraine (Corcoran 2016).

Table 4.3 highlights the absence of Rosneft from the CEE downstream market. The international strategy of Rosneft is more focused on upstream oil. Following the principle of reciprocity known as 'assets for assets' (Belyi 2009), Rosneft has used its partnership with international oil companies in Russia to expand its upstream operations globally. After its failure to buy a 25 per cent share in the Croatian state oil company INA (Poussenkova 2010),

Table 4.3 Russian oil companies' main investments in CEE and Baltic countries

	Company	Filling stations	Oil exploration and production	Oil pipeline	Oil refinery	Russian company
Bulgaria	Neftohim Burgas	X			X	Lukoil
Czechia	Conoco Petrol Stations (1)	X				Lukoil
Estonia	Lukoil-Eurodek (2)	X				Lukoil
Lithuania	Mazeikiu Nafta (3)				X	Yukos
Hungary	MOL (4)			x (gas transmission system)	X	Surgutneftegas (2009)
Poland	Conoco Petrol Stations	X				Lukoil
Romania	Petrotel Lukoil	X			X	Lukoil
Slovakia						Lukoil
	Transpetrol (5)			X		Yukos
Slovenia		X			X	Lukoil

Sources: Henderson and Radosevic (2003); Goldman (2008).

Notes: (1) In 2014 Lukoil sold all its filling station in Czech Republic, mainly to MOL. (2) Oil product terminal. (3) Now owned by the Polish company Orlen. (4) In 2011 the Hungarian government repurchased the 21.1% stake from Surgutneftegaz. (5) In 2009 the Slovak government repurchased the 49% stake from Yukos, which had filed for bankruptcy.

its main investment in downstream oil in the EU was the acquisition of a 50 per cent stake in Germany's Ruhr Oel's joint venture (Henderson 2012).

4.6.2 The specific issue of natural gas: energy security at stake

CEE countries are more exposed to the 'Russian risk' with regard to gas than oil, the latter being a genuinely international market. Given the nature of the gas industry – network industry, relative weight of transmission costs in the overall price, two-way dependence between producer and consumer-countries induced by the specific nature of assets – the interdependence developed during the Soviet era is still subject to considerable inertia. Some countries remain very dependent on Russian gas because of the route taken by gas pipelines built during the Soviet era. CEE countries still import large amounts of natural gas from Russia. The rate of dependence on Russian gas varies from 100 per cent in Bulgaria to 50 per cent in Czech Republic (see Table 4.4). Furthermore, economic factors also contribute to sustaining high levels of dependence on Russian imports. Due to the proximity of these markets, relatively low

Table 4.4 Dependence of CEE countries on Russian gas, 2014

Country	Volume (Gm^3)	Russian imports/ total imports (%)	Russian imports /consumption (%)
Bulgaria	2.8	100	100
Estonia	0.4	100	100
Latvia	1.0	100	100
Lithuania	2.5	100	100
Hungary	5.4	64.3	64.3
Poland	9.1	55.8	55.8
Czech Republic	8.0	75.2	
Slovakia	4.4	100	100

Sources: Gazprom, 2015 annual report; BP Energy statistical review, 2015.

production and transport costs, Russian gas is extremely competitive for these countries. This is particularly true of Poland, Czech Republic and Slovakia, all three major transit countries for Russian gas on its way to Western Europe.

Gazprom has adopted two strategies in the region. The first one is the expression of price-based market power. Gazprom derives an essential share of its profits from exports and one may assume that its prime aim is to maximise gas rent, and consequently its profits in Europe. Accordingly, in non-competitive environments, the firm seeks to impose what may be seen as 'unfair prices'. Such strategies are part and parcel of behaviour which Jonathan Stern (2014) qualifies as a 'profit-maximizing monopolist'. This is wholly consistent with the goals of the Russian state which is determined to maximise fiscal revenue from hydrocarbons in order to balance its budget.

The second strategy deployed by Gazprom may be construed as a 'response' to the liberalisation of EU gas markets and the creation of a competitive environment, organised by the 1996 and 1998 directives and the third EU Energy Package of 2009. Gazprom is trying to move further downstream in the European market to guard against the price and volume risks brought about by EU liberalisation. To secure, enlarge and perhaps better capitalise on its exports, a natural-gas supplier may be tempted by greater downstream involvement, reaching at least as far as wholesale trade. This strategy, which involves acquiring assets in transport, storage and distribution companies, or even large gas consumers (typically electricity utilities), enables a producer to sell their product without passing through competitive wholesale markets (Eikeland 2007) and, thus, obtain greater profit. Downstream integration is a way of recovering the margin of intermediate operators on various downstream segments. In CEE this strategy has particularly focused on purchasing large shares in long-distance transport networks, primarily leading to Europe (the best example is Gazprom's share in the EuroPolGaz which operates the Yamal pipeline to Europe; see Table 4.5). Through this type of investment

Table 4.5 Gazprom's main investments in CEE and in the Baltic states

Country	Date	Joint-venture	Gazprom share (%)	Nature of joint venture
Bulgaria		Overgas	50	Natural gas transport services, marketing
Estonia	1992	Eesti Gaas	37.5	Transport and distribution. In January 2014 Eesti Gaas sold off a gas grid operator, EG Vorguteenus. Vorguteenus Valdus purchased the whole firm. Gazprom subsequently took a 37.03% stake in Vorguteenus Valdus, while retaining a 37.03% share in Eesti Gaas.
Hungary	1994	Panrusgaz (MOL)	40	Marketing and distribution. MOL finalised the sale of its shares to E.ON in 2006, who later sold to MVM Hungarian Electricity in 2014.
	2006			Share in E.ON Földgáz Storage and E.ON Földgáz, and in regional gas and electricity suppliers under the terms of an agreement with E.ON concerning its assets in MOL
	2013			E.ON has concluded an agreement to sell its 100% stake in E.ON Földgáz Trade and E.ON Földgáz Storage to MVM Hungarian Electricity.
		Borsodchem	25	Petrochemical production
Latvia	1997	Latvijas Gaze	34	Marketing and distribution
Lithuania		Stella Vitae	30	Marketing and distribution
		Lietuvos Dujos Amber Grid (2013)	37.1 37.1	Transport, marketing and distribution
Poland	1993	EuroPolGaz (PGNiG)	48	Transport (gas pipeline; Yamal-Europe)
		Gaz Trading (PGNiG)	16	Marketing and trading, gas and LNG
Czechia		Gas-Invest	37.5	Marketing, distribution and trading
		Vemex	33	Trading
Slovakia		Slovrusgaz (E.ON)	50	Transport and marketing

Source: Author.

Gazprom also hopes to secure and control its supply lines to Western Europe, even if the construction of Nord Stream has made this approach less important.

4.6.3 Questioning Gazprom strategy

Gazprom's efforts to move further downstream have been hindered by the interests and energy policies of CEE countries. On the grounds of energy security the latter have sought to restrict investments by the Russian gas company.[6] The determining factors in this process, previously discussed with regard to investments in the oil supply chain, play an even more important part in the case of gas. For many states, moves by Gazprom to take control of gas networks or distribution companies can only increase and sustain the vulnerability of their national gas system. Such moves would enable Gazprom to raise barriers blocking market-entry, thus limiting diversification policies in these countries while enabling the Russian company to fix prices in line with its market power (Smith 2004).[7] We should nevertheless point out that many countries have sought to diversify their sources of gas supply, either by finding new suppliers, such as Norway, or via the Liquefied Natural Gas (LNG) spot market, or by developing the shale gas industry (as in Poland, for instance). It now seems that divergent energy policies are taking shape in the region, and these hinge for a large a part on how Russia engaged in the gas supply. Some countries, such as Bulgaria and Hungary, are keen to obtain a cheaper supply and have consequently sought closer ties with Russia, witnessed by their determination to continue the South Stream project despite EU opposition.[8]

The other factor underpinning the concern about Gazprom's downstream investments relates to the close links between the political and economic determinants of its pricing strategy. Although it is a central issue, it is difficult to reach any definite conclusion on the relative weight of these two determinants. According to Stern (2014) the data on long-term contracts signed by Gazprom reflects its determination to set prices corresponding to its market power in all importing countries. In contrast, Ukraine and Belarus show that it may also use gas prices as a political weapon in the service of Russian foreign policy.

However, it seems to be increasingly difficult to use gas prices for political ends – made possible by Gazprom's market power – in the EU. The Community's free-market policies, designed to bring Gazprom's behaviour into line with prevailing norms by promoting competition, diversifying supply and integrating national markets in a single whole, are beginning to bear fruit (Goldthau and Sitter 2015). Competition policy seeks to limit the market power of Gazprom by allowing the development of a competitive fringe. In this respect, the construction of LNG terminals (3 Gm^3 in Lithuania), as well as better interconnection between eastern and western Europe via Germany, increase the threat of new entrants in some of the region's markets.[9] These developments have forced Gazprom to accept re-negotiation of certain contracts while tending to decrease the price differential between countries. Russia's withdrawal from the provisional application of the Energy Charter Treaty announced in 2009 ended EU attempts to export the community energy acquis to Russia and in so doing create a common energy market integrating the EU's suppliers (Cameron 2010; Keating 2012). EU competition policy nevertheless impacts on the behaviour of Gazprom in the EU market, gradually reducing its market power.

Furthermore, the third EU Energy Package, in particular the rules on unbundling[10] and the Third-Country reciprocity clause have made life extremely difficult for Gazprom's industrial and international-growth strategies, above all due to the impact of these measures on attempts to adapt through downstream integration. The rules on unbundling make it impossible for a producer and supplier such as Russia also to act as a transmission system operator in an EU member state (Willems et al. 2010). In addition, the Third-Country reciprocity clause, also known as the 'anti-Gazprom clause', opens the way for discriminatory treatment of foreign investments. Companies held by shareholders located outside the EU must demonstrate that they will not jeopardise EU energy security, before they can operate in the Union. Russia sees these two rules as a real barrier to its investments in the EU energy sector. Renegotiation of the gas-transit contract between Poland and Russia is a good illustration of the implications of this rule. Until now EurRoPol Gaz, a joint-venture between Poland's PGNiG and Gazprom, managed the part of the Yamal gas pipeline located in Poland. Henceforth it will be in the hands of the Polish operator Gaz-System.[11]

4.7 Conclusion

This contribution sets out to clarify the determinants and modalities by which Russian companies played a part in structuring the energy complex of CEE countries. In so doing we have sought to supplement state-centred analysis of realist inspiration. The Soviet legacy explains both the incentive for Russian companies to develop operations in downstream oil and gas in these countries and why, given the vulnerability of national energy systems, target countries tend to see such developments as a threat to their security. In this respect, the mid-2000s may be seen as a turning point, with the downstream growth strategies of Russian energy suppliers increasingly called into question. Lukoil, for instance, is now disengaging from several CEE countries. As for Gazprom, the economic and institutional changes in the EU market have significantly complicated its downstream growth and its use of strategic pricing.

Notes

1 The Council for Mutual Economic Assistance (Comecon) was the economic federation set up to organise trade between the planned economies of the Soviet Union and Eastern and Central European countries. Trade was governed by special mechanisms in terms of price formation and settlement (transferable rouble).
2 Also, the following: Eastern Oil Company (1994), Onako (Orenburg Oil Company, 1994), Sibneft (1995).

3 In addition to these holdings, there was a group of organisations whose status was very ambivalent, primarily Norsi Oil (started in 1995) and the Central Fuel Company (1997). They lack any real integration, simply regrouping various entities with no clear connection.
4 New gas operators have thus gradually emerged in the unusual context of parallel markets, one with regulated prices, the other not (Ahrend and Tompson 2004). One supplies gas to households at regulated prices, Gazprom being its sole supplier. Other industry, such as the electricity sector, also uses this market, but on the basis of quotas negotiated with Gazprom. Over and above these negotiated quantities, supplied at regulated prices, consumers may resort to a 'free' market, with unregulated prices.
5 To diversify production and reserves geographically Lukoil led the way among Russian companies towards international development, by means of investments in exploration and production. CEE countries, with their limited petroleum resources, were concerned by such expansion.
6 A clear instance of this trend was the refusal, in the 2000s, by the Romanian state to allow Gazprom to take a stake in its two gas distribution companies Distrigaz Sud and Distrigaz Nord when they were privatised. Instead its preference went to GDF and E.ON.
7 The inquiry launched by the European Commission focuses on 'abuse of [Gazprom's] dominant market position in breach of EU antitrust rules'. Apart from the matter of prices, the inquiry carried out by the DG for Competition concerns strategies which may seek to partition markets and prevent diversification of gas supplies. It covers the Baltic countries, Poland, Hungary and Bulgaria. According to the Commission the contracts Gazprom has signed with companies in these countries contain territorial restrictions forbidding exports, destination clauses which hinder competition and are contrary to EU rules. It has also been alleged that Gazprom negotiated deliveries in exchange for commitments on transport infrastructure. European Commission press release of 22 April 2015.
8 The agreements with these countries did not comply with prevailing EU rules on gas pipeline networks.
9 See 'Eastern Europe: Russian gas price ceilings' *Energy Economist*, No. 406, August 2015, pp. 7–16.
10 Unbundling involves separating, in legal or accounting terms, the various segments of the gas supply chain, to prevent vertical integration, seen as a barrier to new operators.
11 The latter pledged to allow TPA operation for the pipeline's unreserved capacity (Poland and Russia reach compromise deal with EU on long-term gas supply and transit, *Gas Matters*, Dec.–Jan. 2011).

References

Ahrend, R. and Tompson, W. (2004). 'Russia's Gas Sector: The Endless Wait for Reform?', *Economics Department Working Paper*, No. 402. (Paris: OECD).
Belyi, A. (2009). 'Reciprocity as a Factor of the Energy Investment Regimes in the EU-Russian Energy Relations', *Journal of World Energy Law & Business*, 2(2), pp. 117–128.
Balmaceda, M.M. (2013). *The Politics of Energy Dependency. Ukraine, Belarus, and Lithuania between Domestic Oligarch and Russian Pressure.* (Toronto: University of Toronto Press).
Binhack, P. and Tichy, L. (2012). 'Asymmetric Interdependence in the Czech-Russian Energy Relations', *Energy Policy*, 45, pp. 54–63.

Braun, A. (2012) 'Resetting Russian-Eastern European Relations for the 21st Century', *Communist and Post-Communist Studies*, 45(3–4), pp. 349–400.
Cameron, F. (2010). 'The Politics of EU-Russia Energy Relations', in K. Talus and P. Fratini (eds), *EU-Russia Energy Relations*. (Brussels: Euroconfidential), pp. 25–38.
Corcoran, J. (2016). 'Currency Crash Hits Russia's Foreign Assets', *Petroleum Economist*, March, pp. 42–43.
Dannreuther, R. (2013). *International Security. The Contemporary Agenda*, Second Edition. (Cambridge: Polity Press).
Dienes, L. (2004). 'Observations on the Problematic Potential of Russian Oil and the Complexities of Siberia', *Eurasian Geography and Economics*, 45(5), pp. 319–345.
Duncan, P. (2007). '"Oligarchs", Business and Russian Foreign Policy', *Economic WP No. 83*. (London: Center for the Study of Economic and Social Change in Europe).
Eikeland, O. (2007). 'Downstream Natural Gas in Europe – High Hopes Dashed for Upstream Oil and Gas Companies', *Energy Policy*, 35(1), pp. 227–237.
Fedorov, Y. (2013). 'Continuity and Change in Russia's Policy toward Central and Eastern Europe', *Communist and Post-Communist Studies*, 46(3), pp. 315–326.
Goldman, M. (2008). *Petrostate. Putin, Power and the New Russia*. (Oxford: Oxford University Press).
Goldschmidt, N. and Zweyrnert, J. (2006). 'The Two Transitions in Central and Eastern Europe as Processes of Institutional Transplantation', *Journal of Economic Issues*, 40(4), pp. 895–918.
Goldthau, A. and Sitter, N. (2015). *A Liberal Actor in a Realist World. The European Union Regulatory State and the Global Political Economy of Energy*. (Oxford: Oxford University Press).
Gustafson, T. (1989). *Crisis amid Plenty. The Politics of Soviet Energy under Brezhnev and Gorbachev*. (Princeton; NJ: Princeton University Press).
Gustafson, T. (2012) *Wheel of Fortune. The Battle for Oil and Power in Russia*. (London: The Belknap Press of Harvard University Press).
Hare, P. and Muravyev, A. (2002). 'Privatization in Russia', *Research Paper Series*, 25 (Russian-Europe Centre for Economic Policy).
Hedlund, S. (2001). 'Property without Rights: Dimensions of Russian Privatisation', *Europe-Asia Studies*, 53(2), pp. 213–237.
Henderson, J. (2013). 'Competition for Customers in the Evolving Russian Gas Market'. NG 73. (Oxford: Institute for Energy Studies).
Henderson, J. (2012). 'Rosneft – On the Road to Global NOC Status?', OIES Working papers, WPM 44. (Oxford: Institute for Energy Studies).
Henderson, J. (2011) 'The Strategic Implications of Russia's Eastern Oil Resources, OIES Working papers', WPM 41. (Oxford: Institute for Energy Studies).
Henderson, J. and Radosevic, S. (2003). 'The Influence of Alliances on Corporate Growth in the Post-Soviet Period: Lukoil and Yukos', Working Papers Series, No. 34. (London: Centre for the Study of Economic and Social Change in Europe).
Hoff, K. and Stiglitz, J.E. (2004). 'After the Big Bang? Obstacles to the Emergence of the Rule of Law in Post-Communist Societies', *American Economic Review*, 94(3), pp. 753–763.
Keating, M.F. (2012). 'Re-Thinking EU Energy Security: The Utility of Global Best Practices for Successful Transnational Energy Governance' In C. Kuzemko, A.V. Belyi, A. Glodthau and M. F. Keating (eds), *Dynamics of Energy Governance in Europe and Russia*. (Basingstoke and New York: Palgrave Macmillan), pp. 86–105.

Khartukov, E. and Starostina, E. (2000). 'Russia's Oil Privatization is More Greed than Fear', *Oil & Gas Journal*, 98(27), pp. 30–32.
Khripunov, I. and Matthews, M.M. (1996). 'Russia's Oil and Gas Interest Group and Its Foreign Policy Agenda', *Problems of Post-Communism*, 43(3), pp. 38–48.
Kryukov, V.A. (2001). 'Who is the Boss in the Oil House?'. *EKO*, November.
Kryukov, V. and Moe, A. (1998). 'Joint Management of Oil and Gas Resources in Russia', *Post-Soviet Geography and Economics*, 39(7), pp. 588–605.
Lane, D. and Seifulmulukov, I. (1999). 'Structure and Ownership' In D. Lane (ed.) *The Political Economy of Russian Oil*. (Lanham; MD: Rowman & Littlefield), pp. 15–45.
Locatelli, C. (2014). 'The Russian Gas Industry: Challenges to the "Gazprom Model?"', *Post-Communist Economies*, 26(1), pp. 53–66.
Locatelli, C. and Rossiaud, S. (2011). 'A Neo Institutionalist Interpretation of the Changes in the Russian Oil Model' *Energy Policy*, 39(9), pp. 5588–5597.
Locatelli, C. (2006). 'The Russian Oil Industry between Public and Private Governance: Obstacles to International Oil Companies' Investment Strategies' *Energy Policy*, 34(9), pp. 1075–1085.
Locatelli, C. (2003). 'The Viability of Deregulation in the Russian Gas Industry', *Journal of Energy and Development*, 28(2), pp. 221–238.
Newnham, R. (2011). 'Oil, Carrots, and Sticks: Russia's Energy Resources as a Foreign Policy Tool', *Journal of Eurasian Studies*, 2(2), pp. 134–143.
Orban, A. (2008). *Power, Energy, and the New Russian Imperialism*. (Westport; CT: Praeger Security International).
Pleines, H. (2009). 'Developing Russia's Oil and Gas Industry. What Role for the State?' in J. Perovic, R. Orttung and A. Wenger (eds), *Russian Energy Power and Foreign Relations. Implications for Conflict and Cooperation*. (London: Routledge), pp. 71–86.
Pleines, H. (2006). 'Russian Energy Companies in the Enlarged European Union' in A. Wenger, J. Perovic and R. Orttung (eds), *Russian Business Power. The Role of Russian Business in Foreign and Security Relations*. (London: Routledge), pp. 47–66.
Poussenkova, N. (2010). 'The Global Expansion of Russia's Energy Giant', *Journal of International Affairs*, Spring/Summer, 63(2), pp. 103–124.
Roland, G. (2000). *Transition and Economics: Politics, Markets and Firms*. (Cambridge; MA: MIT Press).
Smith, K.C. (2004). *Russian Energy Politics in the Baltics, Poland, and Ukraine. A New Stealth Imperialism?*. (Washington; DC: Centre for Strategic and International Studies).
Skyner, L. (2006). 'The Regulation of Subsoil Resource Usage: the Erosion of the "Two key" Principle and Its Inclusion into the Framework of Civil Law', *Review Central and East European Law*, 2(4), pp. 127–157.
Stern, J. (2014). 'The Impact of European Regulation and Policy on Russian Gas Exports and Pipelines' in J. Henderson and S. Pirani (eds), *The Russian Gas Matrix: How Markets are Driving Change*. (Oxford: The Oxford University Press).
Tompson, W. (2008). *Back to the Future? Thoughts on the Political Economy of Expanding State Ownership in Russia*. (Cahier de Russie, CERI).
Willems, A., Sul, J. and Benizri, Y. (2010). 'Unbundling as a Defence Mechanism against Russia: Is the EU Missing the Point?' in K. Talus and P. Fratini (eds), *EU-Russia Energy Relations*. (Brussels: Euroconfidential), pp. 227–244.
Yafimava, K. (2015). 'Evolution of Gas Pipeline Regulation in Russia: Third Party Access, Capacity Allocation and Transportation Tariffs'. *OIES Paper No. 95*. (Oxford: Oxford Institute for Energy Studies).

Part II
Case studies

Part II
Case studies

5 Czech Republic

Rick Fawn

5.1 Introduction

Determining how 'energy secure' the Czech Republic is, drives at two vexing questions: for any country that is deficient of utter energy self-reliance, what can it do to minimise its energy dependence or vulnerability? And, thereafter, how much dependence or vulnerability is reasonable? This chapter commences by establishing the Czech Republic's energy mix and how dependent it is on external suppliers and supply lines. This contribution determines that from the onset of its post-1989 independent foreign policy, Czechoslovakia and subsequently the Czech Republic commendably sought diversification of its energy mix and its energy sources, and built infrastructure to lessen the impact of supply interruptions, particularly those from Russia. Furthermore, its government has stopped foreign takeovers of some strategic industries, namely again by Russian interests.

The chapter then turns to explaining the paradox of relative energy security vis-à-vis Russia and, what we might term, sycophancy towards Russia. This is found not primarily in energy-economic terms, but through three considerations: the structure of the Czech energy sector, including privatisation and the opportunities for corruption, and the highly fragmented nature of the Czech political system.

5.2 The state of energy supplies

In 1991, then-Czechoslovak president Václav Havel mused about his future vision for a prosperous, democratic country. Among the many features that Havel cited were, perhaps quaintly, a multitude of family-run pubs and bakeries. But the surrealist playwright also hard-headedly pictured the country with a guaranteed, secure supply of energy (Havel 1991).

How has the Czech Republic faired since? The media often lump the Czech Republic together with its neighbours, who are primarily if not entirely reliant on Russian energy supplies. This perception pierces the core issue of energy security: what constitutes realistic sufficiency, or when does energy dependency become that? The Czech Republic depends on Russian sources for gas, and currently has contracts for Russian supply of nuclear fuels. True, therefore, the Czech Republic needs some Russian energy. But not wholly. And as a small, resource-poor landlocked country, it has taken substantial measures since 1990 to diversify supply and to change its energy mix, and is the least dependent on Russian energy of any former Soviet bloc country.

The Czech Republic's only major natural resources are brown coal and uranium, the latter once extremely important to the Soviets; but even with so, the Czech Republic imports nuclear fuel. It produces a small amount of high-quality oil, from fields in Moravia, but which fulfils no more than 2 per cent of domestic consumption. Coal, however, still supplies 39 per cent of the Czech Republic's total primary energy source, and the resource itself remains entirely in state control (IEA 2014: 130).

In other areas of energy, however, Communist-era Czechoslovakia, a heavily industrial part of the Soviet bloc, was overwhelmingly dependent on Soviet supplies of gas and oil. Soviet gas supplies to Czechoslovakia began in 1967 and the country was tied infrastructurally, and seemingly inexorably, into a Soviet-era delivery system. Even so, Communist Czechoslovakia simultaneously invested in the southeast European, Adria oil pipeline, which ran through Yugoslavia (principally supplying industries in many of its constituent republics) and extending to Austria and Hungary. The post-Communist Czechoslovak government was intent, on the one hand, to retain trading relations with soon-to-be former bloc countries, but on the other hand, to reduce that eastern energy dependency. In 1992 the Czechoslovak premier visited Croatia and with his counterpart sought to safeguard the Adria pipeline from further damage in the escalating fighting that became the Yugoslav wars of secession. Both leaders also suggested that the emerging six-country regional cooperation initiative called the *Hexagonale* should build a common gas pipeline and also work for the integration of their region into the European energy distribution system (CSTK 1992: 12).

Although that initiative came too late, and could not supply much in any case, it demonstrated Czechoslovak/Czech concern and imagination for increasing its energy security, including reduction of its reliance on Russia. A 1997 deal with Norway significantly reduced the dependence on Russian gas, which up to that point had supplied 100 per cent of the Czech Republic's gas. Considered at the time to be expensive, and highly criticised by (as we shall see, the pro-Moscow) Premier Václav Klaus, the Norwegian deal was later praised when the 2009 Russia–Ukraine gas dispute resulted in reduced gas supplies to Europe. That said, the Czech Republic remains reliant on Russia for, generally, 75 per cent of its gas, although this dependency can vary, with, for example 2012 requiring 66 per cent Russian gas (see, for example, Dickel 2014: 9). The Czech Republic remains under contract with Gazprom for gas deliveries until 2035. Of course, that could offer Moscow potential leverage over Prague. At the time, the deal and the amount of supply (similar to several other countries) was deemed not only to facilitate Gazprom's dictation of prices but also to 'give Moscow more political influence' (see Roškanin 2008: 9; Ośrodek Studiów Wschodnich 2007: 8).

The Czech State Energy Policy, adopted in 2015, pronounces that 'the Czech Republic has already adopted and continues to adopt a series of measures to ensure gas security – a considerable proportion of gas supplies is imported on the basis of long-term contracts, from diversified sources, with diversified transport routes also available' but recognises continued supplies of Russian natural gas (Czech Ministry of Industry and Trade 2014: 15). This is reflected in the fact that although the Czech Republic enjoys far better energy security for some fuels than the EU average, it remains more dependent on foreign gas imports than the EU average (European Commission 2011).

That said, the Czech Republic has undertaken further measures since the 1990s to ease its Russian dependency and to lessen the impact of any supply interruptions. Among these have been construction of gas pipelines and facilities to ensure reverse flows and the expansion of Czech gas storage, now having Europe's second largest facility, allowing for 2.3 billion cubic meters of gas. RWE Gas Storage, part of the German conglomerate that owns much of the gas supply infrastructure in the Czech Republic, planned to develop further storage capacity that could hold 4.3 billion cubic meters, providing six months' domestic consumption.

All six Czech underground storage facilities have been maintained at full capacity, a measure described as both necessary to meet peak wintertime demand but also explicitly as serving in an 'irreplaceable strategic role in increasing energy security enhancing the country's energy security' notably after the Ukrainian crisis of 2014 (see RWE 2014, quoting the Czech Minister of Energy). These preparations proved their worth immediately during the 2009 Russian–Ukraine gas war, when supplies to the EU were disrupted. Not only was the Czech Republic consequently unaffected but the crisis allowed Prague, as two leading Czech analysts concluded, to secure 'some political points', using its gas stores to support beleaguered neighbours as a 'gesture of solidarity' (Binhack and Tichý 2012a: 59–60). Czech special ambassador for energy, Václav Bartuška, confirmed that Czech energy supplies would be sufficient to survive non-transit of gas through Ukraine, a measure he fully expected would occur (quoted in Kahn and Lopatka 2014). The International Energy Agency (IEA), previously critical of Prague for lacking strategic reserves or fuel switching potential in a gas crisis, also noted the prompt Czech planning response after the crisis (IEA 2010).

Despite all of these measures, the Czech Republic is still generally perceived to be heavily dependent on Russian gas. Indeed, about 75 per cent of the 8.3 billion cubic metres (bcm) of Czech gas demand in 2012 was fulfilled by Russian imports and much of its purchased Norwegian gas is actually Russian in origin, thanks to a system of gas trade swapping (Butler 2017: 18). This apparently explains its (and Slovakia's and Austria's) hesitation to agree to harsher EU sanctions against Russia over the Ukrainian–Russian crisis (Peacock 2014).

Such perceptions notwithstanding, the Czech government has also undertaken steps to lessen reliance on Russian oil. In 2013, 64.3 per cent of the

Czech Republic's crude oil came from Russia, although this is down from the near-total dependence in the late communist and early post-communist period. Other sources of crude oil are principally from post-Soviet Caucasus and Central Asia, with Azerbaijan now supplying 25.3 per cent and Kazakhstan a further 9.5 per cent, while Algeria provides just 0.9 per cent (Czech Ministry of Industry and Trade 2014). Prague has particularly sought to enhance relations with Azerbaijan, as highlighted by a presidential visit in 2015. The Czech Republic has also sought to reduce oil consumption generally (including through alternative energy), for example, importing 7.3 per cent less oil in 2013 than in 2012.

Czech planning for oil-delivery diversification extends back to the immediate post-Communist period of 1990, when Prague pressed for what became the Ingolstadt – Kralupy nad Vltavou–Litvínov pipeline (IKL). The logic behind it suggested that existing pipelines were insufficient, but also that Hungary and (the eventually independent) Slovakia would compete against the Czech Republic. The IKL was opened in 1996, and now carries one-third of Czech oil imports (IEA 2014: 133). It is deemed to have been 'a particular advance in terms of Czech geopolitical security' (Černoch 2013: 40). Beyond developing alternative sources Czech efforts at oil diversification extend to strong support for alternative pipelines. As non-Russian Eurasian energy supplies to the Czech Republic already suggest, Prague has pressed for the Transalpine pipeline (TAL) which brings oil through Italy, Austria and Germany, and TAL was connected to the IKL pipeline. Further supply diversification came with the June 2014 agreement with Poland. That extends the STORK II pipeline from Poland's Baltic Sea terminal to bring non-Russian, namely Middle Eastern oil, to the Czech Republic.

In addition to infrastructural enhancements, Prague generally exercises strategic ownership. Widely publicised is the fact that MERO ČR, the company that owns the Czech sections of oil pipelines and storage facilities, is for strategic reasons wholly owned by the Czech state (MERO 2015).

Apart from oil and gas, a sector where Russian influence is evident is nuclear energy, however, this is a sector where Czech strategic control is limited. In 2006 Russian interests replaced American to become the exclusive supplier of nuclear fuel to the Temelín nuclear power plant's two reactors, in an agreement to expire in 2020. The Czech Republic's other facility, Dukovany, similarly owned by the state-energy conglomerate, České Energetické Závody (ČEZ), was already Russian-supplied. However, rather importantly and elaborated presently, the Czech Republic has managed to deflect serious Russian interests in its nuclear energy sector.

Overall, the Czech energy mix, infrastructure and supply demonstrates ambiguities regarding its energy (in)dependence towards Russia. A three-stage periodisation of post-1989 wider Czech energy policy helps to explain that, and specific developments with Russia will be integrated into those periods.

5.3 Periodisation: change and continuity in Russian–Czech energy relations

Russian–Czech energy relations do not lend themselves to tidy periodisation. Rather periodisation comes from developments within Czechoslovakia/Czech Republic, from the influence of EU accession, and then from particular broader events in Czech–Russian relations. Those caveats made, three periods would be: first, from 1990 to 1997, the principal characteristics of which would be the specificity of the Czechoslovak/Czech privatisation process, one that is quite separate of any Russian consideration, but the process and end result of privatisation left substantial opportunity for Russian (and other) political influence. The second period runs from 1997 to approximately 2007, and is governed by the influence on Prague of EU accession. The third period, starting roughly in 2008, is framed by Czech perceptions of energy security and crises, and those often but not always in respect of Russian actions.

5.3.1 Period 1: 1990–1997

The first phase runs from the onset of the early post-Communist period to the end of the Klaus government, in 1997, and concerns the entirety of the early transition privatisation period. Czechoslovakia/Czech Republic was a frontrunner of privatisation. The ultra-freemarketeer federal finance minister, Václav Klaus, claimed that he would privatise almost all of the country's assets, and swiftly. In this otherwise decisive period, energy ownership, however, was largely and intentionally left alone. The revolutionary privatisation was concentrated on small and medium enterprises. Additionally, when Klaus became the first prime minster of the new Czech Republic, between 1992 (still before the end of the federation) and 1997, his government, in a bid to avoid a popular backlash, retained public subsidies for energy, as well as public transport and rents, while removing them from almost all of other sectors, amounting to 80 per cent of consumer spending. Rather than privatising the energy sector, Czech energy conglomerates were instead broken down into smaller companies, but these still remained under state control. How these entities were vulnerable to corruption, both domestic and foreign, and also unduly able to influence political life, will be outlined later in the chapter.

5.3.2 Period 2: 1997–2007

We turn now to the second period, which was defined by EU influence on the Czech Republic. Throughout the accession process the EU sought to encourage further deregulation and privatisation of the Czech energy sector. Across the accession countries the EU pressed for energy privatisation, and some post-communist countries, foremost Hungary, accepted that pressure. The Czech

Republic (and Slovakia) were the most resistant with vested interests, concerns for control over strategic sectors, as well as concern for increased consumer costs.[1] The EU influence worked regarding gas, so that the OECD could recognise that European Directive 2003/55/EC had encouraged the unbundling of the previously vertically integrated sector (OECD 2012: 129). As a result, in 2006, the Czech Republic stated that it had 'fully liberalized its market in electricity and partly opened up its market in gas' (Ministry of Industry and Trade 2006). The EU impact on Czech energy ownership has otherwise been limited. Brussels was only partially successful in influencing Prague on energy privatisation, with much of energy production and distribution left instead in state hands.

5.3.3 2008–present

The third period relates to crises in Russian–EU energy relations, which can be said to date from 2008–2009. The closure of Russian energy supplies transiting Ukraine, to be sure, was an EU-wide dilemma. The 2009 crisis, for example, which so badly affected neighbouring states, was one that Czech Republic endured relatively well. Nevertheless, it pushed for greater multilateral activism in the EU. The Czech Foreign Minister declared: 'The main lesson learned from this crisis is that Russia and Ukraine aren't reliable suppliers. Europe must think about alternative sources and pipelines' (Czech Government 2009). Reactions to the Ukrainian–Russian crisis which broke out in 2013 have also had an (ambiguous) impact on bilateral relations, but do not constitute a watershed.

Significant also is that the Czech Republic experienced distinctive negative, even threatening, relations with Russia which coincided with that broader crisis. Just before that predicament, Prague had accepted the US request to host sections of a Central European–based anti-missile defence system. Moscow immediately protested the move, with the Russian president, Dmitrii Medvedev, pronouncing 'we will not be hysterical about this, but we will think of retaliatory steps' (BBC 2009). Czech reliance on Russian energy could be inferred. In August 2009 Prague expelled two Russian diplomats. Usually a symbolic matter, these expulsions were taken to be far more significant. The Russian Foreign Ministry called the act 'another provocation' from Prague (cited in Radio Praha 2009). That, however, built on Czech anxieties dating formally (if not before) from 2007, when the Czech Intelligence Services claimed that the majority of the 200 Russian 'diplomats' at its Prague embassy were spies attempting to influence Czech political, military and business interests. In 2009, Czech media reported that expulsions were related fundamentally to Russian activities directed at Czech energy and nuclear power interests (iDnes.cz 2009). The peculiarities of Czech–Russian relations benefit from being understood in the context of Czech ownership and (non)privatisation of the energy sector. These characteristics are now delineated.

5.4 Privatisation, ownership and the possibilities for corruption

Having determined that energy privatisation has been very uneven in the Czech Republic, and that key sectors remain in Czech government control, the chapter turns its attention to the general levels of corruption in the Czech Republic and the scope and capacity for Russian influence. We need to acknowledge that determining the extent of Russian influence is challenging for the best-resourced officials, let alone the removed, lone observer and that acts of undue political influence and outright corruption do not intentionally materialise publically. Nevertheless, the contours of a permissive political–economic Czech environment allow us to understand the potential for such scenarios, and illustrations from various Czech actors offer indications of the possibilities for such interactions between Czech energy interests, including Russian, and political elites.

5.4.1 Energy sector, elites and failed energy privatisation

Where privatisation has occurred – particularly regarding gas supply – it has generally resulted in foreign-ownership and that ownership has been subject to investigation. For example, German-owned 'RWE Supply & Trading CZ' is the main importer of Russian natural gas into the Czech Republic. Natural gas is delivered under a long-term contract signed in October 1998, which extends to 2035.

The main Czech actor within the energy sector is České Energetické Závody, abbreviated to ČEZ, which is then, with some unintended but important irony, pronounced 'Chezz', making the nickname of the Chezz Republic. With 70 per cent of the energy sector in its hands, and the ČEZ Group being the largest company, the Czech Republic has been nicknamed by some commentators as the ČEZ Republic. Based on 2014 total assets, the conglomerate ranks fourth in terms of energy and resources in CEE; by market capitalisation, however, ČEZ is the largest energy company in CEE, and has become one of Europe's major electricity providers (Deloitte 2015).

ČEZ has repelled domestic and EU efforts at restructuring and changes in operations. In the early 1990s ČEZ was broken down into distinct companies for production, transmission and distribution. It managed, however, to retain control over major subsidiaries. In 2000 ČEZ was meant to be privatised, and considering its worth, attracted bids from world energy giants. But the process was conducted in what a leading Czech energy analyst calls an 'unclear manner'; all bidders were eventually excluded or withdrew and the state continued to run ČEZ (Černoch 2013: 49). A privatisation effort reoccurred in 2002, again attracting some interest from foreign energy consortiums, but the inclusion of other energy facilities, such as nuclear power, and annual purchases of brown coal (as mentioned, coal itself also being owned by the Czech state), dissuaded them (see 'CZEC Group', no date). Only a minority of shares, now 30 per cent, were eventually divested. The privatisation of ČEZ that was undertaken was conducted in a manner called 'unclear', and 'very hard to judge' (Černoch 2014: 43–44). A leading investigative journalist could, at best, conclude that ČEZ's political influence was not incomparable to that of state energy companies in Russia (Macháček 2008), where overlap between state and energy company personalities and interests are 'extreme' (e.g. Bremmer 2010: 108). *The Economist* has been forthright, writing in 2010 that 'though nominally state-run, many see the power flowing the other way: from CEZ's board into politics' (Economist 2010).

A proposition, then, is that because Czech energy privatisation largely left key assets in the Czech government's hands, the Czech Republic has enjoyed relative immunity from foreign, including Russian pressure. It may even be that ČEZ is too large, even for Russian interests to gain direct control or ownership. Nevertheless, Czech government ownership remains a target for external influence, and one made additionally susceptible because of a combined Czech political-business environment of general corruption and of political fragmentation.

5.4.2 Czech political-business environment of general corruption and of political fragmentation

Business and trade interests could account for some of the Czech 'softness' towards Moscow. The general climate of corruption in the Czech Republic, sadly, suggests that political influence is purchasable. A 2014 EU study found that 95 per cent of Czechs deemed corruption a problem, and 71 per cent of companies called it the primary obstacle to conducting business (European Commission 2014: 3). Transparency International ranks the Czech Republic as more corrupt than several post-Communist neighbours, and just above Bahrain, Jordan, Lesotho, Namibia, Rwanda and Saudi Arabia, as Table 5.1 shows:

Table 5.1 Transparency International, Corruption Perceptions Index 2014: Results

2015 (ranking out of 175 countries)	Country
35	Poland
39	Lithuania
	Slovenia
47	Hungary
53	**Czech Republic**
54	Slovakia
55	Bahrain
55	Jordan
55	Lesotho
55	Namibia
55	Rwanda
55	Saudi Arabia

Source: Transparency International, 2014.

However, a visible link between corruption and the Russian presence is not evident. The US State Department is positive regarding a level-playing field in the Czech Republic:

> There are no general restrictions on foreign investment, although limits exist within certain sectors, for example in airport services. The Czech Republic attracts a great deal of FDI for its size, and has taken strides to diversify its traditional investments in engineering into new fields of research, development and innovative technology. The Czech Republic is a success story among former communist countries, often out-performing its fellow central and eastern European states.
>
> (US Department of State 2014)

However, the energy sector is criticised by the OECD and the European Commission. The OECD has called for general continuation of privatisation in the Czech Republic and in 2014 noted that public ownership of energy remained 'substantial'. The OECD also considers competition to be limited, prompting concerns over 'issues of level playing fields, including problems of implicit subsidies, cross-subsidies from protected market activities, and political risks' which also limit possibility for others to enter the market (OECD 2014: 57). The European Commission has occasionally issued objections, demands and even fines relating to problems in the management of Czech energy. In 2009 the Commission raided ČEZ offices, documentation then seized was used in a further (though inconclusive) 2010 probe into market control (FT 2010). The Commission later issued concerns that ČEZ used its dominant market position to limit capacity in the transmission network to exclude competition. A legally binding settlement was agreed in 2013 (European Commission 2013).

The environment for corruption is but only one part of the explanation of the Czech–Russian energy paradox; the fragmentation of the Czech political system provides the remainder.

5.5 Czech political fragmentation and Czech sycophancy with Russia

Although a gigantic topic, the established indications of the permissive environment for corruption in the Czech Republic should provide some sense of how energy interests, domestic and foreign, could influence politics. That environment was created by the post-Communist Czechoslovak/Czech privatisation process of the 1990s. In sum, the economic liberalisation project under Czechoslovak Finance Minister and then Czech Prime Minister, Václav Klaus, placed no limits on the market. His mantra, repeatedly cited, was that 'dirty money' did not exist.[2] Then, in the last weeks of his 10-year presidency, Klaus invoked his right, for the first time, to issue a pardon. Those exempted included the elderly facing certain sentences and those whose alleged crimes were under investigation for multiple years. Many exempted included leading figures charged with corruption. Klaus maintained that he had no one in mind in issuing the amnesty. While many petty criminals were pardoned, a leading Czech commentator also noted that Klaus's general amnesty provided exemption for leading economic suspects from further criminal investigation (Macháček 2013).

In 2003 the OECD commended Czech authorities for increased efforts to try more cases of corruption; a practice which it deemed 'likely to increase public awareness and have a detrimental effect on shady practices' (OECD 2003: 16). Ten years later, however, in its most-recent report, the OECD expressed deep concerns, including the 'regrettably low level of awareness of the foreign bribery risks'; utter non-participation of Czech companies in the OECD's on-site studies, and lack of awareness of corruption reporting and compliance measures to tackle the risks of foreign bribery. Among many other concerns, the report also noted that the judicial system was susceptible to 'possible political pressures over prosecutorial decisions' that could influence both investigations and prosecutions concerning foreign bribery (OECD 2013: 5). Some examples give indications of the permissiveness of this environment.

As intimated, ČEZ seems to hold considerable sway over politicians. One notable case was the holidaying of several leading Czech politicians, representing different major parties, with ČEZ chairman, Martin Roman, who, unrelatedly, stepped down as ČEZ CEO in 2011, and then from its advisory board in 2013. He had been investigated by Czech corruption police for 'criminal abuse of information'. When he was also investigated by the European Commission, it was alleged that he lobbied the Czech Republic's commissioner, Štefan Füle, to influence the findings (Kenety 2012). More generally, the ZIndex developed at Charles University determined that two-thirds of the €13.7 billion public spending between 2006 and 2010 was not even tracked in the government's official procurement database. Additionally, some 14 per cent of all public tenders had only a single bidder, and these all fell short of both OECD and the Czech Regional Development Ministry criteria (see: ZIndex 2011; Economist 2011). That the possibility for corruption and political influence exists seems evident. This raises a question about what the possible links between Czech political-energy dynamics and Russian influence might be.

5.6 Visible (and invisible) links between corruption and the Russian presence in the energy sector

Despite low trade and certain decisions to exclude Russian bids in strategic sectors of the Czech economy, the depth of Russian economic influence may be considerable, including on Czech politicians. In the year before his death, Havel said that Russian interests in the Czech Republic were 'undoubtedly influencing the behavior of various Czech political parties and politicians', adding, 'I've seen several cases where the influence started quietly and slowly began projecting onto our foreign policy. I can only advise serious discretion and great caution' (quoted in Feifer and Whitmore 2010).

Klaus's views become salient again, now regarding Russia. Klaus opposed as uneconomical the deal that made Norway the alternative supplier of gas to the Czech Republic, and which is credited with preventing the country from being heavily impacted by the 2009 gas crisis. Klaus had his anti-EU and anti-climate change book translated into Russian by courtesy of Lukoil, which also hosted him in Moscow for its launch, when he should have been signing the Lisbon Treaty (he noisily opposed the Treaty, but eventually signed it as the last of the EU member state leaders to do so). While Klaus fumed about the deal creating a Norwegian alternative, Radio Free Europe/Radio Liberty (RFE/RL) instead called the measure the Czech Republic's 'Final Step in Energy Independence' (Naegele 1997). Czech journalist, Jaroslav Plesl, commented in 2010 that 'The Russians want the European Union to be as weak as possible, and for that purpose, Klaus serves their interests well', while RFE/RL summarised that Klaus was 'moving ever closer' to Russia and Putin (Feifer and Whitmore 2010). Out of office since 2003, Klaus nevertheless co-authored on his official website, a justification for Russia's annexation of Crimea, even stating that Russians could be 'happy', and rejecting Western references to 'annexation' (Klaus and Weigl 2014).

Presidential sycophancy towards Russia continued under Klaus's presidential successor, Miloš Zeman. Russian media used Zeman's comments as evidence that an EU leader supported Moscow's annexation of Crimea, and urged others to follow (RT 2014). Zeman denounced the sanctions against Russia at the 2014 World Public Forum, an event organised by Putin's personal friend, the oligarch, Vladimir Yakunin. So pointed have been Zeman's statements that Czech foreign policy analyst, Vít Beneš, designated Zeman 'a president who is openly advocating the official position of the Kremlin' (quoted in czech.cz 2015). Upon the announcement of the Minsk agreement over fighting in Ukraine and before the ceasefire had even been implemented, and unlike other EU leaders, Zeman immediately called for EU sanctions to be lifted. Czech Premier, Bohuslav Sobotka, by contrast, called Zeman's pitch rash, and added that evidence of a ceasefire was necessary first. Defence Minister Martin Stropnický criticized Zeman's decision to attend the Russian military parade in Moscow commemorating the seventieth anniversary of the defeat of Nazism, using the polite but condemning language of 'unfortunate' to describe the president's insistent deviation from the practice of other Western leaders (novinky.cz 2015).

Czech presidents since 2003 have adopted pro-Russian policies, which places them at odds with, or even hostile towards those of the EU. Recent governments have shown elements of division on energy issues, on the Ukrainian crisis and on broader European–Russian and Euro-Atlantic relations. These may be motivated by Russian interests, and certainly allow for their exploitation by the Russian government, as the contents of Kremlin-allied media outlets demonstrate.

Any Russian influence or sympathy in the Czech Republic may be also possible through the fact that governments – and indeed parliament and the constellation of political parties – change significantly and rapidly in the Czech Republic. That said, state-controlled ČEZ has donated to both major political parties, the Civic Democratic Party and the Social Democrats. Even if foreign political/business influence can be found at the party-political level, national interests seem nevertheless to be met, as a substantial Czech study between 2006 and 2010 concluded (Binhack and Tichý 2012b; Tichý 2011). If political changeover seems like a soft entry point, another perspective quite simply is that the Czech political system remains centred on a very few individuals. Leading Czech journalist, Jaroslav Plesl, explained: '[i]f you want to influence politics here, you need to do business with only a very few people, and you can pretty much control the country, that systemic political characteristic, is something the Russians have been able to exploit' (quoted in Feifer and Whitmore 2010). How much this practice occurs in the energy sector remains indeterminate, although issues have arisen.

A debate over a particular ownership case started in 2014, when the Luxembourg-based consortium, LetterOne, founded in 2013 by Russian billionaire investor, Mikhail Fridman, announced it would offer €5.1 billion to buy DEA, the oil and gas subsidiary of RWE which controls substantial Czech energy production. The deal was criticised in Germany amid tensions between Russia and Western nations over the Ukrainian crisis. Nevertheless, the German government still approved the trade deal (DW 2014). Questions were also asked as to how a new Czech storage facility for nuclear waste fuel from Temelín was awarded to a company registered in Liechtenstein, whose director was Russia's honorary consul and believed to be 'under Russian control' (Feifer and Whitmore 2010).

Despite potential Russian influence over the Czech Republic, the Czech government has rebuffed Russian business interests across a variety of sectors, not just energy, explicitly citing strategic reasons. For example, Aeroflot was excluded from bidding in the privatisation of the Czech airline ČSA for fear of 'handing over to the Russians a key industrial player' (Wesolowsky 2011).

Indeed, suspicions of Russian business interests in the Czech Republic have always been present since the end of Communism. Czech intelligence services have outright accused Russian business activity as a cover for spying. The annual report for 2013 stated that Russia's intelligence services have a 'clear priority [to]…consolidate and further expand its capacity of influence in the country'. It further warned that 'the number of intelligence officers under diplomatic cover at the Russian diplomatic mission was extremely high and is complemented by [further] intelligence officers', who come to the Czech Republic 'as tourists, experts, academics, businessmen, etc.' (see Foy 2014). Foreign analysis has shied away from suggesting outright corruption between Klaus and Russian energy interest, but nevertheless has suggested a 'substantial degree of influence exercised by Russia's energy companies' across the post-Communist region (Smith 2010: 9). Zeman's connections to Russian interests are also apparent. The most remarkable example must be that his key adviser, Martin Nejedlý, founded in September 2007 and headed Lukoil Aviation Czech, the Czech branch of Russia's Lukoil. This company then immediately also won the contract to supply fuel to ČSA, the Czech national airline, at Prague's main airport (aktualne.cz 2015). In 2014, the company was fined 27 million Czech crowns for missing fuel. Zeman only said he might consider dismissing Nejedlý from his presidential advisory position (iDnes.cz 2014b).

Such Russian infiltration might inflame Czech sentiments towards Russia. It also should hardly make any Russian 'business' welcome in and of itself. Havel's warnings are all the more important, as ownership of significant energy companies in the Czech Republic appears unknown or is cloaked in multiple layers of ownership (see the example given in Feifer and Whitmore 2010).

Czech responses to Russian influence over the energy sector are further illustrated by events in the third period explored within this chapter. In 2009 energy import supplies from Russia to the Czech Republic fell. At the time, Czech observers attributed that to the Czech agreement to host the radar portion of a proposed US missile defence system. Russian authorities, however, maintained that the drop in supply was not political, but due to pipeline maintenance. Czech Prime Minister, Mirek Topolánek, said in response, 'I want to believe that reasons which the Russian supplier states are only technical' (quoted in De Quetteville 2008). The Czech Foreign Ministry distanced itself from any connection between missile defence and the stoppage, specifically stating: 'We don't want to say if this is related' (quoted in Kramer 2008). The Russian government, however, was stridently undiplomatic in its desire to retaliate against Prague for its participation in missile defence. Dmitrii Medvedev declared 'We are extremely upset …. We will not be hysterical about this, but we will think of retaliatory steps' (quoted in Kramer 2008). The exact cause of the Russian stoppage continues to be debated in the Czech Republic (Hynek and Střítecký 2010). Irrespective, an upside emerged for Prague from the 2009 crisis: official publications commend that 'The crisis in the beginning of 2009 occurred during the Czech Presidency of the EU, which responded by initiating discussions regarding increases in gas security and by opening a broader discussion about a possible additional gas pipeline to the EU' (see the publication supported by Ministry of Foreign Affairs of the Czech Republic, the Confederation of Industry of the Czech Republic and the Confederation of Employers' and Entrepreneurs' Associations of the Czech Republic: *Czech Business & Trade* 2009: 16).

That said, some contemporary regional commentaries implied that the Czech presidency was not successful in dealing with this issue: 'Czech president Vaclav Klaus presided [over] the EU-Russia summit in Chabarovsk (23–24 May) where Russia refused to give any guarantees against possible future crisis concerning the Russian gas supplies' (www.visegrad.info, 2014). The Czech Republic is keen to present a coherent Central European (namely, a Visegrád) policy within the EU. However, Visegrád's energy policy is hardly known within the EU, let alone bearing influence (Fawn 2014; also Nosko and Thim 2011). Dealing coherently with Russia is also very hard. As Czech analyst Michal Kořan (2014) summarised: '[t]he V4 position on Russia… has always been a taboo as there was a tacit agreement on disagreement about Russia'. The Hungarian government's business overtures, including over nuclear technology, make a regional policy towards Russia additionally difficult. Nevertheless, the Ukrainian crisis has seen Czech interest in using Visgrád intensify. In a major speech in May 2014, Prime Minister Sobotka called energy diversification key and noted that V4 countries share similar positions and should cooperate and concentrate on the development of north–south energy corridors (Vláda České republiky 2014).

The impact of the Ukraine crisis has been considerable for the Czech Republic, but not in the way we might expect. The principle result has been for the government to use the crisis to reaffirm support for use of non-renewables: Czech brown coal and nuclear energy. The Ukraine crisis, explained Czech Industry and Trade Minister Jan Mladek in October 2014 'will lead to certain emphasis on those sources'. Indeed, in the post-Communist period Czechoslovakia and the Czech Republic have strongly defended the country's use and expansion of nuclear energy, especially against foreign objections (see: Fawn 2006). Bilateral working arrangements with France concluded in 2012 that it was 'more than ever strategically vital to maintain and enhance European knowledge in the field of nuclear engineering' (Ministry of Industry and Trade 2012). The Ukrainian crisis has reinforced such commitment to Czech energy diversification, and is evident in how Prague has since addressed its reliance on Russian nuclear fuel.

Russia's Rosatom constituted one of two main bidders for the construction of two more units at the Czech Republic's Temelín nuclear power station. The other contender was the Japanese-owned, but US-based, Westinghouse. Regardless, in April 2014 the Czech nuclear power company ČEZ cancelled the tender for construction of two power units. Was that a coy way of ensuring no Russian influence? Several Czech sources suggest that the Russian bid was unfavourable on technological and safety grounds and Westinghouse enjoyed high-profile Western support, including from US Secretary of State, Hillary Clinton, during an official visit to Prague. In other words, the Czechs already had substantive grounds not to accept the Russian bid. Some accounts even suggest that the Czech government used the tenure cancellation to exclude Russia specifically because of its role in Ukraine. Nuclear power is important in the Czech Republic, producing 35 per cent of its electricity (although Slovakia relies on it for 55 per cent and Hungary 50 per cent). The Czech Republic has six reactors, whereas Hungary and Slovakia each have four, and Bulgaria and Romania each two. As important as Russian supply has been to Czech reactors, the Czechs have taken steps that not only limit Russian influence but also, with the cancellation of Temelín expansion, affront Russian interests. Czech Defence Minister Stropický made that point clear already in early March 2014, expressing incredulity at Russian companies bidding for the Temelín expansion because of Russia's loss of credibility as a stable trading partner (iDnes.cz 2014a). The early efforts of Westinghouse to test nuclear fuels long before the tender for Temelín re-opens also suggests renewed Czech willingness to challenge Russian interests.

Although Russia's TVEL also has an extension possibility of the existing agreement to supply Temelín to 2025, in early 2016 the US-based Westinghouse secured a deal to test and license nuclear fuel for Temelín, a provision characterised as 'a view to a future tender for nuclear fuel supply', and the Russian contract being viewed as a concern for Czech security (Radio Praha 2016b and 2016a). How different a reading is that from 2010, when RFE/RL commentators warned 'Moscow is playing for an industry that's been promoted as central to securing the country's energy independence: nuclear power. A Russian company is bidding for the biggest nuclear energy deal in history, and many believe it will win' (Feifer and Whitmore 2010). The Russian ambition, however, continues. The 2014 Czech Intelligence Services annual report warned 'Russia does not consider its ongoing interest in Czech nuclear power engineering as fighting a losing battle. This interest has only become less conspicuous' (BIS 2014). The Czech government nevertheless continues to confront that challenge.

In terms of broader strategy, also, Czech officials within the EU institutions have been (or quickly become) very strong advocates of EU policy generally on energy, as separate from relations with and especially sanctions against Russia. Czech energy analysts support the belief that common EU strategy will secure the Czech Republic in the event of future Russian interruptions of gas or oil deliveries (Binhack and Tichý 2012a: 62).

Former Czech PM, Mirek Topolánek, is cited in current official Czech publications to illustrate long-standing and current Czech intentions within the EU:

> For a long time we have been advocates of a strong joint Energy Policy. It is natural that if the European Union fails to acquire energy raw materials from different sources, its freedom and independence will be threatened.... A joint Energy Policy and limitation of energy dependence is an absolute must for the European Union.

5.7 Conclusion

The Czech Republic seems relatively well-positioned against a Russian energy weapon. Although post-Communist Czechoslovak and Czech governments were never hostile towards the USSR/Russia (despite historical reasons to be so), they have also taken a decidedly moralist stance in foreign relations. Havel, for example, was an outspoken critic of Russian practices in Chechnya; Czechs gave refugee status to Chechens and hosted international NGOs and exiled Chechen media. Czech governments generally have prided themselves for supporting international law and a Helsinki-based European order.

However, Russian financial influence is neither overwhelming nor have Czech authorities hesitated previously to challenge its potential growth or expansion into strategic sectors, including aviation and nuclear power. Why, then, does the Czech Republic appear so accommodating towards Russia at key points? Its fragmented foreign policy partly accounts for this. Different members of the same cabinet take different views on Russian actions (Stropický versus Sobotka), as do different parts of the government (MFA/Energy Ambassador versus ministers; cabinet vs presidents).

That may just be a result of bureaucratic or organisational politics. It could also be a (commendably) calculating strategy – domestically, warning of dangers while simultaneously reassuring the public; regionally, giving welcome encouragement to both the EU and to Russia, and more internationally, by accommodating otherwise discordant EU and American policies towards Russia. That, however, may be giving too much credit. Ultimately, the case of the Czech Republic demonstrates that relative energy security – that is, being less dependent than other post-Communist states on Russian supplies – does not immunise a country from Russian influence. But in the Czech case, that influence is made much more possible by domestic practices, namely those of selective privatisation, pervasive corruption, and a divided political system. No matter how sufficient energy security may be defined, those three factors in the Czech Republic make energy insecurity greater.

Acknowledgements

I would like to acknowledge Eamonn Butler and Wojciech Ostrowski, who were not only thoughtful and effective in organising this project, but also offered suggestions and insights to this chapter far beyond those to be expected from volume editors. James Otčenášek and Zuzana Stuchlíková provided kind help securing some materials. My thanks to all and exemption from any responsibility.

Notes

1 For details of more general comparative post-communist state behaviour, see Buzar (2007: 54–55).
2 For an early assessment, see: Pehe (1991); Husák (1997); and Myant (2003).

References

Aktualne.cz (2015). 'Czech energy security under influence of Russian Lukoil', 21 January, available at: http://zpravy.aktualne.cz/czech-energy-security-under-influence-of-russian-lukoil/r~i:article:658447/, accessed 1 December 2016.
BBC (2009). 'Q&A: US missile defence', 20 January 2009, available at: http://news.bbc.co.uk/1/hi/world/europe/6720153.stm, accessed 19 July 2017.
Binhack P. and Tichý L. (2012a). 'Asymmetric Interdependence in the Czech-Russian Energy Relations', *Energy Policy*, 45, pp. 54–63.

Binhack, P. and Tichý, L. (2012b). 'Česká debata o vnější dimenzi energetické bezpečnosti a národní zájem' [The Czech debate on the external dimension of energy security and national interest], *Central European Political Studies Review*, 1, pp. 90–128.
BIS [Bezpečnostní informační služba] (2014). *Annual Report of the Security Information Service for 2014*. (Prague: BIS).
Bremmer, I. (2010). *The End of the Free Market: Who Wins the War Between States and Corporations?* (New York: Penguin).
Butler, E. (2017). 'Central Europe', G. Stang (ed.) *Securing the Energy Union: Five Pillars and Five Regions*. Series: Institute for Security Studies reports (32). (Paris: EUISS), pp. 17–23.
Buzar, S. (2007). *Energy Poverty in Eastern Europe: Hidden Geographies of Deprivation*. (Farham: Ashgate).
Černoch, F. (2013). 'The History of the Czech Energy Sector', in T. Vlček and F. Černoch (eds), *The Energy Sector and Energy Policy of the Czech Republic*. (Brno: MUNI Press).
CSTK (1992). 11 May, reproduced as 'Calfa, Klaus Hold Talks With Croatia's Greguric', in *Foreign Broadcast Information Service*, 15 May 1992, p. 12.
'CZEC Group' (n.d.), available at: http://ec.europa.eu/enlargement/archives/seerecon/infra structure/sectors/energy/documents/profiles/corpprof-cez.pdf, accessed 11 June 2015.
Czech Business and Trade (ed.) (2009). Issue 9. (Prague).
czech.cz (2015), 'Analyst: Timing of "Alternative" Visegrad Group not Ideal', 29 January, available at: www.czech.cz/en/Aktuality/Analyst-Timing-of-alternative%E2% 80%9D-Visegrad-Group-no, accessed 19 July 2016.
Czech Government (2009). 'Czech Presidency faces up to Gaza and gas dispute', 29 January, available at: www.vlada.cz/en/media-centrum/aktualne/czech-presidency-fa ces-up-to-gaza-and-gas-dispute-52572/, accessed 19 July 2016.
Czech Ministry of Industry and Trade (2014), 'Oil 2013', 22 May 2014, available at: www.mpo.cz/dokument148974.html, accessed 19 July 2016.
Deloitte (2015). Central Europe Top 500: Seeds for Growth: 500 Companies and 18 Countries. Available at: www2.deloitte.com/content/dam/Deloitte/global/Documents/ About-Deloitte/central-europe/ce_top500_2015.pdf, accessed 19 July 2016.
De Quetteville, H. (2008). 'Russian oil supplies to Czech Republic cut after missile defence deal with US', *The Daily Telegraph*, 14 July.
Dickel, R., E. Hassanzadeh, J. Henderson, A. Honoré, L. El-Katiri, S. Pirani, H. Rogers, J. Stern and K. Yafimava. (2014). *Reducing European Dependence on Russian Gas: Distinguishing natural gas security from geopolitics*. (Oxford: Oxford Institute for Energy Studies).
DW (2014). 'Berlin approves sale of RWE oil and gas unit to Russia', 22 August, available at: www.dw.com/en/berlin-approves-sale-of-rwe-oil-and-gas-unit-to-russia/a -17871657, accessed 19 July 2016.
The Economist (ed.) (2010). 'No Minister', 8 April.
The Economist (ed.) (2011). 'Czech politics: State capture', 2 November.
European Commission (2011). 'Czech Republic. Report from DG Energy'. Available at: www.energy.eu/country_overview/Czech_Republic_2011.pdf, accessed 19 July 2017.
European Commission (2013). 'Antitrust: Commission accepts commitments from CEZ concerning the Czech electricity market and makes them legally binding', 10 April. http://europa.eu/rapid/press-release_IP-13-320_en.htm, accessed 19 July 2016.
European Commission (2014). 'Annex. Czech Republic to the EU Anti-Corruption Report'. (Brussels: EC). Available at: http://ec.europa.eu/dgs/home-affairs/what-we-

do/policies/organized-crime-and-human-trafficking/corruption/anti-corruption-repor t/docs/2014_acr_czech_republic_chapter_en.pdf, accessed 19 July 2016.

Fawn, R. (2006). 'The Temelín nuclear power plant and the European Union in Austrian-Czech relations', *Communist and Post-Communist Studies*, 39(1), pp. 101–119.

Fawn, R. (2014). 'Visegrad's place in the EU since accession in 2004: "Western" perceptions', *International Issues & Slovak Foreign Policy Affairs*, 23(1–2), pp. 3–24.

Feifer G. and Whitmore, B. (2010). 'Czech power games: How Russia is rebuilding influence in the former Soviet Bloc'. *RFE/RL*, 25 September.

Foy, H. (2014). 'Spies of Warsaw return as east-west tensions rise'. *FT.com*. 31 October, available at: www.ft.com/cms/s/0/60bc4b0e-6034-11e4-98e6-00144feabdc0.html#a xzz3Im3FpawG, accessed 19 July 2016.

FT (ed.) (2010). 'Brussels probes Czech energy market plan'. 17 September, available at: www.ft.com/cms/s/0/db82b3e4-c1c5-11df-9d90-00144feab49a.html#axzz4L5vYifrR, accessed 19 July 2016.

Havel, V. (1991). *Letní přemitání*. (Prague: Odeon).

Husák, P. (1997). *Budovwinteráni kapitalismu v Čechách*. (Prague: Volvox Globator).

Hynek, N. and V. Střítecký. (2010) 'Energetická bezpecnost podle ceských atlantistů', in P. Drulák and V. Střítecký (eds), *Hledání českých zájmů: mezinárodní bezpečnost*. (Prague: Institute for International Relations). pp. 80–101.

iDnes.cz. (2009). 'Za vyhoštěním ruských agentů stálo české jádro, nikoli radar'. 7 September, available at: http://zpravy.idnes.cz/za-vyhostenim-ruskych-agentu-stalo-ceske-jadro-nikoli-radar-plo-/domaci.aspx?c=A090906_222213_domaci_anv, accessed 19 July 2016.

iDnes.cz. (2014a). 'Je těžko představitelné, že Rusové dostaví Temelín, řekl ministr obrany'. 3 March, available at: http://ekonomika.idnes.cz/stropnicky-pochybuje-o-tom-ze-rusove-dostavi-temelin-pf1-/ekonomika.aspx?c=A140303_153831_ekonom ika_fih, accessed 19 July 2017.

iDnes.cz (2014b) 'Lukoil, který vede Zemanův poradce, dostal od státu pokutu 27 milionů', 16 June, available at: http://zpravy.idnes.cz/pokuta-pro-lukoil-nejedly-zema n-dnx-/domaci.aspx?c=A140616_064803_domaci_skr, accessed 19 July 2017.

IEA. (2010). *The Czech Republic: Oil and gas security 2010*. (Paris: IEA). Available at: http://www.iea.org/publications/freepublications/publication/czech_2010.pdf, accessed 19 July 2016.

IEA. (2014). *Energy supply security 2014*. (Paris: IEA). Available at: http://www.iea. org/media/freepublications/security/EnergySupplySecurity2014_TheCzechRepublic. pdf, accessed 19 July 2017.

Kahn, M. and J. Lopatka (2014). 'Reuters summit – "Foolish" to expect Russian gas via Ukraine this winter – Czech energy envoy', *Reuters*, 29 September.

Kenety, B. (2012). 'ČEZ deals being probed by anti-corruption police'. *Česká pozice* 22 February, available at: http://ceskapozice.lidovky.cz/cez-deals-being-probed-by-anti-corruption-police-ftx-/tema.aspx?c=A120217_140028_pozice_57190, accessed 19 July 2016.

Klaus V. and J. Weigl (2014). 'Let's start a real Ukrainian debate'. 15 April, available at: http://www.klaus.cz/clanky/3553, accessed 19 July 2017.

Kořan, M. (2014). 'Debating V4: Divided we fall…'. Central European Policy Institute, 4 July, available at: www.cepolicy.org/publications/debating-v4-michal-koran, accessed 19 July 2016.

Kramer, A.E. (2008). 'Czechs see oil flow fall and suspect Russian ire on missile system'. *The New York Times*, 12 July.

Macháček, J. (2008). 'Konec ruského ČEZ' ('The End of the Russian ČEZ')', 14 July, originally published in *Respekt*, available at: http://janmachacek.webgarden.cz/rubriky/homepage/respekt-cz/konec-ruskeho-cez, accessed 19 July 2016.

Macháček J. (2013). 'Ke Klausově a Nečasově amnestii'. *Hospodářské noviny*, 9 January, available at: http://blog.ihned.cz/c3-59083570-06b000_d-59083570-06b000_d-59083570-ke-klausove-a-necasove-amnestii, accessed 1 November 2015.

MERO (no date), available at: www.mero.cz/en/, accessed 1 November 2015.

MERO (2015). 'The Ministry of Finance appointed new members of the Board of Directors of the MERO company', 15 January 2015, available at www.mero.cz/files/TZ-MF-MERO_en.pdf, accessed 1 November 2015.

Ministry of Industry and Trade (2006). *Národní zpráva České republiky o elektroenergetice a plynárenství za rok 2005*, 'Report on the status of implementation of the requirements arising from the provisions of Directives 2003/54/EC, 2003/55/EC and 2004/67/EC', 19 September, http://www.mpo.cz/dokument22631.html, accessed 19 July 2016.

Ministry of Industry and Trade (2012). *Czech-French Energy Working Group Extends Co-operation*, 31 January, available at: www.mpo.cz/dokument101645.html, accessed 19 July 2016.

Ministry of Industry and Trade (2014). *State Energy Policy of the Czech Republic*. (Prague).

Myant, M. (2003). *The Rise and Fall of Czech Capitalism*. (Aldershot: Edward Elgar Publications).

Myant, M.R. (2010). *The Rise and Fall of Czech Capitalism: Economic Development in the Czech Republic, 1989–2002*. (Aldershot: Edward Elgar).

Naegele, J. (1997). 'Czech Republic: Norwegian Gas Deal Final Step In Energy Independence'. *RFE/RL*, 9 March.

Nosko, A. and M. Thim. (2011). 'Energetická spolupráce na subregionální úrovni: případ V4' [Energy cooperation at the subregional level: The case of the V4] in P. Binhack and L. Tichý (eds), *Energetická bezpečnost ČR a budoucnost energetické politiky EU*. (Prague: Institute for International Relations).

novinky.cz. (2015). 'Účast Zemana na přehlídce v Moskvě není šťastné rozhodnutí, tvrdí Stropnický', 22 April, available at: http://www.novinky.cz/domaci/364933-ucast-zemana-na-prehlidce-v-moskve-neni-stastne-rozhodnuti-tvrdi-stropnicky.html, accessed 19 July 2016.

OECD. (2003). *OECD Economic Surveys: Czech Republic*. (Paris: OECD).

OECD. (2012). *Inventory of Estimated Budgetary Support and Tax Expenditures for Fossil Fuels 2013*. (Paris: OECD).

OECD. (2013). *Phase 3 Report on Implementing the OECD Bribery Convention in the Czech Republic*. (Paris: OECD). Available at: http://www.oecd.org/daf/anti-bribery/CzechRepublicphase3reportEN.pdf, accessed 19 July 2017.

OECD. (2014). *OECD Economic Surveys: Czech Republic 2014*. (Paris: OECD).

Ośrodek Studiów Wschodnich. (2007). *Gazprom in Europe: Faster Expansion in 2006*. February, Warsaw, available at: http://osw.waw.pl/files/gazprom_w_europie_2006_eng.pdf, accessed 10 June 2016.

Peacock, M. (2014). 'Jaw jaw and war war', Reuters, 2 September, available at: http://blogs.reuters.com/macroscope/2014/09/02/jaw-jaw-and-war-war/, accessed 10 June 2016.

Pehe, J. (1991). 'The Issue of 'Dirty Money' in the Privatization Process'. *Report on Eastern Europe*, 18 October, No. 1–4.

Radio Praha. (2009). 'Czech Republic expels two Russian diplomats for alleged espionage'. 18 August.
Radio Praha. (2016a). 'Nuclear fuel supply contract being prepared for Temelín'. 22 January.
Radio Praha. (2016b). 'Westinghouse signs deal with Czech utility ČEZ for testing fuel for Temelín', 29 February.
Reuters (2014). 'Factbox: How EU's eastern members depend economically on Russia', 24 March 2014, available at: at www.reuters.com/article/2014/03/24/us-ukraine-crisis-east-sanctions-factbox-idUSBREA2N0Q020140324, accessed 19 July 2017.
Roškanin, M. (2008). *Expansion of Gazprom into Europe: Where is the Threat?* (Prague: Association for International Affairs).
RWE (2014). 'RWE's Czech underground storage facilities are full', 9 September 2014, available at: www.rwe.cz/en/about-rwe/press-and-news/press-releases-5045/, accessed 10 June 2016.
RT (2014). 'EU should recognize Crimea as part of Russia – Czech president', 7 April 2014, available at: www.rt.com/news/czech-president-crimea-eu-881/, accessed 5 Novermber 2015.
Smith, K.C. (2010). *Lack of transparency in Russian energy trade: The risks to Europe.* (Washington, DC: Center for Strategic and International Studies).
Tichý, L. (2011). 'Formování společné energetické politiky Evropské unie a fungování vnitřního trhu s energiemi v zájmu České republiky', in V. Střítecký (ed.), *Česká zahraniční politika: mezi politickým (ne)zájmem a byrokratickou efektivitou.* (Prague: Institute of International Relations Prague).
Transparency International. (2014). *Corruption perceptions index 2014* (Berlin: Transparency International), available at: www.transparency.org/cpi2014/results, accessed 19 July 2017.
US Department of State. (2014). *2014 Investment climate statement – Czech Republic*, available at: http://www.state.gov/e/eb/rls/othr/ics/2014/226944.htm, accessed 19 July 2016.
Wesolowsky, T. (2011). 'Russia reconquers Eastern Europe via business'. *The Christian Science Monitor*, 17 November 2011.
Visegrad.info. (ed.) (2014). 'Visegrad countries and Russia', available at: www.visegrad.info/v4-eu-russia-relations/factsheet/visegrad-countries-and-russia.html, accessed 19 July 2017.
Vláda České republiky. (2014). 'Premiér Sobotka na fóru GLOBSEC: Dlouhodobá spolupráce V4 v rámci obrany je důležitá', 15 May, available at: www.vlada.cz/cz/clenove-vlady/premier/projevy/premier-sobotka-ukrajinska-krize-zintenzivni-spolupraci-na-energeticke-bezpecnosti-v4-118762/, accessed 19 July 2017.
ZIndex. (2011). available at: http://wiki.zindex.cz/doku.php?id=vypocet_zindexu, accessed 19 July 2017.

6 Romania

Anca-Elena Mihalache

6.1 Introduction

The purpose of this chapter is to analyse Russian involvement in the Romanian energy sector. The chapter argues that the key to understanding the dynamics governing the Romanian–Russian energy relationship is the legacy of Ceausescu's policies, which aimed at gaining economic and political independence from Moscow during the communist era. The chapter further argues that during the transition period, the emerging capitalist class used the legacy discourse of economic independence in order to block both Russian and Western capital from entering the country, thus reinforcing isolationistic tendencies. The key purpose of this strategy was a division of state assets between domestic post-socialist interest groups. This approach resulted in the poor management of the energy sector throughout the 1990s. Leading on, the chapter demonstrates that Russian limited investments in the Romanian energy sector were not driven by any political agenda but were rather aimed at making quick profit. Thus, the behaviour of Russian companies was not in any way different to those of domestic actors. The chapter concludes by arguing that Romania's EU accession added a new layer of complexity to the energy arena. After 2007, the Romanian policy makers, on the one hand, had to fix a mismanaged and badly damaged energy sector, and on the other, had to keep pace with EU's standards, which they were now expected to implement.

While the discussion in the chapter will focus on the developments of the last 25 years or so, it is important to remember that the Romanian oil and gas business goes back to 1857 and as such has a very long history. In the years preceding the Second World War, the country's thriving oil sector had attracted capital from the largest international investors of the time: Standard Oil, Deutsche Bank, the Rothschild family and Royal Dutch Shell (Buzatu 2009: 30). Between 1911 and 1920 Romania had the fifth largest oil production in the world and then ranked seventh in the following decade (Ivănuş et al. 2008: 267). During the Second World War, Romania was a major energy exporter, supplying Germany with around 58 per cent of its oil imports. The importance of Romania in providing oil to Germany resulted in its main oil refineries becoming targets of the allied campaign and were heavily bombed.

This meant that Romania entered the post-war period with over half of its major oil and gas industry destroyed (Stout 2003: 318). Furthermore, the country was faced with a highly cumbersome reparations and post-war debt payment arrangement with the USSR, which lasted until the second half of the 1950s. The arrangement was important, because it was one of the key determinants of Romania's gradual pursuit of a policy of independence from Moscow. A revived Romanian oil and gas industry was identified as essential for successful realisation of this independence policy. This policy is key to understanding the Romanian energy sector in the post-1990 period to which we will now turn.

6.2 The Romanian energy sector: an overview

A balanced energy mix, state control over strategic assets and reduced import dependency are the three main pillars of Romanian energy security.

6.2.1 Energy mix

Romania's energy mix is both diverse and balanced. The system is not import dependent on any one energy type or source. Even though electricity production and demand have varied widely over past decades, this has always been in tandem with the country's economic performance, and the share of the mix by external importers has remained relatively constant. Electricity production has often also exceeded demand with the surplus exported.[1]

Romania's coal, natural gas and oil is mainly extracted locally. Lignite production even surpasses domestic demand[2] and the surplus is exported (Ministry of Energy 2016: 46). Only pit coal[3] needs to be imported, but given the low volatility and liquid nature of international coal markets, this does not represent a threat to energy security (Ministry of Energy 2016: 47). The main vulnerability for the coal sector is the increasing age of assets, and repairs and maintenance often results in numerous temporary shut downs (Ministry of Energy 2016: 34).

Approximately 40 per cent of the electricity mix is produced from renewable sources, of which large-scale hydropower is dominant. Nuclear energy, the third most used source, is generated at the country's two reactors at Cernavodă, which have been functional since 1996 and 2007 respectively, each with a 706 megawatt (MW) installed capacity and a 5 TWh annual production. Both reactors use Canadian technology, with uranium extracted domestically, which means that the nuclear sector is neither dependent on Russian technology nor on uranium imports.[4]

Oil and natural gas make up a smaller share of the electricity mix, but are essential for transportation, domestic heating and serve as basis for the country's fertilisers and petrochemicals industry. Both oil and natural gas demand have varied widely since 2000 due to variations in industrial activity.[5] In the interval 2010–2015, natural gas demand declined from approximately

14 billion cubic metres (bcm) per year to 11 bcm. This means that, as of 2015, demand is almost entirely covered by domestic production, with only minimal volumes being imported from Russia and Hungary. This represents a significant shift from pre-2009 peak demand years, when Romania needed to import from Russia about a third of the natural gas it consumed. A storage capacity of around 3 bcm also contributes to supply security. Domestic oil production, which in 2015 equalled 3.7 megatons (mt), accounts for about 35 per cent of domestic demand (Ministry of Energy 2016: 74). Barring an international oil price shock, import dependency is not a threat thanks to the market's liquidity.

6.2.2 Ownership structure

The Romanian state has kept a majority share in several strategic energy companies. These include, the gas, electric and oil transmission system operators (TSOs) – Transgaz (58.5 per cent), Transelectrica (56.6 per cent) and Conpet (58.7 per cent); all main coal assets – Oltenia Energy Complex (77 per cent) and Hunedoara Energy Complex (100 per cent); the main hydro and nuclear power electricity producers – Hidroelectrica (80.6 per cent), Nuclearelectrica (82.4 per cent), and Electrocentrale Grup. (100 per cent); and the main natural gas producer – Romgaz (70 per cent), which owns and operates the natural gas storage facilities. The state also holds minority shares in most of the energy companies it has privatised: oil and gas producer, refiner and retailer – OMV Petrom (20.6 per cent); oil refiner – Rompetrol Rafinare (44.7 per cent) (part of KMG International, a KazMunayGas company) and electricity suppliers and distribution system operators Electrica (48.7 per cent), Engie (37 per cent), E.On (13.5 per cent) and Enel (37 per cent).

International companies were slow to penetrate the Romanian energy sector during the early transition years. This changed gradually as the Romanian economy became more appealing thanks to sustained economic growth between 2000 and 2008 and again after 2010. French Engie, German E.On, Italian Enel and Czech CEZ now control the bulk of the utilities' market. The oil retail and renewable sectors have also attracted interest thanks to sustained domestic demand and favourable legislation respectively.

Most of the oil retail market is shared between Austrian OMV Petrom, Kazakh KazMunayGas, Hungarian Mol, Azeri Socar and two Russian companies, Lukoil and Gazprom. Lukoil is one of the few foreign investors to penetrate the energy market in the 1990s and it now controls around 20 per cent of the Romanian oil market with operations in refining and retail (Mureşan 2013). It also holds an offshore exploration perimeter in the Black Sea.

Gazprom is a newcomer to the Romanian energy market. It holds its Romanian assets through Serbian Nis (as Nis Petrol Romania), in which Gazprom Neft has a 56 per cent stake. In 2011–2012, via public auction, it was granted exploration and production licences in the western part of the country and has subsequently developed its retail operation by opening a small chain of fuel stations throughout the country.[6]

Other major international investors are American ExxonMobil, holding exploration concessions in the Black Sea and Czech group CEZ which has built Fântânele-Cogealac Wind Farm, the largest onshore wind farm facility in Europe. There is also a multitude of smaller independent investors, both foreign[7] and domestic, in all energy subsectors.

6.2.3 Policy goals

Since joining the EU, Romania has focused on achieving three main energy policy goals: finding alternative oil and gas sources, complying with the EU's 2020 commitments, and fixing the sector's inherited inefficiencies. Although advancement has been made towards achieving these goals, they remain works in progress.

If we examine the policy of identifying alternative oil and gas sources, we can see that while Romania still ranks in the EU's top five Member States for oil and gas reserves,[8] natural decline and insufficient investment have caused production to drop significantly. In response, the government now approaches diversification on two fronts: on the one hand exploring for new sources of hydrocarbons at home and, on the other, rallying to European efforts aimed at diversifying external gas supply sources.

Domestic production has traditionally come from onshore conventional formations, most of which are depleting. One policy response has been to optimise production in mature fields with the help of new technology. The strategy has been employed by both Romgaz and OMV Petrom (Dudău 2014: 4). Exploration for new onshore fields has also showed some success with a new deposit uncovered by the OMV Petrom–Hunt Oil partnership in 2014. A more promising lead has been offshore exploration in Romania's Black Sea continental shelf. The largest discovery to date is an estimated 42–84 bcm of natural gas in the Neptune perimeter, under concession by ExxonMobil and OMV Petrom. Lukoil discovered an additional 30 bcm in September 2015 in a perimeter in which Romgaz also holds a 10 per cent stake. Commerciality decisions on all offshore perimeters are pending and the earliest date that gas could flow from the Black Sea is 2019.

Romania is also estimated to hold 1.4 trillion cubic metres (tcm) in technically recoverable shale gas resources (EIA 2013). After the lifting of a moratorium on shale gas exploration in March 2013, the American company Chevron opened several prospecting wells, but eventually decided to abandon operations in 2015 citing geological difficulties. Public opposition to shale gas also played a role and as will be seen, public opinion has often mattered in energy-related decision-making. The government has since put shale gas policy on hold.

In terms of import sources diversification, Romania fully supported Nabucco West and simultaneously proposed the construction of a Liquefied

Natural Gas (LNG) terminal on its Black Sea coast to be supplied with Azerbaijani gas.[9] Both projects have failed to move beyond the planning phase, thus stalling this angle for diversification of new energy sources. At the same time, Romania has refused to support any of the Gazprom-proposed pipeline projects and continues to favour maintaining Ukrainian transit routes, which also benefit Transgaz, the Romanian TSO.

The most recent proposal for diversification of natural gas sources has proposed to access the Azeri supplied Trans-Adriatic Pipeline (TAP) through the Romania–Bulgaria Interconnector, which would also allow for gas to be transported beyond Romania to Hungary and Austria. This Transgaz-supported project is known as the Bulgaria–Romania–Hungary–Austria (BRUA) Corridor. It also allows for the possibility of exporting Romanian gas from the Black Sea once the infrastructure to connect the offshore perimeters to BRUA has been completed. The project benefits from EU political and financial support and represents one of the more feasible competing options in the region thanks to its smaller size and the fact that it would make use of existing infrastructure.

The main factors that have shaped these policies will be explored in the chapter, but it suffices to say that the constant preoccupation to maintain domestic oil and gas production and to supplement it with non-Russian sources is consistent with a policy of independence, which has been the mainstay of the Romanian energy sector for decades.

6.3 Domestic factors

6.3.1 The communist legacy: 1945–1989

Post–World War II peace talks resulted in the imposition upon Romania of the so-called SovRoms, a series of joint Soviet–Romanian ventures created on a half-share basis and aimed at generating revenue for post-war reconstruction. A total of 16 such SovRoms operated between 1945 and 1956 and covered all strategic sectors from transport to banking. Coal, oil, natural gas and mining/drilling equipment were each covered by a dedicated SovRom. Assets pledged by the Russian side to these joint ventures were formerly 'German assets' in Romania which, according to the Paris Peace Treaties were granted to the USSR (Cioroianu 2013: 144–146).

Under the umbrella of friendly Russo-Romanian cooperation, SovRoms were used by the Soviets to gradually take control over key economic sectors and at the same time quickly and cheaply transfer Romanian resources and assets to Moscow. At this time, some 85 per cent of Romanian exports were sent to the USSR. Economists have estimated that in the 11 years of SovRoms operations the cost to Romania was US$ 2 bn (Roper 2005: 18). When dismantled, Soviet-controlled SovRom assets were taken over by the Romanian state, with the USSR asking for US$ 9 bn as buy-out. Negotiations lowered the amount to US$ 5 bn, which Romania paid by 1970.

In the late 1950s, Gheorghe Gheorghiu-Dej, the Romanian Communist Party leader, in an attempt to rebuild the economy, focused the country's efforts towards developing its heavy industry such as metallurgy, petrochemicals, and heavy machinery production. This industrial-focused policy directly challenged Moscow's vision for the wider Eastern Bloc and culminated with the 1964 rejection of the Valev Plan, an economic project that promoted the specialisation of Eastern European countries in one field alone. Romania was supposed to focus on agriculture (Constantiniu 1999: 462–465). It should be noted that Romania's membership of the Eastern Bloc during the Cold War was a temporary result of the international context. A historic aversion to Russia can be traced back to the Tsarist annexation of Bessarabia (now the Republic of Moldova) in the nineteenth century.

Dej's line of defiance and independence from Moscow,[10] as well as the policy of industrialisation continued under the leadership of Nicolae Ceauşescu who took power in 1965 (Constantiniu 1999: 471–478). Ceauşescu opposed the 1968 Warsaw Pact intervention in Czechoslovakia; visited the United States in 1973; borrowed money from the International Monetary Fund (IMF) and the International Bank for Reconstruction and Development (IBRD); started importing Western technology; and invested in the domestic petrochemical industry with a view to benefiting from quick profits made from rapid expansion.

One of the latter policy's aims was to move the country even further from Russia's sphere of influence on energy matters. To this avail, Ceauşescu improved his relations with the oil rich Middle East. By the end of the 1960s and beginning of the 1970s Romania had built a solid system in which it imported cheap oil from Iran and Libya (but not the USSR) and then made use of its extensive domestic oil refining capacity to produce at low costs final products which were later exported.

The policy, which was based on access to low priced oil, was severely undermined by the 1973 and 1979 international oil price surges. In addition, the 1980s brought low yields on other previous investments at a time when Ceauşescu had decided to take Romania's policy of independence to a new extreme: to pay off the country's entire external debt. Once accomplished, it was hoped, this would give Ceauşescu freedom to run the country's foreign and domestic policies in accordance mainly with Romania's own national interests and goals, without having to comply with conditions imposed by an external power centre, be that Moscow or Washington. The feat, achieved in April 1989, turned out to be a Pyrrhic victory because the sacrifices imposed on the population to realise the service of debt payments were in large part responsible for Ceauşescu's demise in December 1989 (Cioroianu 2013: 270–272).

6.3.2 The transition legacy: 1990–2007

The Romanian energy sector entered a new stage in 1990. A delayed privatisation process undertaken in an atmosphere of nationalism (Ivănuş et al. 2008: 635) and international isolation are responsible for many of the sector's contemporary problems. It was a time of confusion, of trial and error and questionable intent, as well as a time of colossal deals, few of which have favoured the Romanian state.

Unlike other states in the region undergoing transition, the privatisation process in Romania was slow to materialise, and was resisted by the state until the mid-1990s. A new centre–right coalition government, which came to power in 1996, rushed a wave of restructurings and privatisations. However, it was oriented more by political clientelism than by commercial logic. The coalition's frail power-sharing agreement resulted in the frequent change of political appointees to state-owned companies. Romgaz, for example, had five different general directors hold office within a two year period, on top of the many other lower ranked managers who would often be changed (Chisăliţă 2009: 394).

One of the period's defining traits was a strong aversion to foreign influence which served to represent the role of 'external enemy' (Teodorescu et al. 2005: 43) to a country which was being presented in political discourse as a fortress under siege. As is stated in one transition monograph, 'the nationalism of the Romanian political class has been an important factor in all of the country's transitions towards modernity and has had, every time, a solid social base.... Under nationalist slogan there hid economic, social and political interests' (Pasti 2006: 502). In the context of Romania's post-communist transition, one of the main goals was the 'creation of capitalism's new social elites and their demarcation from the rest of the population through the polarization of both income and property' (Pasti 2006: 137). Although they produced impoverishing results, the way privatisations and reforms were undertaken reflected the overall mentality of the 1990s, where opposition to privatisation among the public was strong (Boia 2001: 15).

The limited foreign capital that entered the country at the beginning of the 1990s went mostly to the consumer goods market but had limited access to the privatisation of state-owned companies. The fact that Romania had no outstanding debt to international lenders gave it enough breathing room to set the stage for the democratisation process on its own terms, away from foreign influence or pressure. It only lasted until April 1991 when the first post-communist standby agreement with the IMF was signed.

Two lines of policy action were undertaken in 1990–1991 to deal with the state-owned companies in the energy and heavy industry sectors. First, the state recognised a number of strategically important businesses that would remain in state ownership, albeit operating as Autonomous Administrations (*Regii Autonome*). Two such cases were Petrom, the Petroleum Autonomous Administration and Romgaz, the Natural Gas Autonomous Administration (Ivănuş et al. 2008: 639). Second, the state limited foreign capital to a mixed participation role within domestic companies' capital. Mixed property was, at the beginning of the 1990s, Romania's maximum opening to globalisation, an arrangement that did little to tempt foreign capital investment (Pasti 2006: 314).

The privatisation process was complicated and little understood by most of the population. Everyone over the age of 18 was granted a number of

Ownership Certificates, each of the same value, which could be used for the purchase of shares in the companies to be privatised (that is, those not converted into Autonomous Administrations). However, the population only really had access to 30 per cent of each company's shares with the remaining 70 per cent continuing to be owned by the state.

One type of privatisation that was used at the beginning of the 1990s was Management and Employee Buyout (MEBO). It allowed a company's shares to be sold (through the Ownership Certificates scheme) to a restricted group of people with previous connection to the company. This prevented access for other interested persons, especially foreign investors, and was believed to bring greater efficiency by motivating employees to improve company profitability. In turn, it led to confusion and errors as the shares' value was set by the state, not the market, meaning that they were often set at below-market prices.

Along with the subsequent trading of shares on specialised markets, MEBO left plenty of room for speculators to take advantage of the shares' low prices. Eventually ownership of industrial and energy companies became concentrated in the hands of one individual or small groups of people with privileged access to the company, such as former syndicate leaders. Most privatisations between 1993 and 1996 used the MEBO method resulting in a drop in their profits in the same years (Almos 2002).

6.3.3 'We will not sell our country': the Rompetrol privatisation

The privatisation most illustrative of Romania's isolationist policy's harmful consequences is that of Rompetrol. Created in 1974 as an oil import-export state-owned company, Rompetrol was privatised through the MEBO method in 1993. By 1998 control over the company lay with liberal businessman, Dinu Patriciu, and a group of smaller investors. Two main accusations were brought against them in 2005 when prosecutors first opened a criminal investigation into Rompetrol.

The first was the so-called 'Libya debt' file, one of the most difficult money-laundering cases that Romanian courts have dealt with.[11] In the 1980s, Romania obtained a 20-year concession for an oil field in Libya. The concession was sold in 1992 to Spanish Repsol as the Romanian state did not have the resources to exploit it. The sale was perfected through Rompetrol, at the time still under state control. However, following the privatisation of Rompetrol in 1993, a number of transactions between the company and several firms moved US$85m, originally destined to go to the state, into Patriciu's personal accounts.

The second accusation in the same Rompetrol file was that of market rigging during Rompetrol's April 2004 first day of listing on the stock market (Anghel and Ciocan 2014). Patriciu had leaked secret information over transaction conditions one day before the listing to Sorin Roşca Stănescu, a senator, and Sorin Pantiş, a former communications minister. Eleven people in total, including the senator and former minister were sentenced to jail when the final verdict was announced in 2014.[12] Dinu Patriciu was never jailed as he passed away two months before the verdict was declared. The value of the loss to the state declared in the Rompetrol file was estimated at US$58.5m, which the company and some of the guilty parties had to pay to the Finance Ministry by November 2015.

Between 2007 and 2009 Dinu Patriciu sold Rompetrol to Kazakh Group, KazMunayGas, for a total of US$2.7bn. Its assets by this time included Petromidia, the country's largest oil refinery and the only one with direct Black Sea access; Vega, a smaller refinery; and a European network of fuel stations. Petromidia had been bought from the Romanian state for US$50.5m on the condition that Rompetrol pay the refinery's US$340m debt and invest US$225m in its modernisation. The negotiations for its purchase resulted in a 2003 Emergency Ordinance, which postponed payment, allegedly in support of a strategic investor. The Ordinance also allowed the payment's conversion into bonds.

As a result, US$603m worth of interest-carrying bonds were emitted, to reach maturity in 2010. When the bonds came to term, KazMunayGas, Rompetrol's new owner, only bought back the number of shares it needed to remain a majority shareholder in the refinery. The Romanian state thus ended up with 44.69 per cent of Petromidia's shares, by this point renamed Rompetrol Rafinare. The issue has not been settled to date.[13]

In May 2016, as KazMunayGas was preparing to sell the company to a Chinese private enterprise, CEFC China Energy Company Limited, the Romanian Public Ministry's Directorate for the Investigation of Organized Crime and Terrorism (DIICOT), the country's highest-ranking prosecutors, began an in-depth investigation of what is now called the Rompetrol II file.

The DIICOT prosecutors instituted a freeze worth about €670m over the company's Romanian assets, which was equal to the damages the Romanian state claimed it is owed from Petromidia's privatisation.[14] More specifically, the ability to convert bonds into stock, which was allowed by the 2003 Ordinance, came under question. In July 2016, an international arbitration procedure was called by the Kazakh company against the Romanian state for the handling of the situation.

6.3.4 We will squander it ourselves: Petrotrans and Petromservice

The companies which remained in state ownership proved to be as problematic as those that were privatised. State assets were so poorly administrated that, in one instance, petty theft was enough to bring an entire company to bankruptcy. Fuel theft was widespread in the transition years and one of its main targets was Petrotrans, the company in charge of fuel transport in Southern Romania. The company owned a pipeline network of almost 2000 km connecting refineries to fuel stations and export facilities. The situation was so serious that in 2007 Petrotrans went bankrupt and was unable to find an investor willing to buy its assets, most of which ended up being stolen and sold for scrap iron (Matache 2010).

The company suffered immense losses beginning in 2000–2001 when it became the target of a group of civilians who started dabbling in small-scale fuel theft. However, the scheme grew so large that at one point it had operatives in local police branches and gendarmerie. In 2012 prosecutors at the High Court of Cassation and Justice, the country's highest court, revealed that what started in 2000 at a small scale had become an intricate industry within a mere two years. Of the 56 people imprisoned due to involvement in the scandal, 36 were law enforcement personnel.[15]

The company had been poorly managed from the beginning. In 1996, its activity was terminated by governmental decree and its pipelines transferred to another state-owned business, Petrom. Three months later, the same government listed a non-existent Petrotrans on the stock market for mass privatisation. It turned out that authorities had failed to take its name off the privatisation list on time.[16] Such blunders were not uncommon.

The policy of repeatedly transferring assets from one state company to another, or dividing a company into various small fractions had become a recipe for reform. Romgaz, for instance, saw its storage activity separated from the parent company in 2000 only to have it reintegrated the next year (Chisăliță 2009: 408). Romanian governments used this policy to make the companies leaner and supposedly more attractive to investors, foreign or domestic.

Very few decisions were based on actual impact studies or market needs and fewer still had a long-term vision. For instance, from the mid-1960s, a large share of the country's refining capacity had been built in conjunction with the petrochemical facilities it serviced. This resulted in a series of physically and technologically integrated units, a boon to the communist economy of the time. Arbitrary restructurings broke the link between the two sub-sectors. As the refining units more readily found buyers, the petrochemical industry suffered a significant setback, which resulted in many of its assets being dismantled ahead of time (Ivănuș et al. 2008: 672). Even when they were sold along with the adjacent refinery, petrochemical facilities were still either shut down (as OMV did at Arpechim and Petrobrazi) or sold for scrap iron (as Lukoil did at Petrotel) (Ivănuș et al. 2008: 675–678).

Even more worrisome was the fact that some of the new entities created through these restructurings were used as vehicles for embezzlement. Such was the case of Petromservice, Petrom's mechanical-energetic division. In 1997, the Petroleum Autonomous Administration was transformed into a vertically integrated state-owned company. Apart from eight refineries, all its assets, including the mechanical-energetic division, were inherited by the new National Petroleum Company Petrom (SNP Petrom). In 1998, the division was externalised and took the name of Petroserv. The state held a controlling stake in Petroserv until 2002 when it came under IMF pressure to restructure Petrom and its adjacent businesses in preparation for privatisation.

To avoid the mass layoff of the division's 15,000 employees, Petromservice was created as a commercial company. Its shares were split equally between a Petrom-Employees Association led by syndicate leader, Liviu Luca, and other mainly Petrom employees who held the shares on an individual basis. The company thrived between 2002 and 2005 thanks to a clause of exclusive partnership in its contract with Petrom, which in 2004 was finally privatised in favour of Austrian Group OMV (Ivănuş et al. 2008: 647–648).

In 2005–2006 capital increases opposed by many shareholders effectively resulted in a hostile takeover of Petromservice by Elbahold Limited, an offshore company, controlled by Liviu Luca, the syndicate leader, and financed by businessman, Sorin Ovidiu Vântu. In 2007, three of Petromservice's four divisions, accounting for 9000 of its employees, were bought by OMV Petrom for €328m, an action for which the company was sued one year later by one of its shareholders which judged the price paid as too high. As part of the deal, the remaining business of Petromservice was renamed PSV Company.

In 2009, PSV Company, which in 2008 had announced a record €380m business figure and €45m profit, requested and was granted insolvency (Chirileasa and Matei 2011). Years of trials finally revealed that the money PSV Company received from OMV Petrom had been siphoned out of the business and into a series of smaller firms owned or controlled by the same people who orchestrated the entire deal, the most famous of whom were Sorin Ovidiu Vântu and Liviu Luca. Both individuals were, in July 2016, sentenced to prison for embezzlement and money laundering linked to the case.[17]

Furthermore, poor decision making can be identified by the fact that the mechanical-energetic division separated from SNP Petrom, through a political decision initially, ended up being bought back by OMV Petrom,[18] but as a business decision, and at a cost to the company of €328m.

As these three cases illustrate, many of the challenges facing the sector today have their roots in the transition years. Privatisation and reform, at least in the first part, were undertaken in isolation to which the public acquiesced. As the policy failed to produce welfare and the effects of isolation trickled down to the population through job losses and inflation, a more open policy towards foreign investors began to take shape. Russian Lukoil was the first significant foreign investor in the energy sector to avail of this change in attitude and openness.

6.4 The Russian factor

Despite the official policy of independence held by Romania, some of the country's political elite who continued into post-communist era did have close relations with Moscow during communist years. However, public aversion to Russia ensured Romania's firm distancing from Moscow from the inception of the new democracy. Steps were maintained throughout the transition years and by most decision-makers, in complete accordance with public opinion, to set Romania on a European and trans-Atlantic path. Against this background, Russian financial capital was regarded with stronger suspicion than Western capital, which to some extent explains its limited influence.

At governmental level, the natural gas contracts inherited from the communist regime were kept and they came with the advantage of the infrastructure having already been built and functional. One supply and two transit deals, known as Conventions, had been signed during the communist years.[19] All Conventions were renewed upon expiry in the 1990s.

A subsequent increase in demand in Europe's south led to the signing in 1996 of a third Convention for the extension of transit capacity through Romania towards Turkey and other Balkan states. A new transit pipeline became operational in 2002. Romania also supplemented its own imported volumes through the 1996 Convention and the pipeline to this avail was made operational in 1999.[20]

Overall the terms of these transit conventions have been favourable to the Romanian state thanks to the revenue they generated. Even in later years when the volume of gas transited through the pipelines has been of a lower capacity from when they were built, transit benefits have been maintained as the payment for transit services is proportional with the transit capacity which is not variable (Chisăliță 2014: 163). This explains why the Conventions have been consistently renewed.

Furthermore, the 1996 Convention, which supplemented volumes imported by Romania, solved another problem affecting the balance of the overall national gas transport system. In this case, the north-western part of the country, which was at the time being supplied from fields in Transylvania (the country's main production region), often suffered from low gas pressure and supply interruptions which in turn severely impacted local industry. Russian gas imports allowed the gas from Transylvania to be delivered to the southern and eastern parts of the country thus helping to balance the system's pressure (Chisăliță 2014: 177–180).

Romania also benefits from the fact that the main import and transit pipelines are the property of Transgaz and have a strategic position close to the Black Sea shore. This means that if Romania is ever in a position to export natural gas, then a key element of the necessary infrastructure will be readily available. Reverse flow is another possible option if sufficient volumes are made available in Europe's south. The main point is that they provide inexpensive options for future scenarios, including one in which Ukrainian transit is terminated.

Separate from the transit and supply dealings, a series of privatisation deals in favour of Russian capital have taken place. In the energy sector, the largest asset to be taken over by a Russian company during the main privatisation era was the Petrotel Oil Refinery. It was bought by Lukoil in 1998 for US $53m after debt had forced it to shut down its 6,100-employee operation the previous year despite 93 years of uninterrupted operation (Pîrvoiu 2014). In 1998 and in 2002, some of Lukoil's debt related to the refinery, was either cancelled or granted an extension with the intention to make the company profitable.[21]

Petrotel was closed for 18 months for refurbishment starting in 2002, with expectations high that it would start turning a profit from 2004 when it re-opened. Although one of Lukoil's most technologically advanced refineries, Petrotel still struggles and from 2010 it has been running at a constant loss (Vlad 2014). In 2014 prosecutors started investigating the company for tax fraud and money laundering with a €1.7 bn estimated prejudice (Petrescu and Tobias 2016). At the point of writing the investigation remains ongoing, and much of Petrotel's assets remain under sequester.

Another refinery, RAFO Oneşti, was initially bought in 2001 by a Romanian businessman, Marian Iancu, who, by 2004 had already brought it to bankruptcy. It was bought by a British company, Balkan Petroleum, sold on again two years later to Calder-A. In 2008, the 60-year old refinery had closed its operations, having accumulated a €2bn debt since its privatisation. It was then bought by a Russian businessman, Iakov Goldovski in 2009, only to see its 43 fuel stations sold later that year (Vlad 2015). In 2014, original owner, Marian Iancu, and his collaborators were sentenced to jail for embezzling the company. Then in February 2015 new owner, Goldovski, announced plans to sell what was left of the refinery for scrap iron, unless he could obtain a better price by selling the refinery's assets and utilities at market value (Niculae 2015).

It was the metallurgical sector however, not energy, which attracted most Russian buyers during the privatisation years.[22] From 1990 onwards the entire domestic steel industry was confronted with increasing production costs because of old technology and a drop in domestic demand. In addition, the raw material, iron, became increasingly expensive, and so did utilities. Most of the purchases were made possible by a governmental rush to sell, at whatever cost, a series of companies which, because of accumulated debt, were considered to be a serious burden to the state:

> The sale price of many formerly socialist industrial companies was many times below the value of the materials they were made up of and there existed plenty of instances of companies sold to 'investors' for sums of money smaller than the price obtained through selling the industrial equipment for scrap iron or the sale of the lands where the industrial buildings were built.
>
> (Pasti 2006: 220)

One of the steel sector companies, Combinatul Siderurgic Reşiţa, was sold in 2004 to the Russian company, TMK, for the symbolic sum of €1 on the condition that the buyer took over the company's debt (Nicolescu 2007). There is no better illustration of Russian investors' logic than this case. During the transition years (1990–2007), the assets most vulnerable and available at the lowest prices were the ones targeted by Russian buyers. It is possible to view the RAFO case and, potentially even that of Petrotel, as examples that show how the intention of new owners was never to invest and to reform, but rather to benefit from a quick profit via asset stripping.

Despite the aforementioned cases, Russian capital has in the post-transition era begun to view the energy sector as a suitable investment industry. However, it is important to acknowledge that no Russian company has been able to dominate it and there is no subsector which is covered specifically. Rather Russian capital now mainly follows the same logic of Western investment, looking to cover small and diverse bits of the market, the ones perceived as being on an upward trend and especially the ones that fit the policy targets set by the government.

An example of this has been the engagement of NIS Petrol and Lukoil in oil and gas up-, mid- and downstream sectors. A Lukoil subsidiary, Lukoil Energy and Gas Romania also own and operate a 9 MW solar park situated close to the Lukoil Petrotel Refinery. Separate from all these, there is also an 84 MW wind park in southern Romania, which started in 2011 as an Italian–Russian joint venture but was subsequently divided. Therefore, oil and gas exploration and renewables, both in line with governmental policy goals, are proving attractive to Russian investors.

Russian business in Romania is currently treated on par with domestic or other foreign investment with no proof of it being advantaged or disadvantaged by its origin. The problems they face are the same as those of all other investors, essentially legislative and fiscal uncertainty. Nor is there any proof of privileged relations that they may hold with political parties or decision makers.

Nevertheless, Russian business still often comes under public scrutiny and when it does, it is often accompanied by the reiteration of the murky privatisations of the transition years. Lukoil's 2015 announcement that it has uncovered a natural gas deposit in its Black Sea concession gave rise to suspicion that the volumes could be exported to the detriment of the Romanian state.[23] There was little mention of the fact that production is in no way certain (the announced volumes were just a preliminary estimate) and of the fact that legally and technically no such exports would be possible in the current context.

Furthermore, NIS Petrol's exploratory activity in Western Romania has been delayed by several years. Public protest and local administration reluctance to grant permits forced the company in 2014 to ask for an extension of its concession to finally dig its first exploratory wells. The public's wariness about NIS was further fuelled by fears that the company was drilling for shale gas, a claim that the company has had to publicly deny several times (see Ledrer 2015; Vasilache 2016).

The press also regularly conveys a Trojan Horse fear that Romanian assets belonging to OMV Petrom could end up in Russian ownership (see Dicu 2016; Ionașcu 2016). OMV CEO, Rainer Seele, had to publicly disavow rumours in April 2016 that Petrom assets would be swapped with Gazprom as part of the Nord Stream 2 deal (Pantazi 2016). Usually when Seele's name is mentioned in a press article, he is portrayed as a traditional business partner of Gazprom (see Bostan 2015; Neagu 2015).

This scrutiny is not inconsequential. The first part of the 1990s showed that public opinion matters to large extent in Romania. The mistrust which was the norm for all foreign capital in the 1990s and which now only applies to Russian investment has been proven to have a policy-shaping effect.

6.5 The European factor

Western capital investment into Romania in the 1990s was limited. Volumes were small partially because of the political and administrative resistance put up by the new Romanian capitalist class which opposed what it perceived as the Western capital's offensive, and as Pasti (2006: 191) notes, partially because of a 'lack of interest in a meagrely developed economy' from a capital base that was 'already largely involved in other developing economies such as those of South-America and Asia'. It was only 'after 2001, when EU and NATO accession perspectives solidified through concrete decisions on behalf of European politicians, the annual level of Western investment in Romania constantly verpassed a billion dollars and started to become significant' (Pasti 2006: 191).

Romania became part of the EU in 2007, a date which is considered to represent the end of its transition years. Most privatisations had already been undertaken by this stage and the energy sector, like most others, had already gained a somewhat stable outlook. There were by this time investors, foreign and domestic, in all sectors thanks also to the period of economic growth that the country enjoyed from the beginning of the 2000s.

The largest and most significant privatisation in favour of a Western company was that of SNP Petrom. Its privatisation terms were first debated in 2000 between the centre-right minister, subsequently president of Romania, Traian Băsescu, and a range of international creditors including the IMF, World Bank and the EU. A public tender was only organised four years later in 2004, under the social-democratic government of Adrian Năstase.

Three companies submitted bids, Austrian OMV, American Occidental and Hungarian Mol. Gazprom initially submitted a non-binding proposal, but decided to withdraw from placing a final bid. The subsequent transaction was worth €1.5bn and gave OMV control over 51 per cent of Petrom's shares (Șerbănescu 2004). The rest of the shares were split between the Romanian state and other investors.

Parliamentary elections in 2004 brought a new centre-right government to power just months after the privatisation. Questions were then raised over the price as well as the terms of the deal, with blame being shifted back and forth between the centre-right government and social-democrats who now found themselves in opposition (Horvat 2011).

A Senate Commission in 2006 charged with investigating the terms of the deal concluded that no laws had been breached but that the company had indeed been under-valued. Additional measures were recommended in compensation for both the price and some of the deal's terms. Overall, however, the privatisation was successful, one of the few such cases.[24]

From the end-point of the transition years, EU legislation also gradually began to penetrate the sector and redefine some of its characteristics that had escaped reform. The most significant of these has been the implementation of the Third Energy Package (TEP), particularly electricity and gas markets liberalisation. Romania undertook to de-regulate electricity and gas prices according to a calendar of incremental price growth over a set period which would give consumers the chance to accommodate to the price increase.[25]

The balance is a delicate one and needs to consider several competing positions. On the one hand, companies are disadvantaged by the obligation to supply their product at a regulated price. Natural gas producers feel pressure because their production activity incurs large costs, especially since many are operating mature fields. Electricity producers, especially from coal, are dealing also with increased competition from renewable energy sources (RES) and with EU pressure to cut emissions. Most consumers, on the other hand, do not have sufficient buying power to afford real market prices. The energy sector having been widely underfinanced for at least two decades has failed to undertake the necessary investments and reform. This includes modernising, refurbishing, taking out of use or building new installations, plants and other infrastructure. Energy efficiency measures have been almost ignored, with the energy intensity of Romanian industry 2.5 times the EU average. Furthermore, the full potential to absorb EU funds has not been reached. Unaffordable electricity and gas prices and the subsequent need to subsidise them through a regulated price are a consequence of this situation (Leca et al. 2013: 7).

This is another example where the public has a bottom-up policy-shaping effect and explains why decision-makers from all political affiliations prefer to delay processes resulting in EU legislation only gradually being implemented. It also helps to explain other protectionist measures, such as the obligation for local producers to prioritise the sale of gas to the Romanian regulated market, thus creating a barrier to gas exports. This particular measure faces considerable opposition from Brussels.

The issue of corruption within the energy sector is also being addressed. Romania has been under strong and institutionalised pressure to stymie corruption since it acceded to the EU.[26] The judicial proceedings mentioned above are a result of the judicial reform enacted because of the EU accession.[27] Legislation has also been passed to address the issue of state companies' inefficient management.[28] However, inefficiencies in the sector still exist. Bureaucracy, an inclination for short-term solutions, partial reform and political control over commercial decisions is still felt in some state-owned companies, especially in the coal sector.

Romania's compliance with EU climate targets is adding a new layer of complexity to the sector's problems. For instance, with the view to meeting its 2020 targets, Romania heavily incentivised renewable energy production from 2011 to 2013 through a green certificates scheme.[29] The overwhelming size of the new generation capacity built under the scheme translated into high, unsustainable consumer costs and put pressure on a transmission system technically unprepared for such a boom. As a result, a legislative turn in 2013 reduced the number of green certificates allocated. This, in turn, confused the market and inflicted heavy losses, insolvency risks and debt payment incapacity on many of the previously thriving RES producers.

The failure of bold action showed policy makers that incremental reform is more suited to the sector's needs, even if this means coming under pressure from Brussels on the speed or type of reform. Gradual reform thus seems to be the way in which the sector has managed to reconcile its past indiscretions with integration into the European Union.

6.6 Conclusion

Periods very different in nature have each left a profound imprint on the Romanian energy sector since its inception. Its first decades were an example of international opening. The following half century, policy was oriented towards independence at first, then isolation. With European integration, the sector is coming full circle as the country is trying to regain its international opening and at the same time address its inherited challenges.

A complex interaction of three elements has had the most significant and lengthiest shaping effect: the country's hydrocarbon potential; the intimate relationship between decision-makers and the public; and the policy of independence. The existence of each has allowed for the existence of the others. The policy of independence would not have been possible without an abundance of oil and gas. The hydrocarbon potential allowed the public to believe that such independence was possible and desirable.

Both Gheorghiu-Dej and Ceaușescu had the population's welfare in mind when the policy of independence was conceived. It functioned for several decades, but only whilst the leaders kept an eye on producing welfare which was the only way to hold on to power given the oppressiveness of the communist regime. With the policy of independence already well rooted in mentality, transition elites needed only to activate it, which allowed for the public's unquestioned consent to the poor management of reform and privatisation in the transition years. Welfare however failed to materialise during this period. This explains why the initial isolation of the 1990s was gradually overturned.

Neither European nor Russian influence managed to fully brake these three elements, or triad, which had solidified over time. The Russian factor has had the opposite effect. The triad has only consolidated under its influence. This is why, even though Lukoil was one of the first and few foreign companies to buy energy assets in the 1990s, and even though Russian contact with the sector has been constant, it has never been able to shape policy or change strategic directions of national interest in its favour. On the contrary, policy has been built in such a manner so as to withstand Russian pressure, both current and future, as was exemplified with the natural gas policy goals.

The transition years show that when Russian capital did penetrate the market, it followed the path of least resistance and then acted in the same manner as domestic capital. It had no other agenda than that of a quick gain. The Lukoil case and the failures of Russian capital in the metallurgic industry are case in point. No wonder, therefore, that the current involvement of Russian companies in oil and gas exploration is conveyed with alarmist undertones in the media, and that the Trojan Horse argument is often used against OMV.

The sector's current challenges are therefore more of a legacy effect than the result of Russian influence. The triad which defines the sector has at the most adapted as it has done in relation to the EU. The national oil company was privatised in favour of a Western company, but the privatisation was lengthy and once finalised came under Parliamentary and public scrutiny.

The EU's Third Energy Package is being implemented, but at a much slower pace than Brussels would desire. Climate targets are being pursued, but also overturned or undermined at the first sign of trouble. Western companies have a significant foothold, but the state has also kept stakes in most privatised assets. Adaptation has, therefore, taken the form of half-measures and temporisation, which give the sector a unique shape.

Notes

1 Demand plunged from 60 terawatt-hours (TWh) in 1990 to 40 TWh in 1999 because of the industrial sector's contraction in the transition years. This recovered to reach 49 TWh in 2008. Due to the international financial crisis, it dropped again to 45 TWh in 2009, but then gradually returned to 49 TWh in 2014. In 2015 production peaked at 65.6 TWh, with a final national demand of 52.6 TWh. For more information, please see Ministry of Energy (2016: 33).
2 Production is on average higher than demand by about 10 mtoe/y.
3 A variety of coal with a higher caloric power than lignite.
4 Some reports made reference to the poor conditions in which local uranium mines have been kept, threatening the country's ability to maintain self-reliance over the long term. Still, even though it might prove costly, the problem is solvable and given uranium's international availability, it does not pose a threat to the country's energy security.
5 Natural gas demand fell from 35 bcm to 25 bcm between 1989 and 1991 and oil demand fell from 19 mt to 13 mt between 1990 and 1992 because of industrial shutdowns. The economic recessions of 1996 and 2009, which caused bankruptcies in many industrial sectors, have had the same effect (Ministry of Energy 2016: 74).
6 Gazprom operates fewer than 20 fuel stations, as opposed to Lukoil which operates more than 300.
7 American Hunt Oil, Amromco Energy and Stratum Energy, Italian Gas Plus S.p.A., Dutch Petro Ventures Europe B.V., Portuguese EDP Renovaveis.
8 Denmark, Italy and Romania each hold an estimated 600 m bbl in proved oil reserves, second only to the UK in the EU and third if Norway is counted. Romania is ranked third in the EU in terms of proved natural gas reserves (after the Netherlands and the UK) and fourth if Norway is counted. Oil reserves have dropped from 1 bn bbl in 1995 and natural gas reserves from 400 bcm in 1995 to 100 bcm in 2015. At current production levels, oil and gas reserves would be exhausted in 19 and 10 years respectively (see BP 2016; Dudău 2014: 9).

Romania 111

9 The LNG terminal was envisioned as part of a larger project, the Azerbaijan–Georgia–Romania Interconnector, AGRI, but high costs and the lack of secure volumes to be supplied by Baku make its prospects unlikely.
10 It must be noted that defiance and independence are only accurate in comparison with the policies of other communist countries towards Moscow at the time and not in absolute terms.
11 'Ceaușescu's investment in Libyan oil. Patriciu, the Murzuk, Libya debt', 6 March 2006. Available at: www.hotnews.ro/stiri-arhiva-1187659-patriciu-creanta-din-murzuk-libia.htm, accessed 28 July 2016.
12 The prejudice in the file has been estimated at $58.5 m, which the company and some of the guilty parties still had to pay to the Finance Ministry as of November 2015.
13 A memorandum was signed in 2013 between the Romanian state and the company by which the refinery's debt is forgiven. It will allow the state to only collect US$270m of the sum it credited the group with in 2003. The state will also remain a shareholder in the refinery, with 18 per cent of the shares – the remaining 26.6 per cent are to be auctioned. The social-democrat government, which negotiated this later deal, then tried to pass it through a Parliament vote in 2014, a move that would have exonerated it of any responsibility for the deal in the future. The vote was rejected by the Constitutional Court, which was called to rule by the then president of Romania, Traian Băsescu.
14 'DIICOT sets Lei 3bn freeze on Rompetrol's refinery and fuel stations. Prosecutors say the activity of the 1998-created criminal group culminated with the Ordinance which converted $603m debts to bonds', 9 May 2016. Available at: www.hotnews.ro/stiri-esential-20984015-diicot-pune-sechestru-rafinaria-benzinariile-rompetrol.htm, accessed 10 August 2016.
15 'The High Court to rule on appeal by policemen accused of favoring smugglers', 17 January 2012. Available at: www.romanialibera.ro/actualitate/eveniment/iccj-incepe-judecarea-recursului-politistilor-sectiei-5-acuzati-de-favorizarea-contrabandistilor-250478, accessed 13 August 2016.
16 'Insider. Romania's oil pipeline network abandoned by authorities and left at thieves' discretion', 28 April 2013. Available at: www.digi24.ro/Stiri/Digi24/Special/Reportaj/Din+interior+Reteaua+de+conducte+petroliere+a+Romaniei+abandonat, accessed 13 August 2016.
17 'Sorin Ovidiu Vântu sentenced to six years and two months in prison, Liviu Luca to six years in the Petromservice file', 22 July 2016. Available at: www.hotnews.ro/stiri-esential-21175641-dosarul-devalizarii-petromservice-sorin-ovidiu-vantu-condamnat-6-ani-doua-luni-executare-liviu-luca-6-ani-inchisoare.htm, accessed 13 August 2016.
18 'Petrom bought Petromservice for €328.5m', 19 September 2007. Available at: www.wall-street.ro/articol/Companii/33277/Petrom-a-cumparat-Petromservice-pentru-328-5-mil-euro.html, accessed 12 August 2016.
19 The supply Convention was signed in 1976 as a follow-up to the 1974 General Convention for production and delivery of natural gas from the Russian Orenburg field to all socialist countries, including Romania. Supply began in 1979 once the pipeline became operational. The two transit Conventions were signed in 1970 and 1985 respectively. The first one was signed between the socialist governments of Romania and Bulgaria for transit of Russian gas. Deliveries began in 1974. The second referred to transit of Russian gas through Romania towards Turkey, Greece and other Balkan states. Its pipeline became operational in 1989 (Chisăliță 2014: 157–163, 170–176).
20 The Romanian pipeline network, 12,574 km long, is connected to three neighbouring states, at four interconnecting points: Medieșul Aurit with Ukraine, 4.01 bcm/y import capacity; Isaccea with Ukraine, 8.61 bcm/y import capacity (main import pipeline); Csanédpalota with Hungary, 1.75 bcm/y import capacity and 0.08 bcm/y

export capacity; and Ungheni, with the Republic of Moldova, 0.04 bcm/y export capacity. The reverse flow Giurgiu-Ruse Interconnector with Bulgaria is expected to be finalised in 2016, though it underwent significant delays. It will have 1.5 bcm/y capacity in each direction. Despite talks in recent years of building an interconnector with Serbia, no actual steps have been taken in this direction.

21 Amounting to €208m in 2013, for a €1.24bn turnover. 'Stolen Romania. What hides behind the Lukoil scandal', 15 July 2015, available at: www.digi24.ro/Stiri/Digi24/Special/Romania+furata/ROMANIA+FURATA+Culisele+afacerii+Lukoi l, accessed 12 August 2016.
22 Mechel, a Russian mining and metals company gradually took over five Romanian steel factories between 2002 and 2008. All had been created during communist times in order to produce steel goods for both domestic use and export. Romanian aluminium producer Alro Slatina, one of the largest aluminium producers in South-Eastern Europe, was also privatised in favour of a Russian company in 2002, and so were other strategic domestic assets such as companies producing pipelines, laminated products and special steels, including a gold reprocessing plant.
23 'Lukoil discovered a significant gas deposit estimated at 30 bcm in the Black Sea. The Russians are the ones who will decide what to do with the Romanian natural gas in the Black Sea', 14 October 2015. Available at: http://economie.hotnews.ro/stiri-energie-20503230-lukoil-panatlantic-romgaz-descoperit-marea-neagra-zacament-important-gaze-estimat-30-miliarde-metri-cubi.htm, accessed 10 August 2016.
24 OMV Petrom's business took off as of 2005 and in 2013 it posted a record €1bn profit. In 2013 and 2014, the company was the largest contributor to the state budget, despite having registered €216m in losses in 2004, before the privatisation. See: 'BERD: Petrom's privatization was a success story', 18 November 2014. Available at: www.capital.ro/-berd-privatizarea-petrom-a-fost-o-poveste-de-succes.html, accessed 10 August 2016. See also (Petrescu 2014).
25 The market was split between businesses and industry in one lot (non-household users) and physical persons in another (household users). Electricity and natural gas prices have been deregulated for non-households as of January 2014 and January 2015 respectively. The deadlines for household-users price deregulation are December 2017 for electricity and 2021 (or 2019 at the earliest) for natural gas.
26 Through the Mechanism for Cooperation and Verification, an instrument specific only to Romania and Bulgaria through which their progress in the fields of judicial reform and corruption is being assessed over a series of benchmarks.
27 Returning to the Lukoil Petrotel tax fraud investigation, it is interesting to note also that it was started by a local court upon complaints from the local fiscal authorities. The fact that it was started at county, not national level is the result of the systemic changes that Romanian authorities are undergoing: the administration, even at local level, and the tax authorities in particular are being reformed.
28 In 2011 an Emergency Ordinance set clear corporate governance rules for state-controlled companies from the Administrative Board selection procedure to making financial results public and the decision-making process fully transparent. See (Chirileasa 2012).
29 Under the scheme each RES producer was granted a certain number of green certificates per MWh, according to the type of RES technology used. The green certificates were then sold to distributors, which were in turn mandated to buy them and which include the costs in the end-user tariffs.

References

Almos, T. (2002). *Privatizarea MEBO în România. Procesul de privatizare şi rezultatele împroprietăririi.* (Budapest: s.n).

Boia, L. (2001). *Romania, Borderline of Europe*. First edition. (London: Reaktion Books).
Anghel, I., Ciocan, O. (2014). '"Lotul Rompetrol" intră la închisoare: 23 de ani cu executare şi 13 cu suspendare pentru manipularea bursei în prima zi de listare a Petromidia', 8 October. Available at: www.zf.ro/eveniment/lotul-rompetrol-intra-la-inchisoare-23-de-ani-cu-executare-si-13-cu-suspendare-pentru-manipularea-bursei-in-prima-zi-de-listare-a-petromidia-13370518, accessed 28 July 2016.
Bostan, R. (2015). 'Germanul Rainer Seele a preluat conducerea OMV şi poziţia de preşedinte al boardului Petrom', 8 July. Available at: www.zf.ro/burse-fonduri-mutuale/germanul-rainer-seele-a-preluat-conducerea-omv-si-pozitia-de-presedinte-al-boardului-petrom-14559312, accessed 10 August 2015.
BP. (2016). *BP Statistical Review of world Energy June 2016* (London, BP). Available at: www.bp.com/content/dam/bp/pdf/energy-economics/statistical-review-2016/bp-statistical-review-of-world-energy-2016-full-report.pdf, accessed 19 May 2017.
Buzatu, G. (2009). *O istorie a petrolului românesc*. Second edition. (Iaşi: Casa Editorială Demiurg).
Chirileasa A., and Matei, A. (2011). 'Cum a ajuns în insolvenţă Petromservice, companie cu active şi afaceri de 380 mil. euro? Unde au ajuns cele 328 mil. euro încasate de la Petrom?', 8 November. Available at: www.zf.ro/special/cum-a-ajuns-in-insolventa-petromservice-companie-cu-active-si-afaceri-de-380-mil-euro-unde-au-ajuns-cele-328-mil-euro-incasate-de-la-petrom-8948863/, accessed 13 August 2016.
Chirileasa, A. (2012). 'Aţi auzit de Ordonanţa 109? Este legea care forţează companiile de stat să devină la fel de transparente ca şi cele de pe bursă', 27 January. Available at: www.zf.ro/burse-fonduri-mutuale/ati-auzit-de-ordonanta-109-este-legea-care-forteaza-companiile-de-stat-sa-devina-la-fel-de-transparente-ca-si-cele-de-pe-bursa-9179449, accessed 19 August 2016.
Chisăliţă, D. (2009). *O istorie a gazelor naturale din România*. (Bucharest: Editura AGIR).
Chisăliţă, D. (2014). *Un secol de transport gaze naturale*. (Braşov: Editura Universităţii Transilvania).
Cioroianu, A. (2005). *Pe umerii lui Marx. O introducere în istoria comunismului românesc*. (Bucharest: Editura Curtea Veche).
Cioroianu, A. (2013). *Cea mai frumoasa poveste. Cateva adevaruri simple despre istoria românilor*. (Bucharest: Curtea Veche).
Constantiniu, F. (1999). *O istorie sinceră a poporului român*. Second edition. (Bucharest: Univers Enciclopedic).
Dicu, M. (2016) 'Gazprom vrea să folosească influenţa OMV pentru extinderea gazoductului Nord Stream', 1 April. Available at: www.agerpres.ro/economie/2016/04/01/reuters-gazprom-vrea-sa-foloseasca-influenta-omv-pentru-extinderea-gazoductului-nord-stream-19-13-15, accessed 10 August 2016.
Dudău, R. (2014). *Industria petrolului şi gazului în România: Tradiţie şi oportunitate strategică*. (Bucharest: Energy Policy Group).
EIA (2013). *Technically Recoverable Shale Oil and Shale Gas Resources: An Assessment of 137 Shale Formations in 41 Countries Outside the United States*. (Washington, DC: US Energy Information Administration).
Horvat, C. (2011). 'Traian Băsescu a semnat memorandumul pentru privatizarea Petrom', 11 January. Available at: www.cotidianul.ro/traian-basescu-a-semnat-memorandumul-pentru-privatizarea-petrom-134456/, accessed 20 August 2016.
Ionaşcu, D. (2016). 'Arma energetică: Gazprom vrea să folosească influenţa OMV pentru extinderea gazoductului Nord Stream 2. De ce se opune România proiectului',

2 April 2016. Available at: http://adevarul.ro/economie/business-international/arma-energetica-gazprom-vrea-foloseasca-influenta-omv-extinderea-gazoductul-nord-stream-2-opune-romania-proiectului-1_56ffe79c5ab6550cb88044a6/index.html, accessed 10 August 2016.

Ivănuș, G. et al. (2008). *Industria de petrol si gaze din România*. (Bucharest: Editura AGIR).

Leca, A. et al. (2013). Liberalizarea treptată a piețelor de energie și gaz și impactul acestui proces asupra economiei românești. *Strategy and Policy Studies (SPOS)*, pp.6–13.

Ledrer, C. (2015). 'NIS Petrol: Nu căutăm gaze de șist în Banat!', 13 February. Available at: www.digi24.ro/Stiri/Regional/Digi24+Timisoara/Stiri/NIS+Petrol+Nu+ca utam+gaze+de+sist+in+Banat, accessed 19 May 2017.

Ministry of Energy (2016). *Strategia Energetică a României 2016–2030, cu perspectiva anului 2050. Versiune preliminară supusă consultării publice.* (Bucharest, Ministry of Energy).

Matache, C. (2010). 'Falimentele din "parohia" lui Videanu: nouă societăți deținute de Ministerul Economiei vor dispărea', 3 August 2010. Available at: http://incomemaga zine.ro/articles/falimentele-din-parohia-lui-videanu-noua-societati-detinute-de-minist erul-economiei-vor-disparea, accessed 13 August 2016.

Mureșan, R. (2013). 'Cea mai scumpă benzinărie Lukoil din România', 10 July. Available at: www.businessmagazin.ro/actualitate/cea-mai-scumpa-benzinarie-lu koil-din-romania-11114377, accessed 25 July 2016.

Neagu, A. (2015). 'Rainer Seele, partener de afaceri tradițional al Gazprom, este noul CEO al OMV', 28 March. Available at: http://economie.hotnews.ro/stiri-companii-1 9766893-rainer-seele-cunoscut-partener-afaceri-traditional-gazprom-este-noul-ceo-o mv.htm, accessed 10 August 2016.

Nicolescu, R. (2007). 'Era privatizării pe un euro s-a încheiat', 6 December. Available at: www.money.ro/era-privatizarii-pe-un-euro-s-a-incheiat/, accessed 12 August 2016.

Niculae, A. (2015). 'Rafo se vinde la fier vechi. Angajații, luați prin surprindere', 4 February 2015. Available at: www.evz.ro/rafo-se-vinde-la-fier-vechi-angajatii-luati-p rin-surprindere.html, accessed 12 August 2016.

Pantazi, C. (2016). 'Rainer Seele, seful OMV: Nu am discutat cu Gazprom despre activele Petrom din România. Nu vrem să vindem centrala de la Brazi', 26 April. Available at: http://economie.hotnews.ro/stiri-energie-20960567-rainer-seele-seful-om v-nu-discutat-gazprom-despre-activele-petrom-din-romania-nu-vrem-vindem-central a-brazi.htm, accessed 10 August 2016.

Pasti, V. (2006). *Noul capitalism românesc*. (Iași: Polirom).

Petrescu, R. (2014). 'Zece ani de la privatizarea Petrom. Cum arată compania acum', 17 May. Available at: www.zf.ro/zf-24/zece-ani-de-la-privatizarea-petrom-cum-arata-c ompania-acum-12626237, accessed 15 August 2016.

Petrescu, L. and Tobias, A. (2016). 'Inculpații din dosarul Lukoil au fost scoși de sub control judiciar. Decizia este definitivă', 13 May. Available at: www.mediafax.ro/ social/inculpatii-din-dosarul-lukoil-au-fost-scosi-de-sub-control-judiciar-decizia-este-de finitiva-15320395, accessed 12 August 2016.

Pîrvoiu, C. (2014) 'Cum se poate transforma Petrotel Lukoil din companie privatizată în una naționalizată', 9 October. Available at: http://economie.hotnews.ro/stir i-energie-18272166-cum-poate-transforma-petrotel-din-companie-privatizata-una-na tionalizata.htm, accessed 12 August 2016.

Roper, S. (2005). *Romania: The Unfinished Revolution.* (Amsterdam: Harwood Academic Publishers).
Şerbănescu, I. (2004). 'Consecinţe ale privatizării Petrom', 8 March. Available at: http://revista22.ro/1044/.html, accessed 10 August 2016.
Stout, J. (2003). *Fortress Ploieşti: The Campaign to Destroy Hitler's Oil Supply.* (Havertown, PA: Casemate).
Teodorescu, B., Guţu, D. and Enache, R. (2005). *Cea mai bună dintre lumile posibile. Marketingul politic in România: 1990–2005.* (Bucureşti: Comunicare.ro).
Vasilache A. (2016). 'NIS Petrol, companie de petrol şi gaze controlată de ruşii de la Gazprom, a obţinut licenţa de furnizare a gazelor naturale în România', 16 March. Available at: http://economie.hotnews.ro/stiri-energie-20870676-nis-petrol-compa nie-petrol-gaze-controlata-rusii-gazprom-obtinut-licenta-furnizare-gazelor-naturale-r omania.htm, accessed 10 August 2016.
Vlad, A. (2014). 'Rafinăria Petrotel, cu pierderi de 210 de milioane de euro în 2013, este "găina cu ouă de aur" a ruşilor de la Lukoil', 10 October. Available at: http://adevarul. ro/economie/afaceri/rafinaria-petrotel-pierderi-210-milioane-euro-2013-gaina-oua-aur rusilor-lukoil-1_5437bbe80d133766a8d2a6ab/index.html, accessed 12 August 2016.
Vlad, A. (2015). 'S-a decis soarta RAFO Oneşti: rafinăria ajunge la fier vechi', 18 February. Available at: http://adevarul.ro/economie/afaceri/s-a-decis-soarta-rafo-one sti-rafinaria-ajunge-fier-vechi-1_54e4cc48448e03c0fdbf1d37/index.html, accessed 12 August 2016.

7 Poland

Wojciech Ostrowski

7.1 Introduction

The question of energy security has been high on the Polish political agenda since the early 1990s. Traditionally, a dominant issue has been the country's direct dependency on Russian oil and gas supplies and on the subsequent concern that the Russian state will abuse its position to meddle with Polish political and economic affairs (Paniuszkin and Zygar 2008; Lucas 2008). In the first two decades following the collapse of the Communist regime, the debate regarding the country's energy security has been divided between those who maintained that the Russian threat is eminent, and those who took a more measured, technocratic view. The latter camp has pointed out that in real terms the country's vulnerability has been largely limited to oil, since Poland's electricity system is powered by domestically produced coal, and that dependency on the Russian gas has been grossly overstated (Sharples 2012). Furthermore, Russian capacity to interfere in any significant way has been considerably constrained by the fact that the Polish state has managed to retain significant control over the country's energy companies (Paszewski 2011). Lastly, and most importantly, the energy relationship with Russia has been complex and has been characterised at different periods either by co-operation or conflict. The simple characterisation of Russia as a menacing actor underplays the importance of long periods of co-operation between the two countries (Górska 2009; Zaniewski 2011). Despite a compelling case put forward by the technocratic camp, those who viewed Russia with a significant dose of scepticism had an upper hand in the public debates concerning Polish energy security. It was pointed out that the prevalence of geopolitical considerations in debates about Polish energy has traditionally trumped technocratic considerations (Longhurst and Zaborowski 2007; Leonard and Popescu 2007; Schmidt-Felzmann 2008; Roth 2011).

This chapter argues that the Russian threat – as technocrats have also pointed out – has been overstated, however, geopolitical considerations are not chiefly responsible for the fact that energy security persistently remained high on the national agenda. Rather, Polish domestic politics, the division and infighting between the 'anti-Russian', post-Solidarity camp and the 'pro-Russian', post-Communist camp, coupled with corruption scandals that brought into the open murky dealings between the Russian oil and gas sectors and Polish political actors, have kept generating interest around the question of the country's energy security and further fuelled concerns about Russia's real intentions. The Ukrainian–Russian 'gas wars' in the mid-2000s entrenched a negative view of the Russian oil and gas sectors and gave the energy security debate a truly geopolitical dimension, albeit, not for long. Since the late 2000s the EU has played an important role in the Polish–Russian relationship through facilitating, on the one hand, reconciliation between two parties and on the other, aiding Polish efforts aimed at diversifying away from Russian oil and gas supplies.

This chapter asserts that debates concerning Poland's energy security should be analysed in the context of transition politics. Both the technocratic and geopolitical explanations miss an important dimension that the study of the political struggles and scandals brings to the forefront. Most importantly, domestic politics reveal the corrupted environment of the 1990s and early 2000s, which allowed Polish and Russian political, commercial and private actors to engage in rent seeking activities. The collusion between the two sets of actors had a detrimental effect on the way in which the debate concerning Polish energy security has developed and more broadly on the political and economic relationship between Russia and Poland.

7.2 Energy security, state-owned companies and politicisation of energy

Discussions in Poland about the country's energy security can be narrowed down to two mutually exclusive narratives: a) Poland is insecure and vulnerable and b) Poland is relatively secure. The first view holds that Poland is insecure because the country depends on imports from Russia for 94 per cent of its crude oil demand and for over 60 percent of gas demand. The second view, which argues that Poland is relatively secure, stresses that the electricity sector is heavily reliant on Polish produced coal with nearly all of its generated electricity (around 92–94 per cent) coming from coal-fired power plants (IEA 2011). In this sense, gas, which Poland mainly imports from Russia, is not a critical part of the energy mix (Omelan and Opioła 2012; Bendyk et al. 2015). Furthermore, in the mid-2010s Poland completed the construction of the LNG terminal, which will considerably ease its reliance on Russian gas (Kublik 2014). At the same time, shale gas, a potential game changer in the Polish–Russian gas relationship, is unlikely to be extracted in any commercial quantities before the end of the decade according to the most optimistic scenario (Górski and Raszewski 2014; Kublik 2015).

The situation is very different in the case of oil. Poland imports crude oil primarily from Russia through the Druzhba pipeline. This dependency on one pipeline makes the country vulnerable to potential disruptions. Yet, those less alarmist about Poland's energy security point out that the Naftoport Oil Terminal which Poland built in the mid-2010s with a capacity of 35 million tonnes of crude oil per year could be increased to 50 million tonnes in the event of major problems with the Druzhba Pipeline. Finally, Poland has two large refineries, with a total crude distillation capacity of 493,000 barrels per day that have been modernised over the last two decades (IEA 2014; see also Gawlikowska-Fyk and Nowak 2015).

The privatisation of the Polish state-owned energy firms over the last 25 years has proceeded relatively slowly (Grudziński 2011). The trade unions and powerful interest groups initially resisted the quick privatisation especially in the mining sector; for instance, major Polish oil companies only went public in 1999 and 2005. Today, the Polish state still owns 72 per cent of the Polish Oil and Gas Company (PGNiG), which is practically the only importer of gas and effectively controls the wholesale market. In addition, the state controls 53 per cent of the Lotos Group (refinery and gas stations) and Orlen (refinery and gas stations) through a golden share mechanism (Grudziński 2016). The coal industry, comprising 27 mines, is dominated by three state-owned enterprises (Kasztelewicz 2012).

The degree to which the Polish state managed to retain control over the country's energy companies meant that since the end of the 1990s influence over the energy sector has steadily shifted from Communist-era managers to governing political parties and patrimonial networks that developed around them (Gadowska 2005). Tellingly, in the period from 1990 to 2010 the Polish oil company Orlen went through seven presidents. Those changes often reflected the shifts in the balance of power either between left and right parties or various fractions on the left or on the right. Another symptom of the politicisation of the energy sector was the presence throughout the 1990s and early 2000s of powerful middle-man in the oil and gas sectors, who were affiliated either with the left or right but did not have any previous experience in the energy sector (Matys 2003).

The politicisation of the Polish energy sector throughout the 1990s led to the rise of corruption, which produced a conducive environment for murky dealings between Polish and Russian political and commercial actors involved in the oil and gas sector (Staniszkis 2001; Krasnodębski 2003). In turn, this collusion had a very negative impact on the Polish–Russian energy relationship. For instance, the persistence of middle companies in the oil and gas trade has been seen as proof that the Russian lobby was at work in Poland and actively collaborating with the post-Communists elites. It was assumed that the ultimate aim of the co-operation has been to hamper Polish efforts aimed at diversifying away from Russian oil and gas supplies. The discussion in the following sections will show that Russian–Polish energy relationship have been greatly damaged by the corruption scandals that erupted in the 2000s, but that these relationships have substantially improved since the early 2010s onwards as actors and practices that dominated the 1990s lost influence.

7.3 Polish–Russian energy relationship

The key factors that have shaped the way in which Russian–Polish energy relations have developed since the early 1990s included the issue of privatisation, diversification away from Russian oil and gas supplies, the role of middle companies and corruption scandals in the energy sector. In addition to these factors, the question of Polish–Ukrainian relations and the EU has also played an important role especially since the late 2000s. In essence, the Polish–Russian energy relationship can be broken down into three distinct periods: co-operation in the 1990s, breakdown in the 2000s and rapprochement from 2000s onwards. The current energy relationship took shape at a time when a number of factors created the basis for a more balanced approach. The conditions during the 1990s also supported collaborative solutions, but less so throughout the 2000s when the Russian–Polish energy relationship went through a period of turbulence, only to recover towards the end of the decade.

7.4 Cooperation: 1989–1999

The early 1990s constituted a high point in the Russian–Polish energy relationship with the Polish political establishment openly welcoming Gazprom's 1992 proposal for the construction of a transit pipeline through Belarusian and Polish territory to deliver gas from the giant gas fields on the Yamal Peninsula to European markets. The new pipeline was principally designed to serve the North and Eastern German market and, to a lesser degree, Poland. Another reason for building a pipeline that would cross Belarus and Poland was the circumvention of Ukraine through which nearly all-Russian gas export to Western Europe had passed (Högselius 2013). The Russians argued that Ukraine was becoming an unreliable transit state due to high levels of theft and the risk of interruption to supplies (Victor and Victor 2004: 1).

From the Russian perspective Poland promised to be a new attractive market as it had not been part of the centrally mandated gasification in the 1960s and 1980s and was a country were coal retained a vastly dominant share of energy supply. In 1975 Poland bought from the USSR 2.3 billion cubic metres (bcm), in 1980 this had risen to 4.9 bcm, and in 1990 it had

Table 7.1 Polish-Russian Energy Relationship 1989–2015

	State Ownership	Corruption Scandals	Middle Companies	Diversification	The Role of the EU	Ukrainian Factor
1989–1999	High	Low	High	Low	Low	Low
1999–2009	High	High	High	Low	High	High
2009–2015	High	Low	Low	High	High	High

Source: Author.

reached 7.8 bcm. The Russian thinking was in line with plans drawn up by Polish policy makers, who, as early as 1990, called for the signing of new long-term contracts with the then USSR. Poland also began negotiations with other gas exporting countries (most importantly Norway) (Uchwała Sejmu RP 1990). The new long-term contract with Gazprom on gas would replace deficient agreements concluded in the 1980s, aid the expansion of the domestic pipeline network and provide additional budget revenues. It was also argued that the pipeline would help to tie Poland to Germany's gas market and initiate a transition towards cleaner electric power generation (Górska 2009: 6). The Russian proposed pipeline gained momentum when negotiations with the Norwegians came to a halt.

The deal on the new pipeline was signed in mid-1993. Initially it was agreed that the capacity of the completed pipeline would be 67 bcm and that Poland would buy 14 bcm annually (Matys and Smoleński 2001). It should be kept in mind that in 1993 Poland consumed only 10 bcm. Thus, rather unsurprisingly, a number of critics argued that officials responsible for negotiating the deal contracted excessive gas volumes and thereby limited the scope for diversification away from the Russian gas supplies in the future. Another major issue from the critics' perspective was the 'take-or-pay' clause in the contract, which obliged Poland to purchase order quantity even if delivery would not be taken (Górska 2009: 9). That said, criticism was largely confined to left-wing academic and political circles as the deal with the Russians was signed by the post-Solidarity government led by Hana Suchocka while Lech Wałęsa was the sitting president (Krasowski 2012). It was also supported by the incoming post-Communist administration that took over power in late 1993. Yet, the controversies surrounding Polish negotiating tactics and the nature of the deal never entirely went away and 10 years later were heavily criticised in the report issued by the Supreme Audit Office concerning the ways in which Poland obtained its gas supplies (Najwyższa 2004). It should be also mentioned that the total gas consumption by 2001 rose to just 11.4 bcm which was some way off the forecast made by the Polish Academy of Science made in 1993, on which the deal was based, which predicted that the gas consumption would grow by 2010 to around 20 bcm and according to most optimistic scenarios could even increase to 27–35 bcm (Victor and Victor 2004: 27).

The key player on the Polish side was the fully stated-owned Polish Oil and Gas Company (Polskie Górnictwo Naftowe i Gazownictwo, known best by its Polish acronym – PGNiG) which in the early 1990s employed over 42,000 people. The company handled the exploration, production, sale and distribution of gas and was responsible for the construction and repairs of the gas network. It should be also mentioned that at the start of the 1990s the company was in a poor financial state with a 50 per cent drop in the gas consumption and a fourfold increase in the price after in 1991 PGNiG started paying Gazprom in hard currency for its natural gas. Hence, the prospect of being involved in a new major project – the construction of the Polish section of the new pipeline was estimated at 3 billion dollars – was a very attractive proposition (Błaszczyk and Cylwik 1999: 42).

In a configuration in which PGNiG and Gazprom were keen to co-operate it was rather puzzling that EuroPolGaz, owned 48 per cent by PGNiG and 48 per cent by Gazprom, which was set up to construct and operate the Polish section of the pipeline, was joined by the third party Polish marketing company, Gas Trading, which owned 4 per cent of the shares. According to the official explanation this was due to the Polish Commercial Code, which stipulated that at least three shareholders were required in order to establish a joint stock company (Matys and Smoleński 2001). Most controversially, 25 per cent of the Gaz Trading shares were allocated to Bartimpex, a private company owned by Aleksander Gudzowaty, which had acted as an intermediary in barter exchanges with Gazprom since 1992. A few years later, Bartimpex shares increased to 36 per cent (Olczyk 2013; see also Bosacki 2002).

According to Jan Olszewski, Polish Prime Minister between 1991 and 1992, Gudzowaty was considered by the Russians as a skillful go-between and able to facilitate cooperation between Russian and Polish gas companies. Olszewski stated that Gudzowaty, who in the 1970s worked in Moscow on behalf of the Polish textile industry and was responsible for coordinating the sale of Polish produced railway equipment to Russia in the 1980s, was in a position to reach an agreement with the Russians on economic matters that he could not – this despite being in a direct contact with his Russian counterpart Yegor Gaidar in his role as prime minister (Kublik 2013). In the years to come Gudzowaty often boasted in public about his friendship with Gazprom's boss Rem Vyakhirev and about his newly accumulated fortune which by the end of 1990s reached over 1 billion dollars. Gudzowaty himself argued that Russians liked to do business with him because he was trustworthy and never tried to cheat them (Matys and Smoleński 2001). Indeed, some argue that 'without Gudzowaty nothing important could have happened on the Polish gas market' in the 1990s (Olczyk et al. 2013). It was reported that throughout this time members of the PGNiG board had tried to eliminate Gudzowaty and other intermediaries but their attempts were frustrated by Gazprom whose representatives bluntly rejected the idea (Zawisza 2011: 26). However, the special relationship with Gazprom tells only part of the story, for another source of Gudzowaty's political and economic dominance in the Polish–Russian gas trade was based on a network of political contacts that he had built and maintained among Polish political elites both from the right and the left (Górska 2009: 11).

Throughout the 1990s Bartimpex employed 17 ex-ministers who served in the post-Solidarity and post-Communist governments. The ministers Gudzowaty employed were at different stages responsible for industry, privatisation, economy, transport and telecommunication. Some, but not all of them, had begun their careers during the Communist times like Gudzowaty himself (Matys and Smolenski 2001; Solska 2013). Furthermore, the head of Bartimpex contributed some $1 million to Lech Wałęsa's presidential campaign in 1995 (Górska 2009: 11). After Wałęsa lost his presidential bid for re-election,

Gudzowaty switched his alliance from the left to the right and in the next election cycle firmly threw his weight behind the post-Communist incumbent Aleksander Kwaśniewski and his political allies.

The construction of the Yamal-Europe gas pipeline lasted from 1994 to 2006. In the late 2000s, pipeline capacity reached 32.9 bcm, almost half of what was initially intended (Gazprom 2016). The Yamal pipeline undoubtedly increased Polish reliance on the Russian gas, however, given the dominance of coal in generating electricity, the pipeline did not dramatically alter the country's energy security. As mentioned above, Poland sits on Europe's largest coal reserves and produces about 90 per cent of its electricity from hard coal and lignite while in the early 2010s Poland's total natural gas imports amounted to just 12 bcm (IEA 2014). More controversial has been the issue of price, since Poland has paid considerably more for Russian gas than its wealthier counterparts in Western Europe (Piński and Trębski 2003). As late as in the mid-2010s, Poland, along with Czech Republic, was paying $500 per thousand cubic meters of gas, while across the border Germany along with Austria and France paid less than $400. Thus, the lack of diversification in gas supplies did not hamper Polish energy security per se but proved to be very costly, as James Henderson explained: '[Gazprom] essentially acts as discrimination monopolist. If it has a significant market share in a country, or if it can see that a country has limited alternatives, then it prices accordingly' (quoted in Kates and Luo 2014).

To sum up, the Yamal–Europe pipeline would have been built without Aleksander Gudzowaty. Both Russian and Polish states and their companies Gazprom and PGNiG had vested interests in the construction of the new pipeline in the early 1990s. Gazprom inserted Bartimpex into the equation due to its dominant position and presumably because Rem Vyakhirev and his inner circle directly benefited from it (Kramer 2013). On the Polish side Gudzowaty 'protected' his company by building and maintaining a vast network of political backers.

On the outside Bartimpex looked like a classic rent seeking mechanism – in itself not exceptional in the post-Communist space. Furthermore, in Poland corrupted practices were not unique to the gas sector and were common also in other branches of the Polish energy sector. Kaja Gadowska in her study of the Polish coal sector in the 1990s stated: 'the fundamental mechanism serving the survival of the system is the presence of highly developed clientelistic networks and mutual dependencies between individual policy makers, i.e. key actors of the mining sector as well as its economic and political environment. The postponement of reforms serves to maintain opaqueness and facilitate the flow of public funds into private pockets' (2005: 23; see also Woś 2014). Although patron–client relations and widespread corruption were not uncommon, Bartimpex was nevertheless a special case.

Its very existence, the way in which Gudzowaty operated and maintained contacts with the political elites, and his huge fortune inevitably fuelled suspicion that the Polish energy sector was penetrated by the Russia lobby intent on hampering Polish energy security. Konstanty Miodowicz, a counter-intelligence chief through the first half of the 1990s, went as far as to suggest that Gudzowaty was directly connected to the Russian mafia (Wiadomosci dziennik.pl 2009). In short, the damage to the Polish–Russian energy relationship was done.

7.5 Breakdown: 1999–2009

The narrative constructed by right-wing politicians towards the 1990s implied that Russian energy companies had a number of allies among post-Communist politicians who were ready to promote their economic interests. Yet, the reality proved to be much more complicated than this. In late 1999, Rem Vyakhirev wrote a letter to the Polish president Aleksander Kwaśniewski in which he proposed the construction of a pipeline or more precisely an interconnector, commonly referred to as 'peremichka' that would run through the eastern part of Poland along the border with Belarus and Slovakia. The Russians openly stated that the main aim of the pipeline was to bypass Ukraine, which they accused of stealing gas – echoing statements that Gazprom had made in the early 1990s (Andrzejewski et al. 2000). Furthermore, Gazprom said that if Poland would not agree to the construction of the pipeline through its territory, the company would attempt to build a pipeline under the Baltic sea (Zawisza 2011: 32). After initial negotiations between Gazprom and PGNiG, the idea of constructing a pipeline was rejected by the Polish side – indeed Aleksander Kwaśniewski became the most outspoken opponent of the deal (Kublik 2005).

Kwaśniewski's support for the Ukraine, which was reinforced by the then ruling post-Solidarity government was a logical continuation of the Polish foreign policy developed throughout the 1990s which characterised relations with Ukraine as 'a strategic partnership of crucial importance' (Copsey and Pomorska 2014: 423; see also Sienkiewicz 2010). The key objective was for Ukraine to stay on course towards Europe. Although Warsaw made its 'strategic partnership' with Ukraine a principle of its foreign policy, 'the instruments it had, given the traditional low capacity to turn "strategy" slogan into a set of "strategic" instruments, were far too poor for such big challenge' (Kuźniar 2009: 265). Thus, the blocking of 'peremichka' was a way of showing the Ukrainian government and public that the country had friends in the west which would look after her interests. Kwaśniewski personally invested a great deal in maintaining Kiev's pro-European direction. In particular, he put special efforts into persuading Ukrainian President Leonid Kuchma, with whom he met more often than with any other foreign head of state (Kuźniar 2009: 266; see also Kardaś 2013).

The rejection of 'peremichka' by Poland was the first signal that energy relations between Poland and Russia would be rocky in the future and that the period of relative co-operation was coming to the end. At the same time, the case of 'peremichka' showed that even if the Russian lobby existed, its relative strength was limited and unable to overturn key foreign policy objectives set by the Polish state (Tymanowski 2012). Yet, few on the right and centre-right were convinced. As Professor Zdzisław Najder, an adviser to the chief negotiator on European integration in the years 1997–2001, stated: '[i]n the east, we are dealing with a partner who conducts and will conduct a planned, deliberate, large-scale, and all-means foreign policy. For Russia, economic relations with abroad, near and far, are first of all a tool in its global foreign policy' (quoted in Górska 2009: 12; see also Pałasiński 2001). The growing Russian influence in ex-Communist countries of Eastern Europe in the early 2000s convinced many on the centre-right that Russia would most likely use its economic clout. *The Economist* commented at the time: '[t]he story varies country by country, but the basic elements are the same: Russian companies, especially in the energy industries, are awash with cash; and the means that they use in their foreign investments and contacts (and their ultimate ends) are often questionable' (*Economist* 2001; see also Szczęsny 2000). When in 2003 Leszek Miller's post-Communist administration (2001–2004) cancelled a contract in 2003 which had been signed by Jerzy Buzek's previous centre-right government (1997–2001) with Norwegian companies to purchase gas that was to be transported through the so-called Baltic-Pipe, his political opponents asserted that more than sound economic calculations were at play.

In late 1999 the Norwegians announced that they were willing to build a gas pipeline through the Baltic Sea to the Polish coast. The initial declarations between PGNiG, Norwegian Statoil and Danish DONG were signed in 2001 to purchase 74bcm of Norwegian natural gas between 2008 and 2024 (Kublik 2001). Miller and his shadow cabinet opposed the gas contract with Norway from the beginning, and cancelled it after coming to power. In essence, they argued that Poland had enough gas supply contracts in its portfolio and did not need the Norwegian volumes. Furthermore, they also argued that Norwegian gas would be 30 per cent more expensive that the one supplied by the Russians (Zawisza 2011: 22–40).

The economic rationale for building the Baltic-Pipe and purchasing gas from Norway are still debated in Poland today. However, in the early 2000s many on the centre-right pointed out that Gudzowaty was Miller's informal advisor on gas matters and therefore, the contract cancellation – which gave priority to Russian gas – had to be treated with suspicion (Zawisza 2011: 29; see also Wasilewski 2005). Furthermore, the centre-right politicians who often pointed out to Miller's involvement with the so-called Moscow loan affair treated his decisions with a heavy dose of distrust in particular when Russian interests were at stake. In January 1990 the Soviet Communist Party lent the Polish United Workers' Party 1.2 million dollars, which Miller and his political allies allegedly used to build a new post-Communist party SLD (Sojusz Lewicy Demokratycznej, Democratic Left Alliance) (Olczyk 2016). The fact that the Miller-Gudzowaty duo was directly opposing the Norwegian gas deal was seen by right-wing politicians and commentators as an attempt by the Russian lobby to keep Poland in the Russian sphere of influence (RMF24 2001; Piński and Trębski 2005). Others argued that Gudzowaty was indeed interested in blocking the Baltic-Pipe but only because at the time he was pushing for an alternative Bernau-Szczecin project rather than serving Kremlin's wishes, whereas Miller simply fulfilled his election promise (Wiadomosci WP 2002; Kublik 2002).

The case of the Norwegian contract shows the extent to which rent-seeking mechanisms created by the Russian and Polish actors in the 1990s become a real political issue in the Polish energy security debates at the start of the 2000s. Any moves against the gas project proposed by centre-right politicians were inevitably assessed through the prism of the Russian lobby narrative in which Gudzowaty was the key figure. Thus a situation was developing in which any future energy deals with Russia were becoming difficult to negotiate and implement. However, matters in the Russian and Polish energy relationship deteriorated once it emerged that the presence of the rent seeking middle companies was not limited to gas but was also present in the oil sector. The fact that the whole issue came to light as a result of a highly publicised oil scandal was badly damaging for the Russian–Polish energy relationship in the next decade.

7.5.1 Orlengate scandal

At the beginning of the 1990s the Polish oil sector underwent a profound economic crisis: the economic recession, the outdated structure of the Polish oil industry and the lack of modernisation and investments throughout the 1990s were amongst the most significant problems. The initial plans envisioned a vertical integration of the sector through the construction of the Polish Oil Company (Polska Kompania Naftowa, PKN) and steady pace of privatisation. At the same time, the state would stay in control of the industry through retaining a majority stake in the strategic parts of the oil infrastructure. However, due to trade union protests and the negative attitude of the refinery's management towards privatisation as well as the lack of interest on the behalf of Western investors, the plans came to a halt. In the following years Polish governments drafted new strategies for the oil sector, however, key elements stayed the same. Most importantly it was argued that the state should stay in control of the oil sector and that partial privatisation, in particular of the refineries which were in need of huge investments, should go ahead. Towards the end of the 1990s, in the middle of the economic crises, the government decided that the Gdańsk refinery should be privatised as soon as possible. Yet, as before, the western investors showed little interest and only the Russian company Lukoil entered negotiations in the early 2000s. However, politicians from both sides of the political spectrum bluntly rejected the Russian proposition (Paszewski 2011).

The issue of the privatisation of Gdańsk's oil refinery, the country's second-largest, and the Russian offer re-emerged in the mid-2000s when it emerged that Jan Kulczyk, Poland's richest man, had offered to act as a middleman in the sale of the Gdańsk refinery to Lukoil. This proposition was not unusual for Kulczyk to make since he was best known for buying shares in companies held previously by the Polish state and selling them to private investors for lucrative profits (for a detailed analysis see Jaworski 2004). The scandal around the sale of the refinery significantly escalated when it came to light that during his dealings with the Russians, Kulczyk met on several occasions in Vienna with a retired KGB spy Vladimir Alganov, who had been based in Warsaw between 1981 and 1992, in order to discuss the deal (Wagstyl 2004). What made matters even worse was that Alganov was a well-known person in Poland who had been involved in another high-profile political scandal in the mid 1990s which led to the resignation of the then left-wing prime minister Józef Oleksy (Perlez 1996). It also quickly emerged that President Aleksander Kwaśniewski directly supported the sale of the refinery and backed Kulczyk in his efforts whereas Miller's post-Communist government was split on the idea, with some key ministers directly opposing it (Krasowski 2014). All these revelations resulted in a political earthquake on the Polish political scene and led to the creation of a parliamentary committee popularly known as 'Orlengate' (2004–2005). Its proceedings were televised live on the main TV channels and were covered widely in the press (Czuchnowski and Wielowieyska 2004). 'Orlengate' took place in the shadows of another major scandal known as 'Rywingate', which shook Polish society to its core and which involved a top Polish media mogul/major Polish intellectual (Adam Michnik) and a majority of the Polish left-wing political elite (Skórzynski 2003; Zarycki 2009; Król 2015).

During the proceedings of the 'Orlengate' committee, which began looking into various aspect of the Polish energy sector, it emerged that not only had Russian gas but also oil been purchased via powerful intermediary companies since the late 1990s (Czuchnowski 2005). The greatest controversy surrounded the J&S Company based in Cyprus, which was virtually unknown to anyone in Poland but which was responsible for the sale of the majority of Russian oil to two Polish refineries. Perplexed Poles also learnt that two naturalised Ukrainian musicians headed the company. Rather understandably, during the Orlengate scandal, J&S's role on the Polish oil market was often compared to Gudzowaty's company and his dealings with the Russians (Czarkowski 2008). However, there were some important differences. Most importantly, J&S sold oil to Poland at highly competitive prices (Todorowa 2016). This fact in itself would explain why J&S for a period of about seven years was not on the radar of either Polish policy makers or commentators, as opposed to Gazprom and the intermediaries that they supported (Morka 1998). Furthermore, despite a fairly wide consensus in Poland that Gudzowaty was Vyakhirev's stooge, the same type of consensus however, does not exist in the case of J&S with some arguing that the company was a creation of the Russian oil lobby and others stating that it was a Polish idea (Wielowieyska 2015).

The picture that emerged from the Orlengate affair was one of a country run by corrupted politicians who readily collude with a home-grown as well as a foreign oligarchy. According to some commentators, Poland, the country that just joined the EU, started to resemble Ukraine rather than a Western democracy (Indulski et al. 2005). The Orlengate scandal was a watershed moment in the Polish post-Communist history. It marked the end of the post-Communists as a serious political force and destroyed the political careers of those involved, including the prime minister and the president. One could even go as far as to say that the Polish transition can be divided into two periods – one before and after the oil scandal (Millard 2006). Most importantly, the Orlengate opened doors to Law and Order (Prawo i Sprawiedliwość, PiS) and Civil Platform (Platforma Obywatelska, PO) two political parties, that have their roots in the post-Solidarity camp, and which have dominated and shaped the Polish political scene from the mid-2000 onwards (Krasowski 2014: 257; Krasnowski 2016). Orlengate has also cast a long shadow over the Polish energy security debate. In response to the country's energy dilemma, the new parties began drawing ambitious plans regarding new pipelines that would bring oil and gas from Central Asia and other locations and finally end Polish dependency on Russia and Russian interest groups (Tymanowski 2012: 83; Tomaszewski 2011; Roth 2011; Czarkowski 2006). The issue of climate change and alternative sources of energy apart from fossil fuels did not play any part in the discussions (Bednorz 2009; see also Gardiner 2015; Wantuch 2016).

The political fallout from Orlengate meant that the energy security issue stayed high on the country's political agenda despite the fact that there was little room for concern (Tymanowski 2012). After all the Russians never tried to shut down the Druzhba pipeline which has been the real Achilles heel of the Polish energy system. However, by the mid-2000s very few politicians from the new establishment attempted to make a distinction between corruption, the role of the middle companies and energy security (Roth 2011). The sensational reporting around this issue throughout the 2000s fuelled the frenzy (Ostrowski 2010: 250; Bieleń 2012: 29). According to Zbigniew Łucki (2011) this was possible because the Polish public had a fairly poor understanding about energy matters and were not able to distinguish between political rhetoric and reality (see also Łucki et al. 2006). As a result, the Polish–Russian energy relationship, which had been under considerably strain since the cancellation of the 'peremichka' pipeline earlier in the decade, deteriorated further. That said, it should be kept in mind that Poland was not solely responsible for the escalation. The Russian actions in the mid-2000s did very little to resolve doubts. The 2004 Russian–Belarusian gas dispute is a case in point.

On January 1, 2004, following the failure to conclude a new supply contract because of Belarus's refusal to agree to a price increase, Gazprom stopped shipping gas to Belarus. Given its near total dependence on imported gas and with no storage capacity capable of withstanding a stoppage, Belarus took gas out of the Yamal–Europe pipeline. Gazprom responded to this move by cutting flows also via this route for over two days (Yafimava 2011). The effect of the dispute was also felt in Poland which was completely unprepared for such eventuality. The politicians on the right were quick to blame Leszek Miller since he was the one who blocked the construction of the Norwegian gas pipeline under the Baltic Sea. The Russian–Ukrainian 'gas wars' of 2006 and, in particular that of 2009 (Heinrich 2008; Stegen 2011; Kuzemko 2014), simply reinforced what many have assumed. Russia would use the 'energy weapon' to resolve economic disputes and to further its political interests. As long as Poland relied on Russian oil and gas supplies, the country's security was vulnerable.

The Polish accession to the EU in 2004 led to yet another rift in the Polish–Russian energy relations. In the second part of the 2000s Polish politicians had put forward several initiatives in the European forum in a bid to decrease dependence on energy supplies from Russia. This has included a treaty aimed at providing collective assistance in energy-related matters along the lines of the NATO charter, and Poland's support for securing direct gas supplies from Central Asian states which bypassed the Russian territory, such as the European Union–sponsored Nabucco pipeline (Goldthau and Sitter 2014: 16; see also Baev and Overland 2010). The reference to 'NATO', which played well in Poland with the right and centre-right electorate, was in particular provocative and unnecessary. The idea was floated by Polish Prime Minster Kazimierz Marcinkiewicz who in a *Financial Times* guest commentary suggested that: 'the energy security treaty could follow formulas contained in the 1949 Washington Treaty, an agreement that allowed for effective transatlantic co-operation, or provisions of the modified Treaty of Brussels that established the Western European Union in 1948' (Marcinkiewicz 2006). The relationship between Russia and Poland hit rock bottom when in 2006 Radosław Sikorski, then defence minister, famously noted that the construction of the Nord Stream pipeline under the Baltic Sea, which bypassed Poland, echoed the 1939 Molotov-Ribbentrop Pact, a pact that led to the outbreak of the Second World War (Kloth 2006). A very different Sikorski appeared in Berlin in 2011, at the height of the Euro crisis, to make this statement: 'I will be probably the first Polish foreign minister in history to say so but here it is: I fear German power less than I am beginning to fear German inactivity' (Taras 2014: 736).

The second part of the 2000s was high on damaging rhetoric but rather low on actions. The rhetoric became more high pitched in 2006 when Polish Oil Company Orlen bought the Lithuanian refinery Mažeikiai, after Russians had openly stated that they wanted to buy it. The pipeline, which delivers Russian oil to the refinery 'broke' shortly after the sale was completed and forced Poles to supply oil in other, much more expensive ways. The refinery, which Poland purchased at a huge cost, is often hailed as the worst business deal in Polish history (Gwiazdowski 2010). In 2014 alone, Mažeikiai accumulated losses of over 1 billion zloty (Grzeszak 2014). The Mažeikiai deal sealed the breakdown in Polish–Russian energy relations.

7.6 Rapprochement: 2009–2015

The rapprochement with the Russians was facilitated mainly by the failure of Polish policy. The Nord Stream pipeline was built and became operational whereas the Polish backed Nabucco pipeline was scrapped (Goldthau and Sitter 2014: 16; see also Miller 2010). The first signs of how badly misguided Polish attempts at building alternative pipelines from Central Asia had been, became visible at the 2007 energy summit in Poland. The key player in the whole equation, the Kazakh President Nursultan Nazarbayev snubbed the Polish invitation and instead attended a meeting with the Russian and Turkmen counterparts (Kublik 2014). The EU, on its part, rejected Polish suggestions at constructing an 'Energy NATO' and stressed the interdependence and need for cooperation with Russia (Tomaszewski 2011). Furthermore, the European Commission in its documents reminded Poland that the country was more secure than others in the region (Nagy et al. 2009). Poles on their part became disillusioned with the lack of progress in Ukraine after the Orange Revolution and reflected critically on their previous support which had at times been almost unconditional. Yet, overall Poland's involvement with the Ukraine remained high during the rapprochement phase (Szeptycki 2009). Furthermore, Russian companies also halted their efforts aimed at trying to buy parts of the Polish energy infrastructure through shady intermediaries. Another important step was the decision by the Polish centre-right elites to bring to a virtual halt the privatisation of the oil and gas sector and to eliminate potential insecurities that came with it (Dąborowski 2014: 11). At the same time, some started to speculate if Poland would not be better off if it simply sold Mažeikiai to the Russians, since no one else declared an interest anyhow (Gadomski 2010).

The Putin administration also made some reassuring moves towards Poland as it eliminated intermediary companies – a product largely of the 1990s – that dominated the gas and oil trade between the two countries. Aleksander Gudzowaty's spectacular business career came crushing down after the departure of Rem Vyakhirev from Gazprom, his patron on the Russian side. Gazprom's new bosses simply refused to work with Gudzowaty. Furthermore, at the Davos Summit in 2009 Putin assured Polish Prime Minster Donald Tusk that Moscow wanted to sell oil to Poland directly without the participation of any middle companies. The Polish oil company Orlen signed its first contract directly with Rosneft in early 2013 (Kublik 2013). This was a significant move as it clarified the relationship between the two countries and removed an issue which had been a cause of major controversies in Poland and responsible for a whole host of misguided policies. An additional important element that contributed to the change was more relaxed Polish attitude towards foreigners, including Russians, because of 'an increased sense of collective security, in part because of newfound economic confidence' (Taras 2014: 710; see also Nocuń and Brzeziecki 2010). However, the real game changer in the Polish–Russian energy relationship was the construction in the first part of the 2010s of the LNG and Crude Terminal on the Polish coast.

After lengthy delay in 2015, caretaker Prime Minster Ewa Kopacz opened the LNG terminal which allows Poland to import up to five billion cubic meters of LNG per year, covering around a third of the country's demand. If necessary the capacity of the LNG terminal can be boosted to 7.5 billion cubic meters. There is widespread consensus that the gas terminal will be an important leverage that the PGNiG will be able to use in its price negotiations with Gazprom. The first signs of this new found leverage became visible in 2014 when PGNiG sought a 15 per cent reduction in the price of gas during its negotiations with Gazprom citing the terminal as one of the reasons (Martewicz and Strzelecki 2014). The project was partly paid by the EU's European Regional Development Fund and as such was a part of a larger policy put in place by the European Commission following the 2009 gas crisis. The gas crisis served as the impetus for the expansion and modernisation of the gas infrastructure in Central Europe with the LNG being one of the key projects. In addition to the terminal a number of cross border interconnectors were built and specific measures were introduced to facilitate the flow of gas (Dąborowski 2014: 8).

Leading on, in 2014 Poland also started the construction of a Crude Terminal in Gdansk, which was finished by late 2015, at a cost of EUR 96 million and on time. The new facilities can serve approximately 40 million tonnes of oil and refined products, covering not only Poland's needs, but those of other countries too, most importantly Germany. With a full capacity of 375,000 cubic metres, the terminal also gives the Polish refining sector a chance to purchase larger amounts of crude oil at a lower price (Góralski 2016). The newfound strength that the terminal gave Poles was on display in the summer of 2016 when Poland began replacing Russian oil with cheaper Saudi and Iranian oil. Head of Rosneft Igor Sechin said that Russia intended to fight for its share on the European oil market. In short, the Russian–Polish energy relationships entered a very new territory (Gorodyankin and Yagova 2016).

To sum up, in recent years the Polish–Russian energy relationship has been relatively placid. Russia has not attempted to take any radical steps that would fundamentally undermine Polish energy security. Furthermore, various fixers and middle companies, which in the 1990s and 2000s acted as intermediaries in the sale of oil and gas between major Polish and Russian energy companies, have been virtually eliminated, making the energy relationship between the two countries much more transparent and straightforward. Russia has also ended its attempts at trying to buy Polish refineries whereas Poland brought to a halt its attempts at diversifying energy supplies from Central Asia and terminated its policies of accruing energy assets in the post-Soviet space. Further, it has stopped using – at least in energy relations – confrontational language.

The EU played an important role in bringing Poles and Russians together in two ways. First, the EU gave Polish policy makers a sense of greater security, and secondly, the EU, by rejecting the Polish proposals from the mid-2000s for an 'Energy NATO', effectively forced Poland to find some sort of agreement with the Russians. Traditionally, the key discord between Poland and Russia has been over the price that Poland pays for Russian gas (more than Germany and other Western states). However, this situation is likely to change once the LNG terminal will become fully operational. It will give Poland additional leverage in its future negotiations with the Russians and will produce a more balanced outcome. It should be also mentioned here that the Western European spot market has indirectly empowered Central European gas companies with respect to Gazprom. T. Dąborowski (2014: 8) has argued that 'in recent years the Russian suppliers have become reconciled to granting discount and partially modifying its formulas in long-term contracts for supplying Central European countries' (see also Gawlikowska-Fyk 2013; Locatelli 2014).

7.7 Conclusion

Polish energy security was never threatened directly by the Russians. Yet, the issue of energy remained high on the Polish political agenda for the last 25 years. In some ways the Polish position was fully justifiable. In the early 1990s the country had just become independent while energy resources, infrastructure and technical know-how were one of Russia's key assets which, in theory, could be used against Poland. The emergence of middle companies was interpreted and viewed as a possible move by the Russians against the Poles. The fact that post-Communist politicians had close relationships with those companies inevitably fuelled suspicions. Yet, the middle companies were not Kremlin's secret weapon but merely a rent-seeking mechanism set by political and business actors for the purposes of their own enrichment. Unfortunately, the scandals that accompanied those companies, their creation and survival, did real damage to the Polish–Russian energy business relations which however, recovered and are likely to be conducted very differently in the future.

To some extent, the legacy of a relatively stable Polish–Russian energy relationship was visible during the Ukrainian crises of 2014–2015. Whereas Poland advocated strong sanctions against Russia and an increased NATO presence on the eastern flank of the alliance, the issue of energy security has been much lower on the Polish agenda than one would expect given the history of regional energy relations in the 2000s (MacAskill 2017). Rather, the debate in Poland focused on the Ukrainian internal energy situation, unpaid bills and on gas storage capacity, with many commentators also discussing the deeply corrupted nature of the Ukrainian gas trade (Kończuk 2015). Yet, it has to be noted that Poles asked the EU member states to coordinate their energy policy more closely and that they worked towards the reduction of their dependency on Russian gas largely through the construction of a gas storage capacity and gas links with countries that are now most dependent on gas sold by Gazprom (*The Economist* 2014a).

In actual fact the key issue for Polish energy security in the last years was neither Russia nor Ukraine, but the EU's decarbonisation policy (*The Economist* 2014b). Interestingly, Polish policy makers to some extent used the Ukrainian crisis as a bargaining chip in their negotiations with the EU. In 2014, Donald

Tusk argued in the *Financial Times* that 'Europe should make full use of the fossil fuels available, including coal and shale gas. In the EU's eastern states, Poland among them, coal is synonymous with energy security. No nation should be forced to extract minerals but none should be prevented from doing so – as long as it is done in a sustainable way' (Tusk 2014). In short, penalising Poland for relying on coal undermines Polish energy security and plays directly into Russian hands. Overall, Polish policy makers in their initial responses to the Ukrainian crises stressed the need for further integration within the European Union and in May 2014 Radoslaw Sikorski called for Poland to adopt the euro: 'The decision about the eventual adoption of the common currency will not have just a financial and economic character, but rather it will be mainly political, dealing with our security' (quoted in *The Economist* 2014c). Thus far, the most visible and serious repercussions of the Ukrainian crisis have not been in the energy arena but in the Polish decision to move thousands of troops towards its eastern borders and the construction of new military bases over the period of the next few years (Kozubal 2017). This militarisation may have a potentially destabilising impact on future energy relationships in the long run (Balcer and Buraz 2016).

References

Andrzejewski, P., J. Giziński and A. Bogusz (2000). 'Broń gazowa. Ile dla Polski warta jest suwerenność Ukrainy?' *Wprost*, 8 August.

Baev, P. and I. Overland (2010). 'The South Stream versus Nabucco pipeline race: geopolitics and economic (ir)rationales and political stakes in mega-projects', *International Affairs*, 86(5), pp. 1075–1090.

Balcer, A. and P. Buraz (2016). 'Eksperci: Rosja największym zagrożeniem dla bezpieczeństwa Polski', *Rzeczpospolita*, 27 July.

Bednorz, J. (2009). 'Węgiel gwarancją bezpieczeństwa politycznego Polski', *Polityka Energetyczna*, 12, pp. 13–28.

Bendyk, E., M. Popkiewicz, M. Sutowski, U. Papajak (2015). *Polski węgiel*. (Warsaw: Krytyka Polityczna).

Bieleń, S. (2012). 'The possibility of reconciliation in Polish-Russian Relations', *Lithuanian Foreign Policy Review*, 27, pp. 11–34.

Błaszczyk, B. and Cylwik, A. (eds) (1999). *Charakterystyka wybranych sektorów infrastrukturalnych i wrażliwych w gospodarce polskiej oraz możliwości ich prywatyzacji*. CASE.

Bosacki, M. (2002). '"Gazeta" kontra Gudzowaty'. *Gazeta Wyborcza*, 3 February 2002.

Bouzarovski, S. and Konieczny, M. (2010). 'Landscapes of paradox: Public discourses and policies in Poland's relationship with the Nord Stream pipeline'. *Geopolitics*, 15(1), pp. 1–21.

Copsey, N. and Pomorska, K. (2014). 'The influence of newer member states in the European Union: The case of Poland and the Eastern Partnership', *Europe-Asia Studies*, 66(3), pp. 421–443.

Czarkowski, M. (2008). 'Ropa, gaz, mafia i... służb', *Tygodnik Przegląd*, 2 February.

Czarkowski, M. (2006). 'Naftowy poker', *Tygodnik Przegląd*, 30.

Czuchnowski, W. and D. Wielowieyska (2004). 'Komisja śledcza zbada aferę PKN Orlen'. *Gazeta Wyborcza*, 29 May.
Czuchnowski, W. (2005). 'Jest raport komisji ds. Orlenu'. *Gazeta Wyborcza*, 27 September.
Dąborowski, T. (2014). 'Breaking the boundaries. The transformation of Central European gas markets'. *OSW Point of View*, No. 46, December.
The *Economist*. (ed.) (2001). 'Russia's overseas investment. Comrade capitalist', 15 February.
The *Economist*. (2014a). 'Paying the price', 29 April.
The *Economist*. (2014b). 'A different Energiewende', 8 February.
The *Economist*. (2014c). 'Poland's foreign policy. A shaky compass', 10 May.
Gadomski, W. (2010). 'Biznes i "jagiellońska polityka"', *Gazeta Wyborcza*, 31 May.
Gadowska, K. (2005). 'Clientelism in the Silesian Mining Industry' in A. Surdej and K. Gadowska, *Political Corruption in Poland*. (Bremen: Forschungsstelle Osteuropa an der Universität Bremen).
Gardiner, B. (2015). 'When energy independence clashes with public health', *New York Times*. 8 July.
Gawlikowska-Fyk, A. and Nowak, Z. (2015). *Nuclear energy in Poland*. (Warsaw: PISM).
Gawlikowska-Fyk, A. (2013). 'How the European Union is shaping the gas market in Poland'. *PISM* (Policy Paper), No. 8(56), April.
Gazprom (2016). 'Yamal – Europe'. Available at: www.gazprom.com/about/production/projects/pipelines/active/yamal-evropa/, accessed 14 August 2017.
Goldthau, A. and Sitter, N. (2014). 'A liberal actor in a realist world? The Commission and the external dimension of the single market for energy'. *Journal of European Public Policy*, 21(10), pp. 1452–1472.
Góralski, R. (2016). 'Increasing Poland's energy security: PERN opens a new crude oil terminal in Gdańsk'. *CEEP*, No. 4(41). (Brussels)
Gorodyankin, G. and Yagova, O. (2016). 'Exclusive: Oil reshuffle in Poland – Urals out, Iran in'. *Reuters*, 12 August.
Górska, J. (2009). 'Dealing with Power: Poland's Energy Policy Towards Russia, 1989–2004'. *Working Paper Series of the Research Network 1989*, Working Paper 23, pp. 2–30.
Górski, J. and Raszewski, S. (2014). 'Energy Security or Energy Governance? Legal and Political Aspects of Sustainable Exploration of Shale Gas in Poland'. *Oil, Gas & Energy Law Journal* (OGEL), 12(3).
Grudziński, Z. (2011). 'Prywatyzacja sektora paliwowo-energetycznego na rynkach publicznych'. *Polityka Energetyczna*, (14), pp. 59–77.
Grudziński, Z. (2016). 'Spółki sektora paliwowo-energetycznego na warszawskiej Giełdzie Papierów Wartościowych'. *Przegląd Górniczy*, (72).
Grzeszak, A. (2014). 'Czy padnie najbardziej znana polska rafineria? Co można w Możejkach?', *Polityka*, 29 lipca.
Gwiazdowski, R. (2010). 'Z determinacją, do końca', *Forbes*, 3 August.
Heinrich, A. (2008). 'Under the kremlin's thumb: does increased state control in the Russian gas sector endanger European energy security?', *Europe-Asia Studies*, 60(9), pp. 1539–1574.
Högselius, P. (2013). *Red gas: Russia and the origins of European energy dependence*. (Basingstoke & New York: Palgrave Macmillan).

Horne, C.M. (2009). 'Late lustration programmes in Romania and Poland: supporting or undermining democratic transitions?', *Democratization*, 16(2), pp. 344–376.
IEA (2011). *Energy Policies of IEA Countries – Poland*. (Paris: IEA).
IEA (2014). *Energy Supply Security 2014: Poland*. (Paris: OECD/IEA).
Indulski, G., J. Jakimczyk and M. Dzierżanowski (2005). 'Koniec ologarchii', *Wprost*. 18 December.
Jaworski, D. (2004). 'Kim pan jest, panie Kulczyk – sylwetka najbogatszego Polaka', *Gazeta Wyborcza*, 15 July.
Kardaś, S. (2013). 'Rosja reaktywuje "Jamał-2": kolejny bluff czy realny projekt?', *OSW* (Analizy), 10 April.
Kasztelewicz, Z. (2012). 'Blaski i cienie górnictwa węglowego w Polsce', *Polityka energetyczna*, 15, pp. 7–27.
Kates, G. and L. Luo (2014). *Russian gas: How much is that*, 1 July. (Prague: RFE/RL).
Kloth, H.M. (2006). 'Indirect Hitler comparison. Polish minister attacks Schröder and Merkel'. *Der Spiegel International Online*. 1 May 2006. Available at: www.spiegel.de/international/indirect-hitler-comparison-polish-minister-attacks-schroeder-and-merkel-a-413969.html, accessed 16 August 2017.
Konończuk, W. (2015). 'Reforma numer jeden. Dlaczego Ukraina musi zreformować sektor gazowy', *Komentarze OSW*, 9 February.
Kozubal, M. (2017). 'MON: Macierewicz przesuwa czołgi na wschód', *Rzeczpospolita*, 9 March.
Kramer, Andrew E. (2013). 'Rem Vyakhirev, Former Chief of Gazprom, Dies at 78', *New York Times*, 17 February.
Krasnodębski, Z. (2003). *Demokracja peryferii*. Slowo/obraz terytoria.
Krasowski, R. (2012). *Po południu. Upadek elit solidarnościowych po zdobyciu władzy*. (Warszawa: Czerwone i Czarne).
Krasowski, R. (2014). *Czas gniewu. Rozkwit i upadek imperium SLD.wyd*. (Warszawa: Czerwone i czarne).
Krasowski, R. (2016). *Czas Kaczyńskiego. Polityka jako wieczny konflikt*. (Warszawa: Czerwone i Czarne).
Król, M. (2015). *Byliśmy głupi*. Wydawnictwo Czerwone i Czarne.
Kublik, A. (2001). 'Polsko-norweski kontrakt gazowy podpisany'. *Gazeta Wyborcza*, 3 September.
Kublik, A. (2002). 'Rezygnacja z bezpośrednich dostaw gazu z Norwegii zwiększy koszty dywersyfikacji', *Gazeta Wyborcza*, 28 September.
Kublik, A. (2005). 'Rosyjski gaz nie może płynąć przez Polskę', *Gazeta Wyborcza*, 03 July.
Kublik, A. (2014). 'Europa i Polska mocno uzależnione od gazu i ropy z Rosji', *Gazeta Wyborcza*, 24 March.
Kublik, A. (2014). 'Europa i Polska mocno uzaleznione od gazu i ropy z Rosji', *Gazeta Wyborcza*, 24 March.
Kublik, A. (2013). 'Jamalska rura-ostatnia część imperium Gudzowatego', *Gazeta Wyborcza*, 14 February.
Kublik, A. (2015). 'Koncesje na poszukiwanie gazu z łupkow w Polsce', *Gazeta Wyborcza*, 09 February.
Kuzemko, C. (2014). 'Ideas, power and change: explaining EU–Russia energy relations', *Journal of European Public Policy*, 21(1), pp. 58–75.

Kuźniar, R. (2009). *Poland's foreign policy after 1989*. (Leverkusen-Opladen: Budrich Unipress Limited).
Leonard, M. and N. Popescu (2007). *A power audit of EU-Russia relations* (Vol. 9). (London: European Council on Foreign Relations).
Locatelli, C. (2014). 'The Russian gas industry: challenges to the "Gazprom model"?', *Post-Communist Economies*, 26(1), pp. 53–66.
Longhurst, K.A. and Zaborowski, M. (2007). *The new Atlanticist: Poland's foreign and security policy priorities*. (Oxford: Blackwell Publishing).
Lucas, E. (2008). *Nowa zimna wojna: jak Kreml zagraża Rosji i Zachodowi*. Dom Wydawniczy Rebis.
Łucki, Z. (2011). 'Wyzwania energetyczne Polski w świetle spójności społeczno-ekonomicznej', *Nierówności Społeczne a Wzrost Gospodarczy/Uniwersytet Rzeszowski*, (18), pp. 372–383.
Łucki, Z., A. Byrska-Rąpała, B. Soliński and I. Stach (2006). 'Badanie świadomości energetycznej społeczeństwa polskiego', *Polityka Energetyczna*, 9(2), pp. 5–63.
MacAskill, E. (2017). 'Russia says US troops arriving in Poland pose threat to its security', *The Guardian*, 12 January.
Marcinkiewicz, K. (2006). 'Europe's energy musketeers must stand together', *Financial Times*, 2 September.
Martewicz, M. and M. Strzelecki (2014). 'Poland Starts Talks With Russian Gazprom to Cut Gas Price', *Bloomberg*, 5 November.
Matys, M. and P. Smoleński (2001). 'Stajnie Gudzowatego', *Gazeta Wyborcza* (Duży Format) reprinted 1 January 2013.
Matys, M. (2003). *Towarzystwo. Biznesmeni i politycy*, seria "Fakt", wyd. Prószyński i S-ka, Warszawa.
Millard, F. (2006). 'Poland's politics and the travails of transition after 2001: The 2005 elections', *Europe-Asia Studies*, 58(7), pp. 1007–1031.
Miller, L. (2010). *Porażka na własne życzenie*. Leszek Miller 6 January, (Oficjalny Blog Polityczny).
Morka, A. (1998). 'Kto sprowadza ropę do Polski', *Rzeczpospolita*, 30 October 1998.
Nagy, S., S. Rychlicki, and J. Siemek (2009). 'Stan obecny i ewolucja stosunków gazowych Rosji z Unią Europejską i Polską', *Polityka Energetyczna*, 12, pp. 393–422.
Najwyższa I.K. (2004). *Informacja o wynikach kontroli zaopatrzenia w gaz ziemny*. Najwyższa Izba Kontroli, Warszawa, lipiec.
Nocuń, M. and A. Brzeziecki (2010). 'Schodek po schodku', *Tygodnik Powszechny*, 8 June.
Olczyk, E. (2016). 'Leszek Miller: Powinienem pójść na wojnę z Agorą'. *Rzeczpospolita Plus Minus*, 17 July.
Olczyk, E., K. Baranowska and T. Furman (2013). 'Gudzowaty. Człowiek z gazu', *Rzeczpospolita*, 15 February.
Omelan, G. and W. Opioła (2012). *Poland's Energy Balance and its Future. The Case Study of Gas as an Energy Source*. Gospodarka, Rynek, Edukacja, 13 April.
Ostrowski, M. (2010). 'Prasa a polityka zagraniczna', in Bieleń, S. (ed.), *Polityka zagraniczna Polski po wstąpieniu do NATO i do Unii Europejskiej: problemy tożsamości i adaptacji*. Difin.
Pałasiński, J. (2001). 'Dywizja Gazprom: Rosyjski gaz i ropa naftowa kształtują nowy układ gospodarczy i polityczny Europy', *Wprost*, 14 January.
Paniuszkin, W. and M. Zygar (2008). *Gazprom: rosyjska broń*. Wydawnictwo WAB.

Paszewski, T. (2011). 'Polityka państw wobec sektorów nafty i gazu w latach 1990–2010'. *Polityka Energetyczna*, 14, pp. 5–28.
Perlez, J. (1996). 'Polish Premier, Ex-Communist Accused of Spying, Resigns', *New York Times*, 25 Janurary.
Piński, A. and K. Trębski (2003). 'Gazoholicy', *Wprost*, 9 November.
Piński, J. and K. Trębski (2005). 'Gazostrojka', *Wprost*, 31 July.
Piński, J. (2007). 'Miękka inwazja. Rosjanie realizują plan przejęcia polskiego sektora energetycznego', *Wprost*, 1 July.
RMF 24 (2001). 'Antoni Macierewicz, poseł Ligi Polskich Rodzin', 10 December. Available at: www.rmf24.pl/ekonomia/news-antoni-macierewicz-posel-ligi-polskich-rodzin,nId,224512, accessed 14 August 2017.
Roth, M. (2011). 'Poland as a Policy Entrepreneur in European External Energy Policy: Towards Greater Energy Solidarity vis-à-vis Russia?', *Geopolitics*, 16(3), pp. 600–625.
Schmidt-Felzmann, A. (2008). 'All for one? EU member states and the Union's common policy towards the Russian Federation', *Journal of Contemporary European Studies*, 16(2), pp. 169–187.
Sharples, J. (2012). 'Russo–Polish Energy Security Relations: A Case of Threatening Dependency, Supply Guarantee, or Regional Energy Security Dynamics?', *Political Perspectives*, 6(1), pp. 27–50.
Sienkiewicz, B. (2010). 'Pożegnanie z Giedroyciem', *Rzeczpospolita*, 30 May.
Skórzynski, J. (2003). *System Rywina*. (Warsaw: Presspublika).
Solska, J. (2013). 'Dwaj panowie K.', *Polityka*, 8 August.
Staniszkis, J. (2001). *Postkomunizm: próba opisu*. Wyd. słowo/obraz terytoria.
Stegen, K.S. (2011) 'Deconstructing the "energy weapon": Russia's threat to Europe as case study', *Energy Policy*, 39(10), pp. 6505–6651.
Szczęsny, J. (2000). 'Oczy i uszy Moskwy', *Wprost*, 9 April.
Szeptycki, A. (2009). 'Polityka Polski wobec Ukrainy', *Rocznik Polskiej Polityki Zagranicznej*, 1, pp. 156–175.
Taras, R. (2014). 'Russia resurgent, Russophobia in decline? Polish perceptions of relations with the Russian Federation 2004–2012', *Europe-Asia Studies*, 66(5), pp. 710–734.
Todorowa, M. (2016). 'Naftowi gracze'. *Forbes Russia*, 23 May.
Tomaszewski, P. (2011). 'Bezpieczeństwo energetyczne Polski w założeniach programowych Prawa i Sprawiedliwości', *Historia i Polityka*, 6(13), pp. 111–121.
Tusk, D. (2014). 'A united Europe can end Russia's energy stranglehold', *Financial Times*, 21 April.
Tymanowski, J. (2012). 'Bezpieczeństwo polityczne i ekonomiczne w relacjach polsko-rosyjskich'. In S. Bieleń and A. Skrzypek (eds), *Geopolityka w Stosunkach Polsko-Rosyjskich*. (Wydział Dziennikarstwa i Nauk Politycznych, Uniwersytet Warszawski).
Uchwała, S. (1990). 'Uchwała Sejmu RP z 9 listopada 1990 r. w sprawie zalozen polityki energetycznej Polski do 2010 r', *Monitor Polski z*, 43, p. 332.
Víctor, D. and Victor, N.M. (2004). 'The Belarus Connection: Exporting Russian Gas to Germany and Poland', *Geopolitics of Natural Gas Study*, 26.
Wagstyl, S. (2004). 'Polish businessman warns of 'damaging' political attacks', *Financial Times*, 9 November.
Wantuch, D. (2016). 'Resort węgla i smogu', *Gazeta Wyborcza*, 22 July.
Wasilewski, A. (2005). 'Ropociąg Odessa–Brody–Płock i Gazociąg Bałtycki', *Polityka Energetyczna*, 8(1), pp. 63–89.

Wiadomosci W.P. (2002). *Od 2008 r. norweski gaz dla Polski; Miller zapowiada weryfikację kontraktu*. Wiadomosci WP, 3 September.
Wiadomosci dziennik.pl (2009). 'Gudzowaty dawał pieniądze SLD', Dziennik.pl, 24 March.
Wielowieyska, D. (2015). 'Afera orlenowska, Kulczyk i wiele nieścisłości', *Gazeta Wyborcza*, 6 August.
Woś, R. (2014). *Dziecięca choroba liberalizmu*. Wydawnictwo Studio Emka.
Yafimava, K. (2011). 'The June 2010 Russian-Belarusian gas transit dispute: A surprise that was to be expected', *Oil, Gas & Energy Law Journal* (OGEL), 9(3).
Zarycki, T. (2009). 'The power of the intelligentsia: The Rywin Affair and the challenge of applying the concept of cultural capital to analyze Poland's elites'. *Theory and Society*, 38(6), pp. 613–648.
Zawisza, A. (2011). *Gaz dla Polski: zarys historii sektora gazu ziemnego w ostatnich dwóch dekadach w Polsce*. Instytut Sobieskiego.
Zeniewski, P. (2011). 'Poland's Energy Security and the Origins of the Yamal Contract with Russia', *The Polish Quarterly of International Affairs*, 20(2), p. 38.

8 Bulgaria

Dimitar Bechev

8.1 Introduction

Bulgaria is often singled out as one of the most vulnerable countries in Central and Eastern Europe (CEE) from the point of view of energy security. Journalists and foreign policy experts never fail to point out that it receives more than 90 per cent of its natural gas as well as a comparable share of its crude oil from Russia. This assessment is overblown, in that gas accounts for about 13 per cent of overall energy consumption, which is well below the EU average (European Commission 2013). More than 60 per cent of Bulgaria's energy needs are covered by resources other than hydrocarbons imported from the Russian Federation. In addition, the modest volume of imports suggests that diversification of sources is not beyond reach. Bulgaria consumes modest volumes of gas – 3 billion cubic meters (bcm) as compared to 6.7 bcm prior to 1989. The imports are principally consumed by the industrial sector (glass-making, chemicals, ceramics, fertilisers) and the district heating plants in large cities could, at least in theory, be procured from other source countries if cross-border connectivity is enhanced. In cases of severe disruptions, similar to the one in January 2009, heating plants could return online by switching to fuel oil (Kovačević 2009). Crude oil (3.8 million tons annually coming from Russia and Kazakhstan via Novorossiysk) is a globally traded commodity so a cut-off of supply is not a direct threat, though price fluctuations, of course, are a matter of concern for the economy. Last but not least, Bulgaria is also an energy exporter (energy corresponds to 15 per cent of exports as compared to 20 per cent of imports).

What matters for Bulgarian energy security is, in the final analysis, politics and market conditions, rather than resource endowment *per se*. Russian companies occupy commanding heights in the oil and gas business. Gazprom remains the principal external supplier to state-owned utility Bulgargaz.[1] Lukoil is both the largest company in the country and, since 1999, the owner of Neftochim, the sole Bulgarian refinery as well as the largest one in Southeast Europe, outside Greece and Turkey (capacity 145,000 barrels/day). The refining facilities at Burgas allowed Lukoil to build a network of filling stations spreading into neighbouring Serbia, Macedonia and further afield.

Russia furthermore wields influence in the electricity sector. The nuclear power plant (NPP) at Kozloduy (two reactors with a combined capacity of 2000 MW) dates back to the 1970s and runs on Soviet technology. Russia supplies the nuclear fuel and reprocesses it once it is spent. The extensive footprint on energy sector provides Moscow with considerable political leverage in Bulgaria and explains, in no small part, why successive governments in Sofia have sought conciliation rather than confrontation with the Russians (Bechev 2015; Conley et al. 2016). Yet, as we shall see, it has never been a happy relationship and both parties hold grudges against each other.

However, the main threat to energy security stems from state capture and rent-seeking, less so from dependency on Russia. Corruption at various levels, the preeminence of vested interests in the energy sector, the weak regulatory framework, and the insufficient capacity to forge and implement long-term policies are all implicated. In that sense, Russia's preeminence is as much the cause of Bulgaria's predicament as its consequence. Moscow has been in a position to advance its commercial and political interests by taking advantage of local conditions and aligning and collaborating with various domestic players. There is indeed a vicious circle at play where the governance deficit exacerbates external vulnerability, which, in turn, locks in policy capture at home.[2] The EU push to reform the sector, particularly the gas and electricity subsector, and introduce more competition and transparency has yet not succeeded to break this loop, though it does make a difference and therefore is not to be dismissed.

The chapter opens with a general snapshot of the energy sector in Bulgaria. It then looks at its development since 1989 and the role of Russia. Next, the discussion zooms in on three cases where energy security – whether defined as reliability of supplies, affordability of resources and output, or more broadly, transparency and accountability of policy making – has been at stake. They include the politically salient issues of natural gas infrastructure development and the diversification of supplies, the controversies in the oil sector, and lastly the trials and tribulations surrounding the project for a second NPP at Belene. The chapter ends with a brief overview of the most recent developments in the Bulgarian energy sector and concluding remarks concerning the overarching issues of security and insecurity.

8.2 The energy sector as a source of (in)security

Bulgaria is not self-sufficient in terms of energy. It does have certain indigenous resources – primarily low-grade lignite (or brown) coal as well as renewables (hydropower, biomass, solar, wind) – yet generally lacks hydrocarbon deposits, despite the continued drilling in sections of its Black Sea shelf. As a result, solid fuels take up the greatest share in its primary energy consumption (36.3 per cent in 2012), followed by nuclear energy (21.4 per cent) and oil (20.1 per cent). But as imported fossil fuels account for up to one-fifth of the overall volume, each year Bulgaria spends about 13 per cent of GDP to cover its external energy bill (European Commission 2014). That, of course, is a major part of the reason why the country is running a structural trade deficit with Russia, much like more or less all of its neighbours in Southeast Europe.

The Bulgarian energy system is dominated by coal and nuclear, a fact that analysts fixated on Russian gas often overlook. In addition to the Neftochim refinery, the most significant elements include the Kozloduy NPP located on the Danube (1,900 MW capacity) and the Maritsa Iztok complex of thermal power plants (TPPs), with joint capacity of 1,465 MW, and lignite mines close to Stara Zagora (south-central Bulgaria). When it comes to gas, Bulgaria matters as a transit country rather than a consumer. It has hosted a section of the Transbalkan Pipeline delivering Russian gas to Istanbul and western Turkey since the late 1980s. As of the 1990s, it is also connected to the Greek gas network. Bulgartransgaz, a state-owned company, is the sole owner of the infrastructure, having been 'unbundled' from trader Bulgargaz after 2007 in compliance with EU rules. Unlike other post-communist countries, Gazprom has no stake in the trunk pipeline crossing Bulgaria or the distribution network. Attempts to take ownership in the early and mid-1990s, when Rem Vyakhirev was still in charge of the Russian behemoth, ended in failure.

The state remains a critical player in the Bulgarian energy sector, despite the various privatisation waves since the late 1990s. It controls the Bulgarian Energy Holding (BEH), an umbrella structure encompassing Bulgargaz, Bulgartransgaz, Kozloduy NPP, the wholesaler National Electrical Company (NEC), the Martitsa East 2 TPP, and the Maritsa East mines. The private sector is headlined by Lukoil, the three regional power distribution companies (CEZ Bulgaria, EVN, EnergoPro – a subsidiary of E.ON), the U.S.-based AES Corp. and Contour Global which control respectively the Maritza East 1 and the Maritza East 3 TPPs. The state is also represented by the Energy and Water Regulatory Commission (EWRC; until 2015 called the State Energy and Water Regulatory Commission), nominally an independent public regulator but in practice often a political bellwether.

The Bulgarian energy system is ridden with inefficiency. Deindustrialisation in the 1990s, and subsequently the economic slump post-2008, sapped internal demand for both gas and electricity. Yet the country has electricity generation overcapacity – thanks to Kozloduy (about one-third of the volumes) and the lignite-burning stations (another 50 per cent). Neighbouring Turkey, Greece, Serbia and Macedonia absorb 20–30 per cent of Bulgarian output (National Statistical Institute 2016). Against this backdrop, it is puzzling that investment in new capacity is constantly increasing. Part of the explanation lies in the EU. Renewables have experienced a boom since 2007 when the EU legislation to promote transition to low-carbon economy kicked in. In 2009–2013, 1568 MW worth of solar and wind units were installed (Ministry of Economy and Energy 2013). With 14 per cent of electricity generated from renewable sources Bulgaria is well on its way to meet the Brussels-set target for 2020 (16 per cent). But, as elsewhere in Europe, renewables have been controversial. During a wave of protests in early 2013, they became the target of criticism for hiking up household electricity bills. There has been a prolonged battle about subsidies, feed-in tariffs and state levies waged between successive governments and producers.³ However, renewables are only one part of the story. As we shall see, billions were spent on a second NPP. And authorities have allowed inefficient coal and heating co-generation plants, falling short of environmental standards, to operate because of their political connections.

Inefficiency is reflected in consumption patterns too. Relatively cheap electricity has resulted in constantly rising demand by households, in contrast to industry. Data shows that up to 30 per cent of that is used for heating. At the same time, levels of energy intensity remain exceptionally high. Experts at the Centre for the Study of Democracy, a prominent think-tank based in Sofia, estimate that over a half of the energy produced in the country is lost in the processes of transformation, transmission, and distribution, as compared to 30 per cent for EU as a whole (Center for the Study of Democracy 2014: 41). Poor insulation of housing units, particularly prefabricated apartment blocks in cities dating back mostly to the 1970s and 1980s, explains that outcome. It was only in the 2010s that energy efficiency projects entered implementation stage, in line with EU legislation such as the 2012 directive.

Last but not least, Bulgaria faces infrastructure issues. There are deficits both in the high- and medium-voltage transmission networks which reflect the inadequate financial condition of state-owned enterprises such as the Electricity System Operator (ESO) and Bulgartransgaz, as well as disputes between the regulator EWRC and the regional electricity distribution companies (3e-news 2015). Occasional disruptions and blackouts are not a rare occurrence. The gas distribution network is underdeveloped as well, even in comparison with Central Europe. Residential demand is strikingly low – only 6 per cent of the total, a function of the high prices and the underdeveloped grid. As little as 3 per cent of households have access to gas (3e-news 2011).

The root problem, as well as the chief source of energy insecurity, is deficient governance. As we shall see, virtually all major projects in the energy field over the past ten or fifteen years have been marred by corruption scandals. According to one estimate, every fourth public procurement contract is concluded in the sector, with all implications that follow from that piece of statistics (Center for the Study of Democracy 2014: 11). A large share of the contracts is awarded to insiders without proper competition, an issue that caused much tension in the case of South Stream (examined in detail below). Overspending on economically flawed projects and mismanagement has put systemically significant companies like NEC, Bulgargaz and ESO in the red. BEH, as an overarching structure, has not helped improve management and transparency but channeled subsidies to its loss-making parts. That has constrained investment into infrastructure and modernising extant generation capacity (e.g. Kozloduy NPP). Political appointees regularly come and go at the top of state-owned enterprises. There has been a deficit of transparency (e.g. on public tendering, inflating the cost of large-scale investment projects, etc.). EWRC, the regulator, has often come under sustained pressure to keep prices low in order to avoid backlash against politicians. At the same time, private companies with close links to all governments have successfully lobbied to have their output included in NEC's mandatory purchase quotas. To sum up, Bulgaria's state-owned energy sector has been systematically plundered by vested interests, decapitalised because of mammoth infrastructure projects, and hampered by the political elites' unwillingness to radically alter the status quo.

8.3 Change and continuity

Many of the above problems result from path dependency. Bulgaria's energy sector still bears the marks of the communist period and the rapid industrialisation between the 1950s and 1970s. As elsewhere in Eastern Europe, the country witnessed the transformation of its mainly agrarian economy into one dominated by industries like steelmaking and the manufacturing of heavy machinery which relied on the massive import of capital, technology and energy resources from the Soviet Union. The decay of the planned economy in the 1980s and the subsequent bankruptcy and collapse of entire sectors (steel making, heavy machinery, etc.) which had been energy intensive resulted in the emergence of considerable spare capacity, similar to next-door Romania.[4] Electricity exports to neighbours are only a partial fix to this issue.

The post-communist period can be roughly divided into three sub-periods: the initial years between 1989–97, the subsequent decade culminating in EU accession, and the time since 2007. In the first period, despite the sweeping transformation in the political system, the sector remained largely unreformed. Conglomerates like the Multigrup, with strong links to the communist *nomenklatura* and security services dominated the field (Ganev 2007; Glenny 2008). They effectively siphoned off assets from state-owned enterprises relying, amongst other things, on cheap energy inputs. Multigroup also acted as an intermediary for Russian gas imports as well as the electricity exports from Bulgaria. It was a key player in Topenergy, a partnership between Sofia and Gazprom which became an intermediary in the gas sales; and, as in the case of Ukraine and other post-communist countries, was suspected of being a slush fund to buy political favours. Andrey Lukanov, senior socialist politician, former prime minister and sometime board member of the joint company, was assassinated in October 1996; as was Multigroup's boss, billionaire Iliya Pavlov, in March 2003. Through Topenergy and Multigroup, Gazprom aimed to take ownership of the gas transit infrastructure in the country. Even if Bulgaria made remarkable progress since the decay of the early and mid-1990s, the legacy of state capture lives on. It is manifest, *inter alia*, in practices such as the allocation of state contracts without proper tendering and the siphoning off of public funds into large-scale projects of dubious economic value.

The second period, starting with the wave of economic changes following the crisis and hyperinflation of 1996/1997 and ending with Bulgaria's accession to the EU on 1 January 2007, was a time when the energy system saw privatisation, liberalisation, and the influx of foreign investment. Lukoil bought Neftochim Burgas in 1999. Regulatory innovation followed suit: EWRC was established in 1999 and the Energy Law of 2003 introduced the unbundling principle. Regional distribution companies were split from NEC and sold off to foreign investors, with the state initially retaining minority stakes. Needless to say, the Energy Law was to undergo endless modifications depending on the politics of the day. Relations with Gazprom changed too. In late 1997, Russian Prime Minister Viktor Chernomyrdin and Rem Vyakhirev decided to build Blue Stream, Gazprom's first underwater pipeline developed together with Italy's ENI, in order to ship additional volumes to Turkey, foregoing the alternative option – scaling up the Transbalkan Pipeline after acquiring a controlling stake in the Bulgarian section. In 1998, the centre-right government of Ivan Kostov forced Multigroup out from Topenergy, which then became fully owned by Gazprom. However, the intermediary company model survived until 2012, with Topenergy replaced in 1999 by another Russian-Bulgarian firm, Overgaz (Stanev 2016).[5]

Russia was to make a comeback only in the mid-2000s. President Georgi Pârvanov (in office 2002–2012) posited Bulgaria as a major international energy player poised to capitalise on its location as the Kremlin floated plans to bypass Ukraine as a gas transit country. Together, Russia and Bulgaria (re)launched major projects such as the Belene NPP, the Burgas-Alexandroupolis pipeline and South Stream, famously called by Pârvanov as Bulgaria's "grand slam" (Georgiev 2008).

Lastly, the eight years of EU membership have been both a time of continued reform driven in no small part by Brussels. The Second and Third Energy Package kicked in by forcing a protracted process of unbundling in electricity and gas. EU legislation on renewable energy resulted in a rapid expansion of solar and wind power capacity in 2009–2013. However, it has been a time of retrenchment too. Bulgaria is one of the leading member states when it comes to infringement procedures in the field of energy. Reform has been patchy and inconsistent and clientelist networks have thrived. For nearly a decade, state-owned firms deposited their cash in Corporate Commercial Bank (KTB), which grew to become the fourth largest lender. In addition to its diverse portfolio in sensitive sectors such as telecoms and tobacco, KTB funded through soft credits news outlets connected to the so-called New Bulgarian Media Group of politician, tycoon and, for a short period, head of the National Security Agency (DANS), Delyan Peevski. The bank's collapse in the summer of 2014 was caused by a clash between its majority owner, Tsvetan Vassilev, and Peevski. Peevski's construction company, Vodstroy 98, was amongst the subcontractors in South Stream and the cancellation of the pipeline deepened the rift with KTB. A media attack, investigation by the Prosecutor-General's office and bank run ensued. Assets worth up to €2.5 billion – more than 5 per cent of Bulgaria's GDP – were virtually wiped out overnight, with the state borrowing internationally to repay insured depositors.[6] What started from the energy sector ended up as a political scandal and economic shock of considerable proportions.

8.4 Playing along with Russia

Russia played a very significant role in all three periods, yet its influence peaked between 2006 and 2014, that is from the moment Vladimir Putin launched plans for South Stream until it was cancelled following the annexation of Crimea. With nuances, successive Bulgarian governments, dominated by the left, the centre, or the right, saw Russia not as a security threat but a welcome business partner. They relished the prospect to attract fresh investment and mobilise budgetary resources which would then be liable to be redistributed to political clienteles. Both the centre-left represented by the Bulgarian Socialist Party (BSP, in power 2005–2009 and 2013–2014) and the centre-right Citizens for European Development of Bulgaria (GERB, in power 2009–2013 and again 2014–present (2017) treaded a thin line. While accepting cooperation with Russia, they sought to avoid conflict with Western partners or, at times, to 'have the cake and eat it'. Ukraine complicated the balancing act but Bulgarian authorities continue to maintain that South Stream is not off the table and a solution could be worked out to the dispute regarding EU's rules on third-party access. Similarly, Sofia maintains, to this day, that the Belene NPP is feasible.

From a Russian perspective, however, Bulgaria has proven an unreliable partner. Despite political and commercial commitments made in the latter half of the 2000s, the Bulgarian government failed to lobby Brussels for advantageous treatment of joint energy ventures. Moscow, for its part, has kept its part of the deal: reducing the price of gas and accepting Bulgarian companies as subcontractors in South Stream (more below). Yet, Sofia walked out from all three multibillion projects: first the Burgas-Alexandroupolis pipeline in 2011, then Belene in 2012 and, ultimately, South Stream. The sections explore the major joint initiatives developed by Sofia and Moscow.

8.5 Gas: the challenge of diversification

In January 2009 Bulgaria was amongst the countries worst hit by the gas cut-off during the dispute between Gazprom and Ukraine's Naftogaz. Disrupted deliveries hit hard the heating systems in large cities, as well as several industrial enterprises. Reserves at the Chiren storage facility (capacity 0.55 bcm) and the gas extracted domestically – e.g. Cape Galata close to Varna (nowadays largely exhausted) – could not compensate for the shortfall. As elsewhere in CEE, the freeze sent a strong signal for the need to diversify gas supplies away from Russia and invest into cross-border connection and underground storage. Bulgaria has launched plans for interconnectors with all neighbours, including Romania (Giurgiu-Ruse), Greece (IGB, Komotini-Stara Zagora), Serbia (Nish – Dupnitsa) and Turkey. There is already reverse flow capacity (0.36 bcm/yr) with Greece – at the main connection point between the two national grids (Kulata-Sidirokastro).

Beyond ensuring security of supply those projects aim at fostering gas-to-gas competition. This overarching goal to drive down prices is not so much pressing now. Even if Bulgaria pays up to 25 per cent more for its gas compared to Western European countries, oil indexation has made Gazprom's tariffs (currently USD 278 for 1000 cubic meters) vis-à-vis potential competitors. Because of South Stream, Russia offered Bulgargaz a 20 per cent discount on a renewed 10-year contract signed in 2012.[7]

Cheaper gas imports is one of the many reasons, along with bureaucratic inertia and scarce resources, that the interconnectors have been moving with a frustratingly slow pace. Inertia at the level of Bulgargaz is also at play. The incumbent is keen to keep the domestic market off limits for rival suppliers, e.g. Greece's DEPA, having seen its market share shrink after 2012 when Overgaz (partly owned by Gazprom) entered the retail market. The original deadline of late 2015 set for the Bulgaria–Romania link was missed. Work on IGB is yet to kick off, despite the positive market test conducted in 2016 while a MoU on the interconnector with Serbia is still to be concluded at the time of writing. It is potentially the most important project as it will provide a physical connection to the Transadriatic Pipeline (TAP) once it starts shipping Caspian gas in the early 2020s. In September 2013 Bulgargaz signed a 25-year contract with Azerbaijan's SOCAR for one billion cubic metres a year. The Southern Gas corridor, therefore, promises to deliver the much-desired diversification.

Bulgaria has other options too, from Liquified Natural Gas (LNG) to tapping into indigenous resources. However, the prospects are far from clear given the low demand in the country. Plans to import LNG from Turkey and Northern Greece (projects for terminals at Kavala or Alexandroupolis are under discussion) are still a long way from proving economical, and there is no investment forthcoming even if the European Commission has ruled them eligible. Interconnectivity with Serbia brings up an opportunity to link to the projected LNG terminal on Croatia's island of Krk but even that is a theoretical possibility. As for gas deposits in Bulgaria, the Han Asparuh offshore field in the Black Sea prospected by a consortium composed of OMV, Spain's Repsol and Total is yet to prove its potential. Unconventional gas might also be the answer. Yet, exploration in the northeast of the country came to a halt after anti-fracking protests in January 2012 led parliament to impose a comprehensive ban not only on extraction but also surveying. In a nutshell, Gazprom's monopoly position is likely to remain unchallenged at least until after TAP comes online and Caspian gas reaches Bulgaria.

8.5.1 South Stream

Russian dominance on the Bulgarian gas market would have been even more complete had South Stream been built. Whether or not the pipeline would have enhanced energy security by preventing cut-offs such as the one of 2009, politicians and business people alike saw it as a second-to-none opportunity. First, Bulgaria extracted concessions from the Russian side: 20 per cent discount, abolition of the re-export clause in the long-term contract and revising the take-or-pay conditions. Second, and more important, the price of the stretch through Bulgaria kept rising: from EUR 1 bn in January 2008 when the Original Intergovernmental Agreement (IGA) was signed, to EUR 3.3 bn in November 2012, to EUR 3.5 bn in November 2014 (or EUR 4.1 bn, including VAT). In other words, there was business for a range of players. The lion's share, of course, would go to Russia. As early as September 2013, even before the official call was released, the Moscow daily newspaper, *Kommersant*, had floated the name of the winner: Gennady Timchenko's Stroytransgansgaz (Serov et al. 2013). Yet, the subcontractors included a list of Bulgarian companies linked by investigative journalists to virtually all major political parties. Vodstroy 98, was linked to Delyan Peevski. Another partner, Tehnoeksportstroy, was managed by the secretary of ex-President Pârvanov, a prominent champion of energy cooperation with Russia including the Belene NPP (of which more below). A third one, Glavbolgarstroy, was a leading construction company that had done well when the GERB were in government between 2009 and 2013. There were two further companies with ties to the influential First Investment Bank (Capital 2014; Georgiev et al. 2016).

The main question was how to find the money to build the Bulgarian section of South Stream, given BEH's 50 per cent stake in the joint venture with Gazprom. In 2012, the GERB government announced that the Russian company was ready to loan EUR 450 million – to be repaid by the transit fees charged by Bulgaria over a period of 15 years. Later on, in October 2014, the BEH's contribution was scaled up to EUR 620 million and repayment extended to 22 years. Although BEH's commitment was underwritten, in the final analysis, by the Bulgarian taxpayer, there was precious little transparency over the small print of the deal, in that there were no firm guarantees concerning the volumes of gas to flow through South Stream. The talks between the Oresharski government and Gazprom were confidential, on the grounds that they pertained to commercial secrets. That is why the answer of whether and how the investment into South Stream would pay off remains unanswered.

The case of South Stream shed light as much on Bulgaria's dependence on Russia as on the frictions between the two. From Moscow's perspective, Bulgaria had committed to push in Brussels for exempting South Stream from the requirements on third-party access to the pipeline. Moscow refused to apply itself, arguing the IGAs signed with the countries along the route took precedence over the Third Energy Package, having been signed before its coming into force. However, Sofia shrank from pushing Russia's case before the European Commission, as the situation in Ukraine led to the disbandment of the technical talks between Gazprom and Brussels on South Stream and third-party access. What Bulgarian authorities did instead was to dilute EU rules domestically. In May 2014, the parliament amended the Energy Act to exclude the sections of South Stream in its territorial waters from the jurisdiction of EU law.

That was a last-ditch act of defiance without precedent in Bulgaria's short time as member of the Union. The European Commission responded by freezing part of its funding for Bulgaria in June. In response, the government froze the project pending a compromise between Gazprom and Brussels, notably on the thorny issue of third-party access to the pipeline. The Commission's actions deepened the rift in the governing coalition between BSP and the Movement of Rights and Freedoms (MRF) drawing support from the country's ethnic Turks and Muslims. While the Socialists were prepared to fight on for South Stream, MRF saw it as a liability and reached out to GERB, the winner in the recent European Parliament elections. The short-lived Oresharski government resigned at the end of July 2014, having suspended South Stream. The KTB saga developed in parallel. It would not be far-fetched to say that the tensions surrounding South Stream dealt the government a mortal blow, having also destroyed a large bank. In August, Stroytransgaz decided to pull out from the consortium, while Timchenko was included in the list of persons subject to EU sanctions. That alone was a clear sign that the South Stream project was stalling if not already completely stalled.

In 2014, Bulgaria found itself in an unenviable situation. If built, its section of South Stream would have utilised considerable financial resources budgeted and spent with little transparency. If cancelled, Sofia ran the risk of losing income and forfeiting investment already made. There was political cost too, in that Putin named Bulgaria, along with the European Commission, as the main culprit for South Stream's failure after he called off the project in December 2014. Russia announced it will work on an alternative, Turkish Stream, crossing into Turkey and then, through Greece and ex-Yugoslavia, into Central Europe.[8] But this has not been the end of the story. The coalition government led by GERB, installed in October 2014, has toyed with the idea of establishing a trading hub on Bulgarian territory bringing in Russian gas via the Black Sea as well as Caspian gas. It advocated the plan during the inaugural meeting of the High Level Group for Central and South Eastern Europe Gas Connectivity in Sofia (February 2015)[9] and applied to the European Commission for funding. Moscow, for its part, reopened, halfway, talks on South Stream – primarily as a hedge against Ankara in the ongoing bargain concerning Turkish Stream.

8.6 Russian oil

Though the oil business has not been 'securitised' in the way gas is, its role in Bulgarian energy politics is arguably more significant. Russia is an enormously important player on that front too. In October 1999 Lukoil bought a 58 per cent stake in the Neftochim Refinery, increasing its share to 93 per cent in 2005. With large storage facilities and a sea terminal at Rossenets, Lukoil enjoys a near monopoly, supplying competing retailers with refined petrol. It tops the list of large companies in the country and is the most significant contributor of VAT and excise duty to the national budget. The company's dominant position has highlighted its links to the Bulgarian political class, from across the party spectrum. In 2011, Lukoil CEO Valentin

Zlatev stepped in as a facilitator in the talks between the government and the Russian state corporation, Rosatom, concerning the Belene NPP (see below).[10] Bivol.bg, an independent whistle blower website associated with Wikileaks, alleged that the Rossenets terminal is a de facto tax-free trading zone outside the purview of the authorities. In December 2014, the Customs Service declared that the excise collected from Neftochim had declined by €140 million. The 2011 investigation carried out together with the Ministry of Finance was inconclusive. Still, Risk Management Laboratory, a think-tank established by Ivan Kostov who, as prime minister, oversaw the privatisation of Neftochim, points a finger at Lukoil for evading tax and operating a cartel to inflate retail prices of both petrol and diesel just as global prices were plummeting (Risk Management Laboratory 2015). The corollary, of course, is that the extra revenue is in part redistributed to political parties as kickbacks. Lukoil denies such charges and insists Bulgaria's true problem is oil smuggling, avoidance of tax and non-compliance with technical standards by small-scale retailers.

Lukoil's prominence in the domestic market and the lingering suspicions of abuse of its dominant position prove the point that energy security goes beyond the issue of import dependency. At its core is the transparency of the sector and the capacity of state authorities to ensure a sufficient degree of competition for the benefit of consumers. As petrol and diesel, as well as oil derivatives, are much more widely consumed than natural gas the social implications of this case are significant. Cartelisation of the market with the protection of political elites would be a prime example of state capture. While there is no direct evidence that Russia has used Lukoil, a private company, to exercise political leverage, the very fact it is virtually at the centre of the Bulgarian economy suggests that any government in Sofia has the incentive to pursue engagement with Moscow.

8.6.1 Burgas-Alexandroupolis

Bulgaria and Russia were also involved in a project envisioning the construction of an oil pipeline between Burgas and the Greek port of Alexandroupolis. Intended to bypass the congested Turkish Straits, the plan made headway after Greece, Bulgaria and Russia signed an Intergovernment Agreement (IGA) in March 2007. Bulgarian policy makers were reluctant to settle for 5 per cent of the joint venture as per Russia's original proposals from the 1990s. Moscow exerted pressure, leveraging a rival project for a pipeline from Samsun to the Mediterranean port of Ceyhan in Turkey as a bargaining chip. The deal endorsed in 2007 foresaw 51 per cent for a consortium of Russia's Transneft, Rosneft and Gazprom Neft, with 24.5 per cent going to companies in each Bulgaria and Greece. Championed by President Pârvanov and the BSP-led coalition cabinet (2005–2009), Burgas-Alexandroupolis fell apart after running into opposition in the Burgas region and the tourist industry. Given the low transit fees (to be competitive to tanker traffic through the

Bosphorus) and the lack of contracted volumes as well as the political ramifications of having a Russian-owned piece of infrastructure on EU soil, the GERB government made a u-turn and effectively put an end to the project in 2011.

Symbolically, Burgas-Alexandroupolis would have enhanced energy ties between Bulgaria and Russia. But it would hardly have dramatic consequences in terms of energy security, strictly defined. Bulgaria's dependence on Russian crude is a constant. Yet the fact that a project of dubious economic value was rushed through the decision-making machinery and attracted as much political attention speaks volumes of the governance deficit besetting the Bulgarian energy sector.

8.7 Electricity: the case of Belene NPP

Next to South Stream, the story of Belene is the most illustrious example of the linkage between the internal and the external aspect of energy (in)security. But the main issue, yet again, was not whether such a facility was commissioned to Russia but rather why billions of public funds were spent on a NPP in the first instance. The construction of Bulgaria's second NPP after Kozloduy (commissioned in 1974) began in 1985 but was abandoned five years later. Plans resurfaced in 2002, justified by the shutdown of Kozloduy's Units 1–4 between 2004 and 2007, considered unsafe by the EU. The decision to restart Belene found an advocate in Prime Minister Simeon Saxe-Cobourg-Gotha as well as Energy Minister Milko Kovachev (who would go on to be employed by Rosatom's export department after the end of his ministerial career in 2005). In October 2006, with a new coalition government led by BSP in charge, a consortium led by AtomStroyExport (ASE), a subsidiary of Rosatom with Gazprombank holding 49.8 per cent of shares, was awarded the contract to build the NPP. The choice of company appeared a foregone conclusion. Already in February, Energy Minister Rumen Ovcharov declared, after a trip to Moscow, that it would be impossible to build Belene without Russia. More specifically, he argued that the preparatory work in the 1980s made the construction site suitable only for a Russian-made reactor. In fairness, ASE did not face a serious competitor – it could underbid a consortium led by the Czech Škoda Nuclear Engineering, itself owned by Russia's OMZ (counting Gazprombank amongst stakeholders).

Belene courted controversy from the very outset. Critics pointed out that even with Kozloduy 1–4 shut Bulgaria had no need for extra capacity and that external demand was shrinking. There was a concern over the likely breakeven price of electricity (EUR 0.105 per KW/h vs. 0.3 KW/h for Kozloduy's remaining Block 5 and 6) as well as over the safety risks associated with local seismic conditions. Opting for Russian technology also elicited criticism given the already high dependence. The Kremlin might have been after geopolitical gains but there were significant commercial interests at play. ASE and Rosatom embraced Belene as a pioneering project involving Russian technology to be completed on EU soil. Not only would Russia be able to showcase its industrial prowess, but the so-called 'nuclear lobby' within Bulgaria, including consultancy companies (e.g. Risk Engineering), politicians and experts, was poised to draw benefits (Stefanov et al. 2011: 36).

But the NPP ran into trouble as German energy company RWE decided to walk out from its partnership with Bulgaria's NEC in October 2009. A U.S. Embassy cable linked RWE's withdrawal with the company's 'buyer's remorse', after being kept in the dark with regard to the talks between Sofia and Moscow on the financing of NEC's 51 per cent stake in the joint venture (McEldowney 2009).

Russia made full use of this turn of events to strongarm Bulgaria. In the ensuing bilateral talks, it offered Sofia a €2 billion loan in exchange for 80 per cent of Belene. (Then Prime Minister Putin had already earmarked up to €3.8 billion in the annual budget.) Later on, Russia accepted 49 per cent but during Putin's visit to Sofia in November 2010 it quoted a price of €6.3 billion – as against €4 billion agreed in November 2006. That sum was added to the €2 billion already spent on preparatory construction works and services related to the deal, bringing the final figure to close to €9 bn. The long-drawn negotiations led nowhere and Belene was abandoned in March 2012 with the pretext that consultant HSBC had published a negative feasibility study (though, in reality, it turned out the recommendation was that government should continue its search for a strategic investor) (Capital 2012).

The termination of the Belene project caused a stir in domestic politics. BSP and Ataka gathered 770,000 signatures, passing the legal threshold of 500,000 and initiating the first referendum in Bulgaria's post-1989 history. Held on 27 January 2013, it was won by those giving a positive response to the question: 'Should Bulgaria develop nuclear energy by building a second nuclear power plant?' GERB and its allies in parliament managed to drop 'Belene' from the wording. Although low turnout invalidated the plebiscite, it demonstrated that Russia was in a position to exert tremendous influence on Bulgarian domestic politics. A successful referendum would have been legally binding.

Borisov's decision to give up Belene prompted ASE to lodge an arbitration suit in Paris demanding in excess €1.2 billion in compensation. Bulgaria filed its own suit for the amount of €44 million at the Arbitration Court of Geneva. In June 2016, NEC lost, with the court awarding ASE €550 million. The award has strengthened even further Moscow's hand in energy talks with the Bulgarian government. What initially looked like a lucrative business project turned into a political liability of enormous proportions. Sunken costs and the vulnerability to Russia are therefore an incentive for politicians, both left and centre-right, to pay lip service to the Belene project. The continued search for a 'strategic investor' to replace RWE diverts the debate away from the question of EUR 1 bn spent on Belene, not counting the arbitration reward.[11]

8.8 Conclusion

The coalition between GERB and the pro-EU Reformist Bloc inaugurated in the autumn of 2014 promised to resuscitate stalled reforms in the energy sector. Amendments to the Energy Law (February 2015) put restrictions on purchases of electricity from the co-generation heat and power plants. Linked to mining tycoon, Hristo Kovachki, they had been previously able to extend their licenses, buy political favours and avoid public scrutiny (unlike the much debated renewable energy producers).[12] Maritsa East 1 and 3 TPPs agreed to charge lower prices on their long-term contracts with NEC on the proviso that NEC pays all its dues. Meanwhile, EWRC increased prices to industry so as to delay the phase-in of higher bills for households.[13] Predictably, that raised significant concern by special interests in business. Lastly, as of June 2015, households and small industrial consumers were allowed to purchase electricity on the unregulated market, bypassing NEC and the power distribution companies. Greater flexibility is expected to increase the system's efficiency and bring down prices without falling back on various forms of state subsidies. However, there is a long way before transparency and accountability prevails in the energy sector and years and decades of mismanagement and rent-seeking are undone. The underlying problems described above are as pertinent as ever, and are likely to remain so in the observable future. EU pressure is clearly a major part of the solution but, as in other areas, it works only to the extent there is buy-in by political elites and business players.

Energy dependence on Russia, with all security implications that flow from it, is a matter of historical legacy. But state capture in the energy sector has actually made things worse. First, the authorities' record in implementing institutional and policy reforms has not been impressive, to put it mildly, which favours the status quo. Second, large-scale energy projects pushed by political elites and supported by their business allies have been conceived in partnership with Russia, both the top-level leadership and state-owned companies such as Rosatom and Gazprom. Moscow's geopolitical agenda, very salient in South Stream and to some degree in Burgas-Alexandroupolis or Belene, has gone hand in hand with domestic dynamics inside Bulgaria. The net result to the public is financial losses of at least EUR 1 bn, the amount spent on Belene alone, not counting the compensation owed to ASE or the several million euro absorbed as salaries and operational costs linked to South Stream-Bulgaria.

In a sense, securitisation of energy lies at the heart of the problem. All ambitious projects have been justified as strategic means to bolster Bulgaria internationally and only then as a source of profit. The focus on high politics diverts the discussion from more mundane cost-benefit concerns. Projects and policies which have the potential to deliver palpable economic benefits (lower prices, diversification of supplies, market flexibility, and consumer choice) such as cross-border connectivity, strengthening the independence of the regulator, incentivising private sector investment in infrastructure, opening the gas market to competition, closing tax loopholes and enforcing anti-trust regulations lag behind. This in a nutshell is Bulgaria's energy security predicament.

Notes

1 Gazprom signed a 10-year contract with Bugargaz in 2012. The Russian company is also present in the domestic retail market through Overgaz EAD, where it owns half of the stock.
2 There is a third dimension of energy security which is beyond the scope of this chapter but deserves to be acknowledged all the same. It has to do with affordability of energy and energy poverty. Consumers in Bulgaria, one of the poorest members of the EU, pay a premium on their energy bills, notably heating and petrol, and are strongly reliant on subsidized electricity. Thus, about one-third of households are unable to heat their homes adequately and 60 per cent report using wood for cooking (Center for the Study of Democracy 2014: 34).
3 In 2012, (S)EWRC tried to cut down the tariffs and also impose additional levies for accessing the grid. The decision was struck down by the High Administrative Court in March 2013. In December, Parliament voted again to introduce 20 per cent charge on producers (Tsolova 2013).
4 Energy efficiency is very low. In the EU, Bulgaria has the highest electricity consumption per unit of GDP (1003 MW/h per EUR 1000) (Eurostat 2016).
5 Interestingly, Gazprom was prepared to drop Overgaz as early as 2006 but the then Socialist-led government insisted on keeping it as an intermediary.
6 For a compendium of data and analysis on the rise and fall of KTB, see the website developed by the Center for Liberal Strategies (Sofia), Transparency International and the Access to Information Program (AIP) foundation. Available at: www.ktbfiles.com.
7 In the anti-trust case pursued against Gazprom the European Commission alleged that this concession constituted an instance of abuse of monopoly position.
8 IGA for Turkish Stream was signed only in October 2016. It halved the original capacity to 31.5 bcm. Of this volume, 15.75 bcm will go to the Turkish market, putting an end to the transit through the Transbalkan Pipeline. However, whether and how the remaining 15.75 can be delivered to EU consumers is an open question. Any extension of Turkish Stream into Greece has to comply with the EU requirements on third-party access.
9 See European Commission (n.d.), available at: https://ec.europa.eu/energy/en/topics/infrastructure/central-and-south-eastern-europe-gas-connectivity, accessed 16 August 2017.
10 Zlatev, called 'vastly influential kingmaker' in a cable wired by U.S. Ambassador John Beyerle in 2006, has never concealed his close relationship to GERB's leader, Boyko Borisov (Beyerle 2006).
11 In October 2016, prosecutors pressed charges against ex-ministers of energy, Rumen Ovcharov and Delian Dobrev. There are charges against two senior directors at NEC as well.
12 Still, the Bulgarian Democratic Centre, a business party bankrolled by Kovachki, sits in parliament and on occasion supports the governing GERB party.
13 In the summer of 2013, the Oresharski government chose to freeze consumer prices and reduce the deficit by selling Bulgaria's surplus of carbon emissions permits as well as by squeezing money from the power distributors and the renewables sector (slapping a controversial tax along with fees for accessing the grid that was subsequently struck down by the court).

References

3e-news (2015). 'Left without investment the electricity transmission and distribution networks are crumbling', 10 March.

3e-news (2011). 'As Little As 3 Per Cent of households in Bulgaria are gasified', 10 May.
Bechev, D. (2015). Russia's Influence in Bulgaria. New Direction – The Foundation for European Reform, available at: http://europeanreform.org/files/ND-report-RussiasInfluenceInBulgaria-preview-lo-res_FV.pdf, accessed 28 November 2016.
Beyerle, J. (2006). 'Bulgaria's most popular politician: great hopes, murky ties', Cable 06SOFIA647_a, 9 May 2006, available at: https://wikileaks.org/plusd/cables/06SOFIA647_a.html, accessed 28 November 2016.
Capital. (2012). '"Belene" e shtiala da stuva nad 10 352 mlrd'. evro. 23 April 2012, available at: http://www.capital.bg/politika_i_ikonomika/bulgaria/2012/04/23/1813770_belene_e_shtiala_da_struva_nad_10352_mlrd_evro/, accessed 28 November 2016.
Capital. (2014). 'Kompaniya ot kruga na Putin poe "Yuzhen potok" v Balgariya', *Capital Weekly*, 21 March.
Center for the Study of Democracy. (2014). *Energy Sector Governance and Energy (In)Security in Bulgaria*. (Sofia: Center for the Study of Democracy).
Conley, H., Mina, J., Stefanov, R. and Vladimirov, M. (eds) (2016). *The Kremlin playbook, understanding Russian influence in Central and Eastern Europe*. Lanham, MD: Rowman & Littlefield.
Eurostat. (2016). 'Electricity and heat statistics'. Available at: http://ec.europa.eu/eurostat/statistics-explained/index.php/Electricity_and_heat_statistics, accessed 28 November 2016.
European Commission. (2013). 'Member States' Energy Dependence: An Indicator-Based Assessment', *Directorate-General for Economic and Financial Affairs*, Occasional Papers 145, April.
European Commission. (2014). Country Report, Bulgaria, *Directorate General Energy*, available at: https://ec.europa.eu/energy/sites/ener/files/documents/2014_countryreports_bulgaria.pdf, accessed 28 November 2016.
Ganev, V. (2007). *Preying on the State: The Transformation of Bulgaria after 1989*, (Ithaca, NY: Cornell University Press).
Georgiev, A., A. Galya, S. Ilin, S. Popov and J. Popov, (2016), '"Yuzhen potok" i ovladyavaneto na darzhavata', *RiskMonitor*, November. Available at: http://riskmonitor.bg/js/tiny_mce/plugins/ajaxfilemanager/upload/Reports/41_SouthStream_State Capture.pdf, accessed 28 November 2016.
Georgiev, O. (2008). 'Golyan ili tvyrde golyam shlem za Balgariya?', *Capital Weekly*, 18 January.
Glenny, M. (2008). *McMafia: A Journey through the Global Criminal Underworld*. (New York: Afred A. Knopf).
Kovačević, A. (2009). *The Impact of the Russia–Ukraine Gas Crisis in South Eastern Europe*. (Oxford: Oxford Energy Institute).
McEldowney, N. (2009). 'Belene Nuclear Power Plant: More Troubles', Sofia 0069 B. Septel, 7 July. Available at: www.theguardian.com/world/us-embassy-cables-documents/215404, accessed 28 November 2016.
Ministry of Economy and Energy. (2013). 'Bulletin on the State and Development of the Energy Sector in the Republic of Bulgaria', December 2013 [original in Bulgarian] Available at: www.me.government.bg/bg/themes/byuletin-za-sastoyanieto-i-razvitieto-na-energetikata-na-republika-balgariya-2013-g-1294-296.html, accessed 28 November 2016.
National Statistical Institute. (2016). *Energy Balance Sheets 2014*, February.

Risk Management Laboratory. (2015). Osnovatelni sameniya za oshtetyavane na byudzheta na Republika Balgariya s tsenata na suroviya petrol, Mezhdinen doklad, June. Available at: http://www.riskmanagementlab.com, accessed 28 November 2016.

Serov, M., O. Mordiushenko and A. Solodovnikova (2013). 'Gennadii Timchenko saditsya na trubu', *Kommersant*, 21 August.

Stanev, I. (2016). '"Yuzhen potok" kato politicheski proekt i kazus na plenenata darzhava, and a'" in G. Atanaset al, *Yuzhen potok i ovladyavaneto na darzhavata*, RiskMonitor, November.

Stefanov, R., Nikolova, V., Hristov, D., Dyulgerov, A., Gegov, K. and Kaschiev, G. (2011). *Energy and Good Governance in Bulgaria. Trends and Policy Options*. (Sofia: Center for the Study of Democracy).

Tsolova, T. (2013). 'Bulgaria imposes 20 pct fee on solar and wind power', *Reuters*, 5 December.

9 Hungary

Eamonn Butler

9.1 Introduction

Hungary's post-2010 energy policy reflects a renewed statist agenda that adopts a critical attitude to key decisions and actions undertaken during the country's post-communist transition period. According to the Hungarian 2012 National Energy Strategy, the national conservative Fidesz-led government considers it important 'to rebuild those Government positions that were given up in the previous years due to short-term fiscal considerations or even less transparent or meaningful reasons' (Hungarian Government 2012: 7). This suggests that the current government believes the transition period and the various policy developments, including the country's privatisation strategy, did not benefit long-term national interest. As such, the government has made active moves to increase the role of the state across energy company ownership and pricing strategies. This has reversed 20 years of a self-limiting role for the state and reduced the dominance of foreign, capital investors within the Hungarian energy sector.

Underpinning this policy agenda, we can identify several issues which, the government argues, require state oversight. These include, the need to oversee stable, cost-effective security of supply and pricing strategies which balance falling domestic production and growing imports; the need to address perceived concerns about the geopolitical strategies of other countries such as Russia; the need to tackle the problem of un-transparent intermediary companies or foreign investors who benefitted from the opportunities afforded by the privatisation and liberalisation processes; and the need to combat emerging environmental and climate change challenges.

These are commonly accepted challenges within the national energy security discourses of many states, however, critics of the Hungarian government also highlight that there is often a fine line between these broad-based goals and what can be viewed as party political interest; as opposed to national interest. For example, the introduction of cheaper state-controlled tariffs for residential consumers (which have seen cuts of up to 25 per cent) is officially argued to be a pricing issue within broader security of supply debates and essential policy mechanism for tackling energy poverty; but has also been viewed by some governmental critics as a 'sweetener' for electoral support for the ruling party, particularly when price caps and cuts are introduced or extended during election years.

Such perceptions raise questions about trust in general governance and suggest that the contemporary energy sector remains subject to many of the same issues (i.e. corruption, lack of transparency) found in the post-1990/pre-2010 era. If this is the case, then it is possible to ask to what extent recent policy developments are really intended to help address perceived legacy problems of the transition era. It is also possible to ask whether Hungary's energy security remains vulnerable to nefarious influences of different energy sector actors (including energy corporations, national government elites, and supplier states, such as Russia) intent on extracting beneficial gain to the detriment of national interest and security. To help understand this, it is useful to trace the evolution of the country's energy policy and examine the challenges that have arisen in response key developments and attempts to improve energy security from the early transition period to the present.

As with other contributions in this book, the chapter is structured around several time periods. The initial period, 1990–2002, covers the first three post-communist administrations, each of which was led by a different political party. It highlights some of the key challenges of the early transition period, including the introduction of privatisation processes and subsequent corruption scandals. It is also the period in which Russia and Hungary agreed their first and, to date, lengthiest energy partnership – the creation of *Panrusgaz*, a jointly owned, Russian–Hungarian intermediary company with a long-term contract to oversee the purchase of Russian gas from Gazprom.

The 2002–2010 period allowed for a reflection on the previous 12 years and brought to light several new challenges for Hungary's energy policy. The first was that the privatisation of the 1990s and liberalisation of the 2000s had attracted the interest of significant external foreign investors, and that this did not always benefit Hungary's own national energy champions and had reduced the influence of the state within the sector. Second, experiences of the 2006 Russian–Ukrainian gas dispute highlighted the challenge of having a single dominant supplier and limited routes for imports of its primary energy type – natural gas. However, while concerns about having a single dominant supplier were acknowledged, the continuing importance of Russia as a 'strategic partner' and energy provider was also reinforced. The need for multiple energy access routes and suppliers which should include Russia was now emphasised, but the frustrations at the reality of making this happen also come to the fore. For example, it was during this period that we first see examples of Hungary's willingness to criticise the European Union (EU) because of its lack of pace with delivering strategic diversification projects; namely the Nabucco pipeline project. This resulted in Hungary hedging its bets on energy supply by courting all available partners, including Russia. This approach resulted in Hungary choosing to participate in opposing projects at the same time; for example, the EU- and USA-backed Nabucco project, as well as the Russian-backed South Stream pipeline project.

The final period is 2010–present, and here we can see that there has been a clear consolidation of Hungary's pro-Russian status with regard to energy supply, but that this is balanced with an attempt to ensure a strong *Magyarország első* (Hungary First) theme that attempts to reposition the Hungarian state as an effective player within the energy market, with national interest taking priority in terms of driving strategic decisions. The critical challenge for the government, as highlighted in this chapter, is that balancing the pro-Russian and the Hungary First policies is particularly difficult. Accusations of susceptibility to external influences, bribery, corruption and illegal business dealings have as a result become more common and opened the government to significant criticism in areas extending far beyond energy.

9.2 Hungary's energy sector

Hungary's energy mix is varied, with natural gas being the dominant primary energy type. In 2014, natural gas made up 33 per cent of the country's energy use, reflecting its importance for the production of electricity and domestic home heating. Beyond gas, other energy types within the energy mix included oil (28 per cent), nuclear (19 per cent), coal (11 per cent), and renewable energy sources (9 per cent).

The country has some, albeit limited, domestic crude oil and natural gas production. Its oil fields were first discovered in 1937, and the primary field at Nagylengyel has been active since 1955 following its discovery three years earlier. Hungary has not been self-sufficient in either oil or gas since the 1970s and its percentage import dependency has increased since 1990, despite consumption of oil and gas decreasing. This is mainly due to the requirement to top-up depletions in energy reserves created by falling domestic production. According to the International Energy Agency (IEA) in 1990 oil production was 62,000 barrels per day (kb/d) and net imports were 115.5 kb/d, meaning the country was 65.1 percent import dependent for oil. In 2018 production of oil is forecast to be 21.1 kb/d with a net import forecast of 109.1 kb/d resulting in an 84 per cent import dependency (IEA 2014). Natural gas production has fallen by around half from 4,874 million cubic metres per year (mcm/y) in 1990 to a forecast of 2,447 mcm/y in 2018. Despite increased usage for general retail consumption, overall demand for natural gas has fallen due to the improved efficiency of the country's gas-fired electricity power stations. However, as noted above, gas imports have still had to rise to meet the difference from reduced production, resulting in an increase of imports from 6,293 mcm/y in 1990 to a forecast 8,729 mcm/y in 2018. This means that Hungary's natural gas import dependency percentage has risen from 56.4 per cent to 78 per cent (IEA 2014).

Russia is the primary supplier state for both imported oil (77.7 per cent) and natural gas (95 per cent).[1] This heavy reliance on Russia has fuelled concerns among some international and national observers about the dominance of Russia as a supplier – particularly during periods when the reliability of the primary supplier is questioned, such as during the 2006 Russia–Ukraine Gas Crisis, which resulted in a 25 per cent drop in gas imports within the first few days of the dispute. Former Hungarian prime minister, Ferenc Gyurcsány, reflected on these concerns when he said in 2006: 'I would be most thankful if I could diversify our supplies … I can hardly overestimate the risk that Hungary runs. Any prime minister would be a fool if he did not want to diversify or if he bound himself to one supplier' (Dempsey 2007). However, as this chapter will show, Hungarian governments have never expressed genuine concern about Russia being an energy supplier, but rather that the danger comes from having a single dominant supplier and supply route, which might be susceptible to disruption, and that 'additional' – as opposed to 'alternative' – supply routes and suppliers should be considered as the preferred solution. This is important for understanding Hungary's relationship with Russia, which will be explored within the wider context of this chapter.

For other energy types, Hungary is also somewhat reliant on Russia, particularly in the nuclear sector, where the country's Soviet-era nuclear power station (NPS) at Paks, 100 km south of Budapest, is fuelled by Russian company TVEL. Paks was opened in 1982 and consists of four reactors which account for around 53 per cent of electricity generation. There are plans to increase this to 60 per cent. The plant has had its 30-year operational lifetime extended by 20 years and there are currently plans to expand the number of reactors by two.[2] These plans have proven controversial due to the perceived lack of transparency in awarding the contract to build the new reactors to Russia's Rosatom. It is claimed that this reflected overly close relations between the Russian and Hungarian governments and poor judgement in terms of rejecting the 'European way' of tendering business. The specifics of this relationship and the associated deal to build the extension to the Paks NPS is addressed later in the chapter.

Hungary is more-or-less self-sufficient in solid fossil fuels, with almost 90 per cent of the coal used (mainly softer brown coal) produced domestically.[3] Despite this, there has been a reduction in the usage of coal, mainly due to environmental reasons, and many domestic coal mines were closed between 1990 and 2000, prompted by EU accession requirements to end subsidies for unprofitable mines.[4] Some limited EU-approved state support for uncompetitive coal mines, to cover operating losses up to 2014 and mitigate ongoing social and regional problems arising from the closure of mines, has continued.[5] Coal imports come mainly from neighbouring states, Czech Republic, Poland and Russia, although the USA has increased its exports to Hungary recently.

Renewable energy sources (RES) is an area where Hungary has potential, particularly in geothermal energy, but high operating costs, time limited subsidy programmes and few identified development opportunities have restricted investment. The EU has given Hungary a target of 13 per cent renewable energy usage by 2020 and in 2014 just over 9 per cent of the energy mix came from RES, mainly biomass (55 per cent). Wind, solar and hydro power all contribute to the RES mix but are of less importance with lower production outputs. Hungary is committed to meeting its 13 per cent target and has set its own slightly higher national target at 14.6 per cent, which it appears to be on track to meet. However, this is still one of the lower targets among EU member states and nuclear and fossil fuels are likely to remain the preferred energy sources in the immediate to longer term due to their perceived cost effectiveness. As the Hungarian National Energy Strategy 2030 set out clearly: 'For the time being, we [Hungary] cannot afford giving up fossil fuels' (Hungarian Government 2012: 11), therefore relations with nuclear and fossil fuel supplier states, namely Russia, as well as the influences of corporate actors operating in the fossil fuel and nuclear sectors will continue to be important.

9.3 1990–2002: the early transition era

9.3.1 1990–1994

When Hungary's first post-communist government, led by the Hungarian Democratic Forum (*Magyar Demokrata Fórum*, MDF) came to power in the 1990 spring election, it inherited an energy system that was firmly located within the Soviet sphere in terms of east-to-west oil and gas infrastructure and imports, as well as Soviet nuclear technology and fuel. The country also benefitted from a system of subsidised Soviet energy exports, which meant it obtained oil and gas at prices well under the production cost and market value.

Access to cheap energy had enabled the country to develop its industrial base and maintain subsidised pricing for domestic customers during the communist era. One of the first consequences of the transition was the loss of the Soviet subsidies, which resulted in energy prices rising sharply to reflect more realistic market costs. This rise in prices was particularly felt by the country's heavy industry sector and it contributed to the reduction in output and closure of many factories, particularly in steel and machinery production. It was also a shock for the public who, in October 1990, following the introduction of a 60 per cent price rise for home heating gas and refined petroleum products took to the streets in protest. Until recently, the resulting three days of 'gas riot' protests were the largest public demonstration witnessed in Hungary since 1956 and caused the resignation of the then finance minister, Ferenc Rabár (Andor 2000: 47). The need to acknowledge the importance of domestic energy prices for the public has since been a constant theme informing the linkages between foreign policy and domestic economic policy held by all Hungarian political leaders, who are acutely aware of the fact that the public will usually hold the government accountable for any excessive rise in household energy prices – a matter that makes a government administration particularly vulnerable in election years. Examples of consistency on this matter can be found across all three time periods explored in this chapter and for some commentators is a defining rationale for the direction of government energy policy (see Ámon and Deák 2015: 90, 95–96).

The first transition government of the MDF recognised the importance of improving the country's economic credentials and stabilising the economy to promote growth and reduce the need for subsidised pricing schemes for industrial as well as residential consumers. To support this, it established a three-year *Programme of National Revival* in September 1990. This programme included a focus on energy policy, with privatisation of the country's energy system, using foreign and domestic capital, identified as a priority project. Although the government prepared the legal groundwork for privatisation to be introduced, its own early privatisation attempts, despite the best of intentions, were muddled and chaotic as the MDF-led administration struggled with the realities of governance and significant challenges of the social, economic and political changes taking place. The government initially insisted on limiting foreign investment and extending indefinitely the state's ownership stake in utilities companies at 51 per cent. This 'provoked disputes within the coalition on the role of the state in large-scale privatisation' (Freeman 1996) and led to questions being raised about the commitment of the government to privatisation, leading to the 'perception that decision-making was discretionary and not rule-based' (OECD 1997: 56). Within two years of coming to power, only 13 per cent of state-owned assets had been privatised and there was confusion among business leaders and possible investors due to the 'contrasting views, aims and interests' on privatisation strategies expressed within different official government documents (Kiss 1992: 1015). This effectively prevented both domestic and foreign investors, including those from Russia, from gaining easy and cheap access to Hungarian state assets during the first few years of the transition and provided an element of breathing space before a more focused and full-scale privatisation scheme was rolled out by the next administration.

The main problem lay with a lack of expertise within the government, compounded by the internal ideological dynamics of the ruling administration, which was a loose coalition of three conservative, centre-right political parties – the MDF, the Independent Smallholders Party (*Független Kisgazdapárt*, FKgP) and the Christian Democratic People's Party (*Kereszténydemokrata Néppárt*, KDNP). The leading party, the MDF, was itself an association of different political groups which had been bound together in opposition to the Socialist Workers Party during the latter stages of the country's communist era. The MDF struggled to maintain a common vision across a range of policy areas, including economic policy, and this ultimately led to a split, with the party's more right-wing caucus separating to create a new far-right party, the Hungarian Justice and Life Party (*Magyar Igazság és Élet Pártja*, MIÉP). Then following the death in 1993 of the MDF leader, Jószef Antall, the rump party, struggling to command public satisfaction in its approach to governance and a depreciating economy, failed to secure a second term in the 1994 parliamentary elections.

9.3.2 1994–1998

The 1994 election was won by a resurgent Hungarian Socialist Party (*Magyar Szocialista Párt*, MZSP) which agreed to enter coalition with the Alliance of Free Democrats – Hungarian Liberal Party (*Szabad Demokraták Szövestsége – a Magyar Liberális Párt*, SZDSZ), under the guise of a technocratic government of experts capable of bringing order and speed to the transition process. Faced with a country almost at the door of bankruptcy, the MSZP/SZDSZ administration immediately set about developing a new and revised privatisation strategy to release much need capital and pay off mainly western owed external debts that had accumulated from the 1970s and which the previous MDF-led administration had struggled to repay (Hieronymi 2013). It could do this relatively easily because one of the previous administration's successes had been to concentrate 'all ownership rights of the state in efficient and corruption-free institutions, making it easy for potential buyers to negotiate with the authorities in good faith' (Djankov 2015: 3).[6] Recognising the investment opportunities that a free market would offer, the Minister of Finance, Lajos Bokros, who oversaw the introduction in March 1995 of the government's national austerity programme (also known as the Bokros stabilisation package) strongly encouraged foreign investment, particularly for the energy sector and other utility industries which would not only benefit from direct inward financial investment but also from the expert knowledge of new owners. Hungary's success in attracting investment was evidenced by the fact that it would ultimately go on to sell more of its energy sector on 'a per capita basis to foreign interests…than any other post-communist country in the region' (Freeman 1996).

In May 1995, the 'Privatisation Law'[7] was passed and laid the groundwork for the speedy sale of state assets, including the national oil, electricity and gas industry companies, alongside the nuclear power station at Paks (which generated more than 50 per cent of the country's electricity). All were found to be attractive for foreign investors, except for the Paks NPP, where environmental and investment challenges proved to be too much of a risk.

The highest prized of the Hungarian energy companies to be privatised was the oil and gas company, MOL Group (*Magyar Olaj- és Gázipari Nyilvanosan Mukodo Részvénytársaság*, MOL Nyrt.). Created in 1991, the company succeeded the 'National Oil and Gas Trust' and brought together nine communist-era companies. MOL quickly gained national champion status with strong competencies in exploration, extraction and refining of oil. It was also considered to be a competent and well-managed company, capable of leading the way in future regional consolidation of the oil and gas industry.

The company's privatisation process was, however, not uncontroversial. The privatisation process saw the government's ownership reduce to less than 40 per cent by 1997. Commentators argued that this had been done too quickly and that privatisation profits were being used to cover imbalances elsewhere in the government's finances (for example, the social security deficit), rather than investing in growing the economy and industrial base. It was this issue that ultimately led to the resignation of Lajos Bokros in February 1996 (Jeffries 2002: 206). Even earlier than the Bokros resignation scandal, the privatisation of MOL and other energy companies, including the national electricity power company (*Magyar Villamos Művek Zártkörűen működő Részvénytársaság*, MVM) had created controversy and instability among the government leadership and MSZP party elites. The most notable case was that of László Pál, who had been the Minster for Trade and Industry between 1994 and 1995.

Pál played a key role managing the privatisation strategy of state assets via the Privatisation Law that was passed in May 1995. However, on 22 June 1995 he was controversially dismissed from office by Prime Minister Gyula Horn following his failure to support a cabinet vote to increase the percentage size of energy company shares to be offered to foreign investors. Pál had wanted to restrict the amount of foreign ownership, particularly of the electricity companies. Pál was supported by the Confederation of Electric Workers Trade Unions who called a strike in opposition to privatisation plans which would allow a majority foreign ownership stake of MVM. In a bid to prevent any disruptive action, the government agreed to only a 25 per cent sale of MVM to a strategic investor in the first privatisation phase. Ironically, to placate disappointed foreign investors the government agreed to increase the available shares in MOL from 35 per cent to 51 per cent. Government opposition eyebrows were subsequently raised, when it came to light that, despite his perceived opposition to foreign ownership of energy companies while in office, László Pál was to become the Chairman of the Board of Directors of MOL upon leaving his ministerial post.

The controversy surrounding MOL's privatisation did not stop when Pál left office. His successor, Imre Dunai, was to become a central character in a related oil import scandal which the Hungarian press dubbed 'Oilgate'. Unlike many of the post-Soviet republics, Hungary was not indebted to Russia, rather it was the other way around with Russia owing around $900 million to Hungary. It was argued by key figures in the government that one of the easiest and quickest ways to recover this outstanding debt would be to link it to extended oil deliveries via MOL (Felkay 1997: 108). Opposition parties, however, argued that a lack of transparency with respect to the Russian oil import arrangements allowed the socialist-led government to engage in corrupt, 'self-serving' deals that benefitted leading government figures or members of their families (Felkay 1997:107).

The main accusations were levelled at Ottó Hujber, a MSZP member who held a vice-president role in the MSZP's employers' division and sat on the inter-departmental committee that coordinated between the various ministries facilitating Russian debt repayments. This committee also decided which intermediary companies would benefit from contracts to service the debt, including that linked to the energy industry. It turned out that Hujber was the chairman of one of the main beneficiary companies (Gomez and Cleave

1995). Furthermore, a parliamentary investigation into the scandal discovered that 80 per cent of the agreements between the state and beneficiaries servicing Russian debt were with just three companies, all of which were closely associated with the Socialist Party (Balmaceda 2000: 205).

Dunai was forced to remove Hujber from his government position to improve transparency of the debt recovery process; however, he found himself further caught up in the scandal when it was revealed that another intermediary company, Hungarian Finance & Trade Corp. (HFT), which had been awarded the contract to coordinate shipments of Russian oil to Hungary, employed his son, Andras Dunai, as the head of its Moscow office. At the same time Andras Patko, who headed HFT's New York office and who had been deputy finance minister under the last communist government was dismissed because of his close association with the Socialist Party (Brown 1996). The favouritism afforded to HFT was heavily criticised by the opposition and cast the government and its handling of the affair in a negative light, forcing the government to quickly withdraw HFT's authorisation to import oil, resulting in its majority owner, the Hungarian OTP bank closing the company's Budapest and Moscow offices and reducing staff from 30 to four (Brown 1996). A cross-party parliamentary investigation was held into the 'oilgate' scandal and although the main outcome was inconclusive there was agreement that severe irregularities in the work of the inter-departmental commission overseeing the repayment of Russian debt and links to the energy sector did exist (Felkay 1997: 108). Interestingly four boxes of documents belonging to the parliamentary investigation were subjected an 80-year secrecy law, although this was later reduced to 30 years, suggesting that there may be more to the investigation than was made public at the time (OMRI 1996: 35).

At no stage during this period was suspicion levelled at Russia as a leading conspirator in the scandal, with attention concentrated firmly on Hungarian business and political elites. Indeed, relations with Russia were considered to be very good, as evidenced by the agreement to create a Gazprom–MOL jointly owned gas intermediary, Panrusgaz, in 1994. The new company would have control of the Hungarian natural gas import market via a 20-year long-term contract which started in 1996. Although the specifics of the negotiations that established the company, and agreed the contract length and price were not made public (raising questions about whether Hungary achieved the best possible deal), the fact remains that the long-term nature of the agreement highlighted the importance of Russia as a supplier of natural gas. It furthermore reinforced the fact that plans for energy diversification, as outlined in the 1993 Hungarian Energy Policy, were not intended to remove Russia as a strategic partner in the energy supply chain. However, it is important to note that this cordial approach to Russia did not necessarily extend to welcoming Russia's integration into other aspects of Hungary's energy sector, including the ownership structures of energy companies, suggesting that from early on, Hungary's relationship with Russia on energy matters would operate on an open-closed platform.

9.3.3 1998–2002

The MZSP/SZDSZ government lost the 1998 election to a Fidesz-led, centre-right coalition which included the FKgP and the MDF. In terms of privatisation the new government inherited a privatisation programme that was by now well established and the country could already claim that 80 per cent of its Gross Domestic Product (GDP) was created in the private sector with an equal 80 per cent of the country's formerly state-owned enterprises privatised (IEA 1999: 21). Energy companies such as MOL were leading the way as private sector generators of GDP. The significance of foreign investors and Hungary's links to the wider European and international markets was not lost on the Fidesz-led government, which was headed by Viktor Orbán. The new government had no original energy strategy and more or less continued with the priorities and principles set out by previous administrations, particularly where they related to integration into European Markets. As György Matolcsy, Minister for Economic Affairs, commented in 2001, 'The main principles and strategic goals of the 1993 energy policy of Hungary are in line with our European integration aspirations, the implementation of market economy and the increasing expansion of competition. Therefore, the energy policy principles and strategy goals accepted by the Parliament in 1993 still show the direction and are valid today' (Butler 2005). With privatisation of the sector mostly complete, the government's focus was concentrated on embedding Hungary into the European market and preparing for EU membership, which was now firmly on the agenda after the opening of negotiations in 1998. As the Hungarian government noted, 'Hungary's relatively limited natural resources, small domestic market, lack of capital, outdated economic structure and infrastructure make ever wider active participation in international economic and financial circles indispensable' (Török 1998).

Involving private energy companies and consumers in the development of energy policy was considered an important move to keep investors and the public happy as the country moved forward with European integration. The government published its 'Hungarian Energy Policy Principles and the Business Model of the Energy Sector (Resolution 2199/1999 VIII.6)' in 1999 which set out support for the development of a more competitive energy market in line with preparations for electricity and gas liberalisation. The assumption of the government was that security of supply would be guaranteed by being part of the wider European market. 'For this reason, the government placed greater emphasis on nurturing the Hungarian energy sector's competitiveness vis-à-vis Europe than on trying to reduce its external energy dependency through domestic production or conservation' (Poos n.d.).

A defining feature of this Fidesz administration and its leadership, most notably that of Orbán, was the strong anti-Russian sentiment. This could be traced back to Orbán's early political career where he established himself as an opponent of the communist regime. Foreign relations with Russia cooled considerably during this time, with Deák (2006: 46) suggesting that Orbán oversaw an 'ice-age' represented by a 'hostile policy' towards Moscow and Putin. However, while this was the case in many aspects of political and economic relations between the two countries, energy did prove an exception. Considering Hungary's dependence on Russia as the dominant energy supplier and the lack of moves to diversify away from Russia, the relationship did not sour completely. Imports of oil and gas from Russia continued, making up the bulk of trade between the two countries and in 1999 Hungary signed a bi-lateral agreement between state-owned MVM and Russia's Rosatom subsidiary, TVEL, to exclusively provide fuel for the Paks NPP until the end of the plant's operational life. It was clear that energy played an important role in the country's national economy and required the government to walk a careful line, so as not to disrupt it. As a senior representative from the Hungarian Foreign Ministry of Strategic Planning commented in 2002, Hungary's neo-Eastern policy which includes relations with Russia and Ukraine is 'very important for Hungary in terms of its gas and oil' and that effective foreign policy was imperative for the country's economy so it 'cannot afford to let difficulties arise' (Butler 2005: 104–105).

9.4 2002–2010: balancing interests

In 2002, the Hungarian Socialist Party (MSZP) returned to office, once again in coalition with the SZDSZ. There was no immediate concern about the security of the energy sector and the primary focus was on continuing to implement the EU's Third Energy Package on liberalising the gas and electricity market, thus opening the country to further investment from western companies such as Germany's E.ON, which purchased a range of gas trading and storage businesses, including MOL's shares in Panrusgaz. The socialists were also keen to improve relations with Russia and had included within their election campaign the slogan – 'gaining back the Russian markets' (Orbán 2008). It was suggested by Anita Orbán (2008), who would later hold the position of Ambassador-at-Large for Energy Security in the Hungarian Ministry of Foreign Affairs under the 2010–2014 Fidesz government, that the Russians were particularly happy with the return of the MSZP to government and that they 'saw a new opportunity to gain a foothold in Hungary'. She references the congeniality of the relationship and the open and positive comments from the Hungarian socialist leadership towards Russia. For example, Péter Medgyessy, the Hungarian Prime Minister, on a visit to Moscow with some 200 Hungarian businessmen commented that, 'We are happy to receive Russian investors, Russian merchants, we aim at a long-term co-operation' and that there were 'no prejudices against Russian investment in Hungary' (Orbán 2008). A return visit by Russian Prime Minister Mikhail Kasyanov to Budapest in September 2003 also saw him express significant interest in the opportunities that the liberalisation of the Hungarian energy market could afford Russian business, with Gazprom, Yukos, and Lukoil all expressing investment interest.

What possible Russian investment might look like was not clear though. None of the previous Hungarian administrations, even those that were friendly towards Moscow, had actively courted such investment, preferring to focus on attracting the attention of western companies. Even the creation of Panrusgaz had its limitations, since the company did not own any infrastructure and its business model was based around its intermediary status and contracts with Gazprom and MOL. The previous socialist government had also sought to prevent Gazprom's access to the Hungarian gas and oil distribution network. This reflected concern about possible excessive influence of Russia if it controlled Hungary's strategic infrastructure as well as being the country's primary energy supplier. Suggestions which claimed opening its infrastructure system to Russian ownership would result in cheaper gas prices were not readily accepted by either elites or the public because the country was already locked into a long-term contract.

The open-closed approach to Russian relations continued to evolve under the leadership of Ferenc Gyurcsány (2004–2009). He held annual meetings between high-level officials within a formally established Russian-Hungarian Economic Cooperation Commission – the first of its type between Russia and a Central European state. Energy security was central to this renewed relationship, with Hungary increasingly viewing Russia as a strategic partner not only in terms of supply but potentially as a financial investor in new infrastructure projects, most notably the South Stream pipeline, and various other transit and storage facilities.

The need for new transit and storage facilities was reinforced by Hungary's experience of the January 2006 Russia–Ukraine gas crisis. This saw Russia suspend gas supplies to Ukraine as part a payment dispute over the end of subsidised rates of $50 per 1000 cubic metres (kcm) and the introduction of market prices of $230 per kcm. Ukraine subsequently siphoned gas intended for European customers which reduced the amount of Russian gas reaching the EU. Central European states were particularly hard hit, with Hungary claiming to lose upwards of 60 per cent of the gas capacity in its pipelines. Hungary's stored gas was also not enough to make up the difference.

Responding to the shock of disruptions to its gas supply, Hungary introduced the 'Safety Stockpiling of Natural Gas Act (XXVI/2006)' and made moves to build a new underground storage facility that would provide it with an additional 1.2 bcm of storage, equivalent to around 40 days of coverage should imports fail again.

The crisis opened a Europe-wide debate on energy supply security with Russia often cast in the role of an agitator intent on using energy as foreign policy tool or 'weapon'. It would have been easy for Hungary to fall into step with these criticisms and seek to diversify away from Russia as a supplier, but in line with its longstanding attitude towards partnership with Russia, the Hungarian government resisted and sought to reinforce evidence of its trust in Russia as a supplier. Putin visited Budapest at the end February 2006 and brought to the table a number of initiatives including the possibility of building a gas storage hub in Hungary, a scheme that was highly attractive to Hungary considering its vast storage capacity. For Gyurcsány though the main thing was to balance his engagement with the EU's embryonic energy policy and commitment to projects such as Nabucco, while keeping Russia onside. The pragmatic nature of Gyurcsány's position towards Russia was clearly witnessed in some of his public speeches on the matter. For example:

> Europe needs not just a common energy policy, Europe needs an open and goodwill-based cooperation with Russia, and we are linked to one another for long times to come.
>
> (Socor 2006)

> Hungary's bilateral deals with Russia on gas transport and supply 'do not contradict, but rather favour Europe's interests by making energy supplies more reliable and predictable'.
>
> (Socor 2006)

> we are determined to build relations with Russia for a long term ... for which we sometimes must wage a fight in our own country.
>
> (Socor 2006)

> While a member of NATO and the EU, Hungary finds the way to promote its national interests through cooperation with others, including Russia ... Russian-Hungarian relations can serve as an example in this regard.
>
> (Socor 2006)

By 2007, it appeared that Gyurcsány has moved fully into the Russian camp in terms of supporting the Russian-back South European Gas Pipeline. He increasingly became vocal in his criticisms of the slow speed of Nabucco, much to the discontent of many of his European partners. He famously said, 'the Nabucco has been a long dream and an old plan ... but we don't need dreams. We need projects ... If someone could say to me definitely, you would have gas by a certain time, fine, but you can only heat the apartment with gas not with dreams ... chasing dreams is also foolish instead of building on realities' (Dempsey 2007). On the face of it, Gyurcsány was speaking very plainly and as a matter of fact. Nabucco was not looking like a realistic project capable of delivering suitable diversification solutions. At the same time, it was not clear if Russia's plans were any more realistic.

Although Gyurcsány appeared to be open to Russia's pipeline projects as part of the country's diversification plans, the historic closed resistance to Russia's incorporation into the ownership structure of Hungarian strategic commodities continued when it came to light that MOL was the subject of a take-over bid by its Central European rival, Austria's OMV. Both companies would have been a strategic fit and could have helped create a major Central

European energy corporation had the merger taken place, however, Hungary sought to prevent this, viewing MOL as a national champion too important for the country to lose. MOL, supported by the Hungarian government made many moves to block OMV and thwart a full-scale takeover. Concerns had also been raised that OMV might have been operating in a Trojan Horse capacity for Russia and that an OMV/MOL merger would lead to the asset stripping of MOL with the spoils divided between the Austrian and Russian energy companies. These fears were claimed to be justified when, in 2009, OMV sold 21.2 per cent of its shares in MOL to Surgutneftegaz (Surgut) – a privately owned Russian energy company. As with its treatment of OMV, Hungary utilised a series of clever shareholder tactics and legal mechanisms to thwart Surgut's access to MOL in terms of voting rights, board membership and right to access financial data, in the hope that this would force the Russian company to withdraw its interest in MOL and divest of its shareholding (see Butler 2011).

9.5 2010–present: Hungary First

The Hungarian government once again changed hands in 2010, when the now right-wing, national conservative Fidesz party, still led by Viktor Orbán, won office with a super majority of more than two-thirds the seats in parliament. This unprecedented win emboldened the government to reshape the Hungarian political landscape via the introduction of a new constitution, which it claimed was necessary to finish the transition that had stalled under previous socialist administrations.

With regard to energy policy, Fidesz had previously been highly vocal in their opposition to Gyurcsány's warm relations with Russia and Putin. Orbán was well known for his anti-Russian stance that could be traced back to his time as a student and the early days of the transition. Therefore, it was assumed that upon taking office the new Orbán-led government might move to cool relations with the Russians, thus replicating their stance from during their first period of government (1998–2002). This was evidenced by the fact that one of the first actions of the new government was to repurchase 21.2 per cent of MOL shares from the Russian company Surgut, making it the largest single shareholder. It did this in 2011, using an International Monetary Fund (IMF) loan to finance the deal. The government paid €1.88 billion for the shares, a 40 per cent premium on the price paid by Surgut to OMV two years earlier. There were numerous questions raised at the time about the purchase, particularly as it represented a reversal of previous governments' decisions to divest of government shareholdings in the company, including golden shares, as part of the country's application of the Third Energy Package. From a political point of view, the move provided a strong nationalist soundbite reflecting Fidesz's perceived anti-Russian position and permanently removing a Russian company from the ownership structure of one of Hungary's national champions. It also reinforced the new government's nationalist Hungary First attitude and desire to re-establish state ownership of a strategically significant utility, a policy which it would go on to promote via its 2012 National Energy Strategy. It should be noted that the government expressed similar interests in re-establishing control over other strategically significant national utilities and associated infrastructure, including water, transport and telecommunications.

The move to reobtain a sizeable government shareholding in MOL could also be seen as an attempt to tidy up the relationship between Hungary and Russia which had become less cordial since 2009 due to MOL's active refusal to work with Surgut and the Hungarian government's use of the court system and arguments about the transparency of the Russian company to prevent Surgut's right, as a shareholder, to vote at shareholder meetings. This had deeply frustrated the Russian company and government. Hungary was also aware that with its long-term gas contract with Russia coming to the end of its 20-year period, new negotiations over a possible new long-term contract would be due to begin in the immediate future. By removing Surgut and ending the animosity over the company, this would allow Hungary to rebuild more cordial relations in advance of future gas contract negotiations.

The Fidesz government made further moves in 2013 to strengthen its hand in these negotiations when MVM purchased two subsidiary companies from Germany's E.ON, including its Hungarian natural gas trade units and storage facilities. It later also purchased E.ON's 50 per cent share in Panrusgaz. This move enabled the government, by virtue of its full ownership of MVM, to (in)formally access the negotiating table on revisions to gas contracts. These are officially held between the contracting corporate parties, rather than between governmental parties; however, because of the nature of the ownership structures of the MVM and Gazprom, negotiations were effectively able to be held at the highest level. Opposition leaders did question the wisdom of this move to expand MVM as a means to access the negotiating table, suggesting that it should not be assumed that the Hungarians would be able to agree a better deal than a major German energy company. Further concerns about the price paid (HUF 260bn) versus the true value of two subsidiaries, which critics claimed would be much less than the HUF 400bn MVM claimed they were worth,[8] when contractual obligations linked take-or-pay requirements of the existing contract are taken into account.

The extent of the Fidesz-led government's spending spree on energy utilities since it returned to office in 2010 should not be disregarded as insignificant, and it has been suggested that the government turned to underhanded methods to encourage foreign-based owners of key utilities to sell. For example, in 2012 the Fidesz government introduced a HUF 125 per metre utility tax based on the length of a company's transmission infrastructure such as pipelines or cables; it also raised the rate of corporation tax from 8 per cent to 31 per cent and forced through a mandatory 10 per cent cut in fuel tariffs for residential households. Martin Herrman, the Chief Executive of the Hungarian subsidiary of RWE, commented in 2013 that these moves were 'unfair' and a de facto attempt at nationalisation which would discourage future foreign direct investment to the detriment of the Hungarian economy.[9]

Regardless of the economic wisdom of the deal at face value, the purchase of E.ON's holdings in Hungary, as well as other gas trading businesses including the largest Budapest gas utility, Főgáz, which had been owned by Germany's RWE and Budapest City Council, meant that the government was making a clear political statement regarding its declared statist moves to rebuild state ownership of the energy sector. As MVM announced in a press release following the purchase of the E.ON subsidiaries:

> In line with the Government's energy policy and the National Energy Strategy, today we have taken an important step towards cementing Hungary's energy security, as well as strengthening the long-term growth potential of the Hungarian economy. The group has started on a growth path in 2010, and with the two new companies joining us, MVM Group has become the largest, Central European wide significant nationally-owned corporation in Hungary ... As part of its medium-term strategy, MVM has decided to build on its existing assets and expertise by entering market segments that provide a good strategic fit to its core business. Over the last two years, the MVM Group has prepared well for taking a key role in the natural gas market, and is now present in all key areas of the business, from infrastructure to trading.[10]

As a wholly owned state utility company, MVM therefore acts as an important conduit for the Hungarian government's approach to energy management. Unlike MOL which is only partly owned by the state and therefore still subject to the decisions and veto of other shareholders, MVM is not burdened in the same way. As such, the government can more easily influence MVM's strategic direction to suit its own political interests, albeit framed as national Hungarian interests.

Two further examples, where MVM has played an important role in energy policy in the name of national interest and energy security are Hungary's commitment to the South Stream pipeline project prior to its cancellation by Russia in 2014 and the expansion of the Paks nuclear power plant. Both cases tie Hungary closely to Russia and it is therefore not surprising that government opposition leaders, as well as other commentators, have queried the nature of the relationship between the two countries and suggested that Hungary has made itself open to (in)direct Russian influence.

With regard to the South Stream case, Hungary had consistently shown interest in the pipeline since it was first announced in 2007 because it fitted with the idea that the country could diversify energy supply routes without losing access to a primary supplier. This is a position that has been held by all administrations in office regardless of political persuasion. Although when in opposition, attitudes differed. For example, prior to 2010, Fidesz had not explicitly opposed Hungary's involvement in South Stream, it did argue against signing an intergovernmental agreement with Russia to participate in South Stream without the express permission of the Hungarian Parliament and went on to promote the rival EU-backed Nabucco pipeline as a better choice for Hungary (Herranz-Surrallés 2017: 193). However, with the collapse of the Nabucco and truncated Nabucco West proposals, and with South Stream remaining on the table, once in office, Fidesz quickly moved to ensure Hungary's inclusion was secured. It was formally announced in 2012 that MVM would be responsible for building the Hungarian stretch of the pipeline. The project, however, ran into difficulties when the EU declared that the pipeline and bilateral deals to build it were in violation of the Third Energy Package which stipulates that pipelines cannot be owned by natural gas extractors and that third-party access should be guaranteed.

In a bid to get around the EU ruling and ensure that the pipeline would continue to be built, Hungary proposed a new law in November 2014 which suggested that any gas company that is not a certified transmission system operator could build a gas pipeline. It was an intriguing piece of legalese that reinforced Hungary's support for Russia while publically challenging the authority of the EU and the status of the Third Energy Package. Nonetheless, even though it could have perhaps set a precedent for other countries to follow suit, Hungary's move did not stop Russia from abandoning South Stream in December 2014; a decision that Orbán blamed entirely on the EU, highlighting his growing frustrations with Brussels and the idea that the Hungarian state, as a unilateral actor, is constantly being thwarted by 'faceless' EU bureaucrats. This notion has subsequently become a defining characteristic of Orbán's government, and for many observers represents the country's shift out of the European and into the Russian sphere of influence. Although, as Ámon and Deák (2015: 87) note, this shift towards working closely with Russia is not necessarily a 'love affair', but 'rather a business relationship on the political level' driven by the fact that Russia 'remains the cheapest source [of energy] for Hungary' with 'no credible plans to change this situation' (Ámon and Deák 2015: 89).

Nowhere can this shift towards Russia and the relevance of money be more strongly witnessed than in the decision to expand the Paks NPP. Paks is a major generator of Hungary's electricity needs, but the facility is aging and although it was granted a 20-year extension on its original 30-year life span, the Hungarian government has been clear that an expansion and replacement programme would need to be implemented. Paks had never been privatised and remained under the ownership of the state via MVM who decided in 2010 just prior to the election of Fidesz that it would seek to expand the plant. This was even more relevant following the Fukushima incident which reinforced the need for improved nuclear safety. In 2012, the expansion of Paks was made a high priority project for the national economy. The problem was how the expansion, now known as Paks 2, would be funded.

The answer was revealed in January 2014, when the Hungarian and Russian governments announced a deal where Russia's Rosatom would build two new reactors financed by a 30-year €10 billion sovereign loan from the Russian state which would cover 80 per cent of the cost. Hungarian government opposition leaders as well as the EU and USA immediately questioned the transparency and closed procurement nature of the agreement. The fact that the new reactors would use Russian nuclear fuel ultimately led to the European Atomic Energy Community (EURATOM) in March 2015 to block that part of the deal, effectively stalling the whole project until a new contract had been approved and signed. This was an administrative bureaucratic exercise though that did not delay the project any great length of time with EURATOM approving the deal a mere one month later in April 2015. However, at the same time the European Commission started an investigation into possible misuse of Hungarian state subsidies to fund the additional 20 per cent of the cost of Paks 2. While this led to an infringement procedure being enacted based on the agreement that public procurement and subsidy rules had been broken, the Commission did approve the deal in March 2017 based on Hungary's commitment to limit distortion of competition (European Commission 2017).

The big question over the Paks 2 project however remains the involvement of the Russians. As with all previous governments, the Fidesz administration was clever enough to ensure that Russia did not obtain ownership over the new nuclear plant and associated infrastructure; however, Russia does remain completely embedded in the project via its financing, responsibility for the build, the provision of fuel for operational reactors and eventual waste fuel processing. There is a lack of clarity and transparency over how Rosatom will engage with the project – will it be as a contractor, a consulted partner, or the de-facto decision maker? It will therefore be interesting to see if the Hungarians, despite being nominal owners and project managers, can retain control of the project and maximise benefit for Hungary.

9.6 Is there Russian influence?

Although Russia has been effectively 'locked out' of the ownership structures of Hungarian energy infrastructure and corporate enterprise (other than the MOL shares previously held by Surgut), there is growing speculation about the influence of Russia within Hungary, particularly under the post-2010 Orbán-led government. It is difficult to categorically prove that there is direct control over Hungarian decision-making, but influential manipulation would not be outside the realms of possibility considering the high level and increasingly close relations that have developed between the two countries since 2010.

An often-cited example of possible Russian influence was the decision by Hungary to suspend reverse flow gas exports to Ukraine in September 2014. This action came only three days after a high-level meeting between Hungarian and Russian officials, leading to accusations from observers that Russia must have wielded excessive influence over the Hungarian leadership, using them as a political pawn in its wider conflict with Ukraine. For Hungary's part, it claimed that Russia did not influence the decision and that the contract to supply Ukraine was conditional on the technical and available capacity of excess gas which it could resell to Ukraine. The levels of Hungary's own gas storage in September 2014 were considerably lower than other states in the region and Hungary claimed it needed to boost its own Russian imports to fill this capacity before it could restart the exports to Ukraine. Hungary has been keen to stress that it was and remains committed to supporting Ukraine in the spirt of European energy and political solidarity.

Orbán has argued that questions about its actions such as suspending the Ukrainian gas exports, over the funding of Paks 2, or the decisions that were made to support the South Stream pipeline are in effect 'economic questions that have been caught up in geopolitics, military policies and security policies' of the Ukraine–Russia conflict (Field 2014). Building on this, Orbán has consistently sought to stress the 'Hungary First' concept and has stated that his actions in respect to Russia do not mean that Hungary is moving closer to Russia, because in fact 'we don't want to move closer to anyone, nor do we want to distance ourselves from anybody'. 'Hungary', he said, 'wanted to follow policies that were not "pro-Russian", but "pro-Hungarian"' (Field 2014). By claiming that Hungary does not to want to move closer to anyone and it is about being more pro-Hungarian, Orbán unwittingly, or perhaps even wittingly, effectively suspends Hungary's engagement with the European integration process, and runs the risk of being accused of being anti-European. This is certainly a charge that has been increasingly levelled at Orbán in much of the West European media and even among elites within the EU institutions. Ultimately, the biggest problem for Orbán and his government is that difficulty balancing the pro-Hungarian position vis-à-vis with what is an obviously close relationship with Russia. Even if certain Hungarian state policy actions were not intended to be pro-Russian, the reality is that they often appear to the general, and even to the specialist observer, to be pro-Russian. When this is the case, it is possible to ask whether it is actually Russia or Hungary who obtains the better deal, economically and politically.

For some, rather than treating the Paks case as a specific example of corruption, it could just be put down to poor governance and decision making which allowed an opaque deal to open the door to greater Russian influence. However, a more significant case which has raised genuine concern of high-level collusion, if not indeed corruption, between the Russians and the Hungarians is the MET gas trading scandal.

The scheme which operated between 2011 and 2015 saw the Zurich-based intermediary company, MET, purchase gas at a low price on the west European spot market, then via a special contract, resell it at the Hungarian border to MVM's gas trading subsidiary, MVMP, which held the monopoly right to use the Hungarian–Austrian Gas (HAG) pipeline, which connected Hungary with the Central European Gas Hub at Baumgarten. Once MVMP had bought the gas, which would be at a cheaper price than it could buy Gazprom via existing long-term gas supply contract between Russia and Hungary, it transited the gas into Hungary via the HAG which it was able to use for free because of a special decree provided to it by the Hungarian government. At this point MVMP would resell the gas back to MET at an ever so slightly higher cost than it paid, but this was still less than standard wholesale gas price in Hungary. Once MET had control of the gas again it could sell it at the same standard price which Gazprom sold gas via the long-term contract, thus allowing it to make a significant profit.

The scheme, according to observers, could not have functioned without the tacit approval of Russia who controlled the prices of Russian gas purchased on the west European spot market (Hegedűs 2016: 6). By approving the cheaper price for gas which would be resold within Hungary, Russia was accepting that it would undermine its own direct sales via the long-term gas contract. The financial beneficiary of the scheme would be the MET's five shareholders, who include MOL (40 per cent), three Hungarian businessmen – Benjámin Lakatos (24.67 per cent), György Nagy (12.665 per cent) and István Garancsi (10 per cent) – and one Russian businessman, Ilya Trubnikov (12.665 per cent) (Hegedűs 2016: 5). Garancsi is Viktor Orbán's special envoy. Although there is no direct evidence that Orbán has been involved or profited from the scheme, it is evident that the Hungarian government knew about and tolerated it. If the government had taken a hard line, then it would have prevented MVMP reselling the gas back to MET thus ensuring any profits would have benefitted MVM and the Hungarian state rather than going to a group of private Hungarian and Russian individuals. It is in this context that questions of state-led corruption can be alluded to.

9.7 Conclusion

Hungary has experienced a fascinating journey since 1990 in terms of its energy policy and security. It has gone from being a country that embraced privatisation and liberalisation during the 1990s to one that has become increasingly statist and controlling, with the post-2010 Fidesz government rolling back on the privatisation achievements of the early transition era. This has opened Hungary to accusations that it is effectively seeking to renationalise certain strategic national commodities and utilities, including the energy sector. The government has undertaken a large-scale spending spree by repurchasing shareholdings from many different investors in the gas, oil and electricity sectors. This has also led to a reduction in the extent to which foreign companies operate within and influence the Hungarian energy sector.

The Fidesz government has justified this policy as one which places national interest at the core of state action. The chapter refers to this as a 'Hungary First' approach. While there is no doubt that national interest does play a role, we can also assume that party political interests and power politics also play a role in driving Fidesz's approach. The extent to which corruption within the sector exists is not as easy to identify, but there are certainly examples, such as the Paks 2 case and the MET gas trading scandal where poor governance decisions have been made and possible illegal practice, and even corruption are more than likely to exist.

Some commentators have suggested that Hungary's engagement with Russia, as the primary energy supplier across the natural gas, oil and nuclear sectors, has opened it to greater levels of influence and that this has driven some of the policy decisions that have been made, including those that challenge the EU and European energy solidarity. Hungary has sought to portray itself as a voice of reason in terms of justifying Russia's role as an energy partner for not just itself but Europe in general. This is based on a long-standing acceptance among all post-communist Hungarian governments that Russia will remain an important strategic partner and supplier of energy to Europe for some time to come. Indeed, when we look closely at both the period of Gyurcsány premiership and that of Orbán we see that there are actually many similarities in what they say.

Hungary has clearly struggled to balance its nationalist, pro-Hungarian, 'Hungary First' policy with its pro-Russian voice. This has left the country open to accusations that it is particularly vulnerable to Russian influence, however, as the chapter has shown, Hungary has sought to restrict Russian influence when possible, mostly in relation to ownership of energy companies. As such we can see that Hungary uses an 'open to some things, yet closed to others' approach when dealing with Russia. We are unlikely to see an abandonment of this approach any time soon, but what we might see is Russia using other ways to influence and obtain control. One such way is through general investment. It would be ironic to see Hungary rebuild its ownership of the energy sector just to find that its capabilities are curtailed by the flexible engagement of Russia. Paks 2 will be an important case-study to watch and assess how the Hungary–Russia dynamic evolves and whether Hungary can retain full control over the project. If it does not then we can say that the Hungary First approach has failed and that a new approach to dealing with energy will need to be developed.

Notes

1 EU Commission Staff Working Documents, Country Factsheets – 'State of the Energy Union', 2015, available at: http://eur-lex.europa.eu/legal-content/EN/TXT/PDF/?uri=CELEX:52015SC0227&from=EN, accessed 7 June 2017.
2 'Nuclear Power in Hungary' (2017), available at: www.world-nuclear.org/information-library/country-profiles/countries-g-n/hungary.aspx, accessed 4 June 2017.
3 'Fossil Fuel Support Country Note – Hungary' (5 September 2016), available at: http://stats.oecd.org/fileview2.aspx?IDFile=37348365-0442-4dd3-8d38-706eb3ad2dfa, accessed 4 June 2017.
4 For an overview of the EU's regulations on state subsidies for mines, see: EU Commission (2010) 'State aid: Commission proposes Council Regulation on State aid to close uncompetitive coal mines' (20 July 2010), available at: http://europa.eu/rapid/press-release_IP-10-984_en.htm?locale=en, accessed 4 June 2017.
5 'Fossil Fuel Support Country Note – Hungary' (5 September 2016), see note 3.

6 Several corporate governance laws were introduced during the final stages of the communist regime. These included: the 'Law on Economic Association (VI/1988)'; the 'Law on Enterprise Transformation (XIII/1989)'; the 'Law on the State Property Agency (VII/1990)' and the 'Law on the Protection of State-owned Assets (VIII/1990)'. These MDF-led government amalgamated the latter three laws into the Privatisation Act (LIV/1992), helping to speed up the preparations of state-owned enterprises for privatisation (Török 1998: 167).
7 The 1992 'Privatisation Act (LIV/1992)' was replaced by the 1995 Privatisation Law, officially known as the 'Law on the Sale of Entrepreneurial Assets Owned by the State (XXXIX/1995)'.
8 See: Magyar Földgáztároló press release dated 1 October 2013, available at: www.magyarfoldgaztarolo.hu/hu/hirek/SitePages/newsDetails.aspx?NewsID=144, last accessed 3 April 2016.
9 See 'RWE and E.ON selling up in Hungary', 28 March 2013, available at: www.powerengineeringint.com/articles/2013/03/RWE-and-EON-selling-up-in-Hungary.html, accessed 3 April 2016.
10 See 'Two new companies, Hungarian Gas Trade Ltd. And Hungarian Gas Storage Ltd. Join MVM group', 1 October 2013, available at: www.magyarfoldgaztarolo.hu/hu/hirek/SitePages/newsDetails.aspx?NewsID=144, accessed 3 April 2016.

References

Ámon, A. and Deák, A. (2015) 'Hungary and Russia in Economic Terms – Love, Business, Both or Neither?', in *Diverging Voices, Converging Policies*. (Warsaw: Heinrich Böll Stiftung), pp. 83–99.
Andor, L. (2000) *Hungary on the road to the European Union: transition in blue*. (Santa Barbara, CA: Greenwood Publishing Group).
Balmaceda, M.M. (2000) *On the Edge: Ukrainian-Central European-Russian Security Triangle*. (Budapest: CEU Press).
Brown, J. (1996). 'The Hungary Report Brief'. 15 January. Available at: www.yak.net/hungary-report/hr.00044, accessed 3 August 2016.
Bruner, R.E. (1995). 'The Hungary Report Brief', 1(14) 3 July. Available at: www.yak.net/hungary-report/hr.00019, accessed 3 August 2016.
Butler, E. (2005). *The European Union and Eastern Enlargement: Hungary and the Security Lens*. (Glasgow: University of Strathclyde).
Butler, E. (2011). 'The Geopolitics of Merger and Acquisition in the Central European Energy Market', in *Geopolitics*, 16(3), pp. 626–654.
Deák, A. (2006). 'Diversification in Hungarian Manner: The Gyurcsány Government's Energy Policy', *International Issues and Slovak Foreign Policy Affairs*, 15(3–4), pp. 44–55.
Dempsey, J. (2007). 'Hungary Chooses Gazprom Over EU'. *The New York Times*. 12 March.
Djankov, S. (2015). 'Hungary Under Orbán: Can Central Planning Revive its Economy?', Policy Brief. No. PB15–11, July. *Peterson Institute for International Economics*. Available at: http://piie.com/publications/pb/pb15-11.pdf, accessed 1 August 2017.
European Commission. (2017). 'State Aid: Commission Clears Investment in Construction of Paks II Nuclear Power Plant in Hungary', IP 17/464, 6 March (Brussels: European Commission).
Felkay, A. (1997). *Out of Russian Orbit, Hungary Gravitates to the West*. (Westport CT: Greenwood Press).

Field, R. (2014). 'Viktor Orbán: US Pressuring Hungary over South Stream, Paks', *The Budapest Beacon*, 7 November 2014. Available at: http://budapestbeacon.com/public-policy/viktor-orban-us-pressuring-hungary-over-south-stream-paks/14661, accessed 7 October 2015.

Freeman, J. (1996). 'Hungarian Utility Privatization Moves Forward', *Transition*, 2(9), 3 May.

Gomez, V. and Cleave, J. (eds) (1995). 'Newsline'. 8 December 1995. (Prague: Radio Free Europe/Radio Liberty). Available at: www.rferl.org/a/1141065.html, accessed 3 August 2016.

Hegedűs, D. (2016). 'The Kremlin's Influence in Hungary: Are Russian Vested Interests Wearing Hungarian National Colours?', *DGAPkompakt*, 8 February. Available at: https://dgap.org/en/article/getFullPDF/27609, accessed 3 August 2016.

Herranz-Surrallés, A. (2017). 'Energy Diplomacy under Scrutiny: Parliamentary Control of Intergovernmental Agreements with Third-country Suppliers', *West European Politics*, 40(1), pp. 183–201.

Hieronymi, O. (2013). 'Regime Change in Hungary, 1990-2013;1994: The Economic Policies of the Antall Government', in *Hungarian Review*, 8(4).

Hungarian Government. (2012). *National Energy Strategy 2030*. (Budapest: Ministry of National Economy).

IEA. (1999). *Energy Policies of IEA Countries: Hungary 1999 Review*. (Paris: IEA Publications).

IEA. (2014). *Energy Supply Security 2014*. (Paris: IEA Publications), pp.228–243.

IEA. (2017). 'Hungary – Energy System Overview'. *IEA Publications*. Available at: www.iea.org/media/countries/Hungary.pdf, last accessed 2 July 2017.

Jeffries, I. (2002). *Eastern Europe at the turn of the Twentieth-First Century: A Guide to the Economics of Transition*. (London: Routledge).

Kiss, Y. (1992) 'Privatisation in Hungary – Two Years Later', *Soviet Studies*, 44(6), pp. 1015–1038.

OECD. (1997). *OECD Economic Survey: Hungary 1997*. (Paris: OECD Publications).

OECD. (2016). *Fossil Fuel Support Country Note: Hungary*. September 2016. (Paris: OECD Publications).

OMRI. (1996). *Annual Survey of Eastern Europe and the Former Soviet Union: Forging Ahead, Falling Behind*. (London: ME Sharpe).

Orbán, A. (2008). *Power, Energy, and the New Russian Imperialism*. Kindle Edition. (Westport, CT: Praeger).

Poos, M. (n.d.) 'Energy – Decision-Making: Strategies, policies, programs and plans, legislation, policy instruments and regulatory frameworks', Ministry of Economy and Transport, Department of Energy, available at: http://www.un.org/esa/agenda21/natlinfo/countr/hungary/energy.pdf, accessed 3 August 2016.

Socor, V. (2006). 'Putin-Gyurcsány Meeting Steers Hungary's Government on the "Third Path"', *Eurasian Daily Monitor*, 3(174), 21 September.

Török, A. (1998). 'Corporate Governance in the Transition – The Case of Hungary: Do New Structures Help Create Efficient Ownership Control?', in L. Halpen and C. Wyplosz (eds), *Hungary: Towards A Market Economy*. (Cambridge: Cambridge University Press).

Zijlstra, K. (1997). 'Privatisation in Hungary, Poland and the Czech Republic', *Draft Interim Report AP220 EC/EW (97) 8*, NATO Economic Committee. Available at: http://www.nato-pa.int/archivedpub/comrep/1997/9p22oece.pdf, accessed 3 August 2016.

10 Baltic States

Giedrius Česnakas

10.1 Introduction

Following the independence of the Baltic States (Estonia, Latvia and Lithuania) in 1990–1991, energy security across the region has been determined mainly by various processes operating at domestic and intraregional levels, and by the structural conditions defined by Russia and the European Union (EU). At the same time, many of the challenges to energy security in the Baltic States were defined during the Soviet period, when the development of energy infrastructure in the Soviet Union isolated the region from external energy markets in all energy sectors (oil, natural gas, electricity) be it continental Europe or Scandinavia. This preconditioned the possibilities for Russia to engage in energy supply disruptions and manipulate energy prices as a means to exert political and economic influence in the Baltic States post-1991. It is also important to recognise that the region is still within a transitional period, trying to ensure its energy security and national security while integrating into regional and world energy markets.

This chapter seeks to balance discussion of Baltic energy security policy and recognises three aspects, the structures and legacies of the Soviet era, the challenges originating from EU membership, and domestic problems such as corruption. The chapter suggests that these issues do not operate in isolation from each other and have affected the energy markets, projects and political decision-making of the three countries.

10.2 Vulnerabilities of the Baltic States – the systemic pressures

Although each of the three Baltic States has different energy systems, they are often viewed as a single energy region. This is due to commonalities determined by their former inclusion in the Soviet Union, which isolated them from other European energy markets. This separation from these markets allowed for Russia to deal with each Baltic State individually, to punish defection and award compliance with its positions.

Of the three Baltic States, Estonia is the least dependent on Russian energy resources, because it has been able to rely on domestic solid fuels – primarily oil shale (Augutis et al. 2016: 34–5). Estonia is the only country in the world in which oil shale serves as the main fuel for power generation (Raukas 2004). Oil shale burning power plants in the Narva region produce 90 per cent of the country's electricity. The importance of oil shale is evident by the fact it has increased from 60 per cent to 70 per cent of gross inland energy consumption between 1991 and 2014, highlighting the importance of domestic fuel resources from the very early days of independence from the Soviet Union. The problem with the shale oil consumption is the high greenhouse gas emissions and in Estonia CO_2 emissions rose 23 per cent between 2000 and 2014 reflecting the production of 533 kg of CO_2 per US$ 1000 of GDP in 2014, compared with an OECD average of 226 kg (OECD 2017). This means that Estonia is among the most carbon-intensive economies in the OECD. Such reliance on oil shale also has implications for energy waste, with Estonia generating more than double the EU average in hazardous waste per capita, 98 per cent of which comes from the oil shale industry. As an EU member state Estonia is faced with significant climate and environmental targets and it has been argued that the country must reduce its reliance on oil shale to improve environmental standing. This is possible through the increased use of renewable energy sources (RES), or natural gas which currently makes up only 13 per cent of gross energy consumption, and is mainly used for district heating. Natural gas imports to Estonia averaged 0.99 billion cubic metres (bcm) between 1992 and 2013. However, prior to 2014, all natural gas in Estonia was imported from Russia, and in order to diversify imports, Estonia has plans to construct liquefied natural gas (LNG) terminals on its coast as well as to build the Finnish–Estonian gas pipeline, Balticconector.

Latvia has a different energy system compared to Estonia and Lithuania, and is ranked second in energy security. Latvia benefits from sizeable renewable energy access, that mostly comes from three hydro power stations (HPS) on the Daugava river (Keguma, Plavinu, Riga), and which cover about 50 per cent of Latvia's electricity needs. Latvia also has significant potential for biomass as well as wind energy. All natural gas imports to Latvia come from Russia, and in 1991 natural gas covered 32 per cent of gross inland energy consumption, remaining around the same at 30 per cent in 2012 (European Commission 2014). The average annual import of natural gas by Latvia from 1992 to 2013 has been 1.46 bcm. Latvia has the advantage of an underground gas storage facility in Inčukalns, ensuring temporary supply for the Baltic States and Russian regions in case of supply disruptions. Inčukalns can store up to 2.3 bcm of natural gas (this can cover natural gas needs of all three Baltic States for nearly six months). Latvia also imports oil products from oil refineries in Lithuania and Belarus and holds transit country status because export pipelines from Russia to the Ventspils oil terminal were constructed during the Soviet period.

Finally, Lithuania might be considered the more vulnerable of the three countries because of its high dependency on energy supplies from Russia.[1] After the restoration of independence, Lithuania found itself with an energy intensive economy and a unique energy infrastructure. Lithuania's nuclear power plant (NPP) at Ignalina was the main source of electricity and its two 1500 MegaWatt (MW) reactors not only satisfied national needs, but also provided electricity for Latvia, Belarus and Russia (Kaliningrad). Ignalina NPP decreased demand for imports of hydrocarbon fuels because it generated 80–70 per cent of annual electricity production. All nuclear fuel was imported from Russia, but it is essential to mention that nuclear fuel imports are not as vulnerable to supply disruptions and cut-offs in comparison to hydrocarbons. Electricity was also produced at the Elektrėnai heat plant (HP), Mažeikiai HP and smaller HPs, which were fuelled by natural gas and heavy oil imported from Russia via pipelines or rail. Renewable resources have not been significantly expanded and most of renewable electricity was generated at Kaunas HPS. Lithuania's unique infrastructure for electricity generation was further enhanced by the Kruonis hydro accumulation plant (HAP), a pumped storage facility, construction of which began in the Soviet period and was completed in the first decade of independence.

Natural gas accounted for 29 per cent of gross inland energy consumption in Lithuania in 1991, and although the percentage is lower compared to Latvia, Lithuania imported nearly three times as much because of the more extensive district heating and chemical industry. Natural gas consumption has increased since 1991 and in 2012 accounted for 37 per cent of gross final energy consumption. In the period 1992–2013 Lithuania annually imported 2.96 bcm of gas on average, all of which came from Russia. Lithuania is also considered a natural gas transit country, because Russia's exclave territory of Kaliningrad is supplied via the Minsk–Vilnius–Kaliningrad pipeline. This would suggest that the need for regular Russian gas supplies to Kaliningrad would decrease vulnerabilities for Lithuania, however, history has shown that this has not prevented supply disruptions.

The Lithuanian economy is highly dependent on oil imports because its oil refinery in Mažeikiai (currently owned by Polish PKN Orlen), which is the only one in the Baltic States, is one of the biggest contributors to the state budget. Gross inland consumption data suggests that the share of oil reached only 44 per cent, but it does not account for exports of oil products from Lithuania. Lithuania had to import much higher quantities of oil to keep the Mažeikiai oil refinery working efficiently, otherwise it would have significant negative economic impacts for the country and for employment in the region where the refinery is situated. The construction of an oil refinery in the Baltic region would seem illogical because in the Baltic States, Belarus and the western part of Russia there is no significant oil production to supply refineries, but during the Soviet period energy infrastructure was designed to meet energy and political needs of an integrated Soviet Union and ensure Moscow's control. The strategy of Moscow was to integrate oil producing regions in Central Asia and Russia with other regions (having limited resources) to keep the economic integrity of the Soviet Union, dividing the energy sector between republics, while positioning Moscow at the centre to regulate these connections

(Goldman 2008: 7–9). Oil refinery was used as a tool of energy diplomacy to punish Lithuania as it had no alternative supplies to the *Druzhba*2 (Friendship 2) pipeline and needed to be supplied by rail.

The importation of natural gas and oil from Russia by the Baltic States created energy, economic and political dependency. For the most part the Baltic States could be accounted as final consumers with some transit capabilities but without – until recently – any alternatives.

The Baltic States remain members of the Integrated Power System/Unified Power System (IPS/UPS), a synchronous area coordinated by Power Council of Commonwealth of Independent States and controlled by a dispatch in Moscow and part of which is the BRELL (Belarus, Russia, Estonia, Latvia and Lithuania) electricity grind circle. At the beginning of their independent statehood there were no connections to the Scandinavian electricity network NORDEL or the continental European electricity network ENTSO-E (previously UCTE).[2] The IPS/UPS network is controlled by Moscow, though in 2006 the Baltic States created the BALTSO network, but it is more a political agreement rather than an independent network operating in practice, because of the remaining integration in IPS/UPS.

After the Baltic States became members of the EU, Lithuania and Latvia were the least self-sufficient members in energy supplies. Because of the lack of interconnections with other regions the European Commission (2006) in its Green Paper referred to the Baltic States as 'energy islands'.

10.3 Victims of energy diplomacy

The legacy of high dependency on Russian energy resources and a lack of alternatives is often credited with allowing Moscow to use energy as a tool of diplomacy, with the expectation that domestic and foreign policies of the Baltic States will be readjusted to favour Russian interests. Larrson (2006: 190) notes that Russian Foreign Minister First Deputy, Vitalii Churkin, argued that energy supply interruptions were one of the probable options for Russian policy in Estonia, Latvia and Lithuania. This chapter does not contest that such energy diplomacy existed, however, it should not be considered the only driver of Baltic energy security policy.

After its declaration to restore independence on 11 March 1990, Lithuania experienced energy diplomacy, when in April oil supplies were suspended for two and a half months in an attempt to force Lithuania to reconsider the economic consequences of independence and to preserve integrity of the Soviet Union (Janeliūnas 2009: 191). In summer (July–August) 1992 Russia again suspended oil supplies to Lithuania and reduced natural gas supplies by more than 50 per cent because of Lithuanian debts (Česnakas 2012: 159). The debts had accumulated because of an oil and natural gas price spike for the Baltic States following Russia's abandonment of Soviet-era subsidies for countries not part of the Commonwealth of Independent States (CIS). Oil supply disruption was repeated in the autumn and winter of 1992–1993. The supply problems led to even deeper economic downturn, with schools and hospitals often left without heating, while the Ignalina NPP was exploited at maximum capacity to satisfy basic energy needs. More recently, in 2010, Lithuania experienced short-term decreases of natural gas supply because of the dropping pressures in the pipelines as consequences of supply disruptions from Russia to Belarus. Some short-term electricity price spikes have been also experienced because Russia closed some lines for maintenance without any warning.

In the winter of 1992–1993 Russia cut off natural gas supplies to Estonia at the same time as an increase in tense political relations (Mäe 2007: 93), which had emerged following Estonia's adoption of a 'Law on Aliens', which affected the ethnic Russians community in the country (Leijonhielm and Larsson 2004: 126). Unlike in Lithuania, and perhaps because of its domestic oil shale capacity, this suspension of supplies was not successful in influencing Estonia's policy position. However, this did not deter further use of energy as a diplomatic tool. Later that decade, Lithuania faced another round of oil supply cut-offs, but this time for economic reasons. The privatisation of the Mažeikiai oil refinery had attracted considerable interest from Russian energy companies, but Lithuania wanted investors from the West. Throughout the privatisation period, Russian state-owned oil transportation company, Transneft, curtailed oil supplies nine times (Larsson 2006: 185). The oil refinery was sold to the United States (US) based Williams International in 1999, however the supply disruptions did impact the financial viability of the refinery and in 2002 Williams International, the Lithuanian Government and Russian oil company Yukos (which did not fall in line with Kremlin policies), agreed to transfer ownership of the refinery to Yukos. Unfortunately, shortly after the Yukos takeover in 2003, the Lithuanian Government was forced to search for a new investor for fear that the refinery would end up in ownership of one of Russia's state-owned energy companies. Some international companies had expressed interest in buying the refinery, including Kazakhstan's Kazmunaigaz, but the company withdrew its offer after Transneft cancelled an agreement on oil transit, because it wanted to ensure that refinery would be sold to Lukoil (TBT Staff 2005). Mažeikiai was subsequently sold to Poland's PKN Orlen, but the failure of Russia to ensure repairs to the Druzba-2 pipeline from July 2006 prevented piped oil imports to the refinery and instead they had to come by sea, resulting in extra cost.

Oil supply disruptions have been also experienced in Latvia and mainly concern control over oil and associated export infrastructure to the port of Ventspils, operated by Ventspils Nafta. Lukoil and other Russian energy firms did seek to acquire Ventspils Nafta, but after long negotiations the Latvian state, the company's private owners rejected the various offers. It has been claimed that in response, Russia interrupted oil and petroleum supplies to Ventspils throughout 2002 before terminating all oil deliveries in 2003 (Grigas 2013). Transneft diverted oil supplies to the Russian ports of Primorsk and Ust-Luga which received significant infrastructural investment. It is worth noting that some Russian oil companies were interested in continuing to export oil via Latvia, but Moscow rejected their complaints about the lack of access (Lelyveld 2003). The result was that Latvia lost income from oil transit via pipelines, and increased supplies of refined petroleum products thus increasing dependence on supplies from Russia and Belarus.

Disruption to the supply of oil products re-emerged in Estonia in 2007 following the relocation of the bronze statue of the Soviet soldier – a World War II memorial. This included the suspension of the delivery of oil and oil products by Russian Railways in May 2007 (Grigas 2013).

10.4 The challenge of EU membership

Challenges to the energy security of the Baltic States have also emerged as the result of EU membership. In the case of Lithuania this related to 'Protocol No. 4 on the Ignalina Nuclear Power Plant in Lithuania', included in the Treaty of Accession (3 April 2003), which stated that Unit 1 of the Ignalina NPP had to close by 2005 and Unit 2 by 2009. The EU demanded closure of Ignalina because it operated Soviet-designed RBMK reactors, the same that had been installed in Chernobyl. The demand for closure was made despite significant investments to improve technical safety at the plant by Lithuania and the international community. Although the EU agreed to provide financial support for decommissioning – a lengthy and expensive process not without significant financial burden to the state – the closure of Iganlina was a strategic loss for Lithuanian and wider Baltic energy security.[3] This has meant that imports of natural gas have needed to increase significantly to produce electricity domestically and electricity grid imports from Russia and other countries in the BRELL circle (Estonia) have had to increase to satisfy consumer demand not met domestically.

For Estonia, the constantly tightening regulations on greenhouse gas (GHG) emissions threaten electricity production in Estonian power plants fuelled by oil shale. The production of oil shale will have to decrease because of the directives and the EU 2030 Climate and Energy Policy Framework requiring the country to cut greenhouse gas emissions by 40 per cent compared to the year 1990 (European Council 2014). Although Estonia would like to use its advantage in energy production via oil shale, it also will have to continue to diversify its energy portfolio and expand renewable resources and possibly even consider investments in nuclear power. Tighter greenhouse gas regulations also affect electricity and heat production in Lithuania, where the heat production plant in Kaunas, as well as other power plants were designed and constructed when GHG emission regulations were much lower. Without significant investments they will not be able to continue operating and so need to be modernised or replaced, again at considerable financial cost.

10.5 Corruption

Not all the threats or challenges to Baltic energy security can be explained by Russian energy diplomacy or EU accession. Many of the problems the three countries face reflect national or domestic matters, often linked to corruption and a lack of transparency across the sector, where Russia's cooperation with energy companies in the Baltic States has allowed for it to advance its economic and political interests. It is worth noting that corruption in the energy sector is usually associated with Lithuania and Latvia, while Estonia is considered to be more resilient to this vulnerability.

It has already been suggested that the privatisation of the strategically important Mažeikių Nafta oil refinery in 1999 was surrounded in controversy due to the Russian disruption of oil supplies and the purchase by US-based Williams International. It was argued that transparency around the deal, which took two years to agree, was limited and it was not clear what the implications for the Lithuanian economy would be particularly with regard to large liabilities that would be retained by the state. Concern about the economics of the deal led to the resignation of both the Finance Minister, Jonas Lionginas, and the Minister for the Economy, Eugenijus Maldeikis, while Prime Minister Rolandas Paksas resigned in protest at the deal five months after its approval. Paksas was known to have strong connections with Russian business and in 2004 he became the first European president to be impeached on the basis of political impropriety by granting Lithuanian citizenship to a Russian national who had provided a significant donation to Paksas' presidential campaign.

Although it was not entirely clear if any relationship existed between key government officials and Russia with respect to the Mažeikių Nafta privatisation process, there is evidence of engagement with Russia in the wider Baltic energy sector. For example, in the early 1990s numerous private intermediary gas trading companies were established in Lithuania. These companies bought natural gas from Gazprom at a lower price and then sold it to customers and domestic suppliers as well as state-owned companies like Lietuvos Dujos (previously the gas supply monopolist) at a higher price. These companies which included Jangila, Stella Vitae and Dujotekana were so successful that they were able to use their financial capabilities to influence Lithuanian politics via links with political parties (Vitkus 2009: 34–35) and the media. Of course, the potential for such companies to conduct business in Russia depended on the goodwill of the Russian government. Balmaceda (2008: 21) noted how the main gas intermediary in Lithuania, Stella Vitae, was replaced in 2001 by a new company Dujotekana despite the fact Stella Vitae had a gas trading agreement which ran until 2006. It has been suggested that this has happened because the then owner of Stella Vitae, Viktoras Uspaskich, was unable to exert the right influence on Lithuanian politics (Tvaskienė 2009) and therefore the company was not viewed as a suitable vehicle for Russian energy diplomacy. The replacement company, Dujotekana, which was headed by Rimandas Stonys became the near monopolist in Lithuanian natural gas imports (Balmaceda 2008: 20). It is worth noting that among Dujotekana shareholders have been a former KGB officer and Russian citizen, Piotras Vojeika, who initially owned 49 per cent the company, which he later sold to

Stonys. Dujotekana was active in providing financial support for political parties, politicians, and media, leading to questions about its lobbying intentions and possible impact on national security (Smith 2004). In 2006, the State Security Department prepared a report on the connections between Dujotekana and the Kremlin, but the report was mired in controversy with many of the investigators fired and the lead agent who headed the investigation dying under suspicious circumstances in Belarus (Alehno 2012). No legal cases were brought against the company as a result of the report and the media suggest that Stonys used influence within the State Security Department to downplay it. However, despite this, the company's role within the gas import sector has since retracted, dropping from 45 per cent in 2002 to 15 per cent in 2011 and to 1.3 per cent in 2015. One possible reason for this is that Gazprom's increasing dominance in Russia and acquisition of energy companies in the Baltic States such as Lietuvos Dujos (Lithuanian Gas), Latvijas Gāze (Latvian Gas) and Eestigaas (Estonian Gas) have allowed contracts and the gas trade to become more transparent, and in doing so decreased the need for and influence of intermediaries. Despite this increased stability, acquisitions of state-owned gas companies in the Baltic States have not prevented Gazprom from sharply increasing of natural gas prices in the region or applying discriminative discounts when required. The privatisation of Lietuvos Dujos by Gazprom was not fully transparent as the company has been sold at lower price than the assessed company's value.

There also have been cases of corruption in the oil and oil products sector. Smith (2004: 38) has noted, that there have been questionable ties between the former Lithuanian Prime Minister, Algirdas Brazauskas, and Lukoil CEO, Vagit Alekperov. Ivanas Paleičikas, CEO of Lukoil Baltija, was also influential in representing the interests of Lukoil when the Lithuanian government was searching for an investor in the Mažeikiai oil refinery in 2005–2006. There have been a number of accusations of corruption in Latvia, mostly concerning the mayor of Ventspils, Aivars Lembergs, who had connections to Lukoil and owned the majority of Ventspils Nafta. In 2003 Latvia's Deputy Prime Minister, Ainars Slesers, initiated the reopening of the investigation of privatisation of Ventspils Nafta and a month later the Latvian Corruption Prevention and Enforcement Bureau started an investigation of Lembergs' connections with offshore companies in Cyprus (Martina and Bogdanas 2012). This led to the deterioration of relations between Lembergs and the Latvian Government, which was not helped by the 2005 General Prosecutor's Office investigation into Lembergs' abuse of the office. In 2007 he was prevented from fulfilling duties in Ventspils' city Council, but he remains mayor of Ventspils (since 1988) despite short interruptions, and is considered one of the richest men in Latvia.

It has to be stressed that despite allegations of corruption, there have never been any significant cases in which the allegedly corrupt politicians or businessmen have been charged and sentenced, reflecting the fact that despite strong elements of speculation there is limited hard evidence.

10.6 Increasing energy security through sector specific projects

To better understand and define the success of energy security projects in the region it is useful to look at the implementation of energy security projects across a variety of sectors. This allows us to identify key variables in the dynamics of regional cooperation as well as cooperation with the EU.

The oil embargo in the early 1990s showed that access to alternative supplies and supply infrastructure was important. This led to the initiation of the oil import/export terminal in Būtingė (Lithuania) in 1995. The project was completed in 1999 and proved essential during the disruptions in 1998–1999, and following the shutdown of the Druzhba-2 pipeline, when it became the main gateway for oil imports to the Mažeikiai oil refinery, thus contributing to the national economy by reshaping energy supply routes and keeping the refinery operational, albeit with Russian oil.

Beyond the Būtingė project, there were no successful energy security projects in the region prior to membership in the EU. This can be explained by the transitional period in the Baltic States. In the early years of independence, the Baltic States were preoccupied with creation of their core legal systems, the replacement of most Soviet-era law, addressing economic issues in the face of economic downturn and adaptation to market economy principles, overseeing the modernisation of their core industries, as well as addressing existing and emergent social challenges and low living standards. Therefore, the limited financial capabilities of the three countries were not prioritised for energy projects. In the foreign policy arena, the main goal was to improve their position within the international community and obtain membership of NATO and the EU.

The impact of institutions like the EU has been noticeable, with Agnia Grigas (2013: 85) commenting that 'the EU agenda has made it more difficult for Baltic States' governments to backpedal in the face of pressure from political parties and energy interest groups that benefit from the current dependence on Russia'. This allowed projects which challenged Russian influence in the region to be developed, although the active implementation of energy projects which substantially changed the energy system did not really begin until around 2006 when EU membership finally created the prospects for financial as well as political support for energy projects that had previously been lacking.

At the same time domestic variables in the Baltic States had a significant impact on energy security projects. The governments promoted particular energy projects that often reflected their domestic agendas, and with changes in administrations, energy policies also invariably changed, thus preventing efficient implementation of energy projects that required longer periods of development. It is important to note that, in general, governments and parliaments agreed on the core approaches to energy sector development, but projects have been different. The over-politicisation of projects, strong interest groups and in some cases, elements of corruption, prevented short-term success and prolonged certain vulnerabilities.

Finally, it must be addressed that although Estonia, Latvia and Lithuania have declared the need for cooperation in the energy sector in order to achieve energy security for the region as a whole, cooperation is regularly hindered by prioritisation of national interests, reflecting the specific realities of differing energy systems and leading to a situation where the Baltic States usually focus on individual national rather than regional projects.

10.6.1 The nuclear sector

The immediate problem for the Baltic States, not only for Lithuania, after accession to the EU was the decommissioning of Iganlina NPP, which had strategic importance for the whole region in terms of electricity production. The countries in the region had to search for alternative ways of electricity generation, but proposals to construct a new NPP have proven challenging and ultimately unsuccessful because of domestic processes as well as lack of cooperation in the region.

In February 2006, the prime ministers of the Baltic States signed a declaration together to plan and build a new NPP in Lithuania. Later the COEs of Lietuvos Energija (Lithuanian Energy), Eesti Energy (Estonian Energy) and Latvenergo (Latvia Energy) signed a memorandum on the construction of new NPP. These declarations were signed nearly three years after it had become clear that Lithuania would have to close the second Ignalina reactor by 2009. In March 2007, the Lithuanian and Polish prime ministers signed a communiqué to include Poland in the project. However, Poland was never an active member of the NPP consortium, and withdrew its participation in December 2011 preferring to develop plans to construct NPPs on its own territory.

The Lithuanian Government headed by the Social Democratic Party had planned that the new NPP would be constructed in cooperation between domestic private investors and the state, even though there was no domestic investor with expertise in building NPPs or implementing such big investment projects. In December 2007, the minister of economy announced LEO LT (Lithuanian Electricity Organisation) as the Lithuanian investor for the new NPP. The state controlled 61.7 per cent of shares in LEO LT through state-owned companies 'Lietuvos Energija' and 'Rytų skirstomieji tinklai', while private 'VP grupė' (VP group) controlled 38.3 per cent of shares via NDX Energija (NDX Energy) and VST (OSW 2009).[4] This created a monopoly in the electricity sector because a single public and private partnership company now controlled generation, transmission and distribution of electricity, while its subsidiary company was responsible for the implementation of the NPP project. The Competition Council had not provided any conclusions on monopolisation and the European Commission was not informed in advance about the merger of companies. The Law on Nuclear Power Plant was adopted on 1 February 2008, despite strong opposition and questions about whether the law contradicted the Constitution which prohibits monopolies. Civic society groups opposing the law gathered signatures to force a repeal, however it still came into force. The new company *Visagino Atominė Elektrinė* (Visaginas Nuclear Power Plant) was established under LEO LT in 2008 and was directly responsible for implementation of the NPP project.

After the 2008 parliamentary election, the new government headed by the National Union–Lithuanian Christian Democrats started a revision process of the NPP project with the participation of LEO LT. On 2 March, 2009 the Constitutional Court ruled that the Law on the Nuclear Power Plant did not contradict Constitution; however, there were other laws connected to the Law on the Nuclear Power Plant which did (Lietuvos Respublikos Konstitucinis Teimas 2009). At the same time the establishment of LEO LT was declared as constitutional, yet six months later, on 4 September, Parliament voted to dissolve LEO LT. Infrastructure controlled by the company was nationalised and former owner NDX Energija received compensation of €196.94 million.

The Lithuanian government ordered a feasibility study of Visaginas NPP from investment bank N M Rothschild & Sons and multinational law firm Herbert Smith to evaluate its electricity production capacities and selection of foreign investors, as well as the impact of alternative energy projects in the region. The resulting report concluded that the project was economically feasible, but argued that a strategic investor with experience in nuclear energy was needed. Lithuania subsequently began preparations for a strategic investor competition, however, the first competition failed when the single company KEPCO (South Korea) withdrew at the end of 2010. The chairman of the Atomic Energy Commission at the Parliament of Lithuania associated withdrawal of KEPCO with pressure from Russia. After the announcement of a second competition in mid-July 2011, two applications were received; the first from Toshiba–Westinghouse and the second from Hitachi. A special Governmental Commission selected Hitachi who would own 20 per cent of the shares alongside Lithuania (38 per cent), Estonia (22 per cent) and Latvia (20 per cent). The projected cost of the single block NPP was €5 billion and the reactor had to be of 1350 MW, with the electricity generation to be divided proportionally according to owned shares, although there was concern that the NPP capacity would not satisfy the needs of investors.

In March 2012, the Government and Hitachi initialised the concession contract for the construction of Visaginas NNP, however, in July opposition parties in Lithuania voted in favour of a consultative referendum on the construction of the NPP to be held alongside the Parliamentary election on 14 October 2012. The referendum results were 35.3 per cent in favour of the construction of NPP, with 64.77 per cent against (turnout was 52.58 per cent of voters). Due to the referendum's consultative status the future of the Visaginas project was passed to the new government headed by the Social Democrats. However, despite being the party that had originally initiated the project the Social Democrats now expressed no determination to follow through with the project. New Prime Minister, Audrius Butkevičius, stated that the Visaginas NPP was an 'unreal project' (alfa.lt 2012), and analysis by the Lithuanian

Energy Institute presented as evidence for a revised Lithuanian Energy Strategy suggested that, taking into account the price of electricity, the prospects of NPP development in Lithuania were negative (Černiauskas 2013). Yet, despite these criticisms, the Government had no political interests in declaring the project dead, because this would create problems for electoral strategies and with regional partners as well as Hitachi. The NPP project is not even included in the draft of Lithuanian Energy Strategy presented in 2017.

The delays to the Visaginas project did little to promote trust among the consortium partners. This was evident from as early as 2009, when the Estonian Parliament adopted its 'National Development Plan of the Energy Sector to 2020', to train specialists and prepare legislation should Estonia decide to build its own NPP (Tere 2009). Plans for Estonia to construct a NPP by 2023 were even floated, but the 2011 Fukushima Daiichi disaster in Japan forced their reconsideration and a recommitment to the Visaginas project. However, after Prime Minister Butkevičius raised doubts about Visaginas in November 2012, Estonia's President Toomas Hendrik Ilves declared Estonia's disappointment with Lithuania's changing position on the project and that 6.5 years had been lost in negotiations for a project unlikely to be competed (alfa. lt 2012). Reflecting evidence presented in 2013, the 2016 Lithuanian National Energy Independence Strategy argued that Visaginas NPP is not currently 'necessary' for the security of energy supply and it was only at this point that the Minister of Energy declared the Visaginas project would be frozen, highlighting how political processes in one Baltic State create problems for regional cooperation (Minister of Energy 2016).

10.6.2 *The electricity network sector*

The significance of the Visaginas NPP was also diminished by plans to integrate the Baltic States with electricity networks in Scandinavia and continental Europe. This meant the reliance on electricity imports from Russia could be balanced by alternative suppliers from the EU member states with much higher political reliability. LitPol Link, NordBalt, EstLink (1 and 2) – electricity interconnections between Lithuania and Poland, Lithuania and Sweden, and Estonia and Finland – have strategic importance for integrating the Baltic States with ENTSO-E and NORDEL, and desynchronising with BRELL network.

Plans for a submarine electricity cable between Scandinavian and the Baltic States were first proposed in 1990s, but not initiated until 2001 when energy companies representing countries of the regions signed the contract agreement. However, the project stagnated and it was relaunched only in 2005 after Lithuania joined the project in 2004. The first line of Estlink between Finland and Estonia became operational in January 2007. In 2010, the Estlink 2 was initiated with construction finalised by March 2014.

The idea of power interconnection between Poland and Lithuania was suggested in 1998, but was not implemented for domestic reasons. It was only in 2006 that Lithuanian President, Valdas Adamkus, and Polish President,

Lech Kaczynski, signed a joint declaration to build an interconnector and in May 2008 the joint company for the project was established. The plans of Visaginas encouraged moves to advance interconnection between the two countries because Poland sought to import electricity from the NPP. The first transmission line between Elk (Poland) and Alytus (Lithuania) was completed in December 2015. The stalling of the NPP project in Lithuania, and an already developed electricity network in North-Eastern Poland has limited the motivation of Poland to finance the construction of a second transmission line.

In August 2006 transmission grid operators in Lithuania and Sweden agreed to launch a feasibility study for a Baltic Sea regional interconnection. The conclusions of the study were positive, but because the NordBalt project, as it was to become known, was to be regional this raised a question about where the submarine cable should end. Both Latvia and Lithuania expressed interest in the cable ending in their territories. Latvia argued that the cable, if it connected it with Sweden would ensure that each Baltic State would have an interconnection, Estonia with Finland, Latvia with Sweden and Lithuania with Poland. After long discussions and only with the involvement of the EU in 2009 the Baltic States agreed that NordBalt would end in Klaipeda (Lithuania). The agreement was reached when the EU committed to provide funding for Latvia to develop electricity infrastructure to improve connections with Estonia (Vilpišauskas 2011: 29). In January 2009, the EU allocated €175 million for the project. The laying of the cable began in April 2014 and was inaugurated in December 2015. However, the NordBalt interconnection suffered a number of technical issues and transmission of electricity only began in February 2016 and was subsequently disrupted a number of times. Nonetheless, it has allowed for the diversification of electricity supply and the Lithuanian Ministry of Energy has plans to construct a NordBalt 2 interconnection by 2025.

The diversification also led to the creation of free electricity markets and integration of the Baltic markets with the Nordic markets. At the beginning of 2010 the BaltPool free electricity market based on the NordPool Spot rules began operation in Lithuania and Estonia joined a few months later (Molis 2011: 10). In 2012 Lithuania joined the Nord Pool Spot in which Estonia already operated, and Latvia joined in 2013, helping to complete the integration of the Nordic and Baltic electricity markets.

The 2007 Baltic Energy Strategy had outlined plans to integrate the Baltic States with the European Continental Network (UCTE) and begin synchronous operation. While this strategic goal remains unchanged, Baltic State unity has been undermined once more on the level of practical implementation, because Estonia presented an alternative suggestion to integrate with the NORDEL network, which became part of the European Continental Network (ENTSO-E). This suggestion contradicted commitments in the Energy Security Supply Declaration (2015), which stated that 'synchronization through direct interconnections between Lithuania and Poland is a prerequisite' (Lithuanian Ministry of Energy 2015). Estonia wants to proceed with Scandinavian integration because it believes there is a lack of willingness for synchronisation by Poland. Although the energy ministers from each of the participant states have agreed that the decision on which network to synchronise with should be based on the results of two independent studies, with an aim to complete synchronisation by 2025. In June 2017, it was decided that the integration will proceed with ENTSO-E (with Poland), as a number of studies showed that the integration with the Continental European Network is more feasible, while Lithuania expressed moderate positions on Estonia's plans to construct the LNG terminal.

Integration with the European electricity network raises concerns for Russia, who would like to prevent the Baltic States leaving BRELL. In October 2015 President Putin threatened the Baltic States, if they decided to synchronise with other networks, suggesting that they would have to pay fines and cover expenses for Russia, because it will have to restructure the grid and additionally invest in its system, with the Kaliningrad exclave proving a particular challenge. It was suggested that synchronisation of the Baltic States with the European Continental Network would cost up to €1 billion. The independent studies suggest that to switch off the Baltic States from BRELL could cost up to €700 million including converters at the border with Kaliningrad and additional electricity generation sources, while Putin claimed it will cost €2.5 billion (see Fuks 2015; 15min.lt 2015). However, the BRELL treaty signed in 2001 does not foresee financial burdens for any party withdrawing from the treaty provided it gives six-month advance notification (BRELL Agreement 2001).[5]

Although proposals for diversification of electricity supplies were raised in the 1990s, they only became a reality after the Baltic States joined the EU. This shows the political and economic importance of the EU in helping to implement regional projects by providing funding and exerting political pressure on the three states to cooperate when possible. However, the lack of cooperation continues to be exposed in the questions of synchronisation of the Baltic States electricity networks and Russia continues to seek influence in the region's electricity sector, something that is also the case in the natural gas sector.

10.6.3 The natural gas sector

The Baltic States inherited a modern, but isolated natural gas infrastructure. As part of the Soviet Union, the three countries were also part of a single supplier network, but with independence found that they had to establish and privatise national natural gas companies to control import, transportation and distribution. Gas companies in Russia were keen to acquire the gas infrastructure in the Baltic region and as part of the privatisation process, the three Baltic States ended up selling most of the shares in their national gas companies to Russian companies as a consequence of isolation from European networks, reality of existing links and the assumption that by selling to Russian companies it would ensure stability of supply and low prices.

Estonia's AS Eesti Gaas was established in 1992 and initially, the state owned 70 per cent of the shares and in 1993 it started privatisation which was completed in 1999. After privatisation, the largest shareholder in AS Eesti Gaas was Gazprom – 37.02 per cent, E.ON Ruhrgas Energie AG which is strategic Gazprom partner in Germany and shareholder in the Nord Stream pipeline owned 33.66 per cent, Finnish Fortum Oil and Gas Oy owned 17.72 per cent, while Itera Latvia (of Russian capital) owned 9.85 per cent, and minor shareholders owned 1.75 per cent.

The Latvian natural gas infrastructure has strategic importance in the wider Baltic States gas infrastructure, because Latvijas Gaze also owns the Inčukalns natural gas storage facility which can serve as a temporary natural gas supplier for the Baltic States. Latvijas Gaze was privatised in 1997 and a 20-year supply contract with Gazprom was signed. Until January 2016 the biggest shareholder was E.ON with 47.23 per cent,[6] Gazprom with 34 per cent, Latvian Government with 16 per cent, and other investors with 2.77 per cent (Latvijas Gaze 2016).

In 2004 Gazprom purchased 34 per cent of Lithuania's Lietuvos Dujos and later increased its shareholding to 37.1 per cent, while its strategic partner E.ON Ruhrgas bought 34 per cent of shares in 2003 and later increased that to 38.9 per cent, the state retained 17.7 per cent, with the rest being controlled by minor shareholders. There has been an argument that the shares were sold below market price. Gazprom paid only €29 million and E.ON Ruhrgas approximately €33.6 million, yet by 2011 Gazprom's share was worth more than €127 million (delfi.lt 2011).

The expectations of the Baltic States that the inclusion of Russian companies in the ownership structure of their natural gas companies would ensure lower prices or stability of supply has not always been fulfilled. The prices paid for directly imported Russian natural gas increased sharply following the removal of subsidies and since then have often been higher when compared to prices of Russian gas purchased at the German border. The disruption of natural gas supply in other post-Soviet states, including Belarus, Ukraine, Moldova, and Georgia in the period of 2004–2009 also indicated that even Russia's strategic dependence on gas transit does not prevent Moscow from shutting down supplies. The reaction of the EU towards the events in Eastern neighbourhood and the introduction of the Third Energy Package in September 2009 created instruments for ownership unbundling through separation of activities, allowing the Baltic States to move forward with the supply diversification, and abandon *Gazprom*'s monopoly.

Kaveshnikov (2010: 592) argues that 'the Third [energy] Package increased state control over the energy sector' and Česnakas (2013: 130) has also suggested that in order to increase immunity to threats in the energy sector there is a need for expansion of state control in the importing country. The Third Energy Package allowed for the Baltic States to do precisely that and, in doing so, readdress the privatisation processes that they had previously undertaken. As it can be observed, the liberalisation and diversification projects were discussed and implemented at the same time. The Third Energy

Package played to the interests of the Baltic States, because the responsibility for the implementation could be transferred to the EU and to some extent this prevented direct confrontation with Russia, although it did not necessarily work out that way, as Lithuania found out when it sought arbitration against Gazprom's pricing strategy.

10.6.4 Arbitrating energy security

Lithuania sought to implement the Third Energy Package in full and in 2010 the Lithuanian Parliament adopted a law dividing Lietuvos Dujos into two companies – Lietuvos Dujos and Amber Grid. The companies were separated in 2013.[7] While implementing the separation in 2012, Lithuania brought a claim before the Arbitration Institute of the Stockholm Chamber of Commerce (SCC), concerning unfair natural gas prices by supplier Gazprom. Lithuania claimed that Gazprom had made a commitment to supply gas at a fair price, subject to the energy resources market in Lithuania and in accordance with prices of alternative fuels. This had been set out under the privatisation agreement of Lietuvos Dujos, but the gas formula was later changed several times. In 2010 Gazprom provided discounts on gas imports for Estonia and Latvia, but not for Lithuania, because it had implemented the Third Energy package. The suggestion was that Gazprom was using discounts as a 'carrot' and 'stick' tactic to discourage Estonia and Latvia from following Lithuania in a similar way. As it was, both these countries responded by seeking exemptions from the EU gas directive.

In 2014, the SCC ruled that Gazprom did have a conflict of interest in holding shares in Lietuvos Dujos and supplying gas at the same time, but it was difficult the claim that it was not supplying gas at a fair price. The Lithuanian Government argued within the SCC case that Gazprom should be forced to pay €1.4 billion to Lithuania – the sum which it claimed had accumulated as a consequence of overpriced natural gas in the period of 2004–2012 (delfi.lt 2016). In order to justify the positive outcomes of the case at SCC, the Government argued that the claim allowed it to buy Lietuvos Dujos and Amber Grid shares from Gazprom in June 2014 for €120.8 million,[8] complete the implementation of the Third Energy Package, and negotiate a reduced gas price (closer to the level paid at the German border) and for it to be paid retrospectively from 2013 until the end of 2015, allowing a saving of €231.7 million.

In September 2012, the European Commission's Directorate General for Competition began an antitrust investigation against Gazprom pricing practices related to perceived abuse of dominance on the Central and Eastern European gas markets. Lithuanian complaints were behind the initiation of this investigation. In April 2015 the European Commission (2015) stated that 'some of its [Gazprom's] business practices in Central and Eastern European gas markets constitute an abuse of its dominant market position in breach of EU antitrust rules'. The Commission also stated that Gazprom imposed territorial restrictions, and unfair pricing policy.

Lithuania was also the subject of a case bought to the UN Hague Arbitrary Tribunal by Gazprom in 2012. Gazprom argued that Lithuania violated the original privatisation treaty's attraction of investments, but in April 2015 withdrew the case after selling its shares in the Lithuanian company (Fuks and Karaliūnaitė 2015). At the end of 2015 a long-term gas supply agreement with Gazprom also ended, enabling Lithuania to freely choose natural gas importers based on prices, via short-term and spot contracts. Data provided by the Ministry of Energy shows that Lithuania imported only 25 per cent of gas from Russia in the first six months of 2016.[9]

As previously mentioned, Estonia and Latvia had initially sought an exemption from the EU gas directive. In the case of Estonia this did not last and it began to move forward with unbundling from 2012, when it passed a law to sell Eesti Gaas–owned pipelines by 2015. Latvia was the country least favouring unbundling as it enjoyed lower natural gas prices because of Gazprom's dominance and ownership of gas storage facilities. In February 2013, the Latvian Parliament postponed gas market liberalisation. This decision was to some extent related to gas price discounts provided by Gazprom. Arguing that an open market would drive prices up, Latvijas Gaze lobbied the Latvian Parliament to leave the company without separation of activities and to allow Gazprom to remain the sole supplier of natural gas. It was not possible to maintain this position and in February 2016 the Latvian Parliament passed the final amendments to an energy law to liberalise the gas market and break up Latvijas Gaze splitting company into two as of April 2017 (LSM.LV 2016). Latvijas Gaze has argued that the liberalisation timetable was not reasonable and requested the Latvian president to return the law to the Parliament, because in the company's assessment it was 'unconstitutional and contradictory to the Latvian government's obligations to the natural gas company and its shareholders' (LETA 2016).

The implementation of the Third Energy Package has ironically strengthened state power in the energy sector and the liberalisation of the natural gas supply in mid- to long-term perspectives has had a positive effect on moving towards the creation of a fully functioning natural gas market in the region. In fact, moves towards this were already being made in October 2015 when Lithuanian and Latvian ministers signed a memorandum of understanding to create a common natural gas market. Lithuania and Estonia already traded some gas, but because prices are very similar broader trade within the Baltic region was not active. Overall, it has been a combination of national interest and the necessity to adhere to EU decisions that has enabled the Baltic States to move into the market direction in energy sector, often at the expense of Russian business interests.

10.7 Diversification of the natural gas supply

The creation of a natural gas market in the region is impossible if there is only one supplier. The project that created the most discussions between the

Baltic States was the regional liquefied natural gas terminal (LNGT). Of the three countries, Latvia was the least active in searching for alternative natural gas supplies, because of its agreements with Gazprom (Winnerstig 2014: 107) and associated discounts. But Latvia recognised that a regional LNGT would benefit it by providing easy access to the existing and possibly expanded storage facility in Inčuklans. Latvia failed to persuade Estonia and Lithuania to build the regional LNGT in its territory because of their lack of confidence in Latvia, who they believed had traditionally succumbed to Gazprom's lobby (Brauna 2014: 18–20) and that LNGT would serve Gazprom's interests due to its shareholdings in Inčuklans. The model of thinking 'what is ours is safe, what is others' is dangerous' (Česnakas 2013: 133–4) dominated the belief that Riga could never be a suitable location and promoted national project ideas as alternatives. A 2012 study ordered by the European Commission suggested that Finland was the most suitable location for a LNGT in the Baltic region, providing a natural gas pipeline is constructed to Estonia. In 2014 Finland and Estonia announced plans to construct two LNGTs, but the European Commission refused to finance two terminals, thus preventing the project from moving ahead. The Commission also refused to finance any local-scale terminals, because it would likely prevent a common position on a regional project and the financial means would not be used in the most efficient way as projects will duplicate one another.

Research on the possibility of constructing an LNG terminal in Lithuania began in 2004, but it was not until 2010 once it had become clear that negotiations between the Baltic States had stalled that the Lithuanian government decided to implement its own national LNGT project to be based at Klaipėda (Molis and Česnakas 2015: 30–33). Lithuania chose to have a floating storage regasification unit, rather than a land-based LNGT. In February 2014, it was named 'Independence' to indicate the end of dependency on Russian gas supplies and in December 2014 it became commercially operational. The LNGT in Klaipėda was supported by the European Commission which authorised €448 million aid (European Commission 2013). This funding was possible because Lithuania argued that the terminal's regasification capacity of 4 bcm almost matches the annual consumption of gas by the Baltic States and thus could act as a regional hub. Estonia, Finland and Latvia still plan to construct three other LNGTs, but cooperation to share financial commitments and use the Klaipėda LNGT as regional terminal and energy security instrument would probably be more rational. Such an approach is validated by regional gas pipeline development and the development of interconnections with other regions. Such projects include the bidirectional 2 bcm capacity Balticconnector pipeline between Finland and Estonia, which is expected to be completed in 2019.

Other regional pipeline diversification projects include the Gas Interconnector Poland–Lithuania (GIPL) pipeline which is a joint venture between Lithuanian Amber Grid, Polish GAZ-SYSTEM S.A. and the Innovation and Networks Executive Agency. GIPL is intended to allow supply to Baltic

States of 2.4 bcm of natural gas annually, and will also ensure reverse supply of 2 bcm. It was expected that the project would be completed by 2020, while later expansion of the pipeline could allow an increase of gas supply capacity to the Baltic States up to 4.1 bcm (Lithuanian Ministry of Energy 2015). This project is also part of BEMIP and ENTSO-G plan of 2013–2022. However, in September 2016 it was announced that Poland had decided to change the pipeline route delaying the project by 2.5 years. There have been suggestions that the decision to change the route was connected not to the environmental concerns in Poland, but to the Polish oil company, Orlen, and its interest to secure discounts from Lithuanian Railways for the transportation of oil and oil products. Once more this indicates how regional interests are undermined by individual (company) and state interests, hindering more rapid achievement of energy security for the region. Nonetheless, once completed the interconnectors with Finland and Poland will create unprecedented connectivity for the Baltic States enabling natural gas to move in the EU North–South direction and vice versa. At the same time Klaipėda LNGT could serve as a gas transit terminal to other regions outside the Baltic States, and the development of the interconnections will diminish necessity for alternative LNGTs in the region, especially when the decreasing consumption of natural gas in the Baltic States due to the investments in biomass, expansion of wind power and increasing energy efficiency is taken into consideration.

10.8 Diversification of resources in the region

The diversification of natural gas supplies, as well as increasing connectivity in the region's electricity sector only partly completes the story of increasing energy security of the Baltic States. The expansion of renewable energy allows for decreasing imports of natural gas and electricity from Russia and increasing sustainability and security.

The Baltic States have significantly expanded electricity generation from renewable resources. By 2014, Estonia had increased electricity generation up to 14.6 per cent (from 0.6 per cent in 2004), Latvia 51.1 per cent (from 46 per cent in 2004) and Lithuania to 13.7 per cent (from 3.6 per cent in 2004). This was due to the expansion of wind farms, solar generation and increased use of wood fuel and hydropower. Expansion of the consumption of biomass also played significant role in decreasing natural gas consumption in the Baltic States. New district heating systems fuelled by biomass were constructed between 2009 and 2013, and numerous waste fuelled plants were also built.

The expansion of renewable resources changes the energy generation and supply systems in the Baltic States; however, these changes are not associated with big projects linked to the diversification of electricity and gas supplies. EU financial support allows for increasing production of renewable resources and this is expected to continue in relation to EU regulations.

One area where success in maximising the benefits of alternative energy sources has been limited and which highlights the challenges of national decision making is shale gas. It is projected that in the case of Lithuania there might be around 100–120 bcm of technically recoverable shale gas (Natural Gas World 2015). In June 2012, the Lithuanian Geologic Survey announced an international competition for the survey and production of shale gas and shale oil in two prospects in western Lithuania. For the survey and extraction in the prospect Šilutė-Tauragė (where the best possibilities to find resources) only one energy corporation, Chevron (based in the United States), participated and won the competition. A massive campaign against the development of shale gas and oil production which was initiated in by the local NIMBY group gained national attention and was supported by the Lithuanian Green Party (Lietuvos žaliųjų partija). At the same time the Lithuanian Parliament initiated proposals to increase taxation on shale gas and oil extraction to 40 per cent, up from 16 per cent originally. In October 2013 Chevron announced its withdrawal from prospection of shale resources, arguing that the decision was based on the likely unfavourable regulation and taxation environment. It is worth noting that Chevron withdrew from other shale gas projects in Central and Eastern Europe due to falling prices and difficult geological conditions, but national policy decisions have played a significant role, including the wholesale abandonment of exploration and production plans, such as that put forward by Lithuania in 2015.

10.9 Conclusions

In little over a quarter of a century the Baltic States have improved their energy security as crucial interconnection, diversification and renewable resources production projects have been completed or are expected to be completed. The region has become more resilient to the external threats as dependency on Russia's resources has decreased and market-based rules expanded. From being part of a closed Soviet-era energy system, the Baltic States have become integrated into European networks.

Though the European Union exerts significant pressure on the Baltic States, this pressure has led to increasing energy efficiency, resource diversification, contributed to decreasing GHG emissions and, overall, greater self-sufficiency. The EU has also provided a crucial function in increasing energy security for the region through political and financial support, as well as acting as a mediator between Estonia, Latvia and Lithuania when they fail to agree on projects. However, its success can also be limited, particularly when certain projects reflect strong national interests, such as with LNG terminals in the Baltic region.

Despite the need for greater cooperation in the region, the self-interest of the states, as well as domestic political processes have reflected a reality that is not always recognised by external observers who assume that the region maintains a collective sentiment and policy direction on energy security. Gabrielsson and Sliwa (2013: 172) provide a great summary of problems in intraregional cooperation between the Baltic States claiming that 'there is an impression that the Baltic nations were so busy in building relations with partners out of region that they had forgotten to build relations inside the region'. There is a perception of the region as a unit in broader geoenergetic sense, yet problems such as the location of LNG terminal, the NordBalt cable, synchronisation and of course failure to implement the Visaginas NPP project illustrate a lack of efficient cooperation limitation to the extent of the region as a single unit. The causes of problems are many: a desire to host infrastructure within the country; lack of trust in neighbours as well as lack of support on the various issues each of the countries are concerned about; and domestic policy changes particularly between administrations that have changed following an election. The over politicisation of projects, influence of energy companies on politicians, corruption and lack of competences to act in certain areas has also led to problems in ensuring energy security and at times encouraged states to rely on themselves to increase energy security.

The implementation of energy security projects, with the exception of the oil terminal in Būtingė, intensified only after the Baltic States joined the EU. It would be difficult to expect that countries going through a difficult transition period would be able to address all issues, and although energy security was an important issue, it was overwhelmed by other goals. These included integration into the international community, membership of the EU and NATO, stabilisation of the economy and return of growth, addressing social issues and building national institutions. It is logical that energy security was addressed only after problems in these areas have been dealt with more or less successfully.

On reflection, it is clear that while Russia has had influence in the region, it is the continued support of the EU and cooperation within the region that has enabled existing energy security projects to proceed. However, to avoid having excessive infrastructure and white elephant projects that undermine national and regional energy security it will be necessary for Estonia, Latvia and Lithuania to overcome mistrust and self-interest and search for closer cooperation.

Notes

1 With Nordbalt and other projects Lithuania significantly improved it energy security position. Data from 2015 shows that it nearly reached level of security of Latvia and Estonia.
2 ENTSO-E was established on 18 December 2008, connecting UCTE, NORDEL and other transmission system operators. In this chapter ENTSO-E will refer to continental European networks – previously UCTE, while NORDEL will be addressed separately for clarity.
3 Prior to the 2008 Lithuanian parliamentary election there was an initiative to collect 50,000 citizen signatures to force an extension to the operation of Ignalina to 2015, however, the groups failed to collect the required signatures. Instead a binding referendum was held together with the parliamentary election and although 88.59 per cent of participants voted to extend the NPP operation, turnout fell below the legally binding requirement.

4 Lithuanian electricity distribution networks have been geographically divided into two companies Vakarų skirstomieji tinklai (Western Distribution Networks – VST) and Rytų skirstomieji tinklai (Eastern Distribution Networks – EST). In 2003 VST was privatised by NDX Energija, which was owned by major retail group in Lithuania and the Baltic States – VP grupė. The conditions for privatisation set in such a way that only two business groups in Lithuania VP grupė and Achema (the biggest chemical company in the Baltic States) could participate in the competition for privatisation. In 2004, the Law on Electricity Energy artificially boosted value of the VST three times.
5 Agreement between concern 'Belenergo', AS 'Latvenergo', RAO 'UESRussia', AS 'EestiEnergia' and AS 'Lietuvos Energija' on parallel work of energy system, 7 February 2001, available at: http://so-ups.ru/fileadmin/files/company/international/icdevelopment/BRELL/BRELL_Agreement.pdf, accessed 14 August 2017.
6 In January 28, 2016, E.ON owned 18.26 % of shares, while 28.97 % have been sold to European Union infrastructure investment fund Marguerite.
7 In October 2014 Lietuvos dujos was separated into two companies – Lietuvos Dujos responsible for distribution and Lietuvos Duju Tiekimas (Lithuanian Gas Supply) responsible for supply; the company was transferred to the ownership of Lietuvos Energija.
8 E.ON Ruhrgas sold its shares in Lietuvos Dujos and Amber Grid in May 2014 for €113.2 million.
9 Information provided in the correspondence with representative of the Ministry of Energy of the Republic of Lithuania.

References

Alehno, O. (2012). 'Dovydo pergalė prieš Galijotą', *Geopolitika*, 10 November. Available at: www.geopolitika.lt/?artc=5634, accessed 16 August 2017.

Augutis J., V. Leonavičius, R. Krikštolaitis, S. Pečiulytė, D. Genys, G. Česnakas, L. Martišauskas, and J. Juozaitis (2016). *Lithuanian Energy Security: Annual Review 2014–2015*. (Kanus: Vytautas Magnus University, Versus Aureus).

Balmaceda, M.M. (2008). 'Corruption, Intermediary Companies, and Energy Security Lithuania's Lessons for Central and Eastern Europe', *Problems of Post-Communism*, 55(4), July/August, pp. 16–28.

BNS. (2016). 'Lithuania's €1.4bn Claim against Gazprom Rejected by Stockholm Arbitration Court', *delfi.lt*, available at: http://en.delfi.lt/lithuania/energy/lithuanias-14bn-claim-against-gazprom-rejected-by-stockholm-arbitration-court.d?id=71628970, accessed 29 August 2017.

Brauna, A. (2014). 'Gas market. Is it really opened?', *IR*, 2–8 January.

Butkevičius, A. (2012). 'Visagino atominė elektrinė – nerealus projektas', *alfa.lt*, available at: http://www.alfa.lt/straipsnis/15068458/butkevicius-visagino-atomine-elektrine-nerealus-projektas, accessed 29 August 2017.

Černiauskas, Šarūnas (2013). Vis dažniau „neteisingai suprastas" premjeras, *DELFI.lt*, available at: https://www.delfi.lt/news/ringas/lit/s-cerniauskas-vis-dazniau-neteisingai-suprastas-premjeras.d?id=61225173, accessed 14 December 2017.

Česnakas, G. (2012). 'Energy Security in the Baltic-Black Sea Region: Energy Insecurity Sources and their Impact upon States', *Lithuanian Annual Strategic Review 2011–2012*, 10.

Česnakas, G. (2013). 'Energy Security Challenges, Concepts and the Controversy of Energy Nationalism in Lithuanian Energy Politics', *Baltic Journal of Law & Politics* 6(1), pp. 106–139.

ELTA. (2011). 'Išaugo 'Gazprom' dujų eksportas į Europos šalis', *delfi.lt*, available at: http://www.delfi.lt/verslas/energetika/isaugo-gazprom-duju-eksportas-i-europos-salis. d?id=47133627, accessed 29 August 2017.
European Commission. (2006). 'Green Paper: A European Strategy for Sustainable, Competitive and Secure Energy'. *Commission of the European Communities*. Available at: http://europa.eu/documents/comm/green_papers/pdf/com2006_105_en.pdf, accessed 16 August 2017.
European Commission. (2013). 'State Aid: Commission Authorises €448 Million Aid for Construction of Lithuanian LNG Terminal', Press Release, 20 November. Available at: http://europa.eu/rapid/press-release_IP-13-1124_en.htm, accessed 29 August 2017.
European Commission. (ed.) (2014). *EU Energy Markets in 2014*. (Luxembourg: Publications Office of the European Union).
European Commission. (2015). 'Antitrust: Commission Sends Statement of Objections to Gazprom for Alleged Abuse of Dominance on Central and Eastern European Gas Supply Markets', *European Commission Press Release*, 22 April 2015. Available at: http://europa.eu/rapid/press-release_IP-15-4828_en.htm, accessed 29 August 2017.
European Council. (2014). *2013 Climate and Energy Policy Framework*. Available at: http://data.consilium.europa.eu/doc/document/ST-169-2014-INIT/en/pdf, accessed 16 August 2017.
Fuks, E. and Karaliūnaitė, U. (2015). 'Gazprom atsiėmė ieškinį prieš Lietuvą', *DELFI*, 2 April. Available at: www.delfi.lt/verslas/energetika/gazprom-atsieme-ieski ni-pries-lietuva.d?id=67611800, accessed 29 August 2017.
Gabrielsson, R. and Sliwa, Z. (2013). 'Baltic Region Energy Security: The Trouble with European Solidarity', *Baltic Security & Defence Review*, 5(2), pp. 144–184.
Goldman, M.I. (2008). *Petrostate: Putin, Power and the New Russia*. (Oxford: Oxford University Press).
Grigas, A. (2013). 'Energy Policy: The Achilles Heel of the Baltic States', in Grigas, A., Kasekamp, A., Maslauskaite, K., Zorgenfreija, L. and Buzek, J. (eds), *The Baltic states in the EU: yesterday, today and tomorrow*, Studies & Reports No 98, Notre Europe – Jacques Delors Institute, July.
Janeliūnas, T. (2009) 'Lithuanian Energy Strategy and its Implications on Regional Cooperation', in Sprūds, A. and Rostoks, T. (eds), *Energy: Pulling the Baltic Sea Region together or apart?* (Riga: Zinatne). pp. 190–222.
Kaveshnikov, N. (2010) 'The Issue of Energy Security in Relations between Russia and the European Union', *European Security*, 19(4), pp. 585–605.
Larsson, R.L. (2006) *Russia's Energy Policy: Security Dimensions and Russia's reliability as Energy Supplier* (Stockholm: FOI-Swedish Defence Research Agency).
Latvijas Gaze. (2016). 'Shareholder Change – Shareholders and Investors'. Available at: www.lg.lv/index.php?id=199&lid=1747&search=E.on, accessed on 29 August 2017.
LETA. (2016). 'Latvian Parliament Speaker Promulgates Amendments to Energy Law', 22 February. Available at: www.leta.lv/eng/home/important/1339EDE9-B5 DE-F233-5D4D-E2A82BF330CE/, accessed 29 August 2017.
Leijonhielm, J. and Larsson, R.L. (2004). *Russia's Strategic Commodities: Energy and Metals as Security Levers*. (Stockholm: FOI).
Lelyveld. (2003). 'Russia: Moscow Seeks Takeover of Latvian Oil Port', *Radio Free Europe/Radio Liberty*, 12 February. Available at: https://www.rferl.org/a/1102205. html, accessed 17 August 2017.

Lietuvos Respublikos Konstitucinis Teimas. (2009). 'Nutarimai, išvados ir sprendimai', available at: http://www.lrkt.lt/lt/teismo-aktai/nutarimai-isvados-ir-sprendimai/138/y2009, accessed 29 August 2017.

Lithuanian Ministry of Energy. (2015). *Energy Security of Supply Declaration*. 14 January, Riga.

LSM.LV. (2016). 'Gas Utility Shareholders Approve Split by April 2017', 22 March 2016. Available at: http://eng.lsm.lv/article/society/society/gas-utility-shareholders-approve-split-by-april-2017.a174741/, accessed 29 August 2017.

Mäe, A. (2007). 'Estonia's Energy Security and the EU', in A. Kasekamp (ed.), *The Estonian Foreign Policy Yearbook 2007*. (Tallinn: Estonian Foreign Policy Institute). pp. 91–119.

Martina, I. and Bogdanas, R. (2012). 'Inside Vladimir Antonov's Reckless Gamble with the Baltic Banks', *The Baltic Times*, 13 June. Available at: www.baltictimes.com/news/articles/31406/, accessed 29 August 2017.

Minister of Energy. (2016). 'Recommended Key Guidelines of the National Energy Strategy of Lithuania'. Approved by the order of the *Minister of Energy of the Republic of Lithuania*, 24 November, No. 1–314.

Molis, A. (2011). 'Rethinking EU-Russia Energy Relations: What do the Baltic States Want?', *SPES Policy Papers*, February.

Molis, A., and Česnakas, G. (2015). 'Reducing Energy Reliance', *per Concordiam*, 6(2), pp. 30–33.

Natural Gas World (ed.) (2015). 'Lithuania Puts Off Shale Gas Plans Indefinitely', *Natural Gas World*, 3 November. Available at: www.naturalgasworld.com/lithuania-shale-gas-delay-postponed-indefinitely-26145, accessed 29 August 2017.

OECD. (2017). 'Estonia Should Reduce its Oil Shale Reliance for Greener Growth', available at: www.oecd.org/estonia/estonia-should-reduce-its-oil-shale-reliance-for-greener-growth.htm, accessed 16 August 2017.

Raukas, A. (2004) 'Opening a New Decade', *Oil Shale*, 21(1), pp. 1–2.

Smith, K.C. (2004). *Russian Energy Politics in the Baltics, Poland and Ukraine: A New Stealth Imperialism?* (Washington, DC: Center for Strategic & International Studies).

TBT Staff. (2005). 'Intrigue around Mazeikiu Nafta Sale Increases as Kremlin Puts Squeeze on Kazakh Bidder', *The Baltic Times*, 23 November. Available at: www.baltictimes.com/news/articles/14091/, accessed 16 August 2017.

Tere. (2009). 'Estonian Government Confirmed its Plan to Establish a Nuclear Power Plant by 2023', *The Baltic Course*, 26 February. Available at: www.baltic-course.com/eng/energy/?doc=10359, accessed 29 August 2017.

Tvaskienė. (2009). 'Grėsmės šaliai grimzta užmarštin', *Lietuvos žinios*, 21 January. Available at: http://lzinios.lt/lzinios/lietuva/gresmes-saliai-grimzta-uzmarstin/127142, accessed 16 August 2017.

Vilpišauskas, R. (2011). 'National Preferences and Bargaining of the New Member States Since the Enlargement of the EU: the Baltic States – Still Policy Takers?', *Lithuanian Foreign Policy Review*, 25.

Vitkus, G. (2009). 'Russian Pipeline Diplomacy: A Lithuanian Response', *ActaSlavicaIaponica* (26), pp. 25–46.

Winnerstig, M. (2014). *Tools of Destabilization. Russian Soft Power and Non-military Influence in the Baltic States* (FOI). Available at: http://appc.lv/wp-content/uploads/2014/12/FOI_Non_military.pdf, accessed 16 August 2017.

11 Serbia

Milos Damnjanovic

11.1 Introduction

On the face of it, Serbia could be thought of as a country that enjoys a reasonably high degree of energy security. In the simplest of terms, such a conclusion can be drawn from the fact that, compared to most other European states, it imports a relatively small proportion of the sources of energy that it uses. When we compare energy dependency rates for 2013 – which reflect the proportion of energy that a country must import, with a dependency rate of 23.58 per cent Serbia compares very well to the other European Union (EU) member states, where the average dependency rate for the entire EU-28 stood at 53.2 per cent in the same year.

Scratching beneath the surface reveals a more complex picture however. As this chapter will show, vulnerability – primarily understood in the sense of dependency, actual or potential, on other states or actors – is unevenly distributed across the Serbian energy sector. While Serbia is most vulnerable when it comes to natural gas supply, the vast bulk of which must be imported, this represent a relatively low share in the country's overall energy mix. By comparison, the country is almost completely self-sufficient in coal, which accounts for over half of its energy mix.

Energy security is, of course, not just a matter of how self-sufficient a country is in terms of energy resources, but also revolves around questions such as the diversity, or lack thereof, of sources and routes through which it can import energy. It can also be examined through the lens of whether energy companies and domestic natural resources are state-owned – in which case a valid question is, how well managed they are – or, whether they are in private hands – in which case a pertinent question is perhaps to what extent ownership is concentrated or diversified. Here the picture of Serbia's energy security is more worrisome. Imports of natural gas still come from a single source – Russia's Gazprom – and through a single pipeline. Moreover, thanks to a 2008 privatisation deal in which Gazprom bought a controlling stake in Serbian energy company, Naftna Industrija Srbije (NIS), the Russian company controls Serbia's oil and gas extraction, as well as its oil refining capacities and much of its oil retail sector.

In the case of Serbia, as this chapter will show, while it can be said to enjoy a relatively high degree of energy security, there are certain points of vulnerability, perhaps best understood in the sense of the country being susceptible to pressure from outside actors who possess leverage, or potential leverage, over the country as a result of dependency relationships in certain parts of the energy sector. What makes Serbia a particularly interesting case study – and perhaps sets it out from other countries – is the way that political considerations (and gambles) over the last decade have made this vulnerability much more acute, leading to an increase in energy insecurity. This is a direct consequence of the transfer of most of the Serbian oil and natural gas sector into the hands of one (Russian) company – Gazprom.

Having set out the basics of Serbia's energy (in)security, the chapter proceeds by examining three distinct time periods in Serbia's energy relations with Russia, which are, among other things, reflected in the presence or absence of middle companies in the supply of natural gas to Serbia. The bulk of the chapter focuses on what became known in Serbia as the 'deal of the century', the Inter-Governmental Agreement between Serbia and Russia, signed in early 2008. Presented as a great triumph of Serbia's political leadership that would increase the country's energy security and bring huge investments and revenues, the deal was a huge gamble for Belgrade in which it ultimately lost out and increased its energy insecurity by handing over its oil and gas sector to Gazprom. The chapter concludes by addressing the puzzle of why the Serbian leadership embarked on this gamble and why it chose to sell the whole of NIS to Gazprom.

11.2 Serbia's energy (in)security: the basics

When discussing energy security in the Serbian context, it is important to frame the discussion appropriately from the beginning, particularly when it comes to natural gas. Within the overall energy mix of the country in 2013,[1] natural gas accounted for only 12.45 per cent of the energy mix, while crude oil and petroleum products accounted for 23.34 per cent. By contrast, coal amounted for 52.86 per cent of the country's energy mix, the rest coming mainly from hydro and other renewable sources.[2] In terms of import dependence, the picture is mixed; in 2013, primary production accounted for 96.78 per cent of the coal mix and 36.8 per cent of the crude oil and petroleum products mix (the figure is slightly higher if we exclude petroleum products and focus only on crude oil and other hydrocarbons, 40.88 per cent), while the situation was least favourable in the natural gas sector, with primary production accounting for only 22.66 per cent of the natural gas mix.[3] Overall, Serbia meets around two-thirds of its energy needs from domestic sources and production, with coal being by far the most important input.

When it comes to electricity production, only 0.45 per cent of electricity generated in Serbia in 2013 came from natural gas-powered plants. The vast majority (70.89 per cent) was generated by coal-powered plants, while the remaining 28.66 per cent of electricity was generated by hydro or other renewable energy sources (RES).[4] Furthermore, electricity generation and coal mining remain almost entirely in the hands of the state-owned electricity generator Elektroprivreda Srbije (EPS). If we consider natural gas consumption, in 2013 around one-third of natural gas consumed was used in municipal heating plants which provide central heating to households during the winter, while another 37.94 per cent was used by industry. Households consumed only 9.32 per cent of natural gas used, while the remainder was primarily used in the energy sector (for example, oil and gas extraction, or refineries).[5] However, in the context of energy security discussions, it is worth noting that the vast majority of heating plants have the ability to switch to other forms of energy in the event of a natural gas shortage.

Another way of looking at Serbia's energy security is through energy dependency rates, which show the proportion of energy that an economy must import. In this respect, with a dependency rate of 23.58 per cent in 2013, Serbia compares quite well to the EU-28 average dependency rate of 53.2 per cent in the same year (Eurostat 2015). Viewed in this way, Serbia could be said to be reasonably secure from an energy point of view. This is also a significant improvement compared to the period before 2009, when Gazprom came into possession of NIS, the vertically integrated national company engaged in oil and gas extraction, oil refining and retail. For the sake of comparison, in 2005 Serbia's import dependency rate was 35.26 per cent. In the following years, Gazprom invested considerably in NIS's domestic oil and gas extraction, increasing the proportion of domestically extracted natural gas from 11.76 per cent of natural gas used in 2005 to 22.66 per cent in 2013. When it comes to crude oil, the share of domestically extracted crude oil increased from 17.43 per cent in 2005 to 40.88 per cent in 2013.[6] While this certainly decreased Serbia's energy import dependency and by extension increased its energy security, it also means that Serbia's limited reserves of oil and natural gas are being depleted at an accelerating rate. When it comes to oil, according to the Serbian government's *Strategy for the Development of the Energy Sector until 2025*, adopted in late 2015, Serbia's known oil reserves were around 50 million tonnes of oil equivalent (toe). With around 1.1 million tonnes of crude oil extracted in 2013, Serbia's known oil reserves could be depleted in less than half a century if this rate of extraction were maintained.

However, it must be noted that the picture looks less positive when we consider energy transport infrastructure, primarily in the natural gas sector. Serbia currently imports natural gas via a single pipeline, through which Russian gas is piped via Ukraine and Hungary. This severely limits Serbia's options not only in terms of whom it can buy natural gas from, but also how it can receive it. With an annual capacity of around 3.6 billion cubic metres (bcm) and daily capacity of round 11.2 million cubic metres (mcm) on which Serbia can draw upon,[7] the pipeline more-or-less meets Serbia's needs; although in winter months, when demand is at its peak, supply has struggled to keep up with demand historically (Ministry of Energy, Development and Environmental Protection 2013: 36).

Just how dangerous such a situation can be became evident in 2009 when Russia's Gazprom suspended deliveries of gas via Ukraine for 13 days due to a dispute with Ukraine over debt payments for gas supplies. This completely cut off deliveries to many European clients, including Serbia. With no alternative supply routes and extremely limited natural gas storage capacity, Serbian officials were left scrambling to secure alternative deliveries of gas. What limited natural gas was available was reserved for priority users, with the situation being alleviated to some extent when emergency supplies of gas were secured from storage facilities in Hungary and Germany (see Borović 2009a; Borović 2009b; Mihajlović 2009). Since then, the situation has improved because Gazprom and Srbijagas have developed the Banatski Dvor storage facility, which can accommodate 450 mcm of natural gas, providing a buffer against supply shocks (Ministry of Energy, Development and Environmental Protection 2013: 40).

There is also another, more worrying angle to the story, which highlights Serbia's energy dependence not just on Russia, but, ultimately, on one Russian company – Gazprom. In the natural gas sector, Gazprom provides the entirety of Serbia's imports. Nor does Serbia have much independent control over its gas storage capacities. As a result of the 2008 Inter-Governmental Agreement (IGA) between Serbia and Russia, Gazprom gained a 51 per cent stake in the country's only gas storage facility, Banatski Dvor, with the other 49 per cent being held by the state-owned Srbijagas.[8] Admittedly, distribution of natural gas remains in the hands of Srbijagas, which also owns most of the domestic gas transport infrastructure.

However, the state-owned company is among the worst run public companies in Serbia, with accumulated debts in excess of €1 billion (Janković 2014) and whose inability to service them has come to threaten the stability of the public finances (Fiskalni Savet 2013: 7–8). Waste, corruption and inefficiency are just one set of problems within the company. A much bigger problem is that, during much of the recent past, for political reasons – in the interests of maintaining social peace and stability – Srbijagas was forced to sell natural gas on to buyers from the state sector (for example, heating plants or state-owned industry) at prices lower than, or around the same price as, that at which it was purchasing it. Even then, many such buyers failed to pay for the gas delivered by Srbijagas. Successive governments tolerated these practices, preferring to cover Srbijagas's losses through commercial loans for which the state provided guarantees, rather than tackle the root causes of the problem.

The situation is similar in the oil sector, with the vast majority of oil imports coming from Russia and to a lesser extent Kazakhstan.[9] As with natural gas, crude oil is transited to Serbia through one pipeline, the Adriatic Pipeline (JANAF), which brings oil from an Adriatic terminal in Croatia to Serbia's oil refineries in Pančevo and Novi Sad. Unfortunately for Serbia, the story of dependence on Russia and Gazprom does not end there. In late 2008,

Serbia sold a 51 per cent stake in its national oil company, NIS, to *GazpromNeft*.[10] In doing so, Serbia handed over its oil refining capacities along with the biggest network of filling stations in Serbia. More damagingly from an energy security point of view, along with refining capacities, Gazprom also gained control over Serbia's domestic oil and gas production. Through NIS, Gazprom came into possession of *NIS Naftagas*, a subsidiary which had previously (during the socialist period) enjoyed exclusive rights to oil and gas exploration and exploitation in Serbia. As a result, the company owned the concessions to all the known oil and gas fields in Serbia for a period of time ranging from 10 to 25 years, depending on the specific field (see Mihajlović-Milanović 2010).

In sum, Gazprom is not only the (almost exclusive) provider of oil and natural gas imports to Serbia, but also has control of the country's domestic production of both natural resources. It controls the country's oil refining capacities and most of its petrol distribution and retail network and its natural gas storage facilities. An additional source of vulnerability is the heavy indebtedness of Srbijagas to Gazprom.

11.3 (In)dependence from Russia

Serbia's current dependence, and indeed vulnerability, towards Russia, or rather one Russian company, in the energy sector is certainly not the result of historical legacies. As will be illustrated, Russia's involvement in Serbia's energy sector has ebbed and flowed in a manner that has mainly been dictated by how warm or cool political ties between the two countries have been during certain periods. What is clear is that the country's current level on dependence on Gazprom is a direct result of the policies pursued by Serbian politicians, particularly since 2007.

When looking back over the previous two decades, three distinct time periods can be identified when considering the Serbian–Russian energy relationship. Table 11.1 provides an overview of the shifting nature of political relations between Serbia and Russia during three different time periods, along with how certain characteristics of Serbia's energy sector changed in line with the changing nature of this relationship. What is particularly clear is that periods of warm political relations with Russia were accompanied by the presence of Russian intermediary companies involved in the sale of natural gas to Serbia and an increase in the prevalence of corruption scandals in the

Table 11.1 Relations with Russia and Serbia's Energy Sector

	Political Relations	State Ownership	Corruption Scandals	Middle Companies	Diversification	The Role of the EU	Ukrainian Factor
1989–2000	Warm	High	Moderate	High	Low	Low	Low
2001–2006	Cool	High	Low	Low	Low	Low	Low
2007–2014	Warm	Low/decreasing	Moderate	High	Low	Increasing	Increasing

energy sector. It also points to a link between the warming of relations between Russia and Serbia post-2006 and the decreasing state ownership within Serbia's energy sector.

11.3.1 1989–2000

The 1990s were, for the most part, a period of international isolation for Serbia, particularly in relation to the countries of the EU. For much of this time, the country was under international sanctions which either prevented or seriously restricted its ability to import oil and natural gas. While from 1992 to 1996 these sanctions were imposed at an international level by the United Nations (UN) Security Council, during the latter half of the 1990s the sanctions were imposed by the United States (US) and the EU on a bilateral basis in response to the escalating conflict in Kosovo.

During this decade, the Serbian leadership sought to build closer ties with Russia, which was reflected in the energy sector. One of the first examples of Serbo-Russian cooperation in the energy sector was the signing of a bilateral 'Agreement on Cooperation on the Construction of Natural Gas Pipelines in the Federal Republic of Yugoslavia' between the Russian and Serbian governments in April 1996. As a consequence of this agreement, *Yugorosgaz* was set up as a joint company between Gazprom (50 per cent stake) and a number of state-owned Serbian companies which controlled the remaining stake. The company's remit was to develop the gas transport and distribution infrastructure in southern and central Serbia, including the planned construction of the *Niš-Dimitrovgrad* interconnector with Bulgaria (see Mihajlović-Milanović 2008; Padejski 2011). Although Yugorosgaz can be considered an important first example of legitimate Foreign Direct Investment (FDI) and equity in terms of joint ownership of a major energy company in Serbia, there were few moves to extend this model into other areas of the energy sector, which remained state-owned throughout the rest of this period. This, however, did not mean that Russia's engagement in the Serbian energy sector was limited to only this particular project. There was engagement via other means such as secretive intermediary supply companies appearing in the energy sector. In March 1992, *Progresgas Trejding* was established as a joint company between *Gazprom Eksport* and *Progress* (a Serbian state-owned company) for the purpose of acting as an intermediary in the supply of natural gas to Serbia. The company would continue to act as an intermediary until the end of 2000 (Padejski 2011).

11.3.2 2001–2006

Following the overthrow of Slobodan Milošević in October 2000, Serbia's isolation from the West ended abruptly. Successive governments after 2000 wanted to make a clear break with the Milosevic era and reorient Serbia in a firmly pro-European direction, hence relations with Russia were allowed to cool markedly.[11] An important break with the past was the removal of middle companies from natural gas supply contracts with Gazprom, while efforts were made to improve the governance arrangements of state-owned energy companies, particularly by increasing transparency and reducing corruption (Boarov 2000; Padejski 2011).

Although the energy sector remained in state hands, the door was opened to privatisation in this period. According to interviews with Serbian officials and media reports from 2000 and 2001, Gazprom expressed an interest during this period in acquiring ownership of NIS in return for writing off Serbia's natural gas debts, but the offer was rejected (Stepanović 2001; Padejski 2011). Privatisation of NIS was firmly placed on the table thanks to the International Monetary Fund (IMF), which began insisting from early 2005 that the Serbian government initiate the process of privatising NIS in order to complete the Extended Arrangement of a stand-by agreement, previously approved in 2002.[12]

11.3.3 2007–2014

During this period, there was a deepening of ties between Russia and Serbia, primarily driven by political considerations on the Serbian side and economic interests on the Russian side. Serbia was faced with a US drive (supported by major EU countries) to resolve the status of Kosovo through independence from Serbia. Determined to do what it could to oppose and prevent this, Belgrade sought the support of Moscow in the United Nations and other international organisations in order to block Kosovo's independence.

The deepening of political and, in turn, economic ties between Belgrade and Moscow manifested itself in a number of different areas including the energy sector. From 1 January 2007, natural gas supplied to Serbia by Gazprom would once again be bought through an intermediary company, this time Yugorosgaz (Grabež 2008; Padejski 2011). However, deepening ties in the energy sector reached their pinnacle in January 2008 when, less than a month before Kosovo's declaration of independence, Serbia and Russia signed an Inter-Governmental Agreement (IGA) which envisaged the sale of Serbia's national oil company NIS to Gazprom, the construction of a joint gas storage facility in the north of the country and a commitment that the South Stream gas pipeline would be routed through Serbia.[13] On the basis of this agreement, Gazprom gained control of much of Serbia's oil and gas sector, in return for Russian support for Serbia over Kosovo and a commitment that the South Stream pipeline would be routed through Serbia. However, in the face of EU challenges to the legality of the South Stream project, the construction of South Stream was abandoned in late 2014 by the Russian side.

11.3.4 The role of intermediary companies

Intermediary companies in the supply of gas to Serbia of mixed Serbian–Russian ownership have had a colourful and controversial past. Their operations have typically been shrouded in secrecy, hence only fragments of information about them are publicly available. However, a common theme of their presence has always been inflated gas prices along with inflated salaries paid to their management, typically a mix of Gazprom executives and senior Serbian politicians or their representatives.

The first of these companies, as already noted, was Progresgas Trejding. From what is known, the company was set up in 1992 by Gazprom and Serbian (state-owned) Progress, both of which had equal stakes in the company. The initiative appears to have come from two friends and business acquaintances – Viktor Chernomyrdin, then the director of Gazprom, and Mirko Marjanović, then the director of Progress, one of Yugoslavia's biggest foreign trade companies. Interestingly, both would become prime ministers of their countries soon thereafter, positions in which they would remain for most of the 1990s. Based on fragments of information available in the media, it is thought that Progresgas Trejding's fee on natural gas supplied was around 1 per cent (Boarov 2000), or around $19 m in 2000 (Padejski 2011). However, an arguably even bigger problem was that, while Progresgas Trejding was careful to extract its fee, it was less careful about ensuring that gas deliveries from Gazprom were paid for. Indeed, until 2000, when Mirko Marjanović was still prime minister, gas deliveries were often paid from the budget or other state funds. Even so, following the overthrow of Milošević in 2000, the new government found that Progresgas Trejding had accumulated debts towards Gazprom of at least $269 mn by 2001 (Stepanović 2001).

With the democratic changes which occurred in Serbia in 2000, intermediary companies were removed from the supply of natural gas for a period of time between 2001 and 2006, with natural gas being bought directly from Gazprom by NIS, then the Serbian state-owned gas distributor. According to Srboljub Antić, who became the Minister of Energy and Mining in the new, post-Milošević government in 2000, during negotiations in Moscow in December 2000, the Serbian side took a firm stand and made it clear it would not accept the presence of intermediaries in the supply of natural gas (Boarov 2000). Quite why the Russian side was willing to accept this, given that Serbia in any case had no option but to buy natural gas from Gazprom, is not clear, but it is possible that a desire to see repayment of the large debt owed by Serbia for natural gas at that point could have influenced their decision.

An intermediary was once again introduced into the supply of natural gas to Serbia from the beginning of 2007. This time, the intermediary company would be Yugorosgaz, with media reports indicating that its fee was at least 4 per cent on the value of the gas supplied (Grabež 2008; Putniković 2008; Padejski 2011). Why an intermediary company was reintroduced is not clear, but as least one Serbian minister at the time, Mladjan Dinkić, has claimed that the Russian side made a very simple offer which boiled down to 'either Yugorosgaz or no gas' (Grabež 2008). The fact that the Serbian side had little option but to give in to Russian demands vividly illustrates the risks of being overly dependent on one supplier of natural gas and, indeed, the vulnerability which this generates.

In terms of beginning to understand why Yugorosgaz was chosen as an intermediary, it is important to note the changes in the company's ownership structure which occurred in 2006. Having started out in 1996 as a joint company in which Gazprom owned a 50 per cent stake and a number of Serbian state-owned companies owned the remaining stakes, by 2006 a Russian company called Centrex (through its subsidiary Central ME Energy and Gas GmbH) had acquired 25 per cent of shares previously owned by Serbian companies. The ownership structure of this new shareholder in Yugorosgaz is anything but transparent – while there are some claims that it is essentially a Gazprom front company, other sources indicate that the company could be owned by individuals close to senior Gazprom officials and a way of funnelling money to 'high level Russian and Austrian officials' (Kupchinsky 2008; Padejski 2011).

11.4 'The deal of the century'

Dubbed the 'deal of the century' by the Serbian leadership, the Inter-Governmental Agreement (IGA) between Russia and Serbia on cooperation in the area of oil and gas was signed on 25 January 2008 in Moscow.[14] It envisaged the following:

- The routing of (a part of) the South Stream gas pipeline through Serbia, with a minimum capacity of 10 billion cubic metres per year (later increased to 40.5 billion cubic metres);
- Completing the construction of an underground gas storage facility at Banatski Dvor (northern Serbia) on the site of an exhausted gas field, to be operated by a joint company in which Gazprom would have a 51 per cent stake and Srbijagas a 49 per cent stake;
- The sale of a 51 per cent stake in NIS to GazpromNeft at a price of €400 million, with a commitment by GazpromNeft to invest €500 million over a four-year period and a commitment by the Serbian government to retain NIS's monopoly on the wholesale of oil derivatives in Serbia for at least two years.

In arguing that the IGA was equivalent to 'the deal of the century', Serbian and Russian officials, as well as friendly political commentators and analysts in Serbia, put forward a number of arguments centred on the idea that the agreement would increase Serbia's energy security, bring badly needed investment projects and increase state budget revenues considerably (Petrovic 2006, 2012; B92 2012; Radio-Televizija Srbije 2012). When it came to energy security, securing Russian agreement to route part, or all, of South Stream through Serbia was, in itself, proclaimed as a major success, given that originally plans had foreseen that the pipeline would pass through Romania, rather than Serbia, on its way to Western Europe.[15] In this way, Serbia would first secure an additional route for gas deliveries, one that by-passed the problematic Ukrainian route, thus diversifying its options for transporting Russian gas; and second, improve the possibility of accessing larger amounts of natural gas. Meanwhile, the construction of the gas storage facility in northern Serbia was also crucial for Serbia's energy security, as it would allow the country to store gas which could then be used during times of peak demand or as a reserve in case of interruption to the natural gas supply.

It was believed that the construction of the pipeline would bring hundreds of millions of euros in construction contracts, while the additional natural gas supplies that Serbia could access would create the opportunity for major investments in building new gas-powered electricity generation plants, the development of local gas supply networks for households, and opportunities for cheaper energy for industry. Particularly prominent were claims that the Serbian budget would receive over €200 million in earnings from transmission tariffs[16] per year following the construction of South Stream.[17] When it came to NIS, the sale of the company to GazpromNeft would bring badly needed investments and internal reforms necessary to make the company profitable.

Was the IGA really so beneficial to Serbia? From the vantage point of today, it seems that the agreement was anything but beneficial. Serbia's energy dependence on a single company – Gazprom – has increased significantly, given that it has handed over almost all of its gas and oil sector (the exception being gas distributor *Srbijagas*) to it. Meanwhile, in December 2014, Russian President Vladimir Putin announced that *Gazprom* was abandoning South Stream, the pipeline which would have brought Serbia added energy security, huge investments and supposed earnings from transmission tariffs (Walker 2014). In terms of energy security, it is arguably in a worse position today than it was in 2008 – still dependent on a single supplier of gas (Gazprom), a single transport route for gas (via Ukraine and Hungary), with the difference that Gazprom now also owns its domestic oil and gas production and refining capacities, as well as much of its petrol retail network. All of this is only partly offset by the fact that, since taking over NIS, Gazprom has invested in modernising the company's refining capacities and increased domestic oil and gas extraction through additional investments.

The chief initial criticism of the agreement in Serbia was focused on the fact that, at a price of €400 m for a 51 per cent stake, NIS was sold to GazpromNeft at a heavily discounted price (Blic 2008). Indeed, an independent assessment of the value of NIS by Deloitte, commissioned by the Serbian government, valued the entire company at €2.2b (Politika 2008). Moreover, as critics, who included the Serbian Minister of Economy, Maldjan Dinkić, argued at the time, selling NIS at such a low price without any legal or financial guarantees from the Russian side that South Stream would actually be built, was irresponsible (Glavonjić 2008). Other Serbian leaders argued, or implied, at the time that selling NIS to Gazprom was the cost of securing the routing of South Stream through Serbia, the benefits of which would far outweigh the low price at which NIS had been sold. Moreover, they stressed that the word of Russian leaders, Vladimir Putin and Dimitri Medvedev, that South Stream would indeed be built, was sufficient guarantee for Serbia (Borović 2008). The argument that the word of the Russian leadership was worth more than any other guarantees was made by Russian scholars too (Pomorcev 2010: 165). Ultimately, the decision by Russia in 2014 to cancel the construction of South Stream would seem to have vindicated the critics of the way in which the deal was conceived.

From a legal point of view, the IGA has also been found problematic for a number of reasons.[18] In particular, it included a clause which exempts all companies covered within the Agreement (including NIS, Banatski Dvor and the joint company for managing South Stream) from any changes to Serbian tax legislation that would have a negative impact on their operations, stipulating that they will be taxed on the basis of legislation applicable on the date of signing of the Agreement (the duration of the Agreement being 30 years). In practical terms, one of the consequences of this was to freeze oil and gas royalties paid by NIS at their 2008 level of 3 per cent of gross production. Although comparison of international oil and gas tax regimes is no simple matter, by any criteria this figure is very low and more common for a country where oil and gas extraction is state, rather than privately, managed. Taking two neighbouring countries with broadly similar oil and gas tax regimes, in Croatia royalties for oil and gas extraction are at 10 per cent (Ernst and Young 2015) while in Romania extracting at NIS's level would result in royalties of 13.5 per cent for oil and 9 per cent for gas[19] (Ernst and Young 2015; KPMG 2013). Consequently, in 2014 NIS paid around €19 m in royalties to the Serbian government for the oil and gas extracted (NIS 2015). However, under the Law on Mining adopted in 2011, the royalty rate was raised to 7 per cent. Had NIS not been exempted from this change under the IGA, it would have had to pay royalties of approximately €44 m; by comparison, in Croatia, for the same volume of extraction it would have paid approximately €63.2 m in royalties, while in Romania it would have paid approximately €75.8 m.

Other elements of the IGA were also clearly unfavourable to Serbia. Of all the countries participating in South Stream, Serbia was the only one which agreed to the possession of a minority 49 per cent stake in the pipeline to be constructed (Padejski 2011). Nor is it clear that handing over the Banatski Dvor gas storage facility to the Russian side, again with a controlling 51 per cent stake, was in Serbia's best interests, given that relatively modest funds were needed to complete construction of the facility at the time.

Despite all this, could the IGA have been beneficial to Serbia overall had South Stream been constructed? Trying to answer such hypothetical questions is always an unrewarding task, but it is worth considering, particularly as many supporters of the IGA in Serbia still cling to this argument. Leaving aside the possible benefits which could have come from additional natural gas supplies, investments, and the undisputed benefit of an alternative supply route for Russian gas, supporters of the IGA argue that the anticipated earnings from transmission tariffs from South Stream would have more than compensated for the fact that NIS was sold at such a discounted price to GazpromNeft. As noted, Serbian officials and commentators estimated that earnings from transmission tariffs from South Stream would have been over €200 million per year.

Such estimates were likely wildly optimistic. EU legislation, which Serbia is also implementing because of its membership in the Energy Community, has been driving national transmission system operators towards greater transparency in setting natural gas transmission fees (see ACER 2013; European Union 2005, 2009). Thus, the level of tariffs charged must broadly reflect genuine costs of transport (including costs of building and maintaining the transmission network), rather than being arbitrary. Consequently, the space for making huge profits through transmission tariffs has been considerably curtailed. The ownership structure of the planned South Stream pipeline in Serbia together with the fact that the seat of the company was in Switzerland (hence reducing the transparency of its operations) also casts considerable doubt on the scale of these revenues, or at the very least leaves open the possibility that Serbia would have had little control over how much it received from South Stream transmission tariffs (E-Novine 2009)

11.5 Serbian domestic politics and the 'deal of the century'

Given the great imbalances built into the IGA between tangible benefits for the Russian side and very uncertain benefits for the Serbian side, as well as how unfavourably it has worked out in practice, how can we account for why the Serbian side agreed to it? It would be tempting to try to attribute Serbia's acquiescence to Russian pressure and blackmail, but there is neither evidence for this nor much reason to suspect it. Instead, if we want to understand why Serbia pursued such an agreement, we should delve into domestic Serbian politics around the period of its signing and understand the context within which it occurred.

From around 2005, momentum began to build within the international community for the resolution of Kosovo's status. This was based on the sense that the 'limbo' in which this territory found itself – formally still part of Serbia and administered by a UN civilian mission – was untenable. In February 2006, UN-sponsored talks, mediated by the UN Special Envoy, Marti Ahtisaari, began between Belgrade and Pristina, with the goal of ultimately tackling the issue of Kosovo's future constitutional status (Cvetković et al. 2006). Predictably, while the sides made some progress on certain technical issues (such as autonomy for Serbs within Kosovo, whether independent or not), they remained as far apart as ever on the possibility of Kosovo becoming independent or remaining part of Serbia. A year after the talks began, Ahtisaari drew up a draft proposal for a settlement between Belgrade and Pristina, indicating that Kosovo would enjoy statehood, which was rejected by the Serbian side precisely because of this.

What became known as the Ahtisaari plan for Kosovo, envisaging supervised independence, was passed to the UN Security Council in April 2007. While the US and European permanent members strongly backed a resolution that would endorse the Ahtisaari plan for Kosovo's independence, Russia threatened to veto it unless both Serbia and Kosovo agreed. Further talks took place, mediated by a US/EU/Russia Troika in the autumn of 2007, but it became clear that the two sides could not reach an agreement on whether Kosovo would become independent or remain part of Serbia. It also began to become increasingly clear as 2007 dragged on that Russia would use its veto and not permit the passage of a UN Security Council resolution endorsing Kosovo's independence unless Serbia agreed to it. In doing so, Russia provided crucial assistance to Serbia's efforts to block Kosovo's path to independence through the UN (for more detailed accounts see ICG 2007a; ICG 2007b).

In parallel to the talks on Kosovo's future, an intensification of the energy relationship between Russia and Serbia began, along with Serbian agreement to energy deals which were at times clearly unfavourable. During 2006, Serbia and Russia began negotiations on the possibility of the construction of South Stream and its routing through Serbia, as well as the joint development of the gas facility in Banatski Dvor. The Serbian government adopted the draft of a Memorandum of Understanding (MoU) between Serbia and Russia to this effect in July of the same year, whose signing was first scheduled for early August, but then delayed until 20 December 2006.[20] The MoU was only signed after Serbia agreed to the introduction of Yugorosgaz as a middle company in the delivery of gas supplies to Serbia for 2007 (having successfully removed such intermediaries in 2001).[21] Building on the MoU, talks on a wider deal that would see the sale of NIS to Gazprom in return for the routing of South Stream through Serbia and the construction of the Banatski Dvor facility made progress through the course of 2007, becoming public during the visit of Gazprom's CEO, Alexei Miller, to Serbia in October of that year (Boarov 2007). A deal was finally announced in December, and signed in January 2008, less than a month ahead of Kosovo's declaration of independence.[22]

While hard to prove, the most likely explanation for why the Serbian side agreed to sign the IGA with Russia, with all its faults, appears to be that, in doing so, it sought to secure Russian support for Serbia's efforts in blocking Kosovo's independence.[23] This is something alluded to even by opponents of the IGA within the Serbian administration, such as the Minister of Economy, Mladjan Dinkić, who stated in 2008 that he was 'ready to propose that NIS be given to the Russians free of charge if this can protect Kosovo ... but this is nonsense' (Glavonjić 2008). Following Kosovo's unilateral declaration of independence in 2008, although the US and most EU countries recognised Kosovo, Russian support remained crucial to Serbia's efforts to stem the tide of recognitions, both in the UN Security Council and in bilateral dealings with other states. It was the need to maintain this support that appears to have kept Serbia locked into implementing the IGA.

11.6 The role of the EU

The European Union has, in public, taken a back seat in Serbia's energy politics until recently. Only from 2013 did the EU step up open pressure on Serbia over South Stream, within the context of the Third Energy Package. Brussels pointed out that elements of the IGA with Russia relating to South Stream were contrary to the rules of the Third Energy Package which Serbia, even though not a member of the EU, was bound to implement as a requirement of its membership in the Energy Community (Večernje Novosti 2013b). A veiled threat suggested that Serbia's EU accession negotiations could be blocked if it insisted on the construction of South Stream on the previously agreed terms.

By and large, in Serbia, such pressure from Brussels was not seen as being a product of concern about Serbia's energy security, but rather as an attempt to mobilise EU rules in a wider geopolitical struggle between Russia and the EU (Blagojević 2014). In this struggle, Serbia would be the collateral damage, as it would be forced to choose between its desire to join the EU on the one hand and a vitally important energy project, both in terms of energy security and financial benefits, which South Stream appeared to be. What caused particular bitterness, both among the wider Serbian public and many within the political elite, was the firm perception (rightly or wrongly) that the EU was applying double standards, having exempted Nord Stream from the same rules which it was now referring to in order to dispute the legality of South Stream (Al-Jazeera Balkans 2014).

For the Serbian government, this situation represented a considerable problem. On the one hand, it could not afford to jeopardise its efforts to join the EU. Yet on the other, giving in to EU pressure and abandoning South Stream would have been deeply unpopular with large sections of the public, with the potential to undermine popular support for Serbia's EU accession. No less important was the potential schism that such a move could have generated within the Serbian leadership between the more pro-Russian camp of Serbian President Tomislav Nikolic, and the more pro-EU camp of Serbian Prime Minister Aleksandar Vucic. Fortunately for the Serbian government, it was saved from having to make any such difficult choices by Russia's President Vladimir Putin, when he announced in December 2014 that Russia was abandoning the South Stream project (Korsunskaya 2014). Equally fortunately for Serbia, it was Bulgaria that took the brunt of Russian blame for the abandonment of South Stream.

11.7 Conclusion: where next?

The case of Serbia neatly highlights one of the key points that is made throughout this book – rather than viewing Serbian energy security in relation to Russia through a classic realist lens, where energy is a 'first-order' geopolitical tool for the Russian state, we should explore the complex web of domestic politics to get a truer understanding of what is going on. What we find is that rather than Russia deliberately using Serbia's dependence on Russian energy supplies to engineer a situation where it could take control of Serbia's energy sector, the Serbian case shows how a different scenario – namely the political process, initiated by the US and some EU member states, of granting independence to Kosovo – created a fortuitous opportunity for Russia. The need for Serbia to turn to Moscow to block Kosovo's independence gave Russia unexpected leverage over Serbia, which in other circumstances it would not have had. Moscow merely pressed its advantage at this opportune moment in order to acquire Serbia's national energy company. To what extent Serbian officials saw this as a threat to the country's energy security is unclear. In public statements, they certainly sought to present the 'deal of the century' as something that would increase the country's energy security. Yet, regardless of that, at this particular moment in time, the competing political and constitutional priority of blocking Kosovo's independence likely far outweighed any concerns regarding energy security, or indeed insecurity.

Following the demise of the South Stream project, Serbia finds itself in an unenviable position, particularly regarding the security of its natural gas supplies. Having spent the strong bargaining chip that it had in its hands until 2008 – its national oil company, NIS – in a risky gamble to secure the routing of South Stream through Serbia, it lost out, failing to secure this major pipeline, while handing control of its oil and gas sector over to Gazprom. On the political front, Serbia did secure the support of Russia in blocking Kosovo's full independence, where it has had partial success. However, even on this front, it is now Serbia's desire to join the EU which is unequivocally driving it in the direction of accepting Kosovo's independence – if not *de jure*, then certainly *de facto*.

Serbian leaders have since appeared to have been jolted out of their energy security complacency. In June 2015, the Serbian Energy Minister Aleksandar Antić, told the 15th Serbia Economic Summit that the country 'would no longer allow itself to fall in love with a single project' (B92 2015). Since then, old plans for building the Niš-Dimitrovgrad interconnection have been dusted off and catapulted into the highest priority position. If built this would link Serbia to Bulgaria's existing gas network, as well as the proposed 'Eastring' pipeline planned by Slovakia, Bulgaria, Romania and Hungary. Meanwhile, Russia continues to dangle the prospect of a much bigger pipeline which would pass through Serbia on its way to Europe, similar to the South Stream project. This pipeline would transport gas from the planned 'TurkStream' pipeline, via Greece, Macedonia and Serbia, to Hungary and Austria.

Ultimately, the real test of whether Serbian elites have learned their lesson from the South Stream experience will be whether they again in the future choose to place all their eggs in the basket of a single energy project, or whether they seek to truly increase Serbia's energy security by pursuing different projects simultaneously, with the aim of diversifying both the sources of natural gas and oil and the routes by which they arrive in Serbia.

Notes

1. Figures for 2013 remain the most relevant at the time of writing. Severe flooding in 2014 affected coal production and electricity generation, with the result that data from 2014 and 2015 does not provide a representative picture of Serbia's energy mix in normal years, its import dependence or the sources from which electricity is typically generated.
2. Author's calculations based on energy balances data for 2013 published by Eurostat (2015). The figures represent the percentage share of each energy source in the country's total gross inland consumption.
3. Author's calculations based on energy balances data for 2013 published by Eurostat (2015). The figures represent the percentage share of each energy source's primary production in the part of the country's total gross inland consumption derived from that energy source.
4. Author's calculations based on data in 2012 Annual Report of the state electricity corporation, Elektroprivreda Srbije (EPS), in EPS (2014).
5. Author's calculations based on data contained in the Energy Balances Report for 2013 produced by the Statistical Office of the Republic of Serbia. See Republiški zavod za statistiku (2014: 22).
6. Author's calculations based on energy balances data for 2013 published by Eurostat (2015).
7. A small amount of additional capacity is reserved for deliveries of natural gas to Bosnia-Herzegovina.
8. The text of the 'Agreement between the Government of the Republic of Serbia and Government of the Russian Federation regarding cooperation in the sphere of the oil and gas industries', along with related documents, can be found here: www.srbija.gov.rs/vesti/dokumenti_pregled.php?id=179483, accessed 19 December 2015.
9. Data available from the Statistical Office of the Republic of Serbia at: http://webrzs.stat.gov.rs/WebSite/, accessed 19 December 2015.
10. The text of the contract is available at: http://www.srbija.gov.rs/vesti/dokumenti_pregled.php?id=179482, accessed 19 December 2015.
11. While it would be wrong to describe Serbo-Russian relations as being bad at this time, there was certainly very little interest in deepening relations from either side.
12. Privatisation of NIS was not part of the original stand-by agreement, which included more vague references to reform and restructuring of state-owned companies, including those in the energy sector. For more information please see: www.imf.org/external/np/sec/pr/2005/pr05169.htm, accessed 19 December 2015.
13. The text of the 'Agreement between the Government of the Republic of Serbia and Government of the Russian Federation regarding cooperation in the sphere of the oil and gas industries', along with related documents, can be found here: www.srbija.gov.rs/vesti/dokumenti_pregled.php?id=179483, accessed 19 December 2015.
14. Final contracts on the sale of NIS, the creation of the joint company operating the Banatski Dvor gas storage facility were signed on 24 December 2008.
15. On Serbia's efforts to secure passage of South Stream through Serbia see B92 (2007); on Russia's stance that the routing of South Stream was linked to the sale of NIS see Boarov (2007).
16. In domestic Serbian discussions, these were still referred to as 'transit fees', a concept abolished inside the EU from 2004, in favor of the term transmission fees (see ACER 2013).
17. See: Vlaović (2011); Danas (2008); Večernje Novosti (2013a).

18 Among the most comprehensive independent legal analyses of the IGA is that carried out by the International and Security Affairs Centre, a Belgrade based think tank (ISAC 2009).
19 In Romania, royalty rates range from 3.5 per cent to 13.5 per cent for oil and 3.5 per cent to 13 per cent for gas, depending on the volume of extraction; the figures given in the text reflect NIS's level of extraction.
20 'MOU to Give Gazprom Strategic Foothold in Serbia', US Embassy Belgrade Cable, 15 August 2006. Available at: https://search.wikileaks.org/plusd/cables/06BELGRADE1285_a.html, accessed 21 December 2015.
21 'Russia, Serbia Sign MOU on Pipeline, US Embassy Belgrade Cable, 22 December 2006. Available at: https://search.wikileaks.org/plusd/cables/06BELGRADE2062_a.html, accessed 21 December 2015.
22 'Serbia Packages Energy Deal for Russia', US Embassy Belgrade Cable, 20 December 2007. Available at: https://search.wikileaks.org/plusd/cables/07BELGRADE1700_a.html, accessed 21 December 2015.
23 Scholars who take this view include Dušan Reljić (Reljić 2009). The same view is also expressed in diplomatic cables from the US Embassy in Belgrade, see for example: 'Serbs and Russians', US Embassy Belgrade Cable, 3 February 2009. Available at: https://search.wikileaks.org/plusd/cables/09BELGRADE98_a.html, accessed 22 December 2015.

References

ACER (2013). *Transit Contracts in EU Member States: Final Results of ACER Inquiry.* (Ljubljana, Agency for the Cooperation of Energy Regulators).
Al-Jazeera Balkans (2014). 'Srbija upozorena zbog Južnog toka', 4 June. Available at: http://balkans.aljazeera.net/vijesti/srbija-upozorena-zbog-juznog-toka, accessed 22 December 2015.
B92 (2007). 'Srbija: Bolje rešenje za "Plavi tok"', 26 September. Available at: www.b92.net/biz/fokus/intervju.php?yyyy=2007&mm=09&nav_id=265236, accessed 19 December 2015.
B92 (2012). 'Južni tok donosi Srbiji 500 mil. €', 6 February. Available at: www.b92.net/biz/vesti/srbija.php?yyyy=2012&mm=02&dd=16&nav_id=583227, accessed 19 December 2015.
B92 (2015). 'Nema više ljubavi za gas, samo interes', 9 June. Available at: www.b92.net/biz/vesti/srbija.php?yyyy=2015&mm=06&dd=09&nav_id=1002410, accessed 22 December 2015.
Biznis Novine (2008). 'Rumunija se nudi umesto Srbije', 28 April. Available at: www.naslovi.net/2008-04-28/biznis-novine/rumunija-se-nudi-umesto-srbije/655801, accessed 20 December 2015.
Blagojević, D. (2014). 'Južni koridor protiv Južnog toka', *Politika*, 17 May. Available at: www.politika.rs/scc/clanak/293278/Juzni-koridor-protiv-Juznog-toka, accessed 22 December 2015.
Blic (2008). 'Nenadić: Zašto je NIS prodat za 400 miliona evra', 5 March. Available at: www.blic.rs/vesti/ekonomija/nenadic-zasto-je-nis-prodat-za-400-miliona-evra/yrvsdgj, accessed 20 December 2015.
Boarov, D. (2000). '"Progresgas trejding" neće više uvoziti gas', *Vreme*, 521, 28 December. Available at: www.vreme.com/arhiva_html/521/index.html, accessed 19 December 2015.
Boarov, D. (2007). 'Ruski paket aranžman', *Vreme*, 876, 18 October. Available at: http://www.vreme.rs/cms/view.php?id=516418, accessed 20 December 2015.

Borović, R. (2008). 'Potpisivanje energetskog aranžmana sa Rusima', *Radio Slobodna Evropa*, 23 December. Available at: www.slobodnaevropa.org/content/article/1362965.html, accessed 19 December 2015.
Borović, R. (2009a). 'Neka naša zemlja cela ima topla grejna tela...', *Radio Slobodna Evropa*, 7 January. Available at: www.slobodnaevropa.org/content/article/1367426.html, accessed 19 December 2015.
Borović, R. (2009b). 'Ponovo vreba opasnost od gasnih muka', *Radio Slobodna Evropa*, 13 January. Available at: www.slobodnaevropa.org/content/article/1369616.html, accessed 19 December 2015.
Cvetković, L. (2008). 'Gasna mafija krivac za cenu gasa', *Radio Slobodna Evropa*, 17 October. Available at: www.slobodnaevropa.org/content/article/1330780.html, accessed 22 December 2015.
Cvetković, L., Gurović, N. and Repić, A. (2006). 'Najzad oči u oči', *Radio Slobodna Evropa*, 20 February. Available at: www.slobodnaevropa.org/content/news/660288.html, accessed 22 December 2015.
Danas. (2008). 'Velimir Ilić: Južni tok doneće srpskom gradjevinarstvu milijardu evra', 25 January 2008. Available at: www.danas.rs/danasrs/ekonomija/velimir_ilic_juzni_tok_donece_srpskom_gradjevinarstvu_milijardu_evra.4.html?news_id=80368, accessed 20 December 2015.
E-Novine. (2009). 'Gas na dugom štapu', 16 May 2009. Available at: www.e-novine.com/index.php?news=26123, accessed 21 December 2015.
EPS. (2014). *Godišnji izveštaj 2013*. (Belgrade, JP: Elektroprivreda Srbije).
Ernst and Young. (2015). *Global Oil and Tax Guide*. (London: Ernst and Young).
European Union. (2005). 'Regulation (EC) no 1775/2005 of the European Parliament and of the Council of 28 September 2005 on conditions for access to the natural gas transmission networks', *Official Journal of the European Union*, 3 November 2005.
European Union. (2009). 'Regulation (EC) no 715/2009 of the European Parliament and of the Council of 13 July 2009 on conditions for access to the natural gas transmission networks and repealing Regulation (EC) no 1775/2005', *Official Journal of the European Union*, L211, 14 August 2009.
Eurostat. (2015). *Energy Balance Sheets: 2013 data*. (Luxembourg: Publications Office of the European Union).
Fiskalni Savet Republike Srbije. (2013). *Ocena fiskalne strategije 2014–2016 i predlog budžeta za 2014. Godinu*. (Belgrade: Fiskalni Savet Republike Srbije).
Grabež, N. (2008). 'Ili Jugorosgas ili nemate gas', *Radio Slobodna Evropa*, 22 October. Available at: www.slobodnaevropa.org/content/article/1332032.html, accessed 19 December 2015.
Glavonjić, Z. (2008). 'Novi obrt oko prodaje NIS-a', *Radio Slobodna Evropa*, 12 December. Available at: www.slobodnaevropa.org/content/article/1359312.html, accessed 20 December 2015.
ICG. (2007a). 'Breaking the Kosovo Stalemate: Europe's Responsibility', *Europe Report*, No. 185. (Brussels: International Crisis Group).
ICG. (2007b) 'Kosovo Countdown: A Blueprint for Transition', *Europe Report*, No. 188. (Brussels: International Crisis Group).
ISAC. (2009). *Pravna analiza aranžmana izmedju Srbije i Rusije u oblasti naftne i gasne privrede*. (Belgrade: International and Security Affairs Centre).
Janković, M.L. (2014). 'Cela Srbija duguje za gas', *Vecernje Novosti*, 10 November, Available at: www.novosti.rs/vesti/naslovna/ekonomija/aktuelno.239.html:518875-Cela-Srbija-duguje-za-gas, accessed 19 December 2015.

Korsunskaya, D. (2014). 'Putin drops South Stream gas pipeline to EU, courts Turkey', *Reuters*, 1 December, Available at: www.reuters.com/article/us-russia-ga s-gazprom-pipeline-idUSKCN0JF30A20141202, accessed 22 December 2015.
KPMG (2013). *A Guide to Romanian Oil and Gas Taxation*. (Bucharest: KPMG).
Kupchinsky, R. (2008). 'The Shadowy Side of Gazprom's Expanding Central European Gas Hub', *Eurasia Daily Monitor*, 5(217), November, Available at: www.jamestown. org/programs/edm/single/?tx_ttnews[tt_news]=34120&tx_ttnews[backPid]=166&no_ cache=1#.VnXupXtG3Io, accessed 19 December 2015.
Mihajlović, B. (2009). 'Susedi nezamenljivi u gasnoj krizi', *Radio Slobodna Evropa*, 12 January. Available at: www.slobodnaevropa.org/content/article/1369140.html, accessed 16 December 2015.
Mihajlović-Milanović, Z. (2008). 'JugorosGaz – burazerska privatizacija', *Pesčanik*, 17 August. Available at: http://pescanik.net/jugorosgaz-burazerska-privatizacija/, accessed 19 December 2015.
Mihajlović-Milanović, Z. (2010). 'Restrikcije su moguce', *E-Novine*, 15 February. Available at: http://www.e-novine.com/ekonomija/ekonomija-analiza/34932-Restrik cije-mogue.html, accessed 19 December 2015.
Ministry of Energy, Development and Environmental Protection (2013). *Report on the Security of Energy Supply in the Republic of Serbia in the Period From 2011 to 2013*. (Belgrade: Ministry of Energy, Development and Environmental Protection).
NIS (2014). *Annual Report 2013*. (Novi Sad: NIS).
NIS (2015). *Annual Report 2014*. (Novi Sad: NIS).
Padejski, Dj. (2011). 'Srbija i Gasprom od Miloševića do danas', *Republika*, 494–495. Available at: www.republika.co.rs/494-495/20.html#f1, accessed 19 December 2015.
Petrovic, J. (2006). 'Gradnja može odmah da počne', *Politika*, 21 December. Available at: www.politika.rs/sr/clanak/19553/, accessed 11 February 2017.
Petrovic, J. (2012) 'Kreće izgradnja Južnog toka', *Politika*, 6 December. Available at: www.politika.rs/scc/clanak/242251/, accessed 11 February 2017.
Politika (2008). 'Dilojt i Tus: NIS vredi 2,2 milijarde evra', 6 September. Available at: www.politika.rs/sr/clanak/54864/Ekonomija/Dilojt-i-Tus-NIS-vredi-2-2-milijarde-evr a#, accessed 20 December 2015.
Pomorcev, A. (2010). 'Russia Serbia Energy Deal: Two Sides of a Coin' in Petrović, Z. (ed.) *Russia Serbia Relations at the Beginning of the XXI Century*. (Belgrade: International and Security Affairs Centre).
Putniković, J. (2008a). 'Prodaja PGT po scenariju Yugorosgasa', *Balkan Magazin*, 29 September. Available at: www.balkanmagazin.net/energetika/cid163-26511/prodaja -pgt-po-scenariju-yugorosgasa, accessed 22 December 2015.
Putniković, J. (2008b). 'Ima li mafije u prometu gasa?' *Balkan Magazin*, 20 October. Available at: www.balkanmagazin.net/energetika/cid163-20323/ima-li-mafije-u-prom etu-gasa, accessed 22 December 2015.
Radio-Televizija Srbije (2012). 'Koristi od Južnog toka', 16 February. Available at: www.rts.rs/page/stories/sr/story/13/Ekonomija/1046242/Koristi+od+%22Ju%C5%BE nog+toka%22+.html, accessed 19 December 2015.
Rapaić, S. (2009). 'Tržište energenata u Evropskoj Uniji i interesi Srbije', *Medjunarodni Problemi*, 61(4), pp. 515–535.
Reljić, D. (2009). *Rusija i Zapadni Balkan*. (Belgrade: International and Security Affairs Centre).
Republički Zavod za Statistiku (2014). *Energy Balances 2013*. (Belgrade: Statistical Office of the Republic of Serbia).

Savković, M'. (2007). 'Da li je Srbija energetski bezbedna?' *Bezbednost Zapadnog Balkana*, 4, pp. 30–35.
Stepanović, B. (2001). 'Fotelja za Čanka', *NIN*, 2640, 2 August. Available at: www.nin.co.rs/2001-08/02/19127.html, accessed 19 December 2015.
Večernje Novosti. (2013a). 'Korist od Južnog toka stiže sa svih strana', 26 November. Available at: www.novosti.rs/vesti/naslovna/ekonomija/aktuelno.239.html:465491-Korist-od-Juznog-toka-stize-sa-svih-strana, accessed 20 December 2015.
Večernje Novosti. (2013b). 'Brisel zaustavlja "Južni tok"!', 4 December. Available at: www.novosti.rs/vesti/naslovna/ekonomija/aktuelno.239.html:466925-Brisel-zaustavlja-Juzni-tok, accessed 22 December 2015.
Vlaović, G. (2011). 'Tadić: Srbija ce biti glavno energetsko čvoriste u regionu', *Danas*, 21 November. Available at: www.danas.rs/danasrs/ekonomija/tadic_srbija_ce_biti_glavno_energetsko_cvoriste_u_regionu.4.html?news_id=228544, accessed 19 December 2015.
Walker, S. (2014). 'Putin Blames EU as Russia Abandons Plans for South Stream Gas Pipeline', *The Guardian*, 1 December. Available at: www.theguardian.com/business/2014/dec/01/russia-blames-eu-as-it-abandons-plans-for-south-stream-gas-pipeline, accessed 20 December 2015.

12 Conclusion
Central and Eastern European energy security – more than Russia

Eamonn Butler

12.1 The place of Russia in CEE energy security discourse

In recent years, energy security has become one of the most pressing policy issues for the countries of Central and Eastern Europe (CEE). The rise in significance of energy security was evidenced by the noticeable increase of references to energy and a shift in the type of language emanating from the region's capitals; a shift that, for some commentators, reflected a clear securitisation of the subject (e.g. Butler 2011: 630; Roth 2011: 601; Janeliunas and Tumkevic 2013; Johnson and Boersma 2013; Judge and Maltby 2017). At the heart of this shift has been the increased focus on energy within national security discourses. Of course, the relationship between energy and security is not new *per se*. Energy has long been recognised as an existential commodity that underpins modern life (Butler 2016: 27) and governments find it impossible not to have a strategic interest. However, in recent years, the connections between energy and geopolitics of the wider CEE region have become more prevalent, particularly in the context of relations between consumer, transit and supplier states. As this book acknowledges in its introduction by Ostrowski and opening chapter by Dannreuther, realist explanations for why this shift has taken place emphasise the geopolitics of energy and have specifically highlighted CEE vulnerability, stemming from dependence on Russian energy (specifically natural gas) imports, as well as Russia's perceived willingness to use energy as a political tool – witnessed in the 2006 and 2009 Russia–Ukraine gas crises. This has elevated Russia's role within debates on regional and national energy security and policy. References to Russia linking it with terminology such as 'energy weapon', 'energy wars' or 'petro-power' regularly appeared in both academic and journalistic writing in the aftermath of the 2006 and 2009 Russia–Ukraine gas disputes and continue to permeate thinking among some scholars. As Newman (2011: 142) wrote: 'Russia's "petro-power" has become an increasingly clear threat to all the states which buy Russian oil and gas. This is obviously especially true for the small, poor, highly dependent states of what Russians call the "near-abroad"'. Such dependent states do, of course, also include the CEE states. This was reiterated in comments by Natalia Slobodian (2016) who said:

Some experts view 'energy wars' as a post-Soviet space phenomenon, arguing that Russia uses energy as a weapon to further control former USSR states. However, it is wrong to assume that such tools cannot be applied to the EU and NATO member states as well, especially in light of Russia's official declaration about using energy resources and infrastructure in order to 'address national and global problems'. In recent years, Russia has also been using the energy weapon against European countries: the reduction of oil supplies to the Czech Republic in 2008 when Prague signed an agreement regarding the deployment of American missile defense radars on its territory is a case in point. In 2007, Russia suspended the supply of oil and coal to Estonia for one month due to the transfer of a monument of Soviet soldiers, explaining that it was a technical problem related to logistics. In 2015, Russia reduced the oil transit through Lithuanian ports by 20 per cent without giving a reason for it.

A cursory glance at any of the national security strategies from the region acknowledges that energy has become of greater concern for all countries. For example, both the Polish and Hungarian National Security Strategies saw the number of references to energy increase fourfold from those documents published before the 2006 and 2009 Ukraine–Russia energy crises to those published afterwards. Although explicit references to Russia as the main instigator of threat to energy security are generally limited within such official government publications (most likely for diplomacy reasons), they are not completely absent, highlighting the fact that concern about Russia does exist. This was most clearly seen in the 2007 Polish National Security Strategy, which noted how, 'The Russian Federation, taking advantage of the rising energy prices, has been attempting intensively to reinforce its position on a supraregional level' (Polish Government 2007: 6) and that, 'The dependence of Polish economy on supplies of energy resources – crude oil and natural gas – from one source *is the greatest external threat to our security*' [author's emphasis] (Polish Government 2007: 8).

General political and academic debates beyond the strategies also allow for further correlations to be drawn, specifically in relation to dependency. It is important to note that the securitisation of energy at the CEE national level has also informed, and been informed by similar discursive shifts at the EU level, where securitisation of energy debates involving Russia have been linked to moves by the European Commission and EU Member States to develop a more comprehensive Common Energy Policy. This has included justification for the creation of the European Energy Union, evidenced by the fact that achieving security of supply through diversification of energy sources, suppliers and routes is one of the Union's five interlinked and mutually reinforcing dimensions – the others being, completing and managing a fully integrated internal energy market, achieving greater energy efficiency, addressing climate change through meeting decarbonisation goals and supporting research, innovation and competiveness (European Commission 2017).

There is justification for the arguments which acknowledge Russia as a major actor in the European energy sector seeking to utilise its privileged position as the main external energy provider to protect and strengthen its supraregional level dominance. The contributions to this book do not seek to dismiss this fact. Russia is a relevant and important actor, and to all intents and purposes, discussion about its role is hugely important for helping to understanding how energy security and policy approaches to energy have been viewed by scholars and governments since the mid-2000s, if not earlier. However, what the contributors to this book have attempted to do is to look beyond a mere reductionist approach to CEE energy security and policy which sees the Russian state as the puppet master controlling the strings of energy policy across the region. Even when differences in national attitudes towards Russia and energy security policy exist and are acknowledged, the first assumption is often that Russia has orchestrated developments or plays an excessive role, either overtly or covertly[1] as a way to divide and rule the region, thus preventing the emergence of a common European negotiating stance that might undermine or weaken Russia's position. Of course, this does not mean that Russia and its energy companies do not have interests or intentions to operate within the CEE energy sector – they do. However, the various authors contributing to this book suggest that the CEE states also need to be acknowledged as actors in their own right, and that certain circumstances, more often than not completely within the control of the CEE states, actually dictate the extent to which the political and economic environment is conducive for Russian presence and engagement. In other words, Russia's level of involvement with the CEE energy sector is entirely conditional on the decisions and actions taken in the various capital cities, from Tallinn to Belgrade.

12.2 Acknowledging the role of CEE governments

The most important contribution of this book is the rebalancing of energy actor debates to include specific reference to the role played by CEE governments and national actors, including national champions, since the collapse of communism. The contemporary CEE energy landscape has developed over more than 25 years and cannot be assumed to be simply a Soviet-era legacy quirk, which locked the countries of the region into a Soviet and later Russian sphere of energy influence, where pipeline infrastructure, and to a lesser degree, nuclear technology, dictated the direction of energy policy. This is not to say that this did not have relevance and certainly, the close political and economic connections between Moscow and the various CEE capitals did mean that for some of the newly independent states of the region, specifically the Baltic States and those Central European states with high dependence on Russian gas imports, the ties that bound them to Moscow were more than just the physical infrastructure. However, what we see from the discussion presented in this book is that right from the beginning of the post-communist era, governments across the region started to develop their own policy positions and moves to shift themselves out of that sphere or distinguish themselves within it, insofar as they could at that point in time. It is important to recognise that these moves were not necessarily due to any inherent fear of Russia and the potential for it to use energy as a political tool, but rather they reflected the broader political and economic sentiment of the time, which saw the CEE countries orientate themselves more towards the liberal market economy structures of western Europe.

The 'return to Europe' mantra that swept across the region and which underpinned most of the early transition governments' policies enabling political, economic and social transformation, was therefore an important driving force for change, including in the energy sector. It was to western Europe that the countries of CEE looked when undertaking this process, particularly with regard to liberalisation and privatisation. As identified within this book, some were more successful than others, but ultimately, it was the decisions taken at national level which dictated the extent to which Russia and its own newly established national energy corporations were able to benefit from privatisation processes in CEE. What is surprising from the case studies set out in this book, is that the capability of Russia to gain traction in the region's energy sector was actually quite limited, and it is only when expressly invited, as in the early stages of the privatisation process in the Baltic states or in the more recent case of Serbia, that it was able to consolidate and strengthen its involvement and influence.

For most the of CEE states, privatisation of the energy sector was intended to help establish strong, market orientated economies with efficient and effective national actors and opportunities for domestic and foreign investment. There was a preference for western rather than Russian investors, but again this was mainly based on the notion that opening up their energy sector, alongside other strategic sectors – whether that be telecommunications or transport – would enable the CEE states to benefit from a reinforcement of the 'return to Europe' ideal and that it would represent a first major step for their longer-term European integration. Russian investors did exist, but as Rossiaud and Locatelli note in their chapter, they were generally limited to certain low-level investment deals, primarily in the downstream retail business sector; although they also had significant success in capturing the Bulgarian refinery business, which in turn supports Russia's dominance in the retail sector.

The intention behind privatisation was that the potential new owners would transform the sector through injecting both operational business knowledge and the necessary financial capital to enable development; but in some instances, such as the case of Romania, the poorly managed transition process allowed for bad governance practices and corruption to take hold. This created an environment where new owners, who were not always Russian, were able to effectively engage into asset-stripping. Examples of poor governance, corruption and scandals were also witnessed in many of the CEE states, as they struggled to manage the process of transition, but they did not necessarily all result in the same outcome. For example, while corruption was mostly tolerated in Romania, when corruption for individual self-gain was identified in other countries during the early transition period, such as Hungary, then a more direct and challenging tone was taken.

As Terry Cox highlighted in his chapter, the decisions taken during the early transition era pertaining to economic liberalisation and privatisation meant that the overall process was not uniform across the region and different policy approaches to how these changes could be achieved were adopted by different states. In each of the states of the region the way in which the privatisation of the energy sector was carried out did not necessarily differ too much from how that of other sectors was carried out in that same state, since energy was generally seen to be part of the wider economy. Furthermore, for some CEE countries, as shown in the chapter on Hungary, the sell-off of the energy sector offered quick and easy access to the financial capital needed to help pay off Soviet-era debts.

It was clear that different states had different priorities when it came to why and how they carried out privatisation. This goes some way to help explain the differing trajectories of countries across the region and potentially why regional consolidation of sector has not taken place. This is an issue which has significant implications for contemporary energy policy. As said, the decisions and actions of the transition period helped to create a varied energy landscape where the degree of political and economic influence held by certain national corporate energy champions, particularly those in the Czech Republic and Poland, enabled them to better resist demands for the state to completely liberalise their markets and divest of state ownership. It also helps to provide some justification for the shifts in direction of certain government policy towards ownership structures within the sector; something clearly evident in both the post-2010 Hungarian Fidesz Government's move to reverse the previous governmental policy to reduce the percentage of state ownership in energy sector, which it feels went against national interest, and the Polish government's declaration within the 2014 National Security Strategy that 'It is necessary for the state to control the infrastructure of the fuel and energy sector and to expand the supervision and control of the wealth of geological resources of the state' (Polish Government 2014: 55).

12.3 What about the EU?

Although it was never the purpose of this book to explicitly examine the European Union (EU) as a third actor in the CEE energy sector, it can not be ignored. The EU has, in recent years, emerged as an energy actor in its own right, and is often placed on the same level as Russia in terms of the perceived influence and direction it can have across the sector as a whole, particularly in terms of regulation and oversight of the development of the single market, which also includes energy. This has, as Dannreuther suggests in his chapter, resulted in the EU being identified as the champion of the liberal tradition and this places it in direct competition with Russia, resulting in an EU–Russia discourse that lends itself neatly to geopolitical framing. The danger, as Dannreuther, correctly points out, is that the independent agency of the CEE countries can be overlooked. This is important not just in terms of the choices CEE states make in relation to Russia, but also those they make in relation to the EU. This creates the danger of a future where there is a skewed analysis away from the CEE states in terms of their specific relations with the EU. This is relevant because the EU is an actor that increasingly, as the various case studies suggest, will likely have a greater role to play in how CEE states approach energy than it has been given credit to date. This is relevant in the context that EU energy policies have become more prevalent in recent years and the EU has taken on a greater oversight role in managing and regulating CEE state actions in the energy field. All CEE states, for example, have been faced with either the opening of infringement procedures or formal requests from the European Commission to comply with EU legislation on energy, specifically that relating to the Third Energy Package.[2] The fact that the EU has a legal route to hold CEE states accountable for failures in the energy sector, potentially provides it with much greater leverage and power over the CEE than that held by Russia. This places it in a unique position vis-à-vis the CEE states.

To understand how the EU got to this position we need to consider its evolution as an energy actor. The EU's engagement with energy is not new and the European integration project is peppered with examples of energy related projects, whether they be the original European Coal and Steel Community and the European Atomic Energy Community (Euratom) from the 1950s, the production of the Energy Charter Treaty in the 1990s, the creation of the Energy Community in the 2000s, and of course the establishment of the Energy Union in February 2015. Energy dependency has proven in recent years to be one of the major concerns for the EU, recognising as it does the fact that its member states currently import about 53 per cent of all the energy the union consumes, including imports of around 66 per cent natural gas, 90 per cent crude oil, 42 per cent coal and other solid fuels, and 40 per cent nuclear fuel (Butler 2016: 27). Most of these imports come from a small group of countries in the wider European neighbourhood – Russia, Norway and Algeria.

Beyond dependency issues, the EU has acknowledged climate change and the environment, as well as the need to promote market liberalisation as additional rationales for its interest in energy. Prior to the events of the 2006 and 2009 Russia–Ukraine gas disputes, most of the EU's attention was actually devoted to addressing liberalisation and the climate agenda, and these continue to play an important role in its approach to the wider energy sector. Initially, questions about security of supply tended to be framed in the context of market forces, and the need to ensure affordable, regular supplies, on an even playing field for all its members. Russia was considered a viable and reliable supply partner in this respect, and any plans for diversification of suppliers was primarily about opening the market to competitive forces and preventing monopolistic pricing structures, rather than challenging Russia's place within the supply chain.

Prior to 2006, the CEE states generally fell in line with the EU on this position. They often engaged with specific cooperative efforts to support their integration into the wider EU energy market in advance of their membership. In 2002, the Visegrád Group (V4 – comprising the Czech Republic, Hungary, Poland and Slovakia) created the V4 Energy Working Group to support the improvement of co-operation across the V4 energy sector. This would allow the then candidate states to respond to EU demands to improve information exchange in support of market liberalisation, and speed up privatisation strategies, which had stalled in some states. Within the context of the accession process there was a banality in how energy was addressed, with it being viewed as part of the ever-evolving market based system. It was this banality that provided the space that was ultimately filled by the realist, geopolitical discourses that emerged after 2006. It did not, however, mean that these issues went away or became less important. Acknowledging that they still exist is the first step to seeing where future interactions are likely to emerge. Central to these interactions will be a wide variety of actors, not least of all CEE state and corporate actors. Just as this book has attempted to do in relation to CEE–Russia energy relations, understanding how various independent actors at the CEE level view energy issues, what their priorities are, and how their actions inform governance and business decisions will be essential to building a more complete picture of future CEE–EU energy relations.

12.4 And what of Russia?

Just as the EU recognised the role of Russia as an important energy supplier and partner, so too did many of the CEE states. As the chapter on the Baltic states shows, collaboration with Russia was initially acceptable, if there was a possible benefit to the state. The various case-studies in the book have also shown that many other states have been willing to work with Russia and acknowledge it as an important supply partner, suggesting that the economic benefit will often trump political interests. However, recent political developments and the broader securitisation of the energy sector has also at times encouraged politics to take precedence. The fact that for some states economics are more important while for others it is politics that matters, reinforces the fact that national interest priorities do fluctuate and should never be seen as set in stone. The main example of this can be seen by the fact that moves to develop policy which supports the importation of Liquefied Natural Gas (LNG) will, more often than not, prove to be more expensive than direct imports from Russia. It is telling that the only states where LNG imports have been successful or where plans are advanced is in those CEE states which are more concerned about the Russian energy threat – namely Poland and Lithuania, as well as other Baltic states. Expensive LNG may appear to be the acceptable price to pay for greater independence from Russia in these cases. But for other CEE countries, such as Hungary and Bulgaria (though perhaps not for Romania), there is no such push to move away from Russia as a partner. Indeed, the CEE states, often are able to curtail or open Russian access to their markets as and when they want. If for example, they decide that Russian engagement is not warranted then mechanisms to prevent this are usually found – the MOL/Surgutneftegaz case set out in the Hungary chapter is the perfect example of such practice. Of course, when CEE does open itself to Russian presence and engagement, then problems can often be identified or start to emerge, especially when we question the level of transparency of business relations – this has also been most notable in the recent case of Hungary. However, a lack of transparency will often be underpinned by the poor governance decisions taken by the respective CEE states, after all, EU procurement law and other policies provide significant opportunity for greater transparency. As the contributors to this book have shown, the drivers of such decisions and ways of operations will often be rooted in the past actions of central CEE actors and the processes which were set in place early on in the post-communist era.

12.5 Conclusion

This book does not assume to explain every aspect of CEE energy relations. It does, however, acknowledge that we cannot view the region as a single unit of analysis and that explanations for the CEE countries' diverging approaches to the issue of energy security in relation to Russia have, on the whole, to date, followed a well-established narrative developed by a range of scholars who divide the region into groups of actors representing anti-Russian, pro-Russian and neutral bases. The book takes the line that these explanations view energy security predominately through a realist lens with energy used as a geopolitical tool by the Russian state. This means that the complexities of the individual energy systems remain largely understudied in wider literature and that without engaging with them we cannot possibly come to a fuller understanding of the region's energy security including its relations with Russia and the European Union.

The book's contributors have sought to provide nuanced studies of a range of country cases, three Baltic states (Estonia, Latvia and Lithuania), three Central European states (Poland, Hungary and Czech Republic) and three south-east European states (Romania, Bulgaria and Serbia). These studies were tasked with moving beyond a simple realist type of analysis. This proved challenging because realism does have a role to play in understanding the national interest led choices made by states. However, the studies were also able to show through their analysis of different governance structures within the CEE energy sector how conducive environments for Russian presence and influence emerged. Discussion of the post-communist transition, the emergence of a post-socialist elite, the politics of private and state-owned energy companies in the CEE states and moves to respond to the liberalisation agenda of the EU were all scrutinised.

Over the past twenty years the studies of energy security, energy systems and the political economy of oil and gas networks in the post-communist space have overwhelmingly focused on Russia and Central Asia, resulting in a partial picture of the problems faced by other post-communist and socialist countries. By providing a better understanding of the dynamics governing approaches to energy security and policy in the CEE region and the varied political and economic actors involved, this book has hopefully opened up new intellectual avenues for future comparative studies between different parts of the post-Soviet bloc.

It also allows us to recognise that the CEE states have a role to play within the EU. Not all engagement on the energy front will be with Russia. Increasingly, Brussels is holding the CEE states accountable for failing to implement EU law appropriately. This potentially will bring Brussels and CEE states into possible conflict, albeit not the same type of conflict often assumed to exist with Moscow. As EU member states, the CEE countries are able to inform EU energy policy, but if common policy is to work effectively then all participants need to follow the rules. If these do not benefit the national interest of the CEE state, then we can expect attempts to push the acceptable boundaries of non-compliance. Only by fully accepting that CEE states have agency and that their decisions will be grounded in not only current affairs but often past affairs will we be able to navigate and understand the politics underpinning Central and Eastern European energy policy and approaches to security.

Notes

1 See Kupchinsky (2009) for an investigative discussion on the machinations of Gazprom and Russian influence in Europe.
2 For a full list of infringement procedures and compliance requests made by the EU please see the Directorate General for Energy Website, available at: http://ec.europa.eu/energy/en/topics/enforcement-laws, accessed 19 August 2017.

References

Butler, E. (2011) "The geopolitics of merger and acquisition in the central European energy market", *Geopolitics*, 16(3), pp. 626–654.
Butler, E. (2016). 'Pipeline politics and energy (in)security in Central and South-Eastern Europe', in Europa Publications (ed.), *Central and South-Eastern Europe 2017*. Series: The Europa regional surveys of the world. (London: Routledge). pp. 27–31.
European Commission (2017). 'Energy Union and Climate' – Website. Available at: https://ec.europa.eu/commission/priorities/energy-union-and-climate_en, accessed 25 August 2017.
Janeliunas, T. and Tumkevic, A. (2013). 'Securitization of the energy sectors in Estonia, Lithuania, Poland and Ukraine: Motives and extraordinary measures', *Lithuanian Foreign Policy Review*, December, pp. 65–90.

Johnson, C. and Boersma, T. (2013). 'Energy (In)security in Poland? The case of shale gas', *Energy Policy*, 53, pp. 389–399.

Judge, A. and Maltby, T. (2017). 'European Energy Union? Caught between securitisation and 'riskification', *European Journal of International Security*, 2(2), pp. 179–202.

Kupchinsky, R. (2009). *Gazprom's European Web*. (Washington, DC: The Jamestown Foundation).

Newman, R. (2011). 'Oil, carrots, and sticks: Russia's energy resources as a foreign policy tool', *Journal of Eurasian Studies*, 2(2), pp. 134–143.

Polish Government. (2007). *National Security Strategy of the Republic of Poland*. Warsaw.

Polish Government. (2014). *National Security Strategy of the Republic of Poland*. Warsaw.

Roth, M. (2011). 'Poland as a policy entrepreneur in European external energy policy: towards greater energy solidarity vis-à-vis Russia?', *Geopolitics*, 16(3), pp. 600–625.

Slobodian, N. (2016). 'Russia, Ukraine and European Energy Security', *New Eastern Europe*, 26 May. Available at: www.neweasterneurope.eu/interviews/2007-russia-ukraine-and-europe-s-energy-security, accessed 19 August 2017.

Index

Abramovich, Roman 56
Adamkus, Valdas 189–90
Adria oil pipeline 74
Adriatic Pipeline (JANAF) 205
Ahtisaari, Marti 213–14
Alekperov, Vagit 55–6, 57, 62
Alganov, Vladimir 126
Algeria 76
Amable, B. 36
Amber Grid 193
Ámon, A. 171
Antall, Jószef 160
Antic, Aleksandar 216
Antic, Srboljub 209
AS Eesti Gaas 192
AtomStroyExport (ASE) 149
Autonomous Administrations 99–100
Azerbaijan 76
Azerbaijan-Georgia-Romania Interconnector (AGRI) 111n9

Bachneftekhim 54
Balkan Petroleum 105
Balmaceda, M. M. 184
Baltic-Pipe 124
Baltic States: arbitrating energy security 193–4; corruption in 183–5; electricity network sector 189–91; energy mix in 178–80; as EU members 181; European Continental Network and 190; European Union agenda for 186; implementing EU's Third Party Package 192–3; intraregional cooperation between 197–8; as members of Integrated Power System/Unified Power System (IPS/UPS) 181; natural gas sector 191–3; natural gas supply diversification 194–6; nuclear sector 187–9; oil supply disruptions 181–3; regional liquefied natural gas terminal 194–5; renewable energy sources (RES) 196–7; synchronisation with European Continental Network 191; vulnerabilities of 178–81; *see also* Estonia; Latvia; Lithuania
BaltPool free electricity market 190
Banatski Dvor storage facility 205, 212, 214
Barnes, A. 47
Bartimpex 121, 122
Bartuška, Václav 75
Bashneft **58**
Belene nuclear power plant 149–50
Beneš, Vit 83
Binhack, Petr 62
Blue Stream pipeline 143
Bogdanov, Vladimir 55–6, 57
Bohle, D. 38–9, 48
Bokros, Lajos 161
Bokros stabilisation package 161
BRELL (Belarus, Russia, Estonia, Latvia and Lithuania) Network 181, 183, 189–91
Brussels 78, 215, 230
Bruszt, Laszlo 33, 43
Bulgaria: capture economies of 45; corruption in 139; deindustrialisation 140–1; Energy and Water Regulatory Commission 140; Energy Law of 2003 143, 151; energy mix in 138, 139–42; energy system inefficiencies 140–1; European Union accession 142–3; gas diversification challenges 144–7; Gazprom's investments in **65**; hosting Transbalkan Pipeline 140; infrastructure issues 141; Liquified Natural Gas (LNG) 145; nuclear energy and 149–50; path dependency 142; post-communist

period 142–3; as pure neo-liberal regime 39; Russian influence on 138–9; Russian oil companies' investments in **63**; South Stream and 146
Bulgarian Energy Holding (BEH) 140
Bulgaria-Romania-Hungary-Austria (BRUA) Corridor 97
Bulgartransgaz 141
Burgas-Alexandroupolis Pipeline 148–9
Bütingé oil terminal 186

capitalism 35–7, 42–4, 48
capitalist economy 33
capitalist transformation 35–6
capture economies 45–6
CEE *see* Central and Eastern Europe (CEE)
CEFC China Energy Company Limited 101
Central and Eastern Europe (CEE): as autonomous actors 26–7; dependence on Russian gas 63–4, **64**; dependent on Russian gas and oil imports 52; economies, segments of 37–8; energy dynamics with Russia 5; energy mix in 24–6; energy security in 23–9; as EU member states 230; European Union as third actor in energy sector 226–8; gas pipeline network 24; Gazprom's investments in **65**; intentions of privitisation 225–6; international integration economies 36–7; Kremlin's strategy at dominating 7; poor governance decisions 229; post-socialist economies of 40–4; as preferred target for Russian firms 53; property transformation 40–1
Centrex 210
České Energetické Závody (ČEZ) 8, 76, 79–80
česnakas, G. 192
Chernomyrdin, Viktor 59–60, 143, 209
Chevron 197
Churkin, Vitalii 181
Citizens for European Development of Bulgaria (GERB) 150–1
Combinatul Siderurgic Reşita 105
Connolly, R. 34–5
Conventions 104, 111n19
coordinated market economies (CMEs) 36
Corporate Commercial Bank (KTB) 143
corporate state capture 45–6
corruption: in Baltic States 183–5; in Bulgaria 139; in Czech energy sector 7–8, 80–2; definition of 44–5; in Hungary 174–5; in Latvia 185; in oil products sector 185; in Poland 118; in Romania 108, 226
Council for Mutual Economic Assistance 67n1
Crimea 29, 144
Croatia 39, 45
crude oil 117–18
Czechia **63**, **65**
Czechoslovakia 33–4, 41, 74 *see also* Czech Republic
Czech Republic: Adria oil pipeline 74; capture economies of 45; corruption in 80–2; economic liberalisation project 81–2; as embedded neo-liberal regime 39; energy privatisation 77–80; energy supplies, state of 73–6; France and 86; impact of Ukraine crisis on 86; Ingolstadt - Kralupy nad Vltavou-Litvinov pipeline (IKL) 76; liberalised foreign trade 46; natural resources 74; nuclear energy and 76, 86; oil-delivery diversification 75–6; periodisation 77–8; political elites 41; political fragmentation of 81–2; privatisation 48n6 ; reliance on Russian oil 75–6; Russian economic influence in 82–7; Transalpine pipeline (TAL) 76; underground storage facilities 75
Czech State Energy Policy 75

Deák, A. 171
Denmark 110n8
de novo segment of the economy 38
Dinkic, Mladjan 209, 211
downstream integration 64–6
Drahokoupil, J. 36–7
Druzhba pipeline 62, 117–18, 186
Dujotekana 184–5
Dunai, Andras 163
Dunai, Imre 162–3

Eastring pipeline 216
economic elite 42–4
economic nationalism 46–7
Elbahold Limited 103
Elektrènai heat plant 180
Elektroprivreda Srbije (EPS) 204
elite formation 40–2
elite transformation 42–4
embedded neo-liberal regimes 39
energy, as political weapon 17
Energy Charter Treaty (ECT) 20, 66–7

energy prices, affecting Central and Eastern Europe 1–2
energy security: in CEE 23–9; components of 1; in IR framework 23–9; Russia as geopolitical threat to 21
energy wars, as post-Soviet space phenomenon 223 *see also* Russian-Ukrainian gas wars
ENTSO-E 181, 189–91, 198n2
E.ON 169
Estlink 189
Estonia: capture economies of 45; economic restructuring in 34–5; AS Eesti Gaas 192; energy mix in 178–9; exemption from EU gas directive 193, 194; Gazprom's investments in **65**; greenhouse gas emissions 183; implementing EU's Third Party Package 193–4; National Development Plan of the Energy Sector to 2020 189; NordBalt interconnection 190; nuclear energy and 189; oil shale 179, 183; oil supply disruptions 182; political elites 41; Russian oil companies' investments in **63**; Scandinavian integration in 190–1; *see also* Baltic States
European Atomic Energy Community (EURATOM) 172
European Commission (EC) 1, 146–7, 181, 193–5, 223
European Continental Network 190–1
European Energy Union 223
European Union (EU): agenda for Baltic States 186; CEE countries as members of 230; decarbonisation policy 131–2; as energy actor 22–3; Energy Package 67; energy relationship with Russia 22–3; incorporating CEE states 21; as normative power 17; Polish accession to 128; recognising Russia as energy supplier 228; renewable energy legislation 143; role in bringing Russians/Poles together 130–1; Romania as part of 107; Russian energy consumption by 25; Serbia and 215; as third actor in CEE energy sector 226–8; Third Energy Package (TEP) 108, 110, 146, 165, 168, 192–3
EuroPolGaz 67, 121

FDI-based market economies 37
financial nationalism 46–7
Finland 195
foreign direct investments (FDIs) 36

Fridman, Mikhail 84

Gabrielsson, R. 197
Gadowska, Kaja 122
Gaidar, Yegor 59, 121
Garancsi, István 174
Gas Interconnector Poland-Lithuania (GIPL) pipeline 195–6
gas pipeline network 24–5
Gazprom: abandoning South Stream 211; ambitions of 28; breach of EU antitrust rules 68n7; Czech Republic and 74; downstream integration 64; as AS Eesti Gaas shareholder 192; European Commission investigation into 193–4; investments in CEE countries **65**; joint-venture with PGNiG 67; market power 60–1; oil production levels **58**; in Poland 122; pricing strategy 66–7; purchasing Lietuvos Dujos 192; restricting investments 66; in Romania 95–6; shipping gas to Belarus 127; suspending deliveries to Ukraine 205; transit pipeline through Polish territory 119; vertical de-integration of 59–60
Gdańsk oil refinery 125
geopolitics of energy 222
GERB (Citizens for European Development of Bulgaria) 150–1
Glavbolgarstroy 146
globalisation 46–7
Greece 145
Gref, German 60
Greskovits, B. 38–9, 48
Grigas, Agnia 186
Gudzowaty, Aleksander 121–3
Gyurcsány, Ferenc 166, 167

Hall, P. 36
Havel, Václav 73
Hellman, J. 44–5
Henderson, James 122
Herbert Smith Law Firm 188
Herrman, Martin 169–70
Hexagonale regional cooperation initiative 74
Hitachi 188
Horn, Gyula 162
Hujber, Ottó 162–3
Hungarian Democratic Forum 159–60
Hungarian Energy Policy Principles and the Business Model of the Energy Sector 164

Hungarian Finance & Trade Corp. 163
Hungarian Justice and Life Party 160
Hungarian National Energy Strategy 2030 159
Hungarian Socialist Party (MSZP) 165
Hungary: Alliance of Free Democrats-Hungarian Liberal Party 161; anti-Russian sentiment 164–5; Bokros stabilisation package 161; capture economies of 45; Christian Democratic People's Party 160; corruption in 174–5; debt recovery process 162–3; as embedded neo-liberal regime 39; energy mix in 157–9; energy policy 164; Fidesz-led government 164–5, 168–9; gas riot protest 159; Gazprom's investments in **65**; HUF 125 per metre utility tax 169–70; Hungarian Justice and Life Party 160; implementing EU's Third Party Package 165, 168; Independent Smallholders Party 160; insider privatisation 41; MOL Group 161–2; national autonomy of 27; natural gas 163; oilgate scandal 162–3; Paks nuclear power station 158; party political interest vs. national interest 155–6; political elites 40–1; post-2010 energy policy 155; Privatization Law 161–2; public's trust in government 155–6, 159–60; renewable energy sources (RES) 158–9; Russia, as strategic partner 156–8; Russian gas imports 25; Russian influence on 172–4; Russian investment in 165–6; Russian oil companies' investments in **63**; Russia-Ukraine crisis, effects of 158, 166; Safety Stockpiling of Natural Gas Act 166; South Stream and 170–1
Hungary First 168–9, 173, 174

Iancu, Marian 105
Ignalina nuclear power plant 180, 182, 183, 187
Ilves, Toomas Hendrik 189
Ingolstadt - Kralupy nad Vltavou-Litvinov pipeline (IKL) 76
Innes, A. 45
International Energy Agency (IEA) 75, 157
International Relations (IR) theories 5
international segment of the economy 38
Italy, oil reserves 110n8

J&S Company 126

Johnson, J. 47
Johnson, S. 43

Kaczynksi, Lech 189–90
Kasyanov, Mikhail 165
Kaveshnikov, N. 192
Kazakhstan 76
KazMunayGas 101
KEPCO 188
Khodorkovsky, Mikhail 21, 56
Klaipéda liquefied natural gas terminal 195
Klaus, Václav 77, 81–2, 83, 85
KomiTek 54
Kopacz, Ewa 129
Kořan, Michal 86
Kosovo 208, 213–14
Kostov, Ivan 148
Kovachev, Milko 149
Kovachki, Hristo 151
Kruonis hydro accumulation plant 180
Kuchma, Leonid 123
Kulczyk, Jan 125–6
Kwaśniewski, Aleksander 123, 126

Lakatos, Benjámin 174
Laki, M. 43
Latvia: capture economies of 45; corruption in 185; energy mix in 179; exemption from EU gas directive 194; Gazprom's investments in **65**; NordBalt interconnection 190; oil supply disruptions 182–3; political elites 41; Russian gas imports 25; *see also* Baltic States
Latvijas Gaze 192
Lembergs, Aivars 185
LEO LT (Lithuanian Electricity Organisation) 187–8
LetterOne 84
liberal market economies (LMEs) 36
Lietuvos Dujos 192, 193
Lignite production 94
limited-access orders 35
Lionginas, Jonas 184
liquefied natural gas 22, 66, 96–7, 179, 195, 228–9
Lithuania: arbitrating energy security 193; capture economies of 45; electricity generation 180; energy diplomacy experienced by 181; energy mix in 179–80; Gazprom's investments in **65**; implementing EU's Third Party Package 193–4; Law on the Nuclear

Power Plant 187–8; LNG terminal in 195; natural gas consumption 180; nuclear power plant project 187–9; oil imports 180; political elites 41; Russian gas imports 25; Russian oil companies' investments in **63**; shale gas 196–7; *see also* Baltic States
Lithuanian Geological Survey 197
loans-for-shares scheme 56
Locatelli, C. 22
Lotos Group 118
Loveman, G. 43
Luca, Liviu 103
łucki, Zbigniew 127
Lukoil 28, 54, 57, **58**, 61–2, 95–6
Lukoil Energy and Gas Romania 106

Maldeikis, Eugenijus 184
Management and Employee Buyout (MEBO) 100
Marjanovic, Mirko 209
market capitalism 33
Martin, Roderick 37–8, 43–4, 48
Martitsa East 2 TPP 140
Matolcsy, György 164
Mažeikiai oil refinery 128, 180, 184
Mechel 112n22
Medgyessy, Péter 165
Medvedev, Dmitrii 78, 85
MERO ČR 76
Miller, Alexei 214
Miller, Leszek 124–5
Milosevic, Slobodan 207
Minsk-Vilnius-Kaliningrad pipeline 180
Miodowicz, Konstanty 123
Mladek, Jan 86
MOL Group 161–2, 168
Movement of Rights and Freedoms (MRF) 147
Mowscow loan affair 124
Multigroup 142
MVM (power company) 162, 165, 169–71
Myant, M. 36–7

Nabucco pipeline 129, 167, 171
Naftna Industrija Srbije (NIS) 202, 208, 211–12
Nagy, György 174
Nagylengyel 157
Najder, Zdzislaw 124
natural gas production, in Hungary 157
Nazarbayev, Nursultan 129
Neftochim refinery 140, 143, 147–8
Nejedlý, Martin 85

Newman, R. 222
Nikolic, Tomislav 215
Niš-Dimitrovgrad interconnection 216
NIS Petrol 106
N M Rothschild & Sons 188
nomenklatura privatisation 43
non-state actors 27–9
NordBalt project 190
Nord Stream pipeline 128–9, 215
North Atlantic Treaty Organization (NATO) 20
Norway 124

oil production: campaign against 197; companies controlling 56; in Hungary 157; in Lithuania 180; in Romania 93, 95
oil shale 27, 178–9, 182–3 *see also* shale gas
Olszewski, Jan 121
OMV Petrom 106–7
open-access orders 35
Orbán, Viktor 164–5, 168, 173
Organisation for Economic Co-operation and Development (OECD) 78, 81, 82
Orlen oil company 118, 128, 129
Ovcharov, Rumen 149
Overgaz 143

Paks 2 project 171–2
Paksas, Rolandas 184
Paks nuclear power station 158, 171
Pál, László 162
Panrusgaz 163, 165
Pantiş, Sorin 100–1
party state capture 45–6
Pârvanov, Georgi 143
Pasti, V. 107
Patko, Andras 163
Patriciu, Dinu 100–1
Pavlov, Iliya 142
Peevski, Delyan 143, 146
periodisation 77–8
peripheral market economies 37
Petrom 99
Petromservice 102–3
Petrotel Oil Refinery 104–5
Petrotrans 101–2
Plesl, Jaroslav 83, 84
Poland: adopting the Euro 132; capture economies of 45; corruption 118; crude terminal in Gdańsk 130; Druzhba pipeline 117–18; economic crisis in 125; as embedded neo-liberal regime 39; energy mix in 117–18;

Index 237

Gazprom's investments in **65**;
globalisation in 46; insider privatisation
41; opening LNG terminal 129–30;
Orlengate scandal 125–8; perception
of Russian energy threats 26; political
elites 41; privatising Gdańsk oil refinery
125–6; privatising state-owned energy
firms 118; Russian influence on 116,
124–5; Russian oil companies'
investments in **63**; Ukraine and 123,
129, 131; Yamal-Europe gas pipeline
122; *see also* Russian-Polish energy
relations
Polish Oil and Gas Company (PGNiG)
118, 120–1, 130
Polish Oil Company (PKN) 125
political elites 40–1
post-communist change 33
post-socialist regimes: capitalism in 36–7;
economic influences 34–6; political
and social factors in 38–9;
transformation of 33–4; types of 39;
variation in 34–9
post-Soviet Russian-EU relations 19–23
privatisation: elites and 40–2; of Gdańsk
oil refinery 125–6; of Hungary's
energy system 160–2; insider 41; of
Mažeikiai oil refinery 182, 184; mixed-
method 42; of Naftna Industrija Srbije
208; parasitic 43; of Polish state-
owned energy 118; priorities of 225–6;
of Romanian energy sector 98–100; of
Russian oil industry 54–7; spontaneous
43; of state-owned oil companies 32–3;
voucher 40–1
Progresgas Trejding 209
property transformation 40
PSV Company 103
Putin, Vladimir 144, 191, 211, 215

Radio Free Europe/Radio Liberty
(RFE/RL) 83
RAFO Oneşti 105
realist theory 29
remittance and aid-based economies 37
renewable energy sources (RES): in
Baltic States 196–7; in Bulgaria 143; in
Estonia 179; EU legislation on 143; in
Hungary 158–9; promoting 22; in
Romania 108–9; in Serbia 203–4
rent-seeking 117, 122, 125, 131, 139, 151
resource nationalism, global
development of 22
Risk Management Laboratory 148

Roman, Martin 82
Romania: capture economies of 45;
communist legacy in 97–8; complying
with EU climate targets 108–9;
corruption in 108; de-regulating
electricity and gas prices 108; domestic
energy production of 27; economic
restructuring in 34–5; energy mix in
94–5; energy ownership structure 95–6;
energy policy goals 96–7, 109; fuel
theft in 101–2; international
development of 95–6; Management
and Employee Buyout (MEBO) 100;
mixed-method privatisation 42;
national autonomy of 27; natural gas
sources diversification 96–7; oil
reserves 110n8; as part of European
Union 107; pipeline network
111–12n20; post-communist transition
98–100; post-war period 93–4;
privatisation process 98–100; providing
oil to Germany 93; public aversion to
Russia 103–4; as pure neo-liberal
regime 39; reorientation to international
markets 46; Russian influence 103–7,
110; Russian oil companies'
investments in **63**; transit conventions
104, 111n19; transition legacy 98–100,
110; Western capital investment
in 107–9
Romgaz 99, 102
Rompetrol 100–1
Rosatom 148, 171–2
Rosneft 54, **58**, 62–3, 129
Russia: abandoning South Stream project
215; economic influence on Czech
Republic 82–7; energy policy 52–3;
energy supply interruptions by 181; as
geopolitical threat to energy security
21; hydrocarbon sector in 54; inter-
governmental agreement with Serbia
203, 210–13; investments in Hungary
165–6; NATO and 20; oil exports 25;
presidential sycophancy towards 83–4;
privatising oil companies 54–7; as
reliable energy supplier 19–20;
resolving economic disputes 128; as
revisionist state 17, 21; state-control
over oil industry 21; TVEL 87; using
energy as political tool 222
Russian-EU energy relations 78
Russian gas: alternative route for 212–13;
competiveness of 25–6; Czech Republic
and 75; dependence on 52;

downstream integration 64–6; European demand for 22; Norway's dependence on 74; Orlengate scandal 126; Polish reliance on 116–17, 122, 131; production by producer **60**; rate of dependence on 63–4, **64**; Romania and 104, 111n19; South Stream gas pipeline 144–7, 170–1, 208, 210–12; Ukraine as transit country for 21; *see also* Gazprom

Russian oil: in Bulgaria 147–9; political economy of 58–9

Russian oil and gas companies: consolidation process 56; emergence of 54; gas production by producer **60**; industry reform 59–60; international development of 61–3; investments in CEE countries **63**; loans-for-shares scheme 56; by production levels **58**; reforming 54–5; state-owned companies in oil production 58–9; vertically integrated 54

Russian-Polish energy relations: breakdown between 123–8; cooperation in 119–23; legacy of 131; long-term contracts with Gazprom 120; overview of **119**; rapprochement with 128–31

Russian-Ukrainian gas wars 2, 8–9, 86, 128, 158, 166

RussNeft **58**

RWE Gas Storage 75

Safety Stockpiling of Natural Gas Act (Hungary) 166
Saxe-Cobourg-Gotha, Simeon 149
Sechin, Igor 59
Seele, Rainer 106–7
Serbia: domestic politics 213–14, 215–16; electricity generation 203–4; energy dependency 204, 205–6; energy mix in 202, 203–4; energy transport infrastructure 204–5; implementing EU's Third Party Package 215; inter-governmental agreement with Russia 203, 210–13; international isolation for 207; overthrow of Slobodan Milosevic 207; perception of Russian energy threats 26; Russian energy relationship with 206–10, **206**; *see also* Kosovo

shale gas 22, 66, 96, 106, 117, 196–7 *see also* oil shale

Sibneft 61
Sidanko 54
Sikorski, Radosław 128, 132

Slavneft 54, **58**
Slesers, Ainars 185
Sliwa, Z. 197
Slobodian, Natalia 222–3
Slovakia: capture economies of 45; as embedded neo-liberal regime 39; Gazprom's investments in **65**; Russian gas imports 25; Russian oil companies' investments in **63**

Slovenia 36, 48n4, **63**, **80**
Smith, K. C. 185
SNP Petrom 107
Sobotka, Bohuslav 83
Socor, V. 167
Soskice, D. 36
South Stream gas pipeline 144, 145–7, 170–1, 208, 210–12
SovRoms 97
spontaneous privatisation 43
Srbijagas 205
Stanescu, Sorin Roşca 100–1
Stark, D. 34, 43
state-business relations 44
state capture 45–6
state segment of the economy 38
state socialism 32
Stella Vitae 184
Stern, Jonathan 64
Stonys, Rimandas 184–5
Stropnický, Martin 83, 86–7
Stroytrransgaz 147
Suchocka, Hana 120
Surgutneftegaz 54, 57, **58**, 61
Swain, Nigel 43
Szalai, J. 43
Szelényi, Iván 42–3

Tatneft 54, **58**
Tehnoeksportstroy 146
Third-Country reciprocity clause 67
Third Energy Package (TEP) *see* European Union (EU)
Tichy, Lukas 62
Timchenko 147
TMK 105
TNK-BP **58**, 61
Topenergy 142, 143
Topolánek, Mirek 85, 87
Transadriatic Pipeline (TAP) 145
Transalpine pipeline (TAL) 76
Transbalkan Pipeline 140
transformation, of post-socialist regimes 33–6
transit conventions 104

transit states 24–5
Transneft 182
Transparency International, corruption perceptions index **80**
Trubnikov, Ilya 174
Turkey 145
Turkish Stream pipeline 147, 216
Tusk, Donald 131–2
Tyumen Oil Company 54

Ukraine 21, 25, 123
Ukrainian-Russian gas wars *see* Russian-Ukrainian gas wars
unbundling 67
Uspaskich, Viktoras 184

Vântu, Sorin Ovidiu 103

Vassilev, Tsvetan 143
Ventspils Nafta 182, 185
Visaginas nuclear power plant 188–90
Vojeika, Piotras 184–5
voucher privatisation 40–1
Vyakhirev, Rem 121, 143

Wałęsa, Lech 120, 121
Westinghouse 86–7

Yamal-Europe gas pipeline 122
Yugorosgaz 207, 209–10
Yukos 21
Yukos affair 55–7, 61–2

Zeman, Miloš 83–5
Zlatev, Valentin 147–8

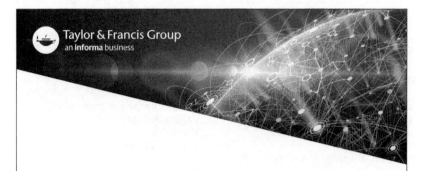